FLIGHTS OF FANCY, FLIGHT OF DOOM

KAL 007 and Soviet-American Rhetoric

Marilyn J. Young
Michael K. Launer

The Florida State University

UNIVERSITY
PRESS OF
AMERICA

Lanham • New York • London

Copyright © 1988 by

University Press of America,® Inc.

4720 Boston Way
Lanham, MD 20706

3 Henrietta Street
London WC2E 8LU England

All rights reserved

Printed in the United States of America

British Cataloging in Publication Information Available

Library of Congress Cataloging-in-Publication Data

Young, Marilyn J., 1942–
Flights of fancy, flight of doom : KAL 007 and Soviet-American
rhetoric / Marilyn J. Young, Michael K. Launer.
p. cm.
Bibliography: p.
Includes index.
1. Korean Air Lines Incident, 1983. 2. United States—Foreign
relations—Soviet Union. 3. Soviet Union—Foreign relations—United
States. 4. Propaganda, American. 5. Propaganda, Russian.
I. Launer, Michael K. II. Title.
E183.8.S65Y67   1989
909'.096454—dc 19   88–28802 CIP
ISBN 0–8191–7225–1 (alk. paper)
ISBN 0–8191–7226–X (pbk. : alk. paper)

To Our Mothers

NOPAC ROUTE R-20 AND THE ACTUAL ROUTE OF KAL FLIGHT 007
Illustration by Terry Graves

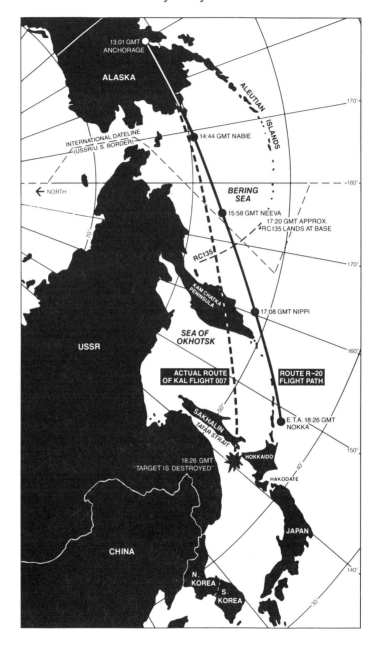

TABLE OF CONTENTS

FOREWORD

As students, respectively, of conspiracy rhetoric and Russian linguistics, we were naturally drawn to developments surrounding the Korean airliner disaster and its aftermath. We were especially intrigued by the obvious attempts of each government to paint the blackest possible picture of the actions and motives of its dominant adversary. Additionally, our interest was piqued by conspiratorial interpretations of US government statements and seemingly inept discussions of the technical issues surrounding the tragedy; in particular we were concerned by wrong-headed analyses of the so-called "KAL Tapes"—assessments which influenced published views of the events of August 31/September 1, 1983. The result is this volume, which we offer primarily as an attempt to analyze the rhetorical development of a tragic situation in the hope that it will contribute to the general understanding of US-Soviet relations, particularly relations in periods of heightened tension.

Dallin and Lapidus have noted:

> The Soviet Union has been the single most important problem for American foreign policy makers since the defeat of Germany and Japan in World War II. It has been the primary cause of … a public state of mind that has fluctuated between an exaggerated optimism about the prospects of Soviet-American collaboration and, more frequently, an obsessive anxiety about the "Soviet threat."[1]

As this book goes to press, the US seems once again caught up in an optimistic phase of this cycle. In contrast, however, in 1983 superpower relations were at a low ebb, reaching their nadir specifically because of the Korean airliner incident. Investigation of the resulting controversy impels us to agree with Halle's rueful declaration: "One is tempted, time and again, to declare that the problems of international relations are fundamentally semantic."[2]

The focus of this study is rhetorical: the use of argumentation; the nature and aims of propaganda, both governmental and nongovernmental; the structure and political applications of conspiracy theory. Accordingly, this study overlaps a variety of disciplines: applied linguistics, criticism, history, political science, and communication. Although available information must be used to assess the veracity of statements and the salience of arguments, we will not concentrate on technical questions about how KAL 007 managed to find itself in mortal danger over Sakhalin Island; nor are we especially concerned with the details of the Soviet interception. At present, however, while we believe that our government and its minions are capable of perpetrating any number of ill-considered acts in defense of 'Liberty and The American Way,' we do not believe there is extant any substantive evidence supporting the notion that KAL 007 was engaged in an intelligence mission for this or any other government.

We recognize Jervis's admonition that evidence is interpreted to fit theories, not the other way around.[3] But the evidence that has been offered as proof for the spy-plane allegation is tenuous—of a type that can be used to support any number of hypotheses, yet which confirms none of them. [This notion is addressed in greater detail in Chapter Six.] At the same time, we do feel that neither the government of the United States nor the government of the Soviet Union approached this tragedy in a forthright manner. In mounting their respective propaganda campaigns, both the Reagan administration and the Andropov government withheld information, distorted the facts, and engaged in the 'creation of truth' to further their own political ends.[4] Although in the international arena the success or failure of one actor to persuade the other impinges on the fortunes of both, we urge the reader to keep in mind that rhetorical assessment is not a zero-sum game: from a critical perspective, the shortcomings of one side do not enhance the performance or the success of the other.

Similarly, we agree with Fisher that the moral quality, or motive, of rhetoric must be investigated by the critic in order to render a judgment.[5] Such a perspective, we argue, is particularly salient for the analysis of conspiracy rhetoric. Nevertheless, contemporary rhetorical theory recognizes that effects may exist independent of moral quality; consequently, we also believe it is possible, for example, to evaluate the impact of releasing corrections to the Soviet pilot tape independent of any moral judgment regarding the act of releasing those emendations.

While we have attempted to be objective, we do not claim to be politically neutral. Indeed, we came to this project tending to believe, at the least, that the US military establishment had taken a posture of benign neglect, passively observing the hapless aircraft and reaping intelligence benefits from the intrusion, confident in the assumption that the Soviets would not dare shoot down unarmed civilians. But we take as an academic article of faith the notion that objectivity is both a function and a necessary component of methodology; it is the means, not the result, of analysis. Jervis's comment about the role of perception in international affairs has relevance to this and similar questions:

> [P]eople who are debating policy should not only realize what they are arguing about but should also ask themselves what possible behavior on the part of the adversary would they take as evidence against the interpretation that they hold. This is especially true of those who see the other as aggressive because ... it is easy to see almost any evidence as consistent with this image.[6]

While no single explanation can be expected to account for all the conflicting evidence, we leave to the reader the task of judging how evenhandedly divergent materials have been brought together in our investigation.

We are particularly interested in the nature and goals of government propaganda, the structure of conspiracy rhetoric as a genre, the effect of transnational broadcasting on communication within the Soviet state, and in communication theory as it relates to both "open" and "closed" societies. As theoretical issues and as the object of case studies, these disparate topics may seem an unwieldy combination, particularly since we do not feel that a single theoretical construct can explain the complex interactions among elements of the KAL story. But all are crucial to developing an understanding of the *Gestalt* of political factors that impinge upon governmental rhetorical behavior under stress. Because of the discrete time boundaries operative in the KAL tragedy, this international incident lends itself to both comprehensive and minute analysis.

We have endeavored to place each component of this analysis into a framework of existing theoretical constructs; consequently, some of the rhetorical theory will seem unnecessary to communication scholars, while some of the political theory may appear superfluous to Soviet area specialists. In reality, the two disciplines are not so far apart, although each seems to operate largely oblivious of the research conducted by the other. For example, what communication theorists have termed "public knowledge" has a cognate in political theory under the rubric of "political culture." Both disciplines are interested in the way political actors use language; thus, what readers from each discipline have often found most interesting in this work is the material and analysis 'from the other side.'

Many individuals have aided us in the course of this research. There are four without whose help this book could not have been written: Jon Lodeesen, Tom Maertens, Jim Oberg, and Jack Reynolds. Many others have gone out of their way to provide documents or to help us find information. Foremost among these have been officials in Washington, including Herb Romerstein, Edward Warner, and Philip Haynes. Ronald Hinckley provided copies of survey questions and responses. A number of journalists and executives in the radio, television, and print news industries shared their particular knowledge and insight, including Natalie Clarkson, Doug Feaver, Sy Hersh, Phil Klass, Todd Leventhal, Victor Navasky, Murray Sayle, and Carolyn Smith. Valuable expertise and hours of good conversation were offered unstintingly by Hal Ewing, truly a twentieth-century Renaissance man, and Roger Wedel. Olga Orshansky, Margaret Jaffie, Al Graham, and Grant Harris never looked askance at our persistent requests for materials; and research librarians at NBC, CBS, and ABC were most helpful in granting access to network news archives. Dr. Sugwon Kang interceded on our behalf before a reluctant editorial board when he might easily have chosen not to. Debbie Launer and our colleagues Curtis Austin, Rich Chapple, Tom King, Ray McKerrow, Bob Newman, Janice O'Donnell, Bill Oldson, Gregg Phifer, and John Poulakos meticulously read many early versions of this manuscript. Patty Casey and Eddie O'Hare of AZUSA Graphics in Washington DC prepared the design and layout of the book; their professionalism and good cheer rescued us from the depths of word processor paranoia. Finally, we would also like to thank a small number of persons who, for reasons of their own, wish to remain anonymous.

Financial support for this project was provided by the Southern Regional Education Board (Atlanta, GA), as well as the Committee on Sabbaticals, the President's Fund, the Office of Graduate Studies and Research, and the Office of the Dean of Arts and Sciences at The Florida State University.

Tallahassee, Florida
April 1988

FOREWARD

NOTES

[1] Alexander Dallin and Gail W. Lapidus, "Reagan and the Russians: United States Policy Toward the Soviet Union and Eastern Europe," in Kenneth A. Oye, Robert J. Lieber, and Donald Rothchild, eds., *Eagle Defiant. United States Foreign Policy in the 1980s* (Boston: Little, Brown, 1983), 191-236, p. 193.

[2] Louis J. Halle, *The Cold War as History* (New York: Harper & Row, 1967), p. 292.

[3] Robert Jervis, *Perception and Misperception in International Politics* (Princeton: Princeton University Press, 1976), p. 156.

[4] The term 'creation of truth' was suggested by Jon S. Lodeesen, Director of US Operations for Radio Liberty.

[5] Walter R. Fisher, "A Motive View of Communication," *Quarterly Journal of Speech*, **56**:2 (April 1970), 131-39.

[6] Jervis, p. 112.

INTRODUCTION

On the night of August 31/September 1, 1983, Korean Air Lines Flight KE007, a scheduled commercial airliner with 240 passengers, was destroyed in mid-air by the pilot of a Soviet Sukhoi-15 fighter. The jetliner had strayed more than three hundred miles off course, twice penetrating Soviet airspace—first over the Kamchatka Peninsula and again over Sakhalin Island, a strategic area north of the Japanese island of Hokkaido. The Korean aircraft, which had been tracked on Soviet radar for two-and-a-half hours, was less than two minutes from international airspace when the Soviet pilot received the order to fire. All 269 persons aboard perished in the Sea of Japan, including United States Congressman Larry McDonald (D-Georgia), chairman of the John Birch Society.

KAL 007, as the plane came to be known, was a Boeing 747 jumbo jet on the second leg of a journey from New York's John F. Kennedy Airport to Kimpo Airport in Seoul, South Korea, with an intermediate stop at Anchorage, Alaska. The Soviet action precipitated an international furor that reminded many observers of the worst periods of 1950s Cold War tension: Why would the Soviet government order the destruction of the airplane and the death of 269 persons? Why was a commercial aircraft spying over restricted Soviet territory in the dead of night?

KAL 007 was shot down at 3:26 am local [Tokyo] time—approximately 2:30 pm (EDT) in Washington DC, and 11:30 am (PDT) in Santa Barbara, California, where President Ronald Reagan had planned to spend a relaxing Labor Day weekend at his ranch. At first, late night network news broadcasts carried a story indicating that a Korean Air Lines jet had landed in Soviet territory. No one seemed to know why this had happened, but it was reported that all passengers and crew were safe.

By the following morning, the real tragedy had become apparent to military intelligence analysts in Washington; Secretary of State George P. Shultz made the announcement at a 10:45 am (EDT) press conference. Initially, Soviet officials denied all knowledge of the incident; 24 hours later they admitted only that air defense forces, the PVO, had attempted to assist an unidentified aircraft to land, but that the craft had "continued its flight toward the Sea of Japan."[1] Thus were the political events set in motion.

President Reagan addressed the nation (and, over Voice of America, the world) on September 3rd and 5th; in the second address, the president played portions of a tape recording of the Soviet pilot tracking and destroying the passenger craft. At the United Nations, emergency sessions of the Security Council were convened on the 2nd and again on the 6th, at which time Council members heard the SU-15 pilot announce to his ground controller:

Пуск произвел. . . .	А цель уничтожена.
[Pusk proizvyol....	A tsel' unichtozhena.]
"I have executed the launch....	The target has been destroyed."

As Ambassador Kirkpatrick addressed the UN assembly, authorities in Moscow released a statement admitting that the PVO had indeed executed orders to "terminate" the flight. On September 9, apparently in response to a deteriorating situation, the Soviet government held an international news conference—which was televised live in the West[2] via hook-up with Intervision, the Soviet bloc TV pool, and, on a tape-delayed basis, even within the Soviet Union itself. Equally unprecedented was the fact that this news conference was conducted by a military official, Nikolai V. Ogarkov, Marshal of the Soviet Union and Chief of Staff of the Soviet Armed Forces. Marshal Ogarkov provided the official Soviet version of events—that the Korean plane was part of a spy mission orchestrated in Washington by the CIA and that the United States government was taking advantage of the situation to cripple the anti-nuclear peace movement in Western Europe and to slander the reputation of the USSR.

Three days later, the United Nations Security Council considered a resolution condemning the destruction of KAL 007. A Soviet veto figured in the nine-to-two vote (there were four abstentions). Charges and counter-charges were traded in the media of both countries for another two weeks, culminating on the Soviet side with a brief, but definitive statement on the issue by Party Chairman and Politburo chief Yuri V. Andropov.[3]

The tragedy that enveloped KAL 007 has provided political analysts and rhetorical scholars a unique opportunity to study a Soviet-American confrontation: it was a situation characterized by few antecedents and a finite starting date. As political events developed over the next four weeks, both the United States and the Soviet Union faced difficult choices regarding closely guarded military and intelligence secrets. The ensuing vacillation between a natural urge for concealment in such matters and the perceived political need for disclosure in this particular instance led to inconsistencies and outright blunders in the rhetorical campaigns waged by each superpower. Nor should one discount the almost reflexive lashing out at one another that, after a decade of more delicately worded detente, had again become the dominant tone of Soviet-American relations during the Reagan presidency. One result of all the controversy and venom was a broadly-based disbelief among the citizenry in both countries regarding the truthfulness of the version sponsored by official organs at home as well as abroad. In the West, this disbelief spawned numerous private attempts to demonstrate US complicity in the deaths.[4] Some felt the American government had probably commissioned the flight; on the other hand, many argued that the vast US intelligence resources in the area surely could have warned the airplane of its predicament. Either way, these versions asserted, the United States should bear at least some responsibility for the events that transpired.

Opinion surveys taken in September, 1983, showed that approximately three-fifths of the American public believed the United States government was withholding information necessary for an accurate determination of what had happened.[5] On the other hand, Radio Liberty polling of Soviet visitors to the West—a sample consisting in large part of members of the Communist Party—demonstrated a significant diversity of belief among the respondents regarding the veracity of the Soviet version.[6] As late as 1986, yet another survey indicated that fully one-fourth of the American public believed the 'spy flight' scenarios.[7]

Evidently neither government was entirely successful in convincing its constituency, foreign or domestic, of the rectitude of its position, despite an extensive and often unprecedented persuasive campaign. Some slippage is to be expected, of course; but 25% is high, even for the US population. Moreover, significant public disagreement among Soviet citizens is still very unusual. In the chapters which follow, we will examine this confrontation over the destruction of KAL 007 and the way in which language and artistic devices were used to present it as a crisis; we will explore the propaganda war and its aftermath—the disaffection from official versions of the truth. We attempt to analyze the rhetorical strategies and assess the rhetorical goals of the primary actors in the KAL 007 story: the government of the United States; the government of the Soviet Union; and the Western conspiratists,[8] as exemplified by the original David Pearson article in *The Nation*.

Our goals are to illuminate the rhetorical behavior of the United States and the Soviet Union in this event, thereby shedding some light on the manner in which rhetoric functions in the two societies; to elucidate how conspiracy theories work rhetorically, which may, in turn, deepen our understanding of the reasons for the attractiveness and rhetorical force of such theories; and to explore the role of propaganda and conspiracy theory in both countries. We hope that this examination will lay a foundation on which future development of a theory of communication for information-restricted societies might proceed.

Part One will examine the US response to the destruction of the Korean Airliner. This section begins with a discussion, in Chapter One, of the role of perception and misperception in superpower relations, focusing on the Reagan Administration and its ideological framework. The following chapter provides a close analysis of official US public communications on the subject of KAL 007. Of necessity, this chapter includes references to the concurrent Soviet reactions, in order to illustrate the relationship between the rhetoric of the two principal actors. Chapter Three considers the question of persuasion versus security: did the US sacrifice public adherence in order to maintain the sanctity of intelligence sources and methods? Specifically, this chapter addresses the issue of the existence of ground-to-air tapes: whether the US possesses, or had access to, recordings of Soviet ground controllers issuing orders to the interceptor pilots who were tracking KAL 007. Finally, in Chapter Four the tapes which are known to exist—the air-to-ground transmissions from the Soviet pilots to their controllers—are examined. The importance of these tapes is underscored by the fact that they constitute the only hard evidence offered by the United States in its prosecution of the propaganda war—for that matter, they are the only hard evidence provided by anyone. Despite the fact that the tapes had been recorded and translated under less than ideal conditions, the English translation became the basis for the US case. The transcript also served as the focal point for much of the speculation found in various scenarios of the shootdown. Yet none of these commentators availed themselves of knowledgeable assistance regarding the Russian text, which was released simultaneously. Our analysis underscores the need for access to the originals of foreign language materials. As Joynt and Corbett point out, "only the correct version of events will enable accurate tests of hypotheses,... for if the data are false or wrongly classified totally false conclusions will be drawn from the 'facts.'"[9]

In Part Two we consider the Soviet position. This section begins, in Chapter Five, with a discussion of important issues in Soviet communication policy: the nature of news reporting; the role of propaganda; communication flow between the state and the citizenry; and the impact of Western transnational broadcasting, particularly Voice of America and Radio Liberty. Also included is a brief discussion of the international climate prevailing in late summer, 1983. Chapter Six evaluates Soviet rhetorical behavior in the immediate aftermath of the shootdown, culminating with Andropov's statement on September 28—the first domestic commentary made by any Soviet governmental (as opposed to military) official. Chapter Seven considers the subsequent public treatment of the event through early 1988, with special attention focused upon the anniversaries. Shifts in the Soviet position are accorded particular emphasis.

Part Three looks at the conspiracy theories that arose around the loss of KAL 007. After an examination, in Chapter Eight, of the genre of conspiratist rhetoric, Chapter Nine focuses on the construction of a particular conspiracy claim involving the Korean airliner, as a vehicle to understanding the rhetorical force and persistence of such theories.

Finally, the Conclusion summarizes the findings of this study, relating the disparate parts to a coherent search for answers in a situation marked by crisis rhetoric and uncertainty. This chapter will provide a synthesis of the rhetorical characteristics of propaganda and conspiratist rhetoric.

The corpus for this study ranges broadly. All official statements of the United States government and its representatives for the period September 1-October 31, 1983, were examined.[10] Special attention was paid to news coverage of the incident broadcast into the Soviet Union by Voice of America, since such broadcasting is perceived there as the official US position. The *New York Times, Los Angeles Times,* and *Washington Post,* as well as the major news weeklies, were scrutinized for both factual information and 'unofficial' statements attributed directly or indirectly to US government representatives.

We examined all Soviet statements promulgated at the United Nations and via the press, radio, and television as well as subsequent press items which appeared sporadically through January 1988. Publications scrutinized include *Pravda* [Truth], *Izvestiia* [News], *Krasnaia zvezda* [Red Star], *Literaturnaia gazeta* [Literary Gazette], *Trud* [Labor], *Sovetskaia Rossiia* [Soviet Russia], *Aviatsiia i kosmonavtika* [Aviation and Astronautics].[11] Again, the critical periods were September/October 1983 and the anniversaries.

Other US and foreign periodical publications were consulted as the need arose. In addition to the seminal David Pearson article, a considerable body of literature espousing the spyplane theory has appeared in the West.[12] A number of articles, often very technical in nature, have been published in the attempt to counter specific claims proposed by the various conspiratists. [These shall be cited in the text as their evidence becomes relevant].[13] Moreover, with each anniversary of the KAL disaster, additional books have appeared in the West,[14] many of which posit a United States conspiracy. A summary of the contents of the major books and monographs appears in the Appendix.

The methodology we have used is grounded in a number of theoretical perspectives, but relies primarily on analysis of argument structure and language use as evidenced in the primary corpus, and, where appropriate, on factual integrity. Specific theoretical constructs are discussed as they become relevant. We adopt the methodological perspective that no single approach is necessarily the most illuminating for all of the types of rhetoric under scrutiny; thus, we have elected to approach each example of discourse in a manner that best accounts for its role in the overall argument. In general, however, the purpose and internal logic of each government's arguments are studied in isolation and in their relationship to those put forth by the other side; arguments propounded by the conspiratists are contrasted with the position of the United States government in light of relevant technical studies.

While the present work does not constitute a treatise on propaganda theory, it is nonetheless necessary to advance a working definition in order to examine what we contend was a propaganda war between the United States and the Soviet Union over the Korean airliner tragedy. In the West, propaganda has acquired a pejorative connotation, resulting in part from the checkered history of such studies in the United States. During World War II, the research emphasis in the

US shifted to development of pro-Allied propaganda, the analysis of Axis propaganda, and concentration on practical explication of persuasive techniques. Quantitatively based studies of persuasion continued to thrive in the post-War era, while the notion of propaganda became more and more identified in the public mind with the enemy.[15]

One of the difficulties encountered in studying propaganda is that of conceptual definition. There seems to be little agreement among scholars as to what constitutes 'propaganda' and no clear distinction between that concept and 'persuasion' or even 'education.' Steinfatt surveyed the major works on propaganda theory, recording eight different definitions, none of which clearly delineates the notion of propaganda from other communication activities.[16]

Although propaganda, education, and persuasion may be overlapping concepts, what separates various forms of communication are the means, or method, each utilizes to achieve its goal. Thus, communication may be persuasive, didactic, or propagandistic depending on the method used, not the setting in which the communicative act occurs. Because they enable us to make these useful methodological distinctions among propaganda, education, and persuasion, we accept the definitional criteria for propaganda suggested by Steinfatt:

1. A desire to hide evidence from public scrutiny;

[As Lee and Lee point out, the propagandist "seldom wants careful scrutiny and criticism."][17]

2. A desire to circumvent or subvert rational processes.

[Steinfatt accepts Bartlett's notion that propaganda operates in a manner that influences people while discouraging them from making any definite search for reasons to adopt the opinions and behaviors advocated. In contrast, (true) education stimulates people to seek to "understand for themselves why they do what they do."][18]

We suggest that these criteria manifest themselves in the form of the communicative act, making it possible to distinguish propaganda from persuasion, education, and other types of communication.[19] In the present case, one can distinguish propaganda, at least in part, by the degree to which it deviates from factual information which was available or which should have been available to the rhetors at the time of the discourse. In this sense, propaganda, as we define it for the purposes of this book, is a subspecies of subversive rhetoric, since it relies on the intellectual coercion of the auditor for its effect.

These ideas are, of course, based on the Western model of communication and, in that respect, suffer from the same narrowness of viewpoint as American understanding of the nature and function of communication in information-restricted societies. The uniqueness of Soviet propaganda lies in Lenin's conception of it as an educational responsibility of the state: it is viewed as a function of government, much as is the duty to administer the bureaucracy or to maintain a national defense.[20] Implications stemming from this notion often are not fully understood, yet, as Kenez points out, "This aspect of the Marxist heritage is the most crucial one for understanding the Bolshevik ... attitude toward propaganda."[21] There is no evidence to suggest that this role has changed materially over the years. While the Soviet state tends to blur possible distinctions among propaganda, persuasion, and education, nevertheless the criteria for identifying propaganda apply equally well to the Soviet model.

In addition to the propaganda analysis, we intend to examine conspiratist rhetoric as a genre of public communication. For purposes of this study, we have defined a rhetorical genre as a combination of situational and formal similarities—a melding, as it were, of content and style.[22] Thus, in our consideration of the conspiracy theories which sprang up around the controversy of KAL 007, we shall look for common methods and techniques, consistent styles and linguistic choices, some of which already have been identified in existing scholarly literature. The unifying concept in this analysis is that of coercion: rhetoric becomes less persuasive and more coercive as it limits the intellectual choices of the auditor. Close textual analysis of argumentative structures, language choices, and other rhetorical devices will be used.

Obviously, the present study relies heavily on the content of news stories and reports, including but not limited to accounts or transcripts of official US briefings and presentations. Some would argue that news reporting does not constitute rhetoric (others would disagree), and certainly in the classical sense they are right. Nevertheless, the process of reporting the news in the US, virtually instantaneous in some instances, becomes part of the text of a rhetorical event: it defines an event, through what is reported and what is not. In effect, the media determine the rhetorical situation.[23] One could argue, for example, that the media were responsible for Reagan's early return to Washington from his Santa Barbara vacation, by creating an image of unconcern with pictures of the president's horseback rides as the background to reports on the shootdown. Certainly, were it not for the present-day capabilities of news reporting, the propaganda war following the KAL disaster could not have taken place. The war was one of words, carried on over television, on the pages of the print media, and in the chambers of the United Nations. Television brought us the first reports of the tragedy, the Shultz press conference, the president's addresses, the United Nations debate, the Moscow press conference of Marshal Ogarkov; transcripts of all of these events were printed in *The New York Times*. To the extent that all rhetorical events are mediated, either electronically or in print, the small screen and the space-borne satellite have replaced the stump and the chautauqua tent as the podiums and auditoriums of our age.

The nature of news reporting in the Soviet Union is more fully developed in Chapter Five. At this point, it is sufficient to point out that Soviet media serve similar functions of issue definition for citizens of that country. Indeed, one might even argue that the context-defining nature of the media is exacerbated in a situation where domestic news is controlled, since virtually all material that appears in the Soviet print and electronic media can be equated with the official views of the government. According to Mickiewicz, "In Soviet society the newspaper was virtually canonized by Lenin and continues to enjoy a prestige in official rhetoric that no other medium can approach."[24] Thus, it is to the Soviet media that we must turn to learn the answer to one of our primary questions: How did the Soviet government handle this specific rhetorical problem? — *does rhetoric include lying?*

Further, with regard to the destruction of KAL 007, it can safely be asserted that without Western transnational broadcasting, no rhetorical situation could ever have been created inside the Soviet Union. Only the insistent barrage of news and commentary from external sources forced the Soviet media to treat KAL 007 as a news story. It is important to remember that as late as 1986, the greatest nuclear power plant disaster in history—the explosion at Chernobyl—was first revealed to the world not by the Soviet Union but by Swedish scientists who detected excess radiation two days after the event and traced its source to the Ukraine. Officials in Moscow knew enough to order the total evacuation of several towns and villages shortly after the accident, but nothing was disclosed either domestically or internationally until after the Swedish announcement.[25] Accordingly, the content of Western news broadcasts beamed into the Soviet Union by radio stations such as Radio Liberty and the Voice of America constitute an indispensable element in the international controversy that raged after the Korean airliner was shot down, for it served as the focal point of Soviet domestic propaganda.

INTRODUCTION

NOTES

[1] *Pravda*, September 2, 1983. Soviet spokespersons later contended that this announcement had, in fact, contained an admission regarding the fate of the airliner, had Western observers only known how to read Soviet news releases; evidently, the phrase "toward the Sea of Japan" was intended to be taken literally.

[2] Cable News Network broadcast the press conference in the United States.

[3] This statement was read over national radio and television on the evening of September 28, 1983, and printed in all daily newspapers the next morning. See: "Zaiavlenie general'nogo sekretaria TsK KPSS predsedatelia Presidiuma Verkhovnogo soveta SSSR Iu. V. Andropova," *Pravda*, September 29, 1983, p. 1.

[4] Most prominent among these was: David Pearson, "K.A.L. 007: What the US Knew and When We Knew It," *The Nation*, August 18-25. 1984, 105-24. See, also, note 13.

[5] *ABC NEWS/WASHINGTON POST POLL*, Survey #0084, September 22-26, 1983. *THE NEW YORK TIMES/CBS NEWS POLL*, September 14, 1983; see: Adam Clymer, "Nation is Confused About Jet Downing, Latest Poll Suggests," *The New York Times*, September 16, 1983, pp. A1, A8.

[6] "The Soviet version of events was accepted by nearly 80% of non-listeners to Western radio, as against fewer than 20% of Western radio listeners [in the sample]." See: K. Mihalisko and R. Parta, *The Korean Airline Incident: Western Radio and Soviet Perceptions*, RFE/RL Soviet Area Audience and Opinion Research, AR 4-84, April 1984, p. 9. Depending on demographic criterion selected, 25-51% of the Soviet urban adult population obtains information on international issues from Western radio (BBC, Deutsche Welle, VOA, RFE/RL). See: *Information Sources and the Soviet Citizen: Domestic Media and Western Radio*, RFE/RL Soviet Area Audience and Opinion Research, AR 5-81, June 1981, pp. 16-20. The authors of both studies caution that all their figures are based on "unweighted frequency counts" of the data and that their sample is "skewed in favor of urban educated males of Russian nationality who are members of the Communist Party." In the authors' opinion, the value of their study is its examination of the "correlations between attitude and source of information"; they explicitly caution against extrapolating their results to the Soviet population at large.

[7] National Strategy Information Center, June 7-11, 1986. See below (Chapter Nine, note 9) for details.

[8] The neologism conspiratists will be used throughout this book in order to avoid the pejorative connotations of the phrase "conspiracy theorists" and the awkwardness of

repeatedly using "conspiracy proponents," "conspiratorialists," "cabalists," or similar locutions.

[9]Carey B. Joynt and Percy E. Corbett, *Theory and Reality in World Politics* (Pittsburgh: University of Pittsburgh Press, 1978), p. 116.

[10]Many of these are contained in *KAL Flight #007: Compilation of Statements and Documents, September 1-16, 1983* (Washington, DC: United States Department of State, Bureau of Public Affairs). Henceforth cited as *COMPILATION*.

[11]Except as noted, all citations from Russian sources were translated by M. Launer. In many instances, Foreign Broadcast Information Service translations exist, but we have often found these to be inaccurate or poorly phrased. [FBIS, which operates under administrative control of the Central Intelligence Agency, provides 'open source' (unclassified) research and translation for units within the Executive branch.] Translations of certain important texts have also been published in the *Current Digest of the Soviet Press*.

[12]Among the more prominent of these "conspiracy" articles are: Tom Bernard and T. Edward Eskelson, "U.S. Spy Plane Capable of Interceding in Attack on Korean Jet," *Denver Post*, September 13, 1983, p. 3B; R. W. Johnson, "007: License to Kill?", *The Guardian*, December 17, 1983, p. 15; Anonymous (P. Q. Mann), "Reassessing the Sakhalin Incident," *Defence Attaché* , June 1984, 41-56; John Keppel, "Was KAL Incident Really an Accident?", *USA Today*, August 31, 1984, p. 10A; Anthony Sampson and Wilhelm Bittorf, "'Sinken auf eins-null-tausend . . . ' Der Todesflug des Korea-Jumbo" ["'Descending to One-Zero-Thousand . . .' Death Flight of the Korean Jumbo Jet"], *Der Spiegel*, September 24 and October 1, 8, and 15, 1984 (four parts); David Pearson and John Keppel, "Journey Into Doubt: New Pieces in the Puzzle of Flight 007," *The Nation* , August 17-24, 1985, 104-110; Sugwon Kang, "Flight 007: Was There Foul Play?", *Bulletin of Concerned Asian Scholars*, 17:2 (1985), 30-48.

[13]Two important publications should be cited here: United Nations Organization. International Civil Aviation Organization, *Destruction of Korean Air Lines Boeing 747 Over Sea of Japan, 31 August 1983. Report of the ICAO Fact-Finding Investigation*, December 1983 [Henceforth, *ICAO REPORT*]; United Nations Organization. ICAO. Air Navigation Commission, *1818th Report to Council by the President of the Air Navigation Commission*, Document C-WP/7809, February 16, 1984 [Henceforth, *ANC REPORT*]. These documents represent the formal investigation of the KAL disaster conducted under UN auspices.

[14]G. Bensi, L. Roitman, and L. Predtechevskiy, *Sachalin--befehl zum Mord. Der erste vollstandige Hintergrundbericht* (Munchen: L. Roitman Verlag, 1983); M. Kalyanasundaram, M.P., *Flight 007* (Delhi: New Literature, 1983); David M. Johnson, *Korean Airlines Incident: U.S. Intelligence Disclosures* (Cambridge: Harvard University, Center for Information Policy Research, 1984), Program on Information Resources Policy. Incidental Paper [I-84-2]; Major-General Richard Rohmer, *Massacre 747* (Markham, Ontario, Canada: PaperJacks Ltd., 1984); Jeffrey St. John, *Day of the Cobra: The True*

Story of KAL Flight 007 (Nashville: Thomas Nelson Publishers, 1984) [this book is really about Congressman McDonald]; Oliver Clubb, *KAL Flight 007. The Hidden Story* (Sag Harbor, NY: Permanent Press, 1985); Alexander Dallin, *Black Box: KAL 007 and the Superpowers* (Berkeley: University of California Press, 1985); Franz A. Kadell, *The KAL 007 Massacre* (Alexandria, VA: Western Goals Foundation, 1985); R. B. Cutler, *Explo 007: Evidence of Conspiracy* (Beverly Farms, MA: R. B. Cutler, 1986); Seymour M. Hersh, *"The Target Is Destroyed"* (New York: Random House, 1986); R. W. Johnson, *Shootdown: The Verdict on KAL 007* (London: Chatto & Windus, 1986) [published in the United States as *Shootdown: Flight 007 and the American Connection* (New York: Viking, 1986)]; David E. Pearson, *KAL 007: The Cover-Up* (New York: Summit, 1987).

The Soviet Union published *"Prestuplenie prezidenta. Provokatsiia s iuzhnokoreiskim samoletom sovershena po prikazu Reigana "* [*The President's Crime: The South Korean Airliner Provocation Was Carried Out On Reagan's Orders*] (Moscow: Izdatel'stvo Agentstva pechati Novosti, 1984). This book is an "abridged translation" of a Japanese study by one Akio Takahasi (a pseudonym). An English text, somewhat different than the Russian and, apparently, the Japanese versions, is available in two editions: *President's Crime: Who ordered the espionage flight of KAL007?* (Tokyo: Ningensha, 1985), distributed by Kinokuniya Book Stores of America; and *Truth Behind KAL Flight 007* (New Delhi, India: Sterling, 1985).

In addition to the Takahasi book, at least two pamphlets and four other books on KAL have been published in Japanese, plus three books in Korean, and one in Greek. Nor should one ignore a lurid French novel, *Le vol 007 ne repond plus* , by Gerard de Villiers (Paris: Librairie Plon, 1984).

[15]For a discussion of the course of propaganda analysis during this period, see: J. Michael Sproule, "The Institute for Propaganda Analysis: Public Education in Argumentation, 1937-1942," in David Zarefsky, Malcolm O. Sillars, and Jack Rhodes, eds., *Argument in Transition: Proceedings of the Third Summer Conference on Argumentation,* (Annandale, VA: Speech Communication Association, 1983), 486-99; also: J. Michael Sproule, "Propaganda Studies in American Social Science: The Rise and Fall of the Critical Paradigm," *Quarterly Journal of Speech,* 73:1 (February 1987), 60-78. Sproule's findings also have been reported in an unpublished paper, "What Ever Happened to Propaganda," presented at the 1987 biennial convention of the World Communication Association, Norwich, England, August 1987.

[16]Thomas M. Steinfatt, "Evaluating Approaches to Propaganda Analysis," *et cetera* , 36:2 (Summer 1979), 157-80, pp. 159-60. Among the definitions that Steinfatt examined were those of Ellul, Lee and Lee, Doob, and Lasswell. Studies of Soviet propaganda, written primarily in the disciplines of political science and history, suffer from the same problem. Kenez, for example, gives the broadest possible interpretation to the notion of propaganda, defining it as "the attempt to transmit social and political values in the hope of affecting people's thinking, emotions, and thereby behavior." While such a broad definition of the term may be appropriate for the Soviet conception of propaganda, which combines education, political indoctrination, and social

mobilization, it is not particularly useful as a conceptual definition for categorizing specific instances. Kenez takes the position that propaganda is "an integral part of the modern world" and that when people object to it, they are usually objecting to "its goals or methods." This statement serves only to emasculate what little value resides in his definition, for, we would contend, propaganda is method. See: Peter Kenez, *The Birth of the Propaganda State: Soviet Methods of Mass Mobilization, 1917-1929* (New York: Cambridge University Press, 1985), p. 4.

[17] Alfred McClung Lee and Elizabeth Briant Lee, *The Fine Art of Propaganda* (New York: Harcourt, Brace, 1939), p. 15. [Quoted in Steinfatt, p. 161.]

[18] F. C. Bartlett, "The Aims of Political Propaganda," in D. Katz, D. Cartwright, S. Eldersveld, and A. Lee, *Opinion and Propaganda* (New York: Holt, 1954), 463-70, p. 465. [Quoted in Steinfatt, p. 162.] Steinfatt notes that the practice of education frequently differs from the ethic expressed in this criterion.

[19] Steinfatt concedes, and we agree, that some education is propaganda; *i.e.*, when education takes the form of attempting to influence or control thought and conduct without also teaching rational processes and critical thinking.

[20] Lenin's theoretical statements regarding the role of propaganda and the nature of the press in a socialist society were expressed in a pamphlet, *Chto delat'?* , the title of which is redolent with symbolism for his audience because it harks back to one of the classics of nineteenth-century Russian intellectual thought. See: V. I. Lenin, *What Is To Be Done?* (New York: International Publishers, 1969).

[21] Kenez, p. 5.

[22] See: Karlyn Kohrs Campbell and Kathleen Hall Jamieson, *Form and Genre: Shaping Rhetorical Action* (Falls Church, VA: Speech Communication Association, 1976). Creps has demonstrated the generic nature of the conspiratist argument. See: Earl G. Creps III, *The Conspiracy Argument as Rhetorical Genre* , Diss. Northwestern University, 1980 (Ann Arbor: UMI, 1981).

[23] As Bennett, *et al.* , observed, "[T]he news media take an active part in the selection, reconstruction, and evaluation of social life. . . ." See: W. Lance Bennett, Lynne A. Gressett, and William Haltom, "Repairing the News: A Case Study of the News Paradigm," *Journal of Communication* , 35:2 (Spring 1985), 50-68, p. 68.

[24] Ellen Propper Mickiewicz, *Media and the Russian Public* , Praeger Special Studies (New York: Praeger, 1981), p. viii.

[25] The Soviet Union's historical reluctance to discuss such topics is well documented in a recent study. See: James E. Oberg, *Uncovering Soviet Disasters. Exploring the Limits of Glasnost* (New York: Random House, 1988).

PART ONE

THE UNITED STATES

PERCEPTION AND MISPERCEPTION

> The United States has two Soviet prob-
> lems. One is the real but manageable
> Soviet threat to our national security
> and international interests.
> The second, and increasingly more
> serious, problem is Sovietophobia, or
> exaggerated fear of that Soviet threat.
>
> *—Stephen F. Cohen*
> *April 9, 1983*[1]

Cohen points out in his perspicacious essay that "Americans have habitually found in the Soviet Union only what they seek."[2] Certainly the present leadership in Washington is no exception. While fear of the Soviets was not created, or even uniquely perpetuated, by the Reagan Administration, its role as a centerpiece of the current Washington outlook is no secret: "the Soviet Union is 'the focus of evil in the modern world.'"[3] The destruction of KAL 007 simply demonstrated the "gulf of mutual antipathy and distrust"[4] that separated a "barbaric" Soviet society from "civilized nations" throughout the world.

Of course, US spokesmen acted as though the character of the event itself provoked the outraged response of the United States and the rest of the world, and at some level that is undoubtedly true. But the significance of perception cannot be discounted; Hugo has emphasized the importance of choice in the development of international disputes:

> [G]overnments have to decide whether or not to identify [an incident] as a cause of dispute by manifesting an objection. If that decision is to be rational, it must be prompted by some prediction of the likely consequences either of declaring a dispute or else of ignoring the incident.... Neither in theory nor in practice is it possible to argue that certain categories of action will invariably arouse objection and that others will not. Similar causes do not have similar effects in international relations.[5]

3

There is little question that the United States publicly treated the destruction of Korean Air Lines Flight 007 as an international crisis. The ensuing confrontation was nearly unprecedented in vitriol, if not in actual prospects for military conflict. Hugo would undoubtedly agree that any decision to manifest an objection—particularly a decision to treat an incident as a crisis—entails certain risks. First and foremost among these certainly is the possible miscalculation of consequences. Worst of all, in this particular instance, it is unclear whether any assessment such as that prescribed by Hugo ever took place. If so, what were perceived as the consequences of ignoring the Korean airliner incident? What goals were sought in manifesting an objection?

The role of the perceptual process—as well as Hugo's point—is underscored by a similar incident that occurred a decade earlier, but which received a very different response: the 1973 destruction of a Libyan passenger airliner over the Sinai Peninsula by the Israeli Air Force. The Israeli action was downplayed as a tragic, but understandable, consequence of nerves frayed by war. Of course, as Holsti has pointed out, there is "an apparently universal tendency to judge the actions of others—and particularly of those defined as enemies—according to different standards from those applied to oneself. Because friends are expected to be friendly and enemies to be hostile, there is a tendency to view their behavior in line with these expectations."[6] Certainly, the labeling of an enemy as such creates public expectations about the classification of a whole series of potential behaviors; leaders violate those expectations at their peril. And the definition of a situation as an international crisis establishes a rhetorical situation, setting in motion public expectations regarding appropriate responses; witness public opprobrium of the discrepancy between Reagan's words and the actions ultimately taken during the KAL "crisis."

Thus, it is fair to ask whether the shootdown of KAL 007 constituted a genuine international crisis, and, if so, what made it so? This is not an idle question: Reagan's two closest advisors, Judge William P. Clark,[7] head of the National Security Council, and Edwin Meese III, White House Chief of Staff, did not deem confirmation of the shootdown, which they received in the pre-dawn hours of September 1, sufficiently urgent to wake the president even though important decisions were being reached concerning the nature of any US response.[8]

Haas recently surveyed scholarly research into the nature of international crisis.[9] He determined that no consensus exists regarding either a conceptual or empirical definition of 'crisis,'[10] but certain ideas do seem to be prevalent. According to Lentner, "[T]ime pressure is the most important element of a crisis from the standpoint of [State Department] decision makers," having been cited by 67.1% of respondents as a factor always involved in crisis situations. The next most frequently cited factor was "uncertainty due to inadequate information."[11] Haas and Brecher both conclude that "unexpectedness is not a central element."[12] Surprisingly, Haas found unexpectedness to be a negatively correlated criterion, while "threat of violence or war" proved to be only the fifth most significant component of a crisis situation.[13]

In all, Haas reviewed two dozen different studies: judging by the published synopses, the destruction of KAL 007 does not conform fully to any one of the definitions proposed in the literature. While no one would claim that the avoidable death of 269 people was unimportant, it is equally true that the situation did not <u>necessarily</u> constitute an international crisis fraught with the possibility of armed superpower confrontation.[14] In this instance, available evidence seems to indicate that trusted presidential confidants, including CIA Director William J. Casey, Undersecretary of State for Political Affairs Lawrence S. Eagleburger, and Assistant Secretary of State for European and Soviet Affairs Richard R. Burt—with probable input from Clark and Meese—made that determination independently and set into motion the ensuing political events. It seems appropriate, therefore, to consider the rhetorical environment created by the individuals advising the president on foreign policy matters.

Mr. Reagan's foreign policy advisors, many of whom were prominent members of the ultraconservative Committee on the Present Danger, have been described as "ideologically oriented crusaders."[15] Tucker also has commented upon the "ideological commitment of the president and most of his principal associates."[16] In addition, with the exception of Professor Richard E. Pipes, who had left the Administration in 1982 to return to Harvard University,

> loyalty to the president and managerial experience account[ed] for most senior appointments dealing with the Soviet Union.... The Reagan administration [has found] itself singularly lacking in individuals at critical policy making or advisory positions who [were] knowledgeable about Soviet affairs.[17]

In part, this situation evolved as a direct consequence of the fact that "the Reagan wing of the Republican party... [has] a paucity of competent foreign policy specialists. This is particularly true of experts on the Soviet Union."[18] Secretary of State George P. Shultz, who replaced General Haig in 1982, remained outside the circle of close presidential advisors, to a great extent simply because, "in contrast to some of the administration ideologues, he espoused a more pragmatic approach to foreign affairs."[19] Yet many observers feel that such diversity of opinion is necessary for effective decision-making. A number of historians and commentators have studied the Kennedy Administration's approach to the Cuban missile crisis as an exemplar of the rational foreign policy decision. Hugo commented on the role of divergent opinions in those policy deliberations:

> [Robert Kennedy] argues convincingly that less correct and far more dangerous choices might have been made in October 1962 if these had not been debated at length, in secrecy and in exhaustive detail among a group of men with sharply conflicting views. His account ... deserves careful consideration by all advocates of the convenience of the quick decisions that emanate from a small group of like-minded men.[20]

Janis, of course, labelled the latter phenomenon 'Groupthink.'[21]

Dallin and Lapidus offer the opinion that the president himself focuses his attention "not on what the Soviet Union does but what it is. Highly determinist in approach,... [he] defines the Soviet system as inherently evil ... [and] sees little prospect for change."[22] Reagan, of course, campaigned for the presidency on a platform of strengthening America's image in the world, overcoming the legacy left by the Carter years: a self-perception of indecisiveness and weakness. Neustadt cautioned about the power of this sort of imagery when he wrote, "The tendency of bureaucratic language to create in private the same images presented to the public never should be underrated."[23] Unfortunately, a rhetorical environment which fosters images of "the evil empire" becomes the proverbial 'self-fulfilling prophecy,' for, as Holsti observes, "When the other party is viewed within the framework of an 'inherent bad faith' model, the image of the enemy is clearly self-perpetuating, for the model itself denies the existence of data that could disconfirm it."[24] Nevertheless, according to Tucker, in the "simple world of the [Reagan] administration" it appears that defense against Soviet military power "has come very close to being a substitute for foreign policy."[25]

In Gaddis's opinion, Reagan has stressed defense over diplomacy in American dealings with the Soviet Union to an excessive degree:

> [O]ne would ... have to go back to the late Truman Administration to find a comparable emphasis upon the accumulation of military hardware and a corresponding degree of skepticism regarding negotiations.[26]

Distrust of negotiation as an instrument for dealing with the enemy is a result of the dichotomous view of the world held by ideologues such as Reagan. Hofstadter discusses the tendency of militant leaders to regard conflicts as ultimate battlegrounds between good and evil, not the subject of negotiation and compromise. "The quality needed is not a willingness to compromise, but the will to fight things out to a finish."[27]

Many historians and political scientists seem to agree on this assessment of Ronald Reagan and the effect his philosophy has had on the quality of advice he receives. According to Dallin and Lapidus, for example, "[h]is choices seem to be based on instinct and deeply rooted prejudices, and his advisers often tend to tailor their recommendations to fit his presumed views and biases."[28] Indeed, the style of the Reagan Administration was characterized by a former senior national security official as "an ad hoc,... shoot-from-the-hip method of making our national security affairs decisions. Our actions are based primarily upon emotion...."[29]

This lack of coherent methodology may explain the "intellectual helplessness occasionally manifest in the administration" and the predilection "to engage in rhetorical political warfare with the Soviet Union."[30] This is the very model of decision-making denigrated by Hugo, who speaks of the necessity for having clear goals in mind when raising a foreign policy dispute: "The decision to manifest an objection ... should not be prompted by a subjective judgement of the nature and quality of the objectionable act, but by considering what [outcome] could be expected if no objection were manifested."[31] Yet, this description of the Reagan situation room conforms with Dowty's opinion that, in general, "decision-makers simply accommodate information to their prevailing perceptions, activating their basic values, instincts, and belief system so as to impose order on a complex and uncertain reality...."[32] Dowty explicitly rejects the "rational actor" and "organizational-institutional" models of decision-making.[33]

A crisis atmosphere is expected to evoke sharp debate, given the importance of decisions taken and the high level of tension.... But ... these debates appear to involve the means to be employed rather than basic policy.... [T]here is little inclination for reconsideration of basic aims.[34]

According to Dowty, during crisis deliberations value concepts and short term policy objectives tend to remain "impervious to new inputs."[35] In the case of the Reagan Administration, "[t]he point of departure is a dichotomous view of the world."[36] Janis warned against this style of decision-making, in which the outcome was a "*group* product, issuing from a series of meetings of a small body of government officials and advisers who constituted a cohesive group."[37] In Janis's study, as a result of in-group pressures "the members of the policy-making group made incredibly gross miscalculations about both the practical and moral consequences of their decisions."[38]

These observations allow one to draw a picture of inexperienced, philosophically rigid, anti-Soviet advisers following the gut-level instincts they share with their president and making crucial decisions in his absence. Nor were these decisions taken in some abstract exercise; rather, the course of superpower relations was being fixed for at least the short-term. As Jones has observed, "if men define situations as real, they are real in their consequences." Moreover, "in determining social reality, beliefs have consequences whether they are true or false."[39] Or, as Harold and Margaret Sprout pointed out over thirty years ago, when one is talking about policy making and the resultant decisions,

what matters is how the policy-maker imagines the milieu to be, not how it actually is. With respect to the operational results of decisions, what matters is how things are,... not how the policy-maker imagines them to be....[40]

From the very inception of the Reagan Administration, the general strategy of political warfare embraced by its foreign policy leadership "implied an effort to isolate the Soviet Union."[41] KAL, of course, provided a remarkable opportunity for implementation of this strategy, because, as Halle wrote, "The ideological view of human affairs ... conforms to the child's image of a world divided between two species, the good (we) and the wicked (they)."[42] The self-confirming nature of this perceptual framework is described by Jervis:

[I]f an actor expects a phenomenon to appear, he is likely to perceive ambiguous stimuli as being that phenomenon. When one
is sure that an object will be present, it takes very little information, or information that bears little resemblance to the object, to
convince one that one is seeing it.[43]

Hence, it should not be surprising that ideologically minded
advisors would follow "the basic attitudes of our American nation,
which always prefers dynamic action to the patient inaction that
foreign relations so often demand; which believes in seizing the
initiative even in situations that give the advantage to those who, by
waiting, retain their freedom of choice."[44] Under the circumstances, it
was natural to revert to the kind of "massive ... verbal assault" with
which, ironically, Soviet representatives at the 1947 Cominform
Congress had initiated the Cold War.[45] Dynamic action required, in this
instance, a verbal attack upon the Soviet Union for perpetrating such
an atrocity. But charges must be backed by evidence—and the need for
evidence brought into play the whole intelligence apparatus of the
United States defense establishment.

Seymour Hersh has documented the role played by William Casey
in shaping the initial Administration assessment of events as they had
transpired over Sakhalin Island.[46] Casey, Hersh reports, relied on the
opinions of Fritz Ermath, the CIA's national intelligence officer for the
Soviet Union and Eastern Europe. Ermath,

who was known throughout the bureaucracy for his rigid anti-
Soviet ideology and for his propensity during crises to
consistently attribute the worst motives to the Soviets ... found
more than enough evidence to conclude that the Soviet
interceptor pilot had identified the aircraft as civilian before
shooting it down. His biases melded perfectly with those of
William Casey....[47]

Casey's role in the political aftermath of KAL raises critical
questions of the function of Intelligence—as an institution—in the
formulation of national policy. Ever since the earliest post-War
discussions of America's need for a centralized intelligence service,
prominent military, political, and diplomatic officials have emphasized the imperative that the functions of collecting and analyzing
intelligence be rigorously insulated from the policy making process.
During Congressional hearings on the establishment of the CIA, Allen

W. Dulles, who later headed the Agency, stated flatly, "The Central Intelligence Agency should have nothing to do with policy." Otherwise, Dulles believed [quite rightly as history has amply demonstrated], it would be too likely that policy makers would be "blind to any facts which might tend to prove the policy to be faulty."[48] General William J. "Bull" Donovan adopted the same position for different reasons; Donovan testified that intelligence functions needed to be centralized specifically because "intelligence must be independent of the people it serves so that the material it obtains will not be slanted or distorted by the views of the people directing operations."[49] Thus, leading military and political figures believed that both collection/analysis and policy determination could be compromised whenever the same individuals or institutions participated in both processes.[50] The primary fear of State Department officials, of course, was that "if intelligence people attuned their minds to policy questions, they couldn't be objective."[51]

In the Reagan Administration, unfortunately, no such fear existed.[52] To an overwhelming extent, it would seem, this fearlessness stemmed from the close personal relationship that existed between the president and the director of Central Intelligence: "One White House official put it simply late last year [1986]: 'Ronald Reagan loves Bill Casey.'"[53]

Woodward described Casey as an "activist director" whose "ability to respond to the yearnings of President Reagan in the policy arena made him one of the most influential figures in the administration." Further, "Casey understood the president's desires." Because of this, the CIA played "as large a role in foreign policy as it ever has."[54] Hersh has documented serious doubts among important intelligence officials regarding Soviet knowledge and intentions during the early morning destruction of KAL 007. But, by anticipating the president's reaction, Casey was able to shape the US response to the tragedy:

> One essential decision was made almost casually. To erase any doubts as to the categorical nature of the American information, Shultz would make clear to the world that the communications intelligence community had the goods on the Soviets; that America and its allies [here, Japan] had the capability to intercept and translate Soviet military communications in the Far East. Such activities are simply not talked about in public.... No one ... [at] the State Department was troubled by the use of [Top Secret communications intelligence] ... because the Soviet wrongdoing

seemed to override any diplomatic or intelligence considerations.[55]

In the process, of course, pure intelligence and the last pretenses to civility became victims of what may be regarded as a convenient, fabricated crisis. The destruction of KAL 007 was handled as a crisis because Reagan's advisors made it into one. It was their premise that the behavior of the Soviet government had followed the "rational actor" model.[56] This assumption created a false reality that accorded with their preconceptions. An undated Defense Department internal briefing paper placed "the KAL massacre within the mainstream of Soviet foreign policy.... The Soviet diplomacy of threats confirms that military might is useful even in circumstances short of war." The memorandum goes on to cite Soviet press statements from the period April 1980—July 1983 as confirmation of the intentionality of Soviet actions and concludes, "The Korean Air Line massacre should be viewed as the latest in a series of Soviet words and deeds designed to intimidate and characterized by contempt for the norms—and reactions—of civilized nations."[57]

Jervis documents the pathological aspects of working from preconceptions in a decision-making atmosphere such as that at the Reagan White House. In this situation, "[a] person may not even begin to come to grips with a large amount of information that could indicate that his views are incorrect, or, in the absence of an open dispute, may fail to notice events of obvious import." Furthermore, the person

> might refuse to discuss the arguments of those who disagree
> with him or be unable to understand simple but powerful con
> siderations that indicate that he is wrong....
> Since intelligent decision-making involves not only the
> weighing of considerations that are brought to one's attention
> but also the active seeking of information, the failure to look for
> evidence that is clearly available and significant constitutes an
> irrational way of processing information.[58]

It would seem that the president and his advisors found it impossible to believe that "the bear from the North" could make so heinous a mistake.[59] Thus, they ignored available evidence that the Soviets were unaware of the civilian status of the aircraft.[60] And Soviet behavior over the next two weeks—the initial denials of any wrongdoing followed by equally fervent denials that the action had been taken by mis-

11

take—certainly did nothing to challenge this interpretation. Hugo's comment about the Pueblo incident is pertinent: "It is the overt attitude rather than the presumed intentions of the government concerned that determines the apparent character of an objectional act."[61]

Nevertheless, in the abstract, one might have expected a more measured, standardized response through organizational channels, especially within the State Department: Hughes found that the "standard operating procedures and incremental decision making of the organizational model are relied on most heavily when the security of the organization [itself] was not threatened."[62] Certainly, the security of neither country was imperiled by the destruction of KAL 007; the only danger was to national image. Unfortunately, however, threats of this sort often bring out the worst in both individual and national character. In this instance, the designation of the tragedy as an international crisis revealed the ideological blinders guiding the actions of the Reagan Administration. As events transpired, a confluence of ideology and policy ill-served the peoples of all of the major actors: the US, the USSR, Korea, and Japan. In the chapters that follow, we will examine in detail the components of what became a propaganda and public relations fiasco for both superpowers.

NOTES

[1]Stephen F. Cohen, *Sovieticus: American Perceptions and Soviet Realities* (New York: W. W. Norton, 1986), p. 17. This essay originally appeared in *The Nation*, April 9, 1983.

[2]Cohen, p. 19.

[3]Cohen, p. 20. Cohen is presumably quoting Reagan.

[4]Grant Hugo, *Appearance and Reality in International Relations* (London: Chatto and Windus, 1970), p. 84.

[5]Hugo, p. 41.

[6]Ole R. Holsti, "Cognitive Dynamics and Images of the Enemy," in John C. Farrell and Asa P. Smith, eds., *Image and Reality in World Politics* (New York: Columbia University Press, 1967), 16-39, p. 17.

[7]Not long ago Theodore Draper reasserted that Clark's influence on the President during this period was unparalleled. Generally accepted as true in 1983, this relationship seems to have been obscured in the intervening years. See: "Reagan's Junta," *New York Review of Books,* January 29, 1987, 5-14, p. 9. Draper notes that General Alexander M. Haig, Jr., then serving as Mr. Reagan's Secretary of State, "was worried by a situation 'in which a presidential assistant [Clark], especially one of limited experience and limited understanding of the volatile nature of an international conflict [at the time the Falklands crisis], should assume the powers of the Presidency.'" See: Alexander M. Haig, Jr., *Caveat: Realism, Reagan, and Foreign Policy* (New York: Macmillan, 1984), cited by Draper, p. 9.

[8]By comparison, Hurwitz notes that President Richard Nixon was not awakened while Henry Kissinger and Alexander Haig decided to put US armed forces on alert during the Yom Kippur War. Hurwitz questions "whether a threat was honestly perceived by US decision-makers or were they simply trying to counteract the effects of the domestic political scandal,"—*i.e.*, Watergate. Bruce Hurwitz, "Threat Perception, Linkage Politics and Decision Making: The October 1973 Worldwide Alert of US Military Forces," *Jerusalem Journal of International Relations,* 7:3, (1985), 135-44, pp. 143, 135. See, also: Henry Kissinger, *Years of Upheaval* (London: George Weidenfield and Nicolson, 1982), p. 585.

[9]Michael Haas, "Research on International Crisis: Obsolescence of an Approach?", *International Interactions,* 13:1 (1986), 23-58.

[10]Haas, p. 52.

[11]Howard H. Lentner, "The Concept of Crisis as Viewed by the United States Department of State," Chapter Six in Charles F. Herman, ed., *International Crises* (New York: Free Press, 1972). [Cited in Haas, pp. 44-46].

[12]Newman, for one, accepted Brecher's criteria. See: Robert P. Newman, "cForeign Policy: Decision and Argument," in J. Robert Cox and Charles Arthur Willard, eds., *Advances in Argumentation Theory and Research* (Carbondale: Southern Illinois University Press, 1982), 318-42, p. 322.

[13] See: Michael Brecher, "'Vertical' Case Studies: A Summary of Findings," in Michael Brecher, ed., *Studies in Crisis Behavior* (New Brunswick, NJ: Transaction Books, 1978), 264-76; and Michael Haas, *International Conflict* (Indianapolis: Bobbs-Merrill, 1978). [Cited in Haas, "Research on International Crisis," p. 47.]

[14]In the first place, Korean Air Lines is not a United States carrier, so that, from a legal standpoint, the proper role for the Reagan administration to assume would have been that of intermediary for South Korea, a US ally which does not maintain diplomatic relations with the USSR. Further, there was absolutely no indication that the destruction of KAL 007 was anything other than an isolated incident, rather than part of a complex of activities that might have threatened vital US interests in the Far East. An analogy might be drawn to the Suez Crisis, which occurred during the Eisenhower administration. While no one would deny that those events constituted an international crisis involving Egypt, Israel, France, and Great Britain, the United States was not directly involved and thus took no action. Even a recent Soviet commentary has recognized that US restraint during the Suez crisis had an ameliorative effect on events:

> The course of any crisis depends on Washington's actions, which can engender and intensify or, quite the opposite, dampen a crisis (such events do happen—one need only recall the 1956 Suez Crisis). . . .

See: V. V. Zhurkin and V. A. Kremeniuk, "Podkhod SShA k mezhdunarodnym krizisnym situatsiiam" ["The US Approach to International Crisis Situations"], in G. A. Trofimenko, ed., "Sovremennaia vneshniaia politika SShA" [*Current US Foreign Policy*] (Moscow: Nauka, 1984), vol. 1, 370-92, p. 372. Interestingly, according to the endleaf information found in all Soviet books, this manuscript went to press less than three months after the KAL 007 incident.

[15]Dallin and Lapidus, pp. 218, 233 [n. 8]. See, also: Robert Scheer, *With Enough Shovels* (New York: Random House, 1982), pp. 144-46, cited therein.

[16]Robert W. Tucker, "The Role of Defense in the Foreign Policy of the Reagan Administration," *Jerusalem Journal of International Relations*, 7:3 (1985), 47-56, p. 54.

[17]Dallin and Lapidus, p. 204.

[18]Dallin and Lapidus, p. 225.

[19]Dallin and Lapidus, p. 203. Shultz's isolation was underscored as the KAL situation developed during the night of August 31/September 1. A State Department official has told us that Shultz was not informed of the loss of the aircraft until, on the way in to work the next morning, he read a report in his briefing book. This scenario was repeated by Hersh in *"The Target is Destroyed."*

[20]Hugo, p. 77. Wilensky presents a somewhat different view of the organizational environment during the Cuban missile crisis. Wilensky's focus at this point in his study is the impact of slogans on policy and his concern was the residue left by the Bay of Pigs fiasco. See: Harold L. Wilensky, *Organizational Intelligence* (New York: Basic Books, 1967), pp. 19-24.

[21]Irving L. Janis, *Groupthink: Psychological Studies of Policy Decisions and Fiascoes,* 2nd ed. (Boston: Houghton Mifflin, 1982).

[22]Dallin and Lapidus, p. 206.

[23]Richard E. Neustadt, *Presidential Power: The Politics of Leadership* (New York: John Wiley & Sons, 1960), p. 139. Quoted by Wilensky, p. 22.

[24]Holsti, p. 17. Holsti cites Henry A. Kissinger, *The Necessity of Choice* (Garden City: Doubleday, 1982), p. 201, for the origin of the term 'inherent bad faith' model.

[25]Tucker, p. 54.

[26]John Lewis Gaddis, "The Rise, Fall and Future of Detente," *Foreign Affairs,* **62**:2 (Winter 1983/84), 354-77, p. 367.

[27]Hofstadter, "The Paranoid Style in American Politics," in *The Paranoid Style in American Politics and Other Essays* (New York: Knopf, 1965), p. 31. Although Hofstadter was writing about extremist rhetoric, the qualities he describes here are characteristic of ideologues in general, of which Reagan is generally conceded to be one.

[28]Dallin and Lapidus, p. 202.

[29]Bob Woodward, "Casey Revived Demoralized CIA," *Washington Post,* February 3, 1987, pp. A1, A9.

[30]Dallin and Lapidus, pp. 205, 206.

[31]Hugo, pp. 63-64.

[32]Alan Dowty, "US Decision-Making in Middle East Crises: 1958, 1970, 1973," *Jerusalem Journal of International Relations,* 7:3 (1985), 92-106, p. 97.

[33]For a discussion of various models, see Barry B. Hughes, *The Domestic Context of American Foreign Policy* (San Francisco: W. H. Freeman, 1978), pp. 7-15.

[34]Dowty, p. 96.

[35]Dowty, p. 100.

[36]Dallin and Lapidus, p. 206.

[37]Janis, p. *viii*.

[38]Janis, p. *viii*.

[39]R. Jones, *Self-Fulfilling Prophesies: Social, Psychological, and Physiological Effects of Expectancies* (Hillsdale, NJ: Lawrence Erlbaum, 1977).

[40]Harold and Margaret Sprout, "Environmental Factors in the Study of International Politics," *Journal of Conflict Resolution*, 1 (Dec. 1957), 327-28. [Quoted in Charles P. Schliecher, *International Behavior: Analysis and Operations* (Columbus: Charles E. Merrill, 1973), p. 88.]

[41]Dallin and Lapidus, p. 220.

[42]Halle, *The Cold War As History*, p. 157.

[43]Jervis, *Perception and Misperception*, p. 153. In fairness, one should note that Jervis believes, generally, that the tendency to measure information against preconceptions and previous experience is both useful and proper. It is when the regular pattern of behavior is not present, as in an accident, or when "deceptive actors take advantage of our expectations" that the tendency can mislead. See: p. 154.

[44]Halle, *The Cold War As History*, p. 306.

[45]Halle, *The Cold War As History*, pp. 151-52.

[46]Hersh, pp. 100 *et passim*. Of a White House Special Crisis Group that met on September 1, 1983 to discuss KAL, Hersh has written, "George Bush may have been the nominal leader of the group, but all involved . . . understood that the real player in the crowd was Bill Casey" (p. 109).

[47]Hersh, p. 100.

[48]Cited by Roger Hilsman, Jr., "Intelligence and Policy-Making in Foreign Affairs," in James N. Rosenau, ed., *International Politics and Foreign Policy* (Glencoe, IL: Free Press, 1961), 209-19, p. 218 [n. 9]. Hilsman was formerly State Department Director of Intelligence and Research.

[49]Quoted by Hilsman, "Intelligence and Policy-Making," p. 210.

[50]"Hilsman found that policy-makers and intelligence officials alike believed that conclusions flowed directly from the facts and that theory was dangerous at the fact-collection stage and unnecessary at the fact-evaluation stage" (Jervis, p. 172 [n. 124]). See: Roger Hilsman, *Strategic Intelligence and National Decisions* (Glencoe, IL: Free Press, 1956).

[51]Hilsman, "Intelligence and Policy-Making in Foreign Affairs," p. 211.

[52]To be sure, the Reagan administration was hardly the first to be burdened by such contamination: since even President Truman frequently complained about the problem, one can assume it to be endemic to the manner in which the Executive branch functions. Nor does the American post-War experience, littered as it is with numerous examples of policy failure caused by intelligence failure, reduce the importance of the problem in the '80s. This, perhaps, is the fundamental message of Seymour Hersh's investigative reporting; see our review of *"The Target Is Destroyed"* in *Washington Book Review*, 2:1 (January 1987), 9-11. Concerning past foreign policy fiascoes, see: Janis. For a thorough discussion of both the intelligence functions of complex organizations (including governments) and past policy mistakes brought on by intelligence failures, see: Wilensky.

[53]Woodward, p. A9.

[54]Woodward, pp. A1, A9.

[55]Hersh, pp. 100-101.

[56]Hughes has observed, "Commentators on the political scene and even political scientists who should know better also frequently adopt the rational actor model when analyzing the decisions made by a foreign country about which little is known." Behavior of the Soviet Union is cited as a specific example (p. 7).

[57]See: Elie D. Krakowski, "The Korean Air Line Massacre: The Broader Context." This unclassified document was provided by the Public Affairs Office, US Department of State. Attesting to the widespread acceptance of this position is a statement by John Lewis Gaddis, who is usually considered to be a 'revisionist' historian. Writing in late 1983, Gaddis offered this opinion: "The recent Korean airliner incident demonstrates once again [the Soviets'] chronic inability to anticipate the effects their own actions have on the rest of the world. . . ." Such a statement makes no sense unless it is assumed the Soviet action was deliberate. See: Gaddis, "The Rise, Fall, and Future of Detente," p. 367.

[58]Jervis, *Perception and Misperception*, pp. 172-73.

[59]Hughes has found it particularly true that the rational-actor model is used to interpret <u>Soviet</u> decision behavior, "especially by those who feel that the basic values and goals of the Soviet Union are ideological" (p. 229).

[60]Hersh's sources had told him that American intelligence "had not developed any specific evidence showing that the Soviets had knowingly shot down an airliner" (p. 84). This assessment was confirmed in January 1988, with the release of documents by Rep. Lee Hamilton. The declassified material stated in part: "[W]e had concluded by the second day that the Soviets thought they were pursuing a US reconnaissance aircraft throughout most, if not all, of the overflight." Rep. Hamilton, in his letter to Secretary of State George Shultz, points out that "the Administration's position was at the time immediately following the incident that the Soviets knowingly shot down a civilian airliner for intruding into their airspace. I am not aware of any change in the Administration's position thereafter." The State Department's reply is an exemplar of what we term 'narrow parameters of truth.' (See: United States Congress. House. Permanent Select Committee on Intelligence, *Declassified Intelligence Assessments of 1983 KAL Shootdown at Variance With Prevailing Administration Statements* [Washington: U.S. House of Representatives, Committee on Foreign Affairs, January 12, 1988]) These documents were provided by Michael van Dorn, a committee staff member. For a more complete discussion of this phenomenon, see Chapter Two.

[61]Hugo, pp. 56-57.

[62]Hughes, p. 227. He cites (p. 228) one study which determined that "even on a security issue such as the status of Berlin, the frequent repetition of crises threatening Western access gradually moved the issue from one dealt with in a crisis atmosphere by [a] small, rational actor-type group [of top governmental officials] to one handled with standard procedures at lower levels." See Charles McClelland, "Access to Berlin: The Quantity and Variety of Events, 1948-63," in J. David Singer, ed., *Quantitative International Politics* (New York: Free Press, 1968), 159-86.

THE MANY GUISES OF TRUTH
(THE US VERSION)

When Secretary of State George Shultz announced to the world that the Soviet Union had shot down Korean Air Lines Flight 007 with 269 people aboard, he set the stage for a superpower argument unique in intensity, as the government of the United States assumed the burden of convincing both its domestic constituency and the international community that the action of the Soviet Union was a natural result of a barbaric communist system.

As a rhetorical event, the KAL "crisis" was self-contained—that is, it had no apparent antecedents and it dominated the news for a finite period of time. These temporal characteristics make it susceptible to analysis using the interactive nature of the notions of text and context, rhetorical situation, and public knowledge.[1] Public knowledge, which is simply the accumulated wisdom of the people, serves as the authoritative ground for political discourse. It renders a public "competent to accredit new truth and value and to authorize decision and action."[2] It provides the framework for any rhetorical situation, defining those exigencies that demand a response, operating as a precondition of rhetorical discourse, part of the perceptual matrix within which that discourse operates. The KAL controversy provides a clear example of a situation requiring a response, in this instance from the US head of state. The Soviet attack on the airplane instantaneously created a rhetorical situation and served as the catalyst for action. With no warning or campaign to provide a framework for such a discussion, public knowledge consisted only of the perceptions regarding both superpowers held by auditors throughout the world. It was left to rhetors such as Shultz and President Ronald Reagan to establish the initial perceptual construct for apprehending and evaluating the Soviet behavior. Accordingly, Reagan established the ideological context, capturing the sentiments of millions of people with his vitriolic denunciation of the Soviet attack, his characterization of the Soviet government as "barbaric," and his pledge to take decisive measures.

From the perspective of rhetorical theory, the case of the Korean airliner also presents a set of anomalies. While public knowledge is relatively stable in the short term, a crisis atmosphere, with its concomitant demand for information, can disrupt this stability. In the environment generated by feelings of crisis, the relationship between text and context, as well as the relationship between rhetors, the rhetorical situation, and public knowledge, exist in a state of flux, altering the dynamic of public knowledge and its authorization process. The unusual circumstance of the secretary of state announcing the shootdown set the scene for such a disturbance in US public knowledge.

In his press conference, Shultz disclosed unprecedented detail about US intelligence capabilities in the Western Pacific.[3] He also revealed that he had not yet talked with Reagan, which meant that a secretary of state, without benefit of consultation, was playing a role most often assumed by presidents: the bearer of bad news about an international crisis. According to *New York Times* reporter David Hoffman, "Shultz had conferred instead with [National Security Advisor William] Clark. Only after Shultz had finished with reporters at the State Department—and was pointedly asked by them if he had talked to Reagan—did the president call to discuss the matter with him."[4] Thus, from the very beginning, the US response to the tragedy demonstrated a lack of coordination that would ultimately vitiate what might have been the greatest propaganda coup for the West since the Cuban missile crisis.

In modern controversies, argument rarely proceeds in an orderly or formal fashion. The norm, rather, is a multiplicity of rhetors, who typically subject auditors to conflicting information even when aligned on the same side of an issue. When the rhetorical situation includes an atmosphere of crisis, one hears a virtual cacophony of pronouncements and official opinion, particularly in the United States. Nevertheless, in the present instance, it is possible to detect a symbiosis in the rhetorical efforts of East and West, a harmonious ebb and flow of charge and countercharge.

This ebb and flow itself underscores how public discourse defines its context: both text and context "are aspects of the interpretation of an audience, and a particular artifact may be used either as text or context at different times."[5] A crisis occurs suddenly from the perspective of the average citizen, who may be uncertain as to the appropriate reaction; people depend on government officials to provide meaning to the event. In selecting a "fitting response," officials attempt to define the context within which the crisis is to be viewed.[6] But the texts of such responses also reshape the context in which the event should be evaluated: "Texts are constituted by their enmeshment in contexts, but contexts are themselves created and sustained by texts."[7] Accordingly, the distinction between text and context becomes blurred.

In the West, intense media coverage provides new and often discrepant information (including the type of data that comes to public attention as the result of press conferences, investigative reporting, congressional hearings, and academic studies), shaping public perceptions, adding to the rhetorical mix and contributing to the dynamism of public knowledge. The result is a mass of detail that overlaps, affects, and perhaps introduces incremental changes to public knowledge but is not yet a part of it. Such texts provide new information, both factual and interpretive, that may act to modify the context in which an event is viewed. This information may be termed 'preknowledge' because it affects the authorization process described by Bitzer, altering what will be considered a fitting response. Depending on the place it is ultimately assigned in the matrix of public perceptions, preknowledge may also change the substance of public knowledge. In a crisis setting, these data consist of the messages created in response to "the urgent need for information,"[8] thereby becoming part of the context of the event, part of the rhetorical situation.

Preknowledge may be actualized into public knowledge through the medium of "shared subjective experience."[9] For example, when television and newspapers reported that the US had in its possession a recorded 'order to fire' from Soviet ground control to its fighter pilots, the American public was presented with a set of facts that seemed consistent with accepted knowledge about US intelligence capabilities.[10] Subsequent denials of the existence of any ground-to-air recordings conflicted with these perceptions. When the denials were offered, they merely conformed to public skepticism, which encompasses the belief that governments always try to protect information about sensitive subjects. Once those expectations were met, however, skepticism about other elements of the official story became more tenable.

In contrast to the situation in the US, it has been common for the media in the USSR to take considerable time announcing disasters; historically, information about tragedies such as airline crashes has been suppressed.[11] In this regard, KAL 007 was no exception: for two days the only news of the shootdown came over the Voice of America and other Western radio stations. This, too, presented an anomalous situation: a factual charge that required a response, but for which no response was forthcoming. Again, a disruption of public knowledge had occurred, this time in the USSR.

It seems likely that public knowledge in a controlled society would be different and would play an entirely different role than in the Western democracies.[12] Where information dissemination is restricted, the authorization process, as Bitzer describes it, is virtually non-existent. Prior to September 1983, little or no interaction had been observed between official public knowledge, upon which rhetorical discourse in Soviet society is based, and the "fund of [historically situated] truths, principles, and values"[13] that make up the unofficial knowledge of the Soviet people. The events that followed the destruction of KAL 007 were important because they attested to a deterioration of the status quo in the USSR: they demonstrate that the Soviet government is not always successful in controlling public information or, therefore, in controlling its domestic rhetorical situation.

Accordingly, this chapter examines American governmental rhetoric surrounding the KAL incident, using Bitzer's concepts in combination with textual analysis to provide a construct for exploring the dynamics of superpower discourse. We trace the development of the United States position regarding the destruction of KAL 007 and examine the role of perception and public knowledge in this international debate. The exposition follows the American rhetorical effort chronologically through September 12, 1983 (when the Soviet Union vetoed a US-sponsored resolution of censure in the United Nations Security Council), and, where appropriate, outlines the Soviet domestic response to this rhetorical campaign.

SEPTEMBER 1-3: INDICTING THE SOVIET ACTION

According to media reports and White House statements, Reagan first learned that the airliner had been shot down at 7:10 A.M. (PDT) on September 1, half an hour before Shultz's press conference began. But this was approximately fifteen hours after the first preliminary intelligence estimate had been transmitted to the National Security Agency and about seven hours after the White House was apprised of it. Judging by this chronology, presidential advisors first considered the event of minor import, not crucial enough to warrant waking the president, and not of sufficient magnitude even for him to talk with his secretary of state prior to Shultz's informing the public of the tragedy. Moreover, they initially judged that the incident did not justify cutting short Reagan's Labor Day vacation. Many correspondents commented on this apparent lack of urgency.

> [O]n "The CBS Evening News," while [Dan] Rather recounted the chronology of the day's traumatic events, a long-range camera showed a picture of the president riding a horse on his ranch, giving the impression that he was oblivious and uncaring even though official White House statements had been strongly worded.[14]

Ultimately, Reagan did return to Washington earlier than expected, because of the impression his continued absence was creating and "the need to demonstrate his personal involvement."[15] Steven Weisman, citing White House Press Secretary Larry Speakes, reported that Reagan had been involved in all the Administration responses and had personally approved the initial statement read by Speakes on September 1: "'As soon as we had the facts, the President was given an update,' Mr. Speakes said. 'When the facts became certain, we apprised the President of it.'"[16]

The domestic political pressure implied in the president's early return to Washington also dictated the tone of his statements. From a rhetorical perspective, this pressure amounts to a sense of inappropriateness in the initial response. Had the president remained on vacation it simply would not have accorded with the public expectation that he take charge of the situation.[17] This is not to suggest that Reagan was not sincerely angry and disturbed by the Soviet action. Rather, "the Soviet attack on Korean Air Lines Flight 007 had reinforced Reagan's basic convictions about the Soviet system: that it lacks the basic moral standards of the West."[18] Nevertheless, as several observers have pointed out, the president had to find a middle ground between the political realities of the nuclear age and the demands of his most conservative constituency and advisers.[19] No doubt, this dichotomy led to the striking difference in rhetorical tone between remarks made by the president himself or his personal representatives and those issued by the State Department and Shultz.

Nevertheless, it was the secretary of state who established the initial context for the American response. In the first official US announcement about the event, Shultz made a careful presentation: though exhibiting anger, he limited himself to the facts known at that time. In addition, he foreshadowed many of the positions the government would maintain throughout the crisis. In his opening remarks, the secretary commented, "At approximately 1600 hours Greenwich Mean Time, the aircraft came to the attention of Soviet radar. It was tracked constantly by the Soviets from that time" [p. 1].[20]

Thus, at the outset, Shultz established the rhetorical position that the Soviet military had ample time to identify KAL 007 as a civilian airliner. The argumentative nature of this point was emphasized when he announced, "the Soviets tracked the commercial airliner for some two and one-half hours" [p. 1]. These statements also revealed that Western intelligence personnel were reading Soviet radar activity. Similarly, the next statement indicated monitoring of Soviet air-to-ground communications (remarks by the fighter pilots to their ground controllers): "A Soviet pilot reported visual contact with the aircraft at 1812 hours. The Soviet plane was, we know, in constant contact with its ground control" [p. 1]. Shultz identified the very moment when KAL 007 had completely disappeared from radar screens. He did not indicate whose radar he was referring to, although it soon became apparent that the plane had been acquired on Japanese military radar shortly before its final descent.

It was unfortunate that the secretary did not think to point out at this juncture that the monitoring (which he clearly implied had occurred) was not carried out in "real time" (that is, by a human operator), but rather (as subsequently claimed) was accomplished automatically by voice-activated recorders and analyzed only later. Such mistakes ultimately blunted the effect of the American rhetorical campaign and contributed to the controversy surrounding allegations of a US role in the incident.

The central question revolved around the natural conflict between politics and security. In a tense situation such as this, the need to reveal hard information in order to marshal world opinion runs the risk of compromising US intelligence assets. In actuality, the KAL incident "produced an unprecedented glimpse into American electronic eavesdropping capabilities."[21] Unfortunately, this unprecedented look wasn't close enough to avoid raising more questions than it answered. Absent a strong statement by Shultz, there was no reason for the American people to understand that the assets which had been disclosed would not enable American intelligence personnel to follow these events as they actually unfolded. This proved to be the major issue that plagued US credibility in the KAL affair. As a result of his desire to make an airtight case, and undoubtedly motivated by genuine anger and revulsion,

Shultz overlooked the caveats and ambiguities that normally accompany discussions skirting the edge of national security issues.

In this instance, even well-informed reporters such as Douglas Feaver of the *Washington Post* operated under the impression that the monitoring had occurred in real time:[22]

> Shultz indicated in his statement yesterday that somebody's radar system knew a great deal about the progress of Flight 007 and the fighters that intercepted it....
>
> In Tokyo, the Japan Defense Agency said its radar showed the plane crossing Sakhalin Island, hundreds of miles west of R20, shortly before the plane was shot down....
>
> [T]here [is no] indication that the pilot radioed for help or sounded alarmed.[23]

In contrast, Getler and *New York Times* reporter David Shribman, who were briefed by Assistant Secretary of State Richard Burt after Shultz's press conference, reported that the monitoring was not accomplished in real time.[24] However, in each instance this information did not appear until well into the article and was not emphasized. Shribman quoted Burt as saying, "American officials did not have 'real-time information.'" It is worth noting the careful manner in which this statement was phrased. As in so many other instances, it prescribed very narrow parameters of truth, for it did not preclude the Koreans or Japanese from having such data.[25]

Not until the next day did Shultz finally deny that monitoring of the tragedy had occurred in real time, a possibility left open by his September 1 statement.[26] Coming at this point, the secretary's denial had the appearance of backing and filling: it was too late to have a positive impact on people's impressions. If nothing else, the primacy effect dictated that the average citizen would remember the elaborate information contained in Shultz's announcement and the monitoring which obviously had enabled the US to compile such a detailed reconstruction of the event; one would be less likely to recall later clarifications of the type Shultz and Burt offered. Thus, public consciousness had developed a preknowledge about this event, based on a collective impression of US intelligence capabilities, that was inadvertently substantiated by Administration officials.

Equally important, the whole episode gave the Soviet Union an opening, allowing them to claim that the United States had followed the entire event and to insist, therefore, that the US could have prevented the disaster, but for political purposes did not choose to do so. Up to this point, the USSR had been typically recalcitrant about the whereabouts of the missing airliner. (Many believe that had the Soviet Union admitted its culpability, apologized, and offered to pay reparations—as Israel and Bulgaria had done years earlier in similar circumstances—the crisis atmosphere surrounding the incident would have dissipated quickly. Instead, the USSR said virtually nothing of substance for the first six days of the crisis).

Shortly after the tragedy, TASS released a brief government statement describing only an attempted interception, which concluded with the "unidentified" aircraft continuing its flight toward the Sea of Japan. It was not until September 6 that the Soviet Union officially admitted having shot down the airliner. By that time it appeared the Soviet government would face the difficult task of orchestrating two campaigns—one for the international front and one for domestic consumption; analysis reveals, however, that most of its effort focused on the domestic audience.

Not surprisingly, Soviet commentators took advantage of the confusion over US monitoring of the flight of KAL 007. O. Piliugin, writing in *Krasnaia zvezda* on September 6, quoted *The New York Times* regarding US surveillance installations in the Western Pacific. He then concluded: "Why didn't US and Japanese air traffic controllers, who followed the South Korean aircraft throughout its entire flight, warn the crew that they were violating the airspace of the USSR?" On September 8, political observer A. Bovin commented in *Izvestiia*:

> [H]ere is what the *Washington Post* reports: "The Federal Aviation Administration and the US Department of Defense had an agreement ... to verify that passenger aircraft were not off course when they left Alaska.... Consequently, there were people who could have helped the "straying" aircraft.

Bovin was actually quoting Feaver's September 2 *Washington Post* article "Dangers of Violating Soviet Airspace Well-Known to Pilots." The citation was taken out of context, and its use by Bovin was clearly designed for maximum impact on an uninformed Soviet audience; Bovin neglected to quote either the title of the article or this passage contained within: "The radar system ... extends coverage about 200 miles from Alaska.... Once a plane goes beyond that 200-mile range, it is on its own for about 3,000 miles, required only to make radio checks with FAA controllers in Anchorage, then with Japanese controllers in Tokyo."

Undoubtedly, this approach strengthened the Soviet position, particularly in the eyes of its own people. Nevertheless, it was not until September 9 that the government of the USSR began a full-scale counterattack in defense of its actions against KAL 007. On that day, Marshal Nikolai Ogarkov, Chief of Staff of the Soviet armed forces, conducted a press conference—most unusual in and of itself. A government representative claimed that the plane was on radar throughout its flight, a claim that was reiterated in all Soviet print media:

> Burt's references to US tracking data in his first contact with us completely refute the position ... that US intelligence agencies ... reconstructed [what had happened] on the basis of data from other sources.
> The US chargé d'affaires in Moscow, in his first contact with the Soviet Ministry of Foreign Affairs, alluded to the fact that radar contact with the plane had been maintained until the very end.

All foreign governments, including those of the unaligned countries represented at the United Nations Security Council, read the US and Soviet press regularly. It can only have been harmful to the American case to have its arguments condemned in the words of its own diplomats.

Thus, a crack had appeared in the air-tight case against the Soviets, a breach of the Americans' own making. For, while Burt's remarks, as reported by the Soviets, did not <u>necessarily</u> preclude reconstructed data, obviously those reconstructions were accomplished very quickly. In the interaction between text and context, discourse of this sort altered the shape of the background against which the scenes were played. One of the long-term consequences of this particular gaffe was the material it gave to the conspiratists, who seized on the monitoring issue as the basis for much of their claim of US culpability.[27]

Shultz's statement on September 1 had anticipated the ultimate American position in a number of ways. In addition to emphasizing the time the Soviets had spent tracking the airliner, Shultz made it clear that US officials were confident they knew what had happened. Moreover, he staked out the moral ground that the US would occupy for the coming weeks: in reference to the Soviets tracking the airliner, he stressed that KAL 007 was a commercial airliner. Later he referred to it as an "unarmed civilian plane," an appellation paraphrased in virtually every succeeding US statement. Shultz himself used variants of this phrase four additional times in response to questions from the press: "commercial airliner"; "unarmed airliner"; "unarmed commercial airliner" (twice) [p. 2]. This characterization was accurate but redundant, a strategic choice designed to underscore the Administration's major argument: the barbaric nature of the Soviet action.

The moral imperative of the US position was summed up when Shultz said: "We can see no explanation whatever for shooting down an unarmed commercial airliner, no matter whether it's in your airspace or not" [p. 2]. The attitude reflected in this comment allowed the Soviet Union little room to maneuver and, thus, ran counter to most diplomatic strategy.[28] In this way, it foreshadowed the coming attempt to gain a political advantage by mustering worldwide condemnation of the Soviet action.

On a number of points, however, Shultz was careful to keep his options open in the face of possibly incomplete information. (Reagan, among others, later closed some of those options.) For example, when asked whether the Soviet Union gave any warning to the airliner, Shultz responded only that there was no evidence that they had done so. When asked whether or not the US knew if the Soviets tried to force KAL to land prior to firing on it with missiles, he stated that he had no information on that point. (However, he did underscore the proximity of the fighter planes to the jetliner and the opportunity for visual identification.) Finally, when asked about the level at which the decision was made to shoot the plane down, Shultz characterized his entire presentation: "I'm relating the facts as we have them at this point, and I can't go beyond the facts that I have here" [p. 2].

A short time after talking with the secretary of state (following the press conference), Reagan released his first statement. Whereas Shultz's remarks laid the ground for the arguments the US would make, Reagan set the rhetorical tone. He began with what was to become the primary rhetorical strategy of the campaign—separating the Soviet Union from the community of civilized nations: "I speak for ...

people everywhere who cherish civilized values in protesting the Soviet attack on an unarmed civilian passenger plane" [p. 2]. The president's rhetorical style established the manner in which the public should interpret and ascribe meaning to the tragedy. He characterized the shootdown as an "appalling and wanton misdeed," terming the Soviet actions "inexplicable to civilized people everywhere." Each of these motifs was elaborated in later speeches and documents both by President Reagan and by US representatives at the United Nations.

Those representatives became involved almost immediately, with Ambassador Charles Lichenstein's letter to the president of the UN Security Council requesting an urgent meeting of that body. The letter essentially reiterated the contents of Shultz's statement, but took the additional step of charging a violation of international law: "There exists no justification in international law for the destruction of an identifiable civil aircraft, an aircraft which was tracked on radar for two-and-one-half hours, and which was in visual contact of Soviet military pilots prior to being deliberately shot down" [p. 3]. The charge of flouting international order is an additional tactic in the strategy of isolating the Soviet Union from civilized nations. Not only was the act wanton and appalling, it was also illegal. The major themes of Soviet culpability were restated as justification for international condemnation of the USSR: the length of time the airliner was on Soviet radar and the physical proximity of the interceptor planes to the jetliner prior to the shootdown. It was on these two claims, with the later addition of the tape of the fighter pilots, that the US based its case.

Reagan, in his speech of September 2, continued in the same vein. His rhetoric took on the characteristics of classic exhortation, described by Black as discourse in which belief follows from an emotional reaction rather than the reverse.[29] Reagan relied on shared public knowledge, not only among the citizens of this country, but of the rest of the world as well: the Soviet government was referred to four times as a "regime," a term which carries decided negative connotations. In one particular paragraph the president again cast the Soviet Union outside the pale, referring to "civilized behavior" and "the tradition of a civilized world," stating that "as civilized societies, we ask searching questions about the nature of regimes where such standards do not apply" [p. 3].

The president variously characterized the shootdown as a "terrorist act," an "atrocity," and "brutality." He drew the contrast between Soviet

29

words and deeds, accused them of flagrantly lying about the "heinous act," and observed, "What can be the scope of legitimate and mutual discourse with a state whose values permit such atrocities?" [p. 3] (How can civilized nations negotiate with barbarians?). In this way, Reagan used tragedy and text to provide a context in which all might view Soviet actions—not only the destruction of KAL, but past and future behaviors as well. Additionally, he justified the inability of the United States to reach accord with the USSR on a variety of issues, both then and in the future, and laid the groundwork for using the tragedy as a springboard to pressure Congress for increased defense spending.

The president gave virtually no sources for his information, an indication of the exhortative nature of his speech. His domestic audience would assume that he has resources for investigation second to none and would, therefore, know whereof he spoke.[30] As Smith has concluded, "The president is, for all intents and purposes, The Source of information on 007. His language reveals a man speaking as if he were an eyewitness to the event."[31] Invoking a long religious tradition of exhortation against evil, Reagan escalated the verbal offensive.

This, then, became the form and tone of the American protest against Soviet barbarism. On September 2, Lichenstein delivered the first statement to the UN Security Council in much the same terms as those used earlier in the day by the president. Expanding upon the theme expressed in his previous day's letter to the president of the Security Council—that the shooting was a violation of international law—Lichenstein said, "Let us call the crime for what clearly it is: wanton, calculated, deliberate murder." Later, the destruction of KAL 007 was termed "this criminal act of mass murder" [p. 4]. In an obvious effort to shape international perceptions of the event, Lichenstein went into considerable detail in recounting the tragedy, noting incidents of Soviet airliners overflying sensitive areas in the United States without adverse consequences, and then describing what one might expect of a civilized government in such situations as this.

Lichenstein elaborated the themes initiated by Reagan, while raising the rhetorical stakes. He cast the United States as a model of civilized behavior, tolerating overflights by Soviet aircraft, filing protests and suspending landing rights rather than firing missiles, thus justifying the revulsion and horror evoked by the behavior of the USSR. Since most nations would prefer to think of themselves as civilized, Lichenstein enveloped them in a cloak of rationality and left the Soviet

Union a lone outcast: "[The Soviet Union] has ... behaved with complete—and I must add, characteristic—contempt for the international community and for even minimal standards of decency and civilized behavior" [p. 5]. By setting up standards of behavior for handling situations such as this one, standards with which any nation would find it difficult to disagree, standards which the USSR had clearly failed to meet, Lichenstein created a means whereby all nations could join in condemnation. The pending action of the Security Council was redefined as the maintenance of world order in the face of uncivilized—indeed, criminal—acts. This isolation of the Soviet Union from the rest of the world quickly became the dominant theme of the American campaign.

The United Nations is rarely presented with an issue in which the debate itself can make a difference in the vote. The Cuban missile crisis was one such unusual situation; the KAL 007 tragedy might have been another. Unfortunately, Lichenstein probably nullified the impact of his strategy—at least as far as the Third World nations were concerned—by going too far, for he concluded with a vivid excoriation of Soviet totalitarianism, a tactic which no doubt served to redivide opinion along ideological lines.

Reagan continued the relentless pursuit of Soviet culpability in his Saturday radio address (September 3), making absolutely clear his intention to isolate the USSR on this issue: "This murder of innocent civilians is a serious international issue between the Soviet Union and civilized people everywhere who cherish individual rights and value human life" [p. 5]. In the same language used the previous day, the president restated the disparity between Soviet words and deeds, and added that this was not the first time that the Soviet Union had fired on a civilian airliner straying over its territory.[32] With this exception, and the omission of the peroration, Reagan's address was a condensed version of Lichenstein's Security Council speech. Coming when it did, the president's speech probably served an epideictic function, more ceremonial than deliberative. Invoking fundamental American distrust of the Soviet Union, Reagan placed the destruction of KAL 007 into the catalog of Soviet crimes and deceptions, reaffirming the context of the US response.

SEPTEMBER 4: THE RC-135

At this point in the chronology, the US position began to deteriorate. On September 4, 1983, Congressional leaders, including Senate majority leader Howard H. Baker, Jr., and the House majority leader, James Wright, attended a White House briefing where they listened to the tape of the Soviet pilots. Immediately thereafter, Wright spoke with reporters and indicated that a US RC-135 reconnaissance plane had been in the vicinity of Kamchatka Peninsula the night KAL 007 was shot down and that the Soviets might have confused the two aircraft.[33] At least one commentator has contended that this remark gave the Soviets the spy-plane argument.[34] Indeed, ample support for this notion exists in the Russian language material concerning the incident.

Later that same day, Larry Speakes was questioned closely by the press about this discrepancy.[35] Speakes insisted that no reference to an RC-135 appeared on the tape of the Soviet pilots; nonetheless, he seemed to admit that reconnaissance planes were aloft as part of routine US surveillance of the Soviet Union and that the US government had considerably more tape than that portion on which the Soviet pilots were recorded:

Q: Did [you] mention to the Congressmen at all that the Soviet pilots were referring to it as an RC-135? [p. 8]

Mr. Speakes: As I say, without going into detail on what is obviously something we don't customarily talk about, that if there was any discussion of it, it was considerably ahead of this effort where the Soviet pilot was in close proximity of the plane, had visual contact with it to an extremely close range....

Q: You mean at some point they might have thought it was, but much later were able to track the plane closer. [p. 8]

Mr. Speakes: It's clear from our evidence, which I will not go into, it's clear from our evidence that the Soviets, for a period of time that extends well beyond this eight minutes, well behind this eight minutes, well in advance of this eight minutes,[36] the Soviets had no reason to doubt that they were tracking a civilian airliner. [pp. 8-9]

Much later in the briefing, a correspondent asked the key question:

Q: Larry, during this period, was there a US reconnaissance plane anywhere near this area, outside the Soviet air space during the period when the KAL flight was around? [p. 16]

Mr. Speakes: I would not say near the area, but the US routinely uses reconnaissance missions outside the Soviet Union in international waters, as do the Soviets use on us. [p. 17]

The question was repeated.

Mr. Speakes: They are [there] routinely, but if there was any case of an observance of a US reconnaissance plane, it was well ahead of this. [p. 17]

The press corps kept coming back to the question of the US reconnaissance plane and the possibility of misidentification on the part of the Soviets.

Q: Your comment earlier that at some point early on the Soviets may have misidentified this aircraft and your subsequent comment that it was not long after that that they discovered there were two different aircraft leaves the impression that at some point there was a US reconnaissance aircraft that the Soviets may have mistaken for the KAL flight. Again,... is that the impression you meant to give, and is that an accurate impression? [p. 21]

Mr. Speakes: Well, we ... routinely have reconnaissance flights in international waters, and I'm not going to be specific about what we had in the area. [p. 21]

Q: About the time period, you're not going to be specific as to whether we had reconnaissance in the area during the period of the KAL flight— [p. 21]

Mr. Speakes: We routinely do so. If you can't read that, you can't see your hands before your face. [p. 21]

Q: If that's the way you want it read, you did say there were two different aircraft. Is that a slip, or you meant to say that? [p. 21]

33

Mr. Speakes: No slip. That's what I said. [p. 21]

Obviously piqued by this insistent questioning regarding US reconnaissance activity, Speakes observed near the conclusion of the press conference: "We have given you more than you ever knew or that we knew about them" [p. 25]. Indeed.

Toward evening, the White House issued a detailed clarifying statement, which indicated that an RC-135 was fulfilling a routine mission off the coast of Kamchatka at the time the Korean airliner was first detected by Soviet radar, two-and-one-half hours prior to the shootdown. The White House claimed that the Soviets were familiar with the flight characteristics of the RC-135, that they had tracked the two planes separately, and that they had first identified the Korean plane as an RC-135 and then as an "unidentified aircraft."[37] The statement reiterated the US contention that the Soviets had ample opportunity for visual identification of the airliner—that the two types of aircraft are in no way similar. Finally, the statement points out that at the time KAL 007 was shot down, the RC-135 had been on the ground in Alaska for more than an hour.[38]

The problem with this episode was that it muddied the waters. Prior to September 4, the US could claim absolutely that the Soviets had sufficient time, on radar and visually, to identify the intruder as a civilian airliner; now there appeared to be some basis for Soviet confusion, despite Speakes's insistence to the contrary. This impression was strengthened by the US government's attempts to clarify the issue, which only served as fuel for those who already believed the US was directly involved, or at least should have been able to warn the ill-fated airliner. The context which gave meaning to this event was subtly beginning to alter its shape.

As it turned out, Wright's revelation, and the alacrity with which it was substantiated by the Reagan Administration (revealing in the process more highly classified information) was tantamount to opening Pandora's box. Not only did this gaffe expose the American position to ridicule at home and among its allies, it also gave the Soviet leaders a wedge to break out of the disastrous public relations maze that had enveloped them.

Soviet commentary in *Pravda* on the morning of Tuesday, September 6 revealed mostly stagnation and the type of 'political invective' indicative of a lack of anything cogent to say. Among customary Soviet tactics employed were *ad hominem* attacks on the character of the US president and the 'slippery slope' fallacy:

> Standing at the conductor's podium [directing] this hysteria is the White House, whose master has outdone himself in his pathological hatred of the Soviet Union and of our people.
>   It is logical to assume that if today [the American government] defends its "right" to instigate flights of an intruder aircraft, then tomorrow it will try to justify with the same recklessness and cynicism the "accidental" launch of death-dealing rockets against foreign territory.

In addition, *Pravda* evoked the spectre of Nazi Germany, a standard safety-net of Soviet ideological rhetoric—World War II and the incredibly heavy toll in human life and suffering endured by the Soviet people serve as a rhetorical icon in the USSR: "Anti-communist hysteria isn't new. These methods are well known, because they completely coincide with those of Hitler's propaganda, which fabricated Poland's 'attack' on Germany forty-four years ago."[39]

But evident, too, were the first glimmers of what was to become an effective counterattack. It is important to consider the timing here. The White House briefing attended by James Wright had broken up shortly after noon, EDT, on Sunday, September 4; the congressman's revelations sent capital correspondents scurrying for their Pentagon sources and necessitated the Speakes press conference in mid-afternoon. Around dinnertime in Washington—after midnight, September 4/5 in Moscow—the White House issued its "clarification."

News of the RC-135 was dutifully broadcast by the Voice of America. According to information provided by Philip C. Haynes, Managing Editor of the News Division at VOA, four news items between 11:30 am and 3:30 pm EDT discussed the fact that tape recordings of Soviet personnel were played to participants in the White House briefing.[40] Then, at 16:58:48, the VOA wire carried this text:

> The (White House) spokesman said the Soviet Union may have initially mistaken the airliner for a U.S. spy plane. He said the United States does routinely carry out reconnaissance flights over international waters near the Soviet Union. But reporters were told no U.S. reconnaissance plane was over Soviet territory

at the time. The spokesman said the airliner was tracked for up to two hours, and was downed well after it should have been recognized as a civilian airliner.[41]

An hour later, VOA reported:

Spokesman Larry Speakes told reporters the United States does routinely carry out reconnaissance flights over international waters near the Soviet Union, just as the Soviets do near the United States. He said the Soviets may have thought the Korean airliner was a U.S. reconnaissance plane, an RC-135, when the Korean aircraft was first spotted on their radar. But he said this was approximately one and a half to two hours before the shoot-down.

And he said that with the visual information obtained by the Soviet fighter pilot in close proximity to the Korean airliner, and the radar information available to the Soviets, when they shot it down they should have known without a doubt that it was a civilian airliner.

Reporters also were told that no U.S. reconnaissance plane was over Soviet territory.[42]

Evening updates carried similar versions, adding that the reconnaissance plane stayed well outside Soviet airspace,[43] and that "the spy plane was about... 1600 kilometers away" when the Korean airliner "was shot down as it emerged from restricted Soviet airspace."[44]

This was the break the Soviet government needed. Its propagandists must have been under tremendous pressure to find a way out of this public relations tupík ('dead end'). There are no written minutes to consult, of course, but it is easy to imagine the ebullient mood that must have prevailed at the daily planning session of the Soviet propaganda leadership on Monday morning.[45]

On Tuesday, *Pravda* quoted CBS television news: "The USSR might have mistaken the airliner for an American reconnaissance aircraft flying off the coast of Kamchatka."[46] Only once prior to this had the Soviets seriously mentioned US military aircraft as the cause of possible confusion. But even that had not occurred until September 4; it, too, had taken the form of a quotation from the foreign press— specifically, the *Sydney Morning Herald* in Australia: "The Soviets might have taken the South Korean aircraft to be a US spyplane because on radar it looks just like a US military reconnaissance aircraft; it might also have been mistaken for a US E4B bomber."[47]

Nothing more was made of this report at the time. During its 8:00 A.M. newscast on September 6, however, Soviet TV raised the issue of the RC-135:

> As has become known from the US press, the Americans not only relentlessly tracked the movements of the intruder by satellite,[48] they also sent into the area their own RC-135 reconnaissance plane, which travelled parallel to the intruder's path. "The report of the presence of a second aircraft has raised new questions concerning this already confusing episode," *The New York Times* admits. In this regard, many observers have asked: was the RC-135 supervising the actions of the other aircraft?[49]

At this point the newscaster quoted Congressman Wright as saying he had heard "several" references by the Soviet pilot to the presence of the RC-135.[50] Once again, the American position had been contradicted, in Soviet eyes, by America's own spokespersons.

During the 4:00 P.M. television newscast that afternoon, Soviet citizens were told that US RC-135s frequently "use foreign civilian airliners as a cover for reconnaissance flights near the USSR." The newscaster then reported that UPI had commented (in the newscaster's words) "spyplanes loaded with electronic equipment literally poise themselves above passenger liners in order to confuse Soviet air defense radar stations. UPI indicates," he continued, "that just such a reconnaissance aircraft was airborne alongside the South Korean aircraft that intruded into the airspace of the USSR and [that] it even intersected its path twice." This report sounded as though the two planes were in close proximity; US accounts differed markedly, claiming that, although the RC-135 had indeed crossed the path flown by Flight 007, the Korean airliner was already a considerable distance away when that intersection occurred.[51] What is important here, however, is that Soviet media were beginning to alter the context in which Soviet citizens might view reports of the airliner's destruction. In the Soviet Union, stories appearing on television or in newspapers carry the presumption of government approval; these items become part of Soviet official public knowledge, thus providing context for future argument. This alteration continued through Ogarkov's press conference September 9.

Later that evening (September 6), at 9:00 P.M., the Soviet government released a "Statement," which was read over the radio and TV and subsequently published the next morning in every major daily newspaper. This statement constituted the first definitive step forward in their campaign to discredit the American version of the KAL incident. It was here, for the very first time, that the Soviet government itself claimed to have monitored the flight of an RC-135 off the coast of Kamchatka Peninsula. John Burns, writing in Moscow on September 6, noted that Washington's disclosure of the RC-135 "seemed to have had a strong influence in shaping the manner in which Soviet explanations of the incident were presented."[52]

Three days later, during the September 9 press conference, Marshal Ogarkov made the first direct Soviet claim that the RC-135 had rendezvoused with KAL 007, flying in tandem with the Korean plane for some ten minutes before the airliner penetrated Soviet airspace. The alleged rendezvous was depicted on Ogarkov's map as a 'double loop' adjacent to the route followed by the airliner. US officials deprecated this assertion, maintaining that the RC-135 had never flown closer than seventy-five miles to the flight path of KAL and had, in any event, departed from the area long before the jetliner approached Kamchatka.[53]

Nevertheless, allegations concerning the activities of the American reconnaissance aircraft—particularly the contested double loop—became the centerpiece of Soviet contentions that the US had sent KAL 007 over sensitive Soviet territory on an espionage mission. Without this damaging evidence, provided by representatives of the United States government itself, the Soviet government undoubtedly would not have succeeded in convincing very many people, either at home or abroad, that the events surrounding the destruction of KAL 007 had occurred in any fashion other than that depicted in the US charges. Public understanding of the event was beginning to shift.

Most importantly for the propaganda war, the possibilities presented by this new revelation provided the beginnings of the explanation demanded by the nations of the world. Soviet rhetoric began to take on the characteristics of the wounded party.

SEPTEMBER 5-8, 1983: RELEASING THE TAPE

In his televised address to the nation on the evening of September 5, Reagan continued to elaborate his charges, using the rhetorical style that had become the trademark of the US response to this tragedy. After making reference to the bereaved families, he recalled the KAL 902 incident of 1978, overflights of US military installations by Soviet and Cuban planes, and the details of KAL 007's last flight. At this point, the president played a small portion of the audio tape of the Soviet pilots (with voice-over translation) and described the scene that the tape recounts. He referred to the Soviet refusal to allow the US to participate in the search for wreckage, relating this to previous massacres in Czechoslovakia, Poland, Hungary, and, most recently, Afghanistan.[54] After describing actions the US was taking in retaliation for the downing, the president then correlated Soviet brutality with the need for a strong US defense system and the necessity for continued negotiation on arms reduction.[55]

Other than the tape and elements of Reagan's personal style (such as the reference to relatives of the dead), there was nothing new here. It was essentially a repetition of the positions both he and other officials had taken earlier. By this point, one suspects, the US initiative had begun to wane, for the world's ability to sustain horror is limited once the horror itself is over. But the tape, with its inherent dramatic interest, rekindled feelings of revulsion and curiosity and added yet another piece to the developing contextual mosaic.

The United States made an effort to capitalize on this reaction with Ambassador Jeane Kirkpatrick's September 6 address to the United Nations Security Council. After vilifying the Soviet Union for lying about the "cool, calculated act," Kirkpatrick played her trump card, the complete tape of the Soviet pilots. The American presentation was designed to produce the maximum dramatic effect: while simultaneous translations echoed in the ears of the delegates, the Russian and English texts appeared together on large monitors especially installed for the day's session. Nothing like this had ever been staged before.[56]

Following the tape presentation, the ambassador made several claims about its contents: (1) the interceptor had the airliner in sight for over twenty minutes before firing the missiles; (2) the interceptor pilot saw the airliner's navigation lights; (3) contrary to Soviet contentions, the pilot made no mention of firing tracer rounds [a fateful

US error here]; (4) there was no indication that the pilot made any attempt to communicate with the airliner or to otherwise signal it; (5) at no point did the Soviet pilots raise the question of the identity of the aircraft [p. 9].[57]

Kirkpatrick's address represented the first direct attempt to refute statements being made by officials of the USSR, and as such it constituted a shift in strategic posture. Prior to this speech, the United States was strictly on the attack; the answering of arguments, however, is primarily a defensive stance which, in this instance, dissipated the moral focus of the US position. In that sense, the Soviet strategy of fabrication had begun to have an effect, for the US had, at this point, shouldered the burden of proof.[58] In retrospect, one can see that this subtle shift in approach did not bode well for US attempts to generate a groundswell of public condemnation and thus to isolate the Soviet Union. Rather, it portended a continued deterioration in the absolute rectitude of the US position.

But there was no immediately discernable result, since at about this time the government of the USSR itself gave new life to the US campaign. While Oleg Troyanovsky, the Soviet ambassador to the United Nations, was blandly attempting to parry US charges at the Security Council meeting, Moscow released the "Soviet Government Statement," cited earlier, and admitted that the PVO, its Air Defense Forces, had "terminated" the flight of KAL 007.[59] Moreover, on the eve of the Madrid human rights conference (which had long been scheduled for the second week in September), Soviet media carried a report that the downing the "intruder aircraft" accorded with the laws of the Soviet Union; and in the future, the report continued, the Soviet Union would comply with those laws.[60] Coming as it did on the heels of Kirkpatrick's impassioned insistence that "international air travel depends on networks of mutual trust that we will not shoot down one another's airliners," [p. 10] the Soviet Union's huffy defensiveness was a serious public relations blunder. It reinforced the Reagan Administration's characterization that "violence and lies are regular instruments of Soviet policy" [p. 10]. In addition, the ill-considered remark gave credibility to the notion that the destruction of Flight 007 was "a deliberate stroke designed to intimidate—a brutal, decisive act meant to instill fear and hesitation in all who observed its ruthless violence" [p. 10]. Soviet timing was terrible.

The United States seized the opportunity to further condemn the Soviet Union, to insist that the statement demonstrated the USSR "is not bound by the norms of international behavior and human decency to which virtually all other nations subscribe."[61] On September 7, the White House issued a statement condemning the Soviet position, claiming it demonstrated that "they will shoot down the next off-course unarmed aircraft that transgresses the territory prescribed by Soviet law" [p. 11].[62] Eagleburger and Shultz made similar remarks to the press. On September 8, Shultz expanded on this position: "This brutal Soviet action has vividly displayed the Soviet Union's lack of concern for the human lives involved" [p. 11].

The Voice of America also continued to broadcast harsh statements into the USSR. The destruction of KAL 007 was called "a gross violation of civilized behavior and a barbarous act of violence."[63] Later it was reported that Eagleburger had "denounced the Soviet statement [of the previous evening] as lies and half-truths."[64]

SEPTEMBER 11, 1983: REVISING THE TAPE

The opening provided by the ill-timed Soviet statements could not, however, overshadow the damage done to the US position by the publication of revisions to the tape transcript. A September 11 State Department news release announced the corrections:

> As part of the policy of the US Government to develop full information on the tragic shootdown of KAL #007 by Soviet forces on August 31, US Government experts have continued to review the poor quality transmission on the tape which was played at the UN Security Council September 6. That review has now been completed. After efforts at electronic enhancement and hundreds of replays of the tape, US Government linguists were able to interpret three passages more clearly as indicated below [p. 13].

Among those corrections was one additional line that seemed to indicate that the Soviet fighter pilot had, after all, fired tracer rounds: "I am firing cannon bursts."

The sincerity of this policy was attested by the timing: the emendations were released the day prior to the crucial Security Council vote on a provisional resolution condemning the Soviet attack. These revisions marked the lowest point in the US campaign for total international denunciation of the Soviet Union.[65] Their cumulative effect, coming on the heels of the impressive performance by Marshal Ogarkov in Moscow two days earlier, can be seen in the UN vote (surely, the goals of Soviet officials in staging the press conference included sowing doubt in world opinion). America's NATO allies (France, the Netherlands, the United Kingdom) unanimously supported the resolution; of course, the Soviet Union and its Warsaw Pact ally Poland voted no. Among the unaligned nations, however, what should have been nearly unanimous condemnation became instead a vote which was effectively five-four; Jordan, Malta, Pakistan, Togo, and Zaire supported the resolution, while China, Guyana, Nicaragua, and Zimbabwe abstained. The abstention by Guyana, whose representative had been installed as Security Council president just prior to KAL's destruction, was particularly embarrassing to the United States.

The corrections made it appear that the US had overclaimed its evidence, obscuring the fact that the quality of the intercept tape was exceedingly poor.[66] Producing a complete, accurate rendering of the content in such a short time was a monumental task; in fact, the military transcribers had performed magnificently. The problem was not that the transcript required reinterpretation in spots, but that the government, in first releasing the transcript, did not assert strongly that the text was incomplete and that analysis was continuing; although certain passages in the transcript had originally been marked inaudible, so that further corrections might have been expected, the US government did nothing to prepare the public for this eventuality. (A better tactic would have been to delay releasing the tape at all until the translation was as complete as possible).

In fact, the corrections did not change the essence of US charges, but as a result the American position lay open to suspicion. Apparently because of the perceived need to move quickly and decisively, the Reagan Administration failed to take the obvious precautions. In our view, this failure proved to be just as damaging as Shultz's initial omission of the caveat against real time monitoring of KAL. In Rohmer's opinion, the release of these corrections "had a profound effect on all the wavering Third World nations that might have gone with the United States and that were apparently prepared to do so up to the time of the announcement."[67] Perceptual closure, however, prevented the State Department from anticipating the effect of the emendations:

If the person believes that his inference is based only on the event itself, he will think that a reasonable man holding a different hypothesis, even though he might not change his mind because of the event, would still admit that the event is best explained by, and counts as evidence for, the first person's view. This consequence of not understanding the inference process multiplies the problem: because people cannot understand how others can claim that the event supports a different conclusion, they become more intolerant of others' positions.[68]

From a rhetorical perspective, the corrections are crucial to understanding the progression of the propaganda campaign. While no one was excusing the USSR, public understanding of the event became clouded: moral certainty gave way to uncertainty. America's carefully constructed contextual mosaic was beginning to crumble.

The manner in which the Soviet government used this propaganda bonanza is most revealing, for it demonstrates more than any other circumstance the fact that Moscow's primary concern at this juncture had become maintenance of its credibility among its own citizenry. In Dallin's view, the "overriding priority" of Soviet strategists was the need for "maintaining the facade of infallibility vis-a-vis its own population and ... forestalling any doubts in the minds of its own elite on whether the system worked."[69] Obviously, Soviet officials had concluded that there was no realistic hope of discrediting the tape transcript in the world arena. No serious attempt to dispute the authenticity of the tape was made in the Security Council, at Ogarkov's press conference, or in the Soviet presentation to International Civil Aviation Organization officials during that UN body's inquiry into the KAL disaster.[70]

Nevertheless, for internal consumption, Soviet propagandists had a veritable field day, concentrating from September 11 through September 14 on this latest American blunder. Although VOA had initially discussed the tape on September 4, and an article in Pravda had mentioned it almost off-handedly on September 6,[71] the first time that the Soviet people had heard an officially sanctioned public discussion of the existence of the taped conversations was during Ogarkov's news conference on the ninth (three days after they had been played before the United Nations); not surprisingly, the many embarrassing questions concerning the tape were deleted from the edited Soviet telecast. But Voice of America and Radio Liberty broadcasts undoubtedly had been reaching many people in major cities such as Moscow and Leningrad, where Western programming is particularly popular. The effect of this uncensored news had to be counteracted, if possible. It was fairly easy to make the Americans look foolish:

> The value of such recordings, which were prepared in the USA, is well known. It is hardly accidental that American Congressman Wright maintained that he heard something when he first listened to the tape, but this segment no longer appeared in the recording that was subsequently distributed. (*Pravda*, September 11)

This is known as having your cake and eating it, too.

> The falsification ... is clear and unconcealed. (*Pravda*, September 12)

> [T]he State Department has announced that it was distributing what it called a "new version" of the transcript of conversations between the Soviet ground control and the Soviet pilot. This raises a legitimate question: has Washington been operating until now with falsified tapes? It was not accidental that during the Moscow press conference it was noted that one could not trust all these 'tapes', since they were faked from start to finish.
> Obviously, Washington has tripped up, is trying to save itself, and, caught in its own lie, has been forced to admit this lie, at least in part. We shall see what comes next. (*Pravda*, September 13)

> State Department representative Romberg announced that specialists had supposedly studied the tape once again and, having spent much time (hurrah for the 'specialists'!), were now able to provide three clarifications and three corrections. Including the clarification that Washington linguists could not previously decipher the words "I am opening cannon fire".... What further 'clarifications' will these foreign Russian language 'experts'— disinformation experts, is more like it—provide in the future? (*Pravda*, September 14)

Who would have thought that the transcript would be released before every possible intelligible statement had been squeezed out?[72] Or that corrections so damaging to the US would be made public the day before a crucial UN vote?

SEPTEMBER 12, 1983: KIRKPATRICK'S SPEECH

Whereas the Soviet Union was intent upon salvaging prestige on its domestic front, having made its best effort in the international arena with the Ogarkov press conference, the United States now had to contend with vacillating world opinion. Its overwhelming moral and political advantage had been considerably eroded by time and circumstance. Kirkpatrick again took the rostrum at the UN on September 12 in an attempt to repair the damage, and immediately went on the attack:

> But even more disturbing than the deed itself has been the behavior of the Soviet Government in the days since it shot down that plane.... Instead of admitting error, it has insisted that no error was made. Instead of taking responsibility for the act, it has lashed out with groundless accusations. Instead of taking steps to ensure against a repetition of such an incident, it has emphasized that it would do the same thing all over again [p. 15].

The ambassador pointed out that the "cannon bursts" were essentially irrelevant; indeed, it was possible that they were not tracer bullets—that is, warning shots—at all, but "regular, normal cannon rounds which are not visible." The point, according to Kirkpatrick, was that there is no excuse whatsoever for shooting down a civilian airliner, particularly one which "was within 60 seconds of leaving Soviet air space" [p. 16].[73] Thus, she attempted to subsume the Soviet position without refuting it—a potentially more effective tactic than the one used in her first address.

The high point of this speech compared the KAL incident to the one in which a Soviet submarine had strayed into Swedish territorial waters. Pointing out the double standard applied by the Soviet government, Kirkpatrick commented disparagingly:

> According to [its] unique interpretation of international law, if a Soviet warship—a warship, mind you—invades the territorial waters of another state, that state cannot even detain the warship but must simply escort it out of its territorial waters. But if a civilian airliner with 269 people aboard happens to stray into Soviet airspace, the Soviet Union is justified in shooting it down, even as it is about to exit that airspace [p. 16] [emphasis in original].

45

In this address, Kirkpatrick returned to the exhortative style exhibited in earlier US discourse. She attempted to persuade through indirection and inference, passing over the facts: Soviet warships <u>invade</u>, civilian airliners <u>stray</u>. The speech transcended such niggling questions as cannon bursts and reconnaissance planes, evoking instead the fundamental truths of the American West: good guys and bad guys, guilt and retribution.[74]

Was she able to recoup the advantage lost by the United States in the miasma of explanations and revelations that followed the initial disclosure of the destruction of KAL 007 and the 269 people aboard? Only history can answer that question. In the short term, however, response to the US request for worldwide action against the Soviet Union was spotty at best. The United States was able to take only limited action itself, in spite of the strong language used by government officials to denounce the Soviet Union. And, certainly, the US was not able to achieve the resounding condemnation of the Soviet Union that it sought. Even in the Security Council, the US barely succeeded in gaining a majority vote for its watered-down resolution.

Furthermore, there remain in the minds of many, both in the United States and abroad, serious questions about a possible US role, whether passive or active, in the tragedy. And (because the 'black box' was not found)[75] the unanswered questions about Flight 007—why it was off course, whether the crew was aware of their location or of the interception—will probably never be resolved.

CONCLUSIONS

These two weeks of international jousting provide a fascinating picture of governments reacting to an extraordinary rhetorical situation. US officials approached the conflict with confidence and seized the opportunity presented by what they perceived as a clear moral imperative to make a political statement to the world. At last the Soviets had committed an act for which there was no provocation, no possible justification! Their true nature could be made clear; the political and military position of the United States could regain some of its former lustre. In vivid terms, using concrete images, American officials exhorted not only their domestic constituency but the entire world to join in condemnation of the Soviet barbarians. That the United States counted on universal revulsion to produce belief in the bankruptcy of the Soviet position is obvious: no traditional arguments were made, only indignant pronouncements; other than the tape, no evidence was presented. The US relied on the fact of the shootdown, the callous manner in which it occurred and was denied, and the dramatic loss of life to produce the necessary belief.

Exhortation requires public authorization of the emotions it evokes, for it depends upon "weighted facts,"[76] which in turn depend on public knowledge to authorize those weightings. Without this engagement, the necessary emotions will not be elicited, belief will not follow, and the exhortation will fail. At this level, US strategy was a qualified success, for it drew on the accumulated wisdom of our time. Since World War II, the United States and its allies have viewed the Soviet Union as the ultimate enemy. Additionally, in a mobile world where air travel has become commonplace, fear of flying lies very near the surface of our collective consciousness. It is surely a truism that, as Kirkpatrick stated, "international air travel depends on networks of mutual trust that we will not shoot down one another's airliners" [p. 10], or, as Shultz put it, "we can see no explanation whatever for shooting down an unarmed commercial airliner, no matter whether it's in your airspace or not" [p. 2]. Without doubt, these two statements captured the sentiments of most of the people in this country, if not the world.

But the strategy was basically flawed, in part because the United States never resolved the dichotomy between political expedience and national security. At critical junctures, the government failed to provide sufficient clarification of intelligence capabilities; as a result, the public was misled. Later attempts to correct misapprehensions had the effect of undermining the American case. In short, the United States handed the Soviet government a scenario of reasonable doubt. Failure to stress at the very outset that monitoring of the Soviet forces was not carried out in real time crippled all subsequent efforts to correct public perceptions. When it became known that an American reconnaissance aircraft, an RC-135, had been patrolling off the coast of the Kamchatka Peninsula, the White House rushed to provide details. The US also claimed to have recorded Soviet radar data that would confirm the flight path of the RC-135 (thus blatantly compromising the security of our intelligence capabilities in this regard),[77] but refused to release this information when the Soviets alleged that the reconnaissance plane had flown a "double loop" in order to rendezvous with KAL 007. This refusal led many to believe the Soviet version. So, having judged early in the campaign that security interests must be sacrificed for political gain, the US ended by squandering both.[78]

At other times (particularly with regard to the transcript errors and to initial revelations concerning the RC-135), the Reagan Administration rushed to provide even more previously secret information. These disclosures further confused an already perplexing situation, and each new revelation gave the USSR a new argument.

From a theoretical perspective what had transpired was a rapidly shifting context in which public perceptions were unable to stabilize. In a crisis atmosphere, the public relies on its accumulated knowledge to define the situation, to put it into comprehensible terms, to determine the most appropriate reaction; to create, as it were, the rhetorical situation in which the rhetor is expected to respond. The rhetorical situation is, thus, a construct of public perception. As soon as the rhetor does respond, however, the elements become interactive. Using text (discourse), the rhetor not only informs, but also establishes the context in which the event should be evaluated.

Bitzer extends the interactive nature of this process to include the relationship between the "fitting response" and the situation that determines what such a response must be.[79] The reaction of the rhetor is, to some extent, constrained by the parameters of the situation, unless the context can be redefined.[80] In clear cases of crisis, the context—and, hence, the reaction—is less ambiguous. As examples, consider Pearl Harbor, the Kennedy Assassination, the Cuban missile crisis. In each instance, the stability and security of the nation were threatened. When national interests are not so directly involved, however, the context is more dubious and conflicting perceptions may weaken the parameters of the rhetorical situation. In these instances, the public seeks additional guidance.

A situation such as the downing of KAL 007 can be handled in a number of ways; for ideological reasons, the Reagan Administration elected to treat it as an international crisis, as a means of exposing the negative side of the Soviet system.[81] Based on his dichotomous view of the world, on his perception of the USSR as evil incarnate, Reagan attempted to establish a context in which the nations of the world could join in a groundswell of condemnation of the Soviet Union, isolating that country from the community of civilized nations.[82]

Thus, the people of the United States, and the world, were urged to view this tragedy as an unprovoked act of wanton murder committed by a government that places no value on human life. The scene played well, given public expectations and the information available. One feature of a crisis atmosphere, however, is the demand for further information; and that spelled the downfall of the Reagan Administration's morality play. For information also re-defines context, and as each new datum entered the public consciousness, the contextual delineation provided by the US slipped further away. The situation was complicated, of course, by multiple texts delivered by multiple rhetors: the revelations by Congressman Wright, the hedging by Larry Speakes, the stories appearing daily in the press and on television turned a clear-cut victory into confusion. While the price was probably greater in terms of world opinion than at home, the Administration never regained the offensive. Momentum had shifted.

The difficulties were two-fold. First, the Administration failed to account for the impact its subsequent revelations (or lack thereof) would have on public perceptions. Once such information entered the public consciousness, it assumed the status of preknowledge, and it had to be taken into account. Not surprisingly, a majority of Americans felt the government was withholding information about KAL 007.[83] To a great extent, this was undoubtedly justified for national security purposes, but public knowledge that the US government routinely deceives its citizens certainly contributed to growing doubts about US complicity in this particular instance.

At every opportunity to halt the shifting context and ebbing public belief, the US government made the inappropriate choice: revealing discordant information, failing to reveal data that could have repudiated competing claims on public acceptance. At the same time, the very success of the Reagan Administration's exhortations against the Soviet Union contributed to the eventual erosion of the US position. On the one hand, the United States was so confident, so righteous, so indignant, it seemed the case against the USSR was unassailable. The level of rhetoric was so elevated that it could not tolerate even minimal slippage. As the contradictions and corrections began to mount, American rhetoric began to sound like bombast.

On the other hand, while the US government repeatedly asked for an explanation from the Soviet Union, it was clear that no explanation would suffice. Indeed, the possibility of explanation was dismissed, almost from the beginning. As Windt pointed out in another context, "[H]ow can reasonable discussion proceed when one group claims to have truth, righteousness, and authority on its side while portraying its opponents as irrational, wrong, and illegitimate?"[84]

Examining the language used by Reagan, Kirkpatrick, and Lichenstein, one is reminded of the dictum expressed by Ogden and Richards: "Words are so powerful ... that by the excitement which they provoke through the emotive force, discussion is for the most part rendered sterile."[85] The accusatory tone adopted by Reagan from the very beginning of the crisis precluded any explanation, mutual truth-seeking, or negotiation. When the president labelled the Soviets "uncivilized" and called them "barbarians," he was limiting the choices of his audience and coercing them into choosing between the USSR and civilized behavior.[86]

The exhortative nature of Administration rhetoric removed it from the realm of persuasion and argumentation. As Balthrop explains, argument "presumes the possibility for arriving at a shared perception of reality. That is, some motivation exists on the part of each participant to want to understand, to arrive at some meaning about the experience, act, or situation that makes sense to those involved."[87] By emphasizing that the US did not know all the answers, Shultz initially left open the door to meaningful dialogue with the Soviets, but the president soon eliminated any possibility in that regard. The carefully preserved options apparent in Shultz's initial statement were rapidly eroded. At every step of the way there seemed to be no coordination of the flow of information, no agreement among military, diplomatic, and White House personnel regarding a concerted, unified plan of action, and no well defined goals beyond embarrassing the Soviet Union.

Not surprisingly, the USSR responded to the coercive elements in Reagan's ideological rhetoric, rather than to the persuasive stance exhibited by Shultz in his initial statement. For as Burgess has commented, "ultimately, the more clearly advocates perceive threats to their moral world and the more openly they are attacked by voices from an alien world then the narrower are their options for strategic choice and invention, resulting in a striking lack of adaptability *within* rhetorics that can prevent resolution of conflict *between* rhetorics."[88]

The Soviet Union, for its part, started out bereft of a reasoned position, reacting to foreign reaction, and initially giving little heed, as usual, to domestic considerations. Although the USSR lost much credibility with Western pacifists, it was able to prey upon US blunders with sufficient effect to negate the worst-case impact its actions might have had upon Third World opinion. What is fascinating about the Soviet situation, however, is the extent to which justifying its actions at home assumed such uncharacteristic importance for Soviet strategists. The Soviet government, too, was exhorting its citizens to adhere to its emerging interpretation of the event. The recollections of other American misdeeds, the visions of World War II, the Ogarkov press conference, all were intended to evoke the weighted facts of classic exhortation. One major difference between the US and Soviet campaigns was that, with the shift in momentum, it seemed that the 'evidence' had begun to support the Soviet version.

Nevertheless, in the wake of the KAL tragedy, the rhetoric of both governments could best be characterized as arational. The United States abandoned rationality in order to win a moral victory over its greatest enemy; the USSR responded in kind because its ideology, coupled with the nature of the verbal attack against its action, severely limited the available rhetorical options. Communicating across cultures in a crisis situation is complicated enough, but the abandonment of rationality only exacerbates the difficulty.[89]

Clearly, this was the situation in the aftermath of the destruction of the Korean airliner. While it is occasionally true that the rhetoric of outrage is merely a veneer, overlaid on meaningful negotiation for the benefit of a specific audience, that does not seem to have been the case in this instance. Certainly, Shultz left open the door for such a circumstance, but it was quickly closed—a fact that ultimately was as much the fault of Soviet intransigence as of American self-righteousness.

NOTES

*A condensed version of this chapter appeared as "KAL 007 and the Superpowers: An International Argument," *Quarterly Journal of Speech*, August 1988.

[1] Lloyd F. Bitzer, "The Rhetorical Situation," in Walter R. Fisher, ed., *Rhetoric: A Tradition in Transition* (East Lansing: Michigan State University Press, 1974), 247-60. Also, Lloyd F. Bitzer, "Rhetoric and Public Knowledge," in Don M. Burks, ed., *Rhetoric, Philosophy and Literature: An Exploration* (West Lafayette: Purdue University Press, 1978), 67-94.

[2] Bitzer, "Rhetoric and Public Knowledge," p. 68.

[3] See: David M. Johnson.

[4] David Hoffman, *Washington Post*, September 2, 1983, p. A14. Hoffman was covering the president in Santa Barbara and filed his report September 1.

[5] Robert J. Branham and W. Barnett Pearce, "Between Text and Context: Toward a Rhetoric of Contextual Reconstruction," *Quarterly Journal of Speech*, 71: 1 (February 1985), 19-36, p. 21.

[6] Bitzer, "Rhetoric and Public Knowledge," p. 85.

[7] Branham and Pearce, p. 21.

[8] Bitzer, "The Rhetorical Situation," p. 255.

[9] Bitzer, "Rhetoric and Public Knowledge," p. 85.

[10] For details surrounding this problem, see Chapter Three.

[11] See: Oberg, "Disasters in the Air," Chapter Eight in *Uncovering Soviet Disasters*.

[12] For a detailed analysis of Soviet rhetoric and the influence of Western radio, see Part II of this study, where political science perspectives are explored. For a discussion of the influence of world view on rhetorical conventions, see Kathleen Jamieson, "The Rhetorical Manifestations of *Weltanschauung*," *Central States Speech Journal*, 27:1 (Spring 1976), 4-14; and P. Albert Duhamel, "The Function of Rhetoric as Effective Expression," *Journal of the History of Ideas*, 10 (June 1949), cited therein.

[13] Bitzer, "Rhetoric and Public Knowledge," p. 68.

[14]Tom Shales, *Washington Post*, September 2, 1983, p. C13. See also: David Hoffman, *Washington Post*, September 2, 1983, p. A14

[15]Hoffman, *Washington Post*, September 2, 1983.

[16]Steven Weisman, *The New York Times*, September 2, 1983, p. A5. Weisman was also covering the president's stay in Santa Barbara. The relevant quotation is: "Mr. Reagan was notified in a telephone call from Mr. Clark at 7:30 p.m . . . that the plane was missing. This was nearly eight hours after Mr. Shultz had reported the plane's disappearance from radar contact." If Weisman was correct, the Department of State knew very quickly after the shootdown that contact with the plane had been lost. Hersh would claim that Weisman is wrong: He has written that Shultz learned of the shootdown only the next morning. See: *"The Target is Destroyed"*, p. 99.

[17]Apparently it was Michael Deaver who convinced the president that public relations considerations required him to cut short his holiday weekend. See: Larry Speakes with Robert Pack, *Speaking Out. The Reagan Presidency from Inside the White House* (New York: Charles Scribner's Sons, 1988), p. 120.

[18]David Hoffman and John M. Goshko, *Washington Post*, September 3, 1983, p. A22.

[19]See, for instance, the comments of: Undersecretary of State Lawrence Eagleburger, quoted by Hoffman and Goshko; Senator Howard Baker, quoted in a wire service compilation, *Washington Post*, September 2, 1983, p. A12; and an editorial in the *Washington Post*, September 2, 1983, p. A20.

[20]*COMPILATION*, p. 1. [Henceforth, bracketed page citations within the text will refer to this document.]

[21]Michael Getler, *Washington Post*, September 2, 1983, p. A17. Getler wrote these words on September 1. Evidently, everyone in the administration except presidential advisers Meese and Clark was taking this situation quite seriously.

[22]See: Thomas Maertens, "Tragedy of Errors," *Foreign Service Journal*, 62:8 (September 1985), 24-31, p. 29. (In a 1986 interview, Feaver confirmed that this was his impression at the time and that he had seen no information which would cause him to alter his opinion.)

[23]Douglas Feaver, *Washington Post*, September 2, 1983, p. A9. Again, Feaver wrote this article on September 1.

[24]Getler; David Shribman, *The New York Times*, September 2, 1983, p. A7. See also: Bernard Gwertzman, *The New York Times*, September 2, 1983, p. A5.

[25]This practice, of course, is widespread. Dallin, commenting that US denials of CIA complicity are self-serving, observes, "A quibbler might also maintain that such a de-

nial did not necessarily cover other U.S. government agencies, such as the [NSA]." See: *Black Box*, pp. 42, 114 [n. 31].

[26]See: *COMPILATION*, p. 5.

[27]It has been claimed by Sampson and Bittorf, for instance, that Shultz participated in a conference call very shortly after KAL 007 went down in the Sea of Japan. For a compilation of material used by conspiratists to justify their argument that the Korean airliner was on a reconnaissance mission planned and executed by the US, see: R. W. Johnson, *Shootdown* ; or Pearson, *KAL 007: The Cover-Up* .

[28]Hugo states, in contrast, that during the Cuban missile crisis, John Kennedy "took as much trouble to preserve the Russian line of retreat as he did to bar their further advance. His policy was so successful that the dispute was terminated in a manner that both governments were able to regard as advantageous" (p. 71).

[29]Edwin Black, *Rhetorical Criticism: A Study in Method*, 2nd ed. (Madison: University of Wisconsin Press, 1978), p. 9.

[30]Terence P. Moran has called this the "if-only-you-knew-what-I-know-you-would-agree-with-my-position" approach. It has become, Moran claims, a standard tactic of presidential rhetoric to rely on "inside information, ... secret knowledge, ... and similar private and non-sharable ways of knowing." See: "Propaganda as Pseudocommunication," *et cetera*, 36:2 (Summer 1979), 181-97, pp. 191, 190.

[31]Donald C. Smith, "KAL 007: Making Sense of the Senseless," (Paper delivered at the annual convention of the Speech Communication Association, Denver, November 1985). Smith analyzed the language choices in President Reagan's comments about KAL 007 and discovered that the most frequent descriptors used by the president were "massacre" (16 times); "tragedy" (11 times); "attack" (6 times); "crime against humanity" and "downing" (4 times each); and "murder", "brutality", and "brutal" (3 times each). Smith's analysis spanned the period 1 September 1983 to 1 January 1984.

[32]This was the first official reference to a 1978 incident involving another Korean Air Lines jetliner, Flight 902.

[33]Hersh contends that Reagan administration officials knew very early that the Soviets did not realize the aircraft was civilian (pp. 84-86). This assessment was confirmed by the Hamilton correspondence released in January 1988. See Chapter One, note 60.

[34]Rohmer, p. 100.

[35]See: "Press Briefing by Larry Speakes," The White House, Office of the Press Secretary, September 4, 1983. Bracketed page citations in the text at this point refer only to this document, not to the compilation of administration statements cited above.

[36]The words "eight minutes" refer to the air-to-ground tape, which was voice activated, thus eliminating silent periods during the 49-minute interception. See Chapter Four.

[37]Senator Baker told the press that the Soviet radar operators must have known which aircraft they were tracking, as evidenced by the fact that they had assigned different numbers to each for tracking purposes and knew each was headed in a different direction. See: Richard Halloran, *The New York Times*, September 6, 1983, A16. This was one of many indications that US military intelligence had monitored Soviet radar operators in the Kamchatka area.

[38]The base for this plane is on Shemya Island in the Aleutians, which is technically in Alaska; most people, upon hearing such a statement, would probably have thought the reference was to a place like Anchorage. See: Murray Sayle, "KE007: A Conspiracy of Coincidence," *New York Review of Books*, April 25, 1985, 44-54.

[39]Peter Millar, reporting from Moscow for Reuter, noted the commentary of Genrikh Borovik on the Soviet evening news program *Vremia*: "'When the Hitlerites made an attack, they forced women and children in front of them,' he said. 'I do not think this comparison is too strong. I think it is just right.'" See: *Washington Post*, September 6, 1983, p. A6.

[40]VOA's news stories are written in English, then translated by the various language sections for broadcast in the vernacular. According to Natalie Clarkson, Chief of the Russian Division, the Russian news broadcast never lags more than three hours behind the wire.

[41]Voice of America, CN-056, September 4, 1983 [16:58:48].

[42]Voice of America, Correspondent Report 2-1339, September 4, 1983 [Reporter: Philomena Jurey] [17:58:52].

[43]Voice of America, CN-063, September 4, 1983 [no time indicated].

[44]Voice of America, no item number, only "subs[titutes for] CN-063", September 4, 1983 [no time indicated].

[45]The Soviet propaganda organization has been described by Lisa Jameson, "Soviet Propaganda: On the Offensive in the 1980's," in Richard F. Staar, ed., *Public Diplomacy: USA Versus USSR* (Stanford: Stanford University Press, 1986), 18-45, pp. 25-27. It is typical of the lugubrious decision-making process inside the Soviet bureaucracy that no plan to capitalize on the RC-135 revelation was approved in time to have a statement prepared for the Monday evening *Vremia* newscast.

[46]V. Zakharov, "Chto kroetsia za 'intsidentom' " ["What's Hiding Behind the 'Incident'"], *Pravda*, September 6, 1983, p. 4.

[47]This citation in *Pravda* incorporated the first appearance of the term 'spyplane' in Soviet commentary.

[48]This was the first mention of satellite involvement. Although the concept was discarded for quite a while, a major story in *Pravda* subsequently highlighted this allegation. See: Marshal aviatsii P. Kirsanov, "Fakty izoblichaiut Vashington" ["The Facts Expose Washington"], *Pravda*, September 20, 1983, p. 4.

[49]This and other citations from Soviet radio and TV broadcasts were translated from Russian language materials provided by Jon Lodeesen.

[50]"Wright . . . told reporters that on the tapes Soviet fighter pilots twice referred to the plane inside Soviet airspace as being an RC-135." See Michael Getler, *Washington Post*, September 5, 1983, p. A9. Since there was absolutely no mention of any foreign aircraft other than the 'target' during the forty-nine minute span covered by the tape of the final interception and destruction of KAL 007, Wright's admission inadvertently revealed the existence of more transcribed conversations than had been known previously. Needless to say, these recordings have never been released. Administration officials have been quoted as saying that the United States possessed fifty-five minutes of tape. See: Steven Weisman, *The New York Times*, September 5, 1983, p. 6.

[51]Both sides attempted to create misimpressions concerning the whereabouts of the reconnaissance plane. See note 38.

[52]*The New York Times*, September 6, 1983, p. A16. During the period September 2-5, *Pravda* had published only six items relating in some fashion to KAL. During the period September 6-9, however, *Pravda* averaged five items per day. The figures for other Soviet newspapers are comparable.

[53]According to Philip Taubman (*The New York Times*, September 3, 1983, p. A6), US information that the RC-135 had never flown within seventy-five miles of KAL 007 came from analysis of Soviet radar activity. The United States never released this evidence, which, if correct, could have totally negated the effect of the Soviet counterattack and salvaged the Third World vote in the UN on September 12.

[54]One might note a similarity of tactics employed by the US and the USSR: both governments are inclined to recite a catechism of transgressions committed by the other.

[55]*COMPILATION*, pp. 6-8. Further bracketed page references refer to this document. On the issue of defense spending, *Pravda* (September 9, 1983, p. 5) again quoted *The New York Times* : "Many analysts expect that Reagan will use the KAL incident to achieve passage of his requests to Congress for greater military appropriations for such programs as the MX missile." This statement echoed a VOA report that Congressmen of both parties "agree the Korean plane incident has strengthened President Reagan's hand in dealing with defense issues, particularly the controversial MX strategic missile program." See: Voice of America, CN-021, September 7, 1983 [06:06:22].

[56] Bernard D. Nossiter, *The New York Times*, September 7, 1983, pp. A1, A15. Also see: Kadell, *The KAL 007 Massacre*, 191-98 *et passim*.

[57] At the same time, Assistant Secretary of State Richard Burt was retreating somewhat from the official American position that the Soviets knew KAL 007 was a civilian aircraft: "We are convinced that aircraft was a commercial airliner and there was a very good chance the Soviet Union fully understood that when they shot it and destroyed it" [emphasis added]. See: Voice of America, Special Report #4-0389, "FOCUS: The Fate of Flight Seven," September 6, 1983 [Reporters: Paula Wolfson and De Smith]. On September 7, VOA reported, "The White House says it has evidence not yet made public to indicate the Soviet Union should have known the plane its fighters shot down last week was a civilian commercial aircraft" [emphasis added]. See: Voice of America, CN-065 [12:55:11]. These reports gain added interest in light of the declassified material released by Congressman Hamilton in 1988. See: note 33 above and Chapter One, note 60.

[58] Zarefsky found this to be a common thread in conspiracy arguments. See: David Zarefsky, "Conspiracy Arguments in the Lincoln-Douglas Debates," *Journal of the American Forensic Association*, 21:2 (Fall 1984), 63-75. Zarefsky suggested that "successful conspiracy arguments shift the burden of proof to one's opponent while minimizing one's own burdens" (p. 73).

[59] This statement was read on *Vremia*, the mid-evening TV news program (9 P.M. Moscow Summer Time—early afternoon in New York). As Marilyn Burger reported later on ABC's *NIGHTLINE*, "Troyanovsky was still repeating the party line, but it was yesterday's party line already being contradicted in Moscow practically at the moment he spoke." See: *ABC NEWS NIGHTLINE, show #608* [transcript], September 6, 1983, p. 4.

[60] "Zakon o gosudarstvennoi granitse SSSR" ["The Law on the USSR State Border"] was promulgated on November 26, 1982 in *Pravda* and *Izvestiia*, pp. 1-3. Article 36 of the law states, in part, "The border troops and Air Defense Forces protecting the USSR state border use weapons and combat equipment . . . against violators of the USSR state border on land or water or in the air . . . in instances in which the violation cannot be stopped or the violators detained by any other means." See: *The Current Digest of the Soviet Press*, 34:51 (January 19, 1983), 15-20, p. 20.

[61] This statement was made by Lawrence Eagleburger, September 6, 1983. See: COMPILATION, p. 10.

[62] The wording of this statement is significant, since the USSR claims a 200 mile offshore limit to its territory.

[63] Voice of America, CN-001, September 7, 1983 [no time indicated].

[64] Voice of America, CN-021, September 7, 1983 [06:06:22].

[65] As Rohmer commented in genuine disbelief, "It was astonishingly incongruous that, although the Soviet Union had shot down the 747 and killed 269 people, the United States should be on the defensive" (p. 172).

[66] Also completely eclipsed was the demonstrable claim that, even today, there is no indication that any other accepted interception procedures were employed by the Soviet fighters prior to firing the missiles. See Chapter Four.

[67] Rohmer, p. 171. But see: Dallin, *Black Box*, pp. 16, 94.

[68] Jervis, *Perception and Misperception*, p. 182.

[69] Dallin, *Black Box*, p. 89. See Chapter Five.

[70] See: Dallin, *Black Box*, p. 12. Toward the end of the September 9 press conference, Soviet First Deputy Minister of Foreign Affairs Georgi M. Kornienko did make a disparaging comment about the authenticity of the tapes. See also: *ICAO REPORT* .

[71] V. Zakharov, "Chto kroetsia za 'intsidentom'" ["What's Hiding Behind the 'Incident'"], *Pravda*, September 6, 1983, p. 4.

[72] While we believe the tape was released prematurely, Speakes—blaming Clark and Casey—thinks it was held too long in order to set up the UN presentation so as to duplicate the drama that had been generated by Ambassador Adlai Stevenson during the Cuban missile crisis. See: Speakes with Pack, pp. 122-23.

[73] Published estimates have ranged from thirty seconds to two minutes. In any event, it was close enough to 'escaping' Soviet territory that, on the map utilized by Ogarkov to demonstrate the alleged path of KAL 007 and the U.S. RC-135, the time of the shootdown is claimed as 1824 GMT, two minutes earlier than that noted in the U.S. transcript for the statement "I have executed the launch. The target is destroyed." This was done to ensure that, in the Soviet version at least, KAL was indisputably flying over Soviet territory—hence still an 'intruder'—when fired upon; but this was a curious move, since no serious allegation disputing the whereabouts of the airliner was ever raised. It is important to remember that a jetliner at cruising speed would require only about eight or nine minutes to completely cross Sakhalin Island.

[74] Zarefsky also suggested that in making a conspiracy argument inference is more persuasive than evidence (See: "Conspiracy Argument," p. 73). While Kirkpatrick was not arguing for a conspiracy, the strategy was effective in this instance.

[75] One published report stated unequivocally that the United States had recovered the black box. Alex Braun, then editor of a specialty trade publication in Palo Alto CA, was told by what he termed "usually reliable sources" within the State Department that the source had inadvertently seen written confirmation of that fact. See: Alex Braun, "Has 007's 'Black Box' Been Found?", *Microwave Systems News*, 13:11 (November 1983), p. 48. If this is true, what the informant saw was a very closely guarded, code-

worded 'CRITIC' message. Braun told us in a recent interview that he contacted his source again about two months later, but the individual refused to discuss the matter further. "A curtain had been pulled down around the topic," Braun said.

The published report attracted a certain amount of attention. Braun received telephone inquiries from the staffs of both CBS news anchor Dan Rather and syndicated columnist Jack Anderson; in each instance, the caller inquired, unsuccessfully, as to the identity of Braun's source. Further, Braun was quoted by Soviet commentator Iu. Bandura. See: "Provokatory u pozornogo stolba," ["Provocateurs in the Stocks"], *Izvestiia,* August 31, 1984, p. 5.

[76]Bitzer, "Rhetoric and Public Knowledge," 84; also see: Charles W. Kneupper, "Rhetoric, Public Knowledge and Ideological Argumentation," *Journal of the American Forensic Association,* 21:4 (Spring 1985), 183-95, p. 186.

[77]Government officials were "appalled" when Lichenstein blandly told the Soviets at the UN, "We watched you watching them" (private communication).

[78]Admiral Stansfield Turner, former CIA director, said, "I was shocked by the amount of detail that the secretary of state gave this morning. . . .The secretary discussed these techniques in greater detail than I've ever heard before in public and certainly gave the Soviets a clear readout on just what those capabilities are in this particular area of the world." Admiral Bobby Inman, former NSA Director, supported the Administration's actions, "[Y]ou always cringe when sources and methods are being exposed. But there are situations that are of sufficient gravity that those who have the authority to declassify, the principal officers of government, make the decision to do so." *ABC NEWS NIGHTLINE, show #604,* September 1, 1983, p. 8.

[79]Bitzer, "The Rhetorical Situation," p. 256.

[80]See: Branham and Pierce, p. 27.

[81]For a comparison of differing presidential treatments of crises, see: James W. Pratt, "An Analysis of Three Crisis Speeches," *Western Speech,* 34:3 (1970), 194-202.

[82]For a discussion of Reagan's world view, as expressed in his speeches, see: Paul D. Erickson, *Reagan Speaks. The Making of an American Myth* (New York: New York University Press, 1985).

[83]*ABC NEWS/Washington Post Poll* (Survey #0084, consisting of 1,506 interviews conducted during September 22-26, 1983). Question 33, "Do you think the Reagan administration has told the public all it should know about the Korean plane incident or do you think the administration is holding back important information?" elicited these responses: (1) Told the public all it should know—32%; (2) Holding back information—59%; (3) No opinion—9%.

[84]Theodore Otto Windt, Jr., "Administrative Rhetoric: An Undemocratic Response to Protest," *Communication Quarterly*, **30**:3 (Summer 1982), 245-50.

[85]Quoted in James R. Andrews, "Confrontation at Columbia: A Case Study in Coercive Rhetoric," *Quarterly Journal of Speech*, **55**:1 (February 1969), 9-16.

[86]Andrews defined coercive rhetoric as discourse which limits the viable alternatives available to receivers of communication (p. 10). See Chapter Eight.

[87]V. William Balthrop, "Argumentation and the Critical Stance," in Cox and Willard, eds., *Advances in Argumentation Theory*, 238-58, p. 246.

[88]Parke G. Burgess, "The Rhetoric of Moral Conflict: Two Critical Dimensions," *Quarterly Journal of Speech*, **56**:2 (April 1970), 120-30, pp. 125-26. See also: V. William Balthrop, "Culture, Myth, and Ideology as Public Argument: An Interpretation of the Ascent and Demise of 'Southern Culture'," *Communication Monographs*, **51**:4 (December 1984), 339-52, p. 350.

[89]Balthrop, "Culture, Myth, and Ideology," p. 350.

DID THE UNITED STATES SUPPRESS GROUND-TO-AIR COMMUNICATIONS?

In charting the ebb and flow of information during the political struggle between East and West over the fate of the Korean jetliner, one sees the United States constantly wavering in its attitude toward revealing military secrets. It is arguably true, on the one hand, that the American government had never before willingly released so much 'compartmented' electronic and communications intelligence. Yet the internal pressures against releasing such information were tremendous: beyond a natural reluctance to do so under any circumstances, leading intelligence officials were rightfully appalled at the almost casual manner with which all-important "sources and methods" were being compromised.[1] For even when spokespersons refused to place the actual evidence in the public domain, enough was said to enable the Soviet government to determine whatever it needed to know about specific American intelligence capabilities. As is so often the case, the only ones left in the dark were the American people.[2]

On one issue, however, the government apparently balked—and that was with regard to the existence of a tape-recorded 'order to fire' or other instructions from Soviet flight dispatchers to the interceptor pilots. It is not at all clear that such 'ground-to-air' recordings actually exist: the governments of Japan and the United States steadfastly deny this; but many reports (which circulated immediately after the jetliner was downed) claimed that they do exist. Because the story behind these stories is itself so fascinating, and because the ground-to-air issue may be the only issue on which the United States actively suppressed the news (by clamping down on talkative Pentagon sources and by denying the accuracy of information it had previously admitted to be true), we will detail in this chapter all the relevant reports that were promulgated during the first week of September 1983. In addition, we will attempt to assess the rationale for stonewalling such information when it would seem that the value of a given US intelligence 'asset' had already been compromised.

As we have noted, one of the features of a crisis atmosphere in the West is the demand for information. Everyone needs or wants details about the event: the government, the press, the public. Only with adequate data can the parties determine the proper context and the appropriate response. The atmosphere surrounding the disappearance of KAL 007 was no exception. The difficulty lies in obtaining <u>accurate</u> information, because conflicting disclosure requirements, lack of hard knowledge, and competition among the media often lead to greater confusion and uncertainty. Hence, it is not surprising that in the early morning hours of September 1, with reporters in three world capitals (Tokyo, Seoul, and Washington) scrambling after facts that might help sort out what had happened, a number of inaccurate stories circulated among the press. One report even stated that the airliner had landed safely on Sakhalin Island. Subsequent information, in particular translation of the pilot tapes, proved this story tragically false.

Some early reports concerning the pilot (or 'air-to-ground') tape also overstated the information it contained. For example, on September 1, a story out of Hong Kong declared:

> The Japanese Defense Agency monitored a message from the pilot of a Soviet MiG-23 which said he was going to fire on a Korean Air Lines jetliner just before a KAL aircraft disappeared early today, the JIJI NEWS AGENCY reported … .
> The agency, quoting official sources, said that the pilot messaged his base on the Sakhalin Island: "I am going to fire a missile. The target is the KAL airliner."[3]

Nothing of this sort was overheard, of course, as the published air-to-ground transcripts indicate, and the story was not repeated. Nor was it picked up by the American daily press.

Other reports, however, had a longer life-span. Most prominent among these was the story that the Japanese Defense Agency had recorded both sides of the conversations between Soviet interceptor pilots and flight dispatchers on the ground. On September 1, Kyodo news service [Tokyo] reported that:

> Japanese military intelligence monitored Soviet radio communication suggesting an air attack by Soviet air forces shortly before a missing Korean Airlines jetliner vanished from radar screens early Thursday morning, military sources said.
> According to the sources, Japanese military intelligence monitored conversation between Soviet aircraft and a ground

based radio station around 3:20 a.m. Thursday Japan Standard Time. The conversation was reported as follows:

> 'Take aim at the target.'
> 'Aim Taken.'
> 'Fire.'
> 'Fired.'

Three similar communications were monitored, the sources said.

Military specialists said that Soviet air force planes are generally controlled by voice command from ground stations. The radio conversation, dubbed as COMINT, is usually monitored by Japanese military intelligence and analyzed, the sources said....

The sources said that the information based on the military monitoring had led to the announcement by the Japanese Government that the jetliner was most likely shot down by the Soviet Union.[4]

This report was picked up by the Western press, and it received considerable play in the United States. NBC News correspondent Jack Reynolds broke the ground-to-air story in the US nearly three hours before George Shultz's press conference. At 8:00 am, September 1, John Palmer reported on *THE TODAY SHOW* that:

Jack Reynolds, our Pentagon correspondent,... told us just a few minutes ago that he has picked up reports, I think, in contacting some of his sources there in Japan, that military officials had picked up word of broadcasts, apparently from Soviet MiG fighters, of course speaking in Russian, and the words, 'you are free to fire,' were heard. [TO STEVEN FRAZIER IN TOKYO:] Anything like that coming your way?

FRAZIER: That's not being released officially. We don't have confirmation of that....[5]

Apparently, the networks had difficulty confirming the story. It was seven hours from the time NBC broke the news until the story was repeated, this time by CBS in a 3:05 p.m. *SPECIAL REPORT*:

RATHER: Appearing angry and concerned at a news conference, Secretary of State Shultz said the Soviets had tracked the airliner for two and a half hours. According to Japanese intelligence sources, the final radio transmissions went like this.

> Ground: Take aim at target.
> Air: Aim taken.
> Ground: Fire.
> Air: Fired.[6]

CBS reiterated this item in their 3:57 p.m. *NEWSBREAK*:

RATHER: Secretary of State Shultz said the Soviets had tracked the 747 jet for 2 1/2 hours before moving in for the kill by air-to-air missile. Japanese intelligence monitored the final Soviet communications.

> Ground: Take aim at target.
> Air: Aim taken.
> Ground: Fire.
> Air: Fired.[7]

and again on the *EVENING NEWS*:

RATHER: Other chilling details of how Flight 007 was destroyed came from intelligence sources. In Japan, sources say monitoring of a conversation between a Soviet SU-15 pilot and Soviet ground controllers shows the following.

> Ground: Take aim at target.
> Air: Aim taken.
> Ground: Fire.
> Air: Fired.[8]

NBC did not repeat the item until their 11:30 p.m. *SPECIAL REPORT*:

MARVIN KALB: The Korean 747 did stray into Soviet air space, crossing Kamchatka, and then Sakhalin, two highly sensitive strategic outposts in the Soviet Pacific. For two and a half hours it was tracked by Soviet jets. One of the jets got close enough to see unmistakably that the 747 was a passenger plane. Still, the following exchange between the Soviet jet and its ground control was picked up by Japanese intelligence.

> Ground: Take aim at the target.
> Air: Aim taken.
> Ground: Fire.
> Air: Fired.[9]

At this point the NBC version conformed to that of CBS (which also included the story in its 11:30 p.m. special).[10]

Meanwhile, the story had begun to appear in the national print media. The first widespread mention occurred in an Associated Press dispatch from Strategic Air Command headquarters at Offutt AFB near Omaha. The wire story, a rewrite of an *Omaha World-Herald* interview with an unidentified Pentagon officer, stated, "[S]urveillance work routinely includes the eavesdropping by U.S. and Japanese intelligence personnel on Soviet military radio transmissions—both ground-to-air and air-to-ground conversations, the officer said."[11] Specific mention of the Japanese information was published in the September 2 edition of *The New York Times* (the earliest possible issue):

> The Japanese news agency Kyodo said a Soviet radio communication had been monitored by Japanese military intelligence that gave this exchange, apparently between the Soviet fighter and its ground station just before the airliner's disappearance:
>
> > "Take aim at the target."
> > "Aim taken."
> > "Fire."
> > "Fired."[12]

and the *Washington Post* of September 3.[13]

Evidently, ABC was the last to get confirmation; they did not broadcast this story until 6:30 p.m., September 2, on *WORLD NEWS TONIGHT*, their regular evening news show. However, ABC stayed with the story longer, rebroadcasting it on September 3:

> TOM JARRIEL: The smoking gun may have been found, according to the Japan Broadcasting Company. That news agency is quoting Japanese government sources as saying Russian ground commanders ordered their interceptor jets to shoot down Korean Airlines Flight 7. According to the Japanese report, Soviet ground control radioed, quote, "take aim at target." The fighter pilot replied, quote, "aim has been taken." Ground Control,

quote, "Fire." Soviet fighter, quote, "missile fired, target destroyed." There is still no confirmation from official US sources of that Japanese report.[14]

CBS and NBC had dropped the story after September 1, although, according to Dallin, there were "initially clear indications" from both Japanese and American sources that both air-to-ground and ground-to-air communications had been intercepted. Dallin further stated that Kyodo News Service released several excerpts in Tokyo on September 1. One of these exchanges included the dialogue reported by the US networks.[15] It should be noted that throughout September 1 and 2, Japan Broadcasting Corporation reported this information on several different occasions, each time citing "both Japanese government and intelligence sources."[16]

What is most interesting about this chronology is the attribution of the story and its relationship to the confirmation process. According to Carolyn Smith, Assistant Director of Political Operations at ABC News in New York, the networks (and, presumably, the print media as well), not wishing to acknowledge one another's work if at all possible, attempt to obtain independent verification of a report before airing it. If corroboration cannot be obtained, the rival network's report is credited; in the absence of such an acknowledgement, one can assume the reporter was able to get the necessary verification. Ordinarily, two independent confirmations are required to air a story, although on a 'breaking' story such as this the producer might air the report with only one source. Moreover, Smith said, no network would repeat an item in a subsequent newscast (as all three networks did in this instance) unless it had been verified in the interim and the producer was certain that it was accurate. As reporters succeeded in reaching their sources, the story became more detailed: CBS correctly identified the type of fighter plane, and ABC managed to get a more precise translation of the pilot's fateful announcement. Thus, the chronology of television reporting implies confirmation of Jack Reynolds's initial story.

In the initial NBC report, the attribution is very vague: "[Reynolds] has picked up reports, I think in contacting some of his sources there in Japan." By 3:05, CBS was crediting the story to Japanese intelligence, thereby indicating that the network had gotten confirmation. Dan Rather, on the CBS EVENING NEWS, waffled a bit on the attribution ("In Japan, sources say"), but by the 11:30 p.m. SPECIAL REPORT, Japanese intelligence was again cited as the source.

Similarly, on September 2, ABC first attributed the report to Japanese intelligence, but the next day watered that down to the Japan Broadcasting Company quoting Japanese government sources. This shift can be accounted for by Tom Jarriel's note that they had no confirmation from official US sources. *The New York Times,* too, referred to Kyodo news agency as the source of their story.[17]

Michael Getler of the *Washington Post* tried to follow up the issue, but Assistant Secretary of State Richard Burt avoided giving unequivocal answers regarding whether or not US officials possessed evidence of a direct order from the ground command to fire on the airliner. Getler, in the end, reported the story as unconfirmed by US sources and attributed it to "a Japanese news agency."[18]

In a recent interview, Jack Reynolds recalled that he was awakened September 1 at 7:30 a.m. (EDT) by an overseas call from an old friend in the Japanese news media. This friend, Reynolds told us, knew someone in the Japanese military who had actually heard the ground-to-air tape. The Japanese reporter said his agency was going public with the information "in the next ten minutes." "And they did," Reynolds stated. Reynolds first called in the story to *THE TODAY SHOW,* as indicated above, then spent the day at the Pentagon trying to get his regular sources there to provide more information regarding the ground-to-air tape and Western knowledge of the 'order-to-fire'. His stateside sources could not confirm the story; however, he noted, "Because of the specific information I had, I did not get a denial." Reynolds said that in the past these people had always told him when he was wrong about something. He continued:

> I felt this was tantamount to an admission. If they know you've got something, they won't lie to you because they don't know where you got your information. If it was definitely not true, my experience was that they would give you some indication that you were barking up the wrong tree.[19]

Reynolds remains convinced the story was accurate. He described his Japanese source as "absolutely impeccable," someone with "no axe to grind," a friend who was just repaying past favors. Moreover, nothing Reynolds subsequently heard or learned contradicted his information. "I was comfortable with it as I got it. I didn't have any problem with it," he said. When asked if he has ever doubted the existence of such ground-to-air tapes, he replied without hesitation, "No, not for a minute."

George Wilson of the *Washington Post* said that he, too, tried to follow up the story but encountered a stone wall, not only at the Pentagon, but at the State Department as well. His usual Air Force contacts provided no help whatsoever. Wilson indicated to us that it was his "working assumption" that the Japanese had the actual tape. He pursued this quite aggressively—"I wanted it badly"—but never managed to obtain a copy.[20]

Philip Taubman of *The New York Times* was equally unsuccessful in obtaining confirmation from State Department officials Richard Burt and John Hughes, who made only very carefully worded denials. According to Getler, Hughes commented that "[t]here was no clearcut transmission like that in the US record of the conversations."[21]

In an intriguing exchange on *THIS WEEK WITH DAVID BRINK-LEY*, September 4, when Sam Donaldson asked Lawrence Eagleburger, US Undersecretary of State, "Have we heard the order to fire yet?", Eagleburger replied:

> Well, you're pushing me on a subject that obviously gets close to being difficult. Let me simply say we know that the aircraft fired, and I can't talk about whether he got an order to fire or not.[22]

And so, the story died in the United States. On September 6, however, Japanese government spokesperson Masaharu Gotoda announced that while Japan had recorded the ground-to-air communications, his government would not release the tape:

> Chief government spokesman Masaharu Gotoda released radio communication from a Soviet fighter, monitored by Japan's Self-Defense Forces....
> Japan and the United States will jointly submit the tape-recorded communication to a session of the United Nations Security Council, Gotoda said.
> Japan has also monitored communication from the ground to the fighter but will not release it, he said.
> This will be enough evidence to prove the Soviet shooting down of the South Korean jet....[23]

Gotoda did suggest, however, that if the Soviet Union persisted in denying responsibility for its actions, Japan might release the tape recorded order to fire.[24]

Within hours, Defense Vice Minister Haruo Natsume denied the existence of the ground station intercepts:

> The Defense Agency has in its possession the taped communication of only the pilot of the Soviet interceptor ..., Defense Vice Minister Haruo Natsume said Tuesday.
> Natsume denied a remark made by Chief Cabinet Secretary Masaharu Gotoda earlier Tuesday to the effect that Japan also had recorded communication of Soviet ground stations with the pilot.[25]

Japan did not release the ground-to-air tape, of course, and from this point on officials reiterated the government's position that no such recordings existed.

According to *The New York Times*, the US government also indicated initially that it had the ground-to-air tapes. Among these statements was one made September 6 by Larry Speakes, in which he alluded to "further evidence" in the possession of US authorities which demonstrated that the Soviets knew KAL was a civilian airliner. This evidence would not be released, however, because, according to Speakes, "it would compromise intelligence sources." Speakes reiterated this position September 7. Interestingly, he also denied that the United States had the ground-to-air tapes. The tapes, he stated, belonged to Japan and it was up to the Japanese to release them.[26] This revelation came after the official Japanese denial that the intercepts existed.[27] Shortly thereafter, however, it was reported in the United States that Japan had suffered significant losses of intelligence data from Soviet sources:

> It has been pointed out that slips of the tongue by U.S. and Japanese officials must have indicated to Moscow that Japan had monitored not only what the pilots said but the hard-to-obtain ground commands to the pilots, official denials notwithstanding. Japanese military officials, however, have been able to prevent the ground communications from being made public.[28]

Johnson reports that these denials by Japanese government officials did not put an end to "continuing reports in the Japanese press that the government did indeed have such tapes. Privately, Japanese intelligence officials admitted that they had the tapes but that it would be too compromising to security to release them."[29]

As late as September 11, in a summary of political events through Ogarkov's press conference on the 9th, reporters for *The Sunday Times* (London) who were critical of most aspects of the American government's version unequivocally maintained that both portions of the Soviet intercept sequence had been recorded:

> There is *no* evidence that a Soviet fighter pilot clearly identified the target to his ground controllers or that ground control knew it was a commercial airliner.
> But The Sunday Times has discovered that Japan's Air Self-Defense Force *did* intercept ground control transmissions—and, furthermore, supplied the recording to the Americans. This second, unrevealed tape contains no reference to the target which would identify it as a harmless civilian airplane. The Americans maintain, however, that they have only the pilot's transmissions.[30]

This statement in *The Sunday Times* was the clearest and most adamant assertion to appear in a major communication medium.

Yet, the US media dropped this ground-to-air portion of the story. No network broadcast a follow-up report, and the item rapidly faded from the print media as well. Aside from Sam Jameson's September 19 Tokyo dispatch, the last known repetition occurred in the September 12 issues of *TIME* and *Newsweek*.[31] Judging by American news coverage, the story had begun to soften on September 3, the point at which ABC's Tom Jarriel reported no confirmation from "official US sources." No newsperson had succeeded in getting Pentagon informants to talk about the matter; evidently, significant pressure had been applied by the government. But the final decision against releasing ground-to-air transcripts came very late in the process, providing further indication of a lack of coordination within the Executive branch. The story of the order to fire, initially broadcast with the earliest reports of the tragedy, was repeated at least five times between 8:00 a.m. and 11:30 p.m. EDT— a span of some 15 1/2 hours—but no denial was issued during this period.[32] The first direct denial apparently came some five days later.

Obviously, too much had already been disclosed.[33] Thus, the primary effect of this indecision may have been to embarrass the Japanese. According to Anthony Sampson:

> The United States reneged on a pledge to Japan to reveal its two-hour radio transcripts of Flight 007 after the Japanese made public their record of the plane's last fifteen minutes. The US thus embarrassed the Japanese, along with exposing their monitoring capability.[34]

Much had been revealed about US capacities, as well. Yet the fundamental question—Did the US or Japan record Soviet ground personnel directing the aerial interception of KAL 007?—has never been answered. It is difficult for a layman to believe, given the extensive intelligence assets focused on the Soviet Far East Command, that the United States could not monitor virtually anything of military significance. This impression is reinforced by previously cited statements that someone did monitor microwave traffic between local sector commanders and higher authorities in Moscow.[35] Indeed, we have been told by a former Air Force intelligence officer that the United States most certainly has several transcripts of these conversations, that at least ten years ago all Soviet ground-to-air as well as air-to-ground transmissions on Sakhalin were available for real-time monitoring from as far away as Anchorage. In addition, a former Army officer who had been stationed at Wakkanai told us that even in the 1950s some Soviet ground stations directly across the La Perouse Strait from Hokkaido could be monitored.

On the other hand, many observers apparently felt that the alleged recording of an order to fire was erroneous.[36] We have directly asked a representative of the US Department of State on several occasions whether ground-to-air transcripts exist and each time have received an unequivocal denial. It is presently the official position of both Japan and the United States that such recordings or transcripts do not exist.

The central question raised by this controversy revolves around the natural conflict between politics and security: revealing hard information in order to marshal world opinion runs a genuine risk of compromising US intelligence capabilities. The policy and security issues are intertwined to such an extent that one must examine them together in order to form an opinion regarding the conflicting evidence that has been assembled in this chapter. If one assumes that the United

States possesses the technical means to have achieved what is claimed, then everything depends on whether or not those assets were appropriately deployed and functioning on the night of August 31/September 1, 1983.

It should be stated clearly that the US does possess such technical means. At the same time, it must be recognized that intercepting ground-to-air radio transmissions is a much more difficult task, from a logistical standpoint, than intercepting air-to-ground. Without getting too technical (thus exhibiting our own ignorance), there are only four ways to situate the appropriate receiving equipment within or near the "cone of radiation" of signals emanating from the ground: in space, in the air, on the Earth's surface, or under the Earth's surface. With regard to monitoring Soviet flight dispatchers, the last two means are severely restricted: the listening post must be located close to the transmitting point.

Presumably, Soviet authorities can determine which American airborne or space platforms, if any, were in an appropriate position to have intercepted the ground-to-air messages. For instance, the US may have had an aircraft aloft that night in the Sea of Okhotsk.[37] If that or another platform could have monitored the transmissions, even accidentally, it is a safe bet that it did so[38]—and the Soviets would have to assume that it had.[39] The problem for American officials can be set forth in the form of a syllogism that hypothetically might be constructed by Soviet officials:

> If the United States has acknowledged eavesdropping while our ground stations directed the tracking and destruction of KAL 007...
> And if we know that there were no satellite or airborne reconnaissance platforms in position to have accomplished this ...
> Then it must be true that the US has situated a surface or subsurface receiving station close enough to our transmitters to succeed in accomplishing this—and we had better start looking around.

This, in real life, is what the spy business is all about. Specific information is perishable—hence, theoretically it is replaceable. [Particularly valuable data may have a very long period of relevance, however.] What intelligence agencies strive most to protect are facts concerning the technical and human collectors from which they obtain information—their much ballyhooed "sources and methods."[40]

How do these considerations affect the issue of ground-to-air monitoring and possible government suppression of the intelligence product? Analogizing from a courtroom situation, we would say that motive and means have been demonstrated, but opportunity has not been established [although guidelines for determining opportunity have been offered]. Still, no smoking gun has been uncovered. All judgments, therefore, are necessarily tentative. Nonetheless, it is our opinion that ground-to-air tapes do (or did) exist, and that somewhere in the US intelligence establishment much more is known about the precise details of Soviet deliberations and actions throughout the two-and-a-half hour interception than has been made public. On this issue, we believe, the US government is justified in not revealing all it knows.

This story may not seem significant on its face; after all, with the pilot tape, the question of whether Soviet ground control had issued an order to fire was moot: there was no doubt that the interceptor pilots had destroyed the civilian airliner.

However, the story illustrates the role played by the US media in shaping rhetorical situations in this country and guiding the interpretation process during times of perceived crisis. Initially, the question of the fate of the airliner was paramount; the earliest stories of recorded conversations established a context of veracity for later pronouncements. Secretary of State Shultz indirectly corroborated the rumors that these tapes existed by announcing the US knew the Soviet plane was in "constant contact with its ground control." Thus, there was an aura of reciprocal credibility enhancement between the secretary's statements and the reports in the media. To the average citizen, there could be no question that American military personnel had recorded every word spoken by every Soviet serviceman who had any connection to the destruction of KAL 007.

Some might argue that the demise of the story also exemplifies the symbiosis between reporters and their government sources: when the government decided to kill the story, the press went along. This is certainly possible, although at least two reporters have indicated that they made a serious attempt to follow-up the question. In the post-Watergate era, it is more likely that the exigencies of Western journalism took over. According to media representatives we have interviewed,

75

the media see their obligation as reporting developments as soon as they can be confirmed. But circumstances change, new information may surface, and today's "truth" can become obsolete. In a rapidly developing story such as the fate of KAL 007, other facts may become more important and the press moves on. The ground-to-air story, then, might simply have died of benign neglect.

CHAPTER THREE

NOTES

[1]In mid-September, Lt. Gen. Lincoln D. Faurer, then Director of NSA, issued a directive forbidding further contact with the news media; he reminded NSA personnel of their legal obligations and threatened them with both loss of security clearance and possible prosecution if his directive were ignored. [In 1986 Faurer's successor, Lt. Gen. William E. Odom, issued a similar order after an excerpt from *"The Target Is Destroyed"* was published in *The Atlantic Monthly*.]

[2]The situation calls to mind a cynical aphorism heard from time to time in the Halls of Washington: "Keeping America Safe from Democracy."

[3]Foreign Broadcast Information Service (henceforth, FBIS), *Daily Report. Japan*, September 1, 1983, p. C2. [BKO11307 Hong Kong AFP in English 1302 GMT 1 Sep 83].

[4]FBIS, *Daily Report. Japan*, September 2, 1983, p. C1. [OWO11609 Tokyo Kyodo in English 1602 GMT 1 Sep 83].

[5]*NBC NEWS TODAY SHOW* [transcript], September 1, 1983, p. 30. According to Tom Shales ["Television's Scramble on the Crisis," *Washington Post*, September 2, 1983, p. C13], Palmer, *THE TODAY SHOW* news anchor, was on the air when Reynolds, NBC's chief Defense Department correspondent, phoned in this report to the control room. Senior producer Marty Ryan relayed the information to Palmer through Palmer's earphone, and Palmer "spoke the words on the air as he heard them from the control room."

[6]*CBS NEWS SPECIAL REPORT* [transcript], September 1, 1983, 3:05-3:09 p.m., EDT.

[7]*CBS NEWS NEWSBREAK* [transcript], September 1, 1983, 3:57 p.m., EDT.

[8]*CBS EVENING NEWS WITH DAN RATHER* [transcript], September 1, 1983, p. 2. This report gains credibility because of the change in identification of the Soviet aircraft, indicating an additional source had been consulted. Initially identified as a MiG-23, the plane was later determined by US intelligence to be an SU-15.

Although it has universally been accepted in the West that the fatal rockets were fired from a Sukhoi fighter-interceptor, at least one high ranking Japanese official disagreed. On September 7, 1983, Agence France Press reported the following in regard to Shinji Yazaki, whom AFP described as the "director general" of a Japan Defense Agency bureau:

At an unusual 2:30 am press conference, Mr Yazaki said that the plane, code-named "805," could be a MiG-23 fighter because of its flying path recorded on the radar screen. (U.S. officials have identified aircraft "805" as a Sukhoi-15 and said a MiG-23 accompanied it on the attack as an observer.) But Mr Yazaki noted that the MiG-23 fighter had a greater flying range than the SU-15 and Japanese officials have said that only a MiG-23 could have stayed aloft so long before hitting its target.

See: FBIS, *Daily Report. Japan*, September 7, 1983, p. C1 [OWO70319 Hong Kong AFP in English 0138 GMT 7 Sep 83].

[9]*NBC TV NEWS NETWORK REPORT* [transcript], September 1, 1983, 11:30 p.m., pp. 1-2.

[10]The *CBS NEWS SPECIAL REPORT* : "THE DEATH OF FLIGHT 007," which was televised at the same time, opened with the following commentary by Dan Rather [transcript, September 1, 1983, 11:30 p.m., p. l.]:

The words were picked up early Thursday morning, Tokyo time, by Japanese intelligence officials.

Ground:	Take aim at the target.
Air:	Aim taken.
Ground:	Fire.
Air:	Fired.

At 3:26 a.m., Korean Air Lines Flight Seven disappeared from the screens.

[11]"Pentagon Officer's Report: U.S. Eavesdropped as Jetliner Was Attacked," *Los Angeles Times*, Late Edition, September 1, 1983, p. 1.

[12]Robert D. McFadden, *The New York Times*, September 2, 1983, p. A4. The identical nature of these reports may be interpreted in two contradictory ways: either the story is true and confirmed, or the reporters, faced with deadlines and no independent confirmation, had resorted to a practice known as "black-sheeting"—filing a consistent story, one which was essentially a group effort. For a discussion of "black-sheeting," see: Robert P. Newman and Dale R. Newman, *Evidence* (Boston: Houghton Mifflin, 1969), p. 136; and Felix Greene, *A Curtain of Ignorance* (Garden City, NY: Doubleday, 1964), p. xvii.

[13]William Chapman, "Flight 007; South Koreans Demand Soviet Apology, Indemnity," *Washington Post*, September 3, 1983, p. A23. The source cited by Chapman is *Asahi* newspapers quoting Japanese military sources. This article, which was filed from Seoul, also appeared in the *International Herald Tribune*, September 2, 1983, p. 1.

[14]*ABC WORLD NEWS TONIGHT WEEKEND REPORT* [transcript], September 3, 1983, p. 1. It is interesting to note that the final transmission of the fighter pilot in this

version more closely approximates the remark on the official transcript released by the United States and first read to the nation by President Reagan on September 5. That transcript says, "I have executed the launch. The target is destroyed."

[15]Dallin, *Black Box*, p. 110.

[16]Johnson, *Shootdown*, p. 169.

[17]It is curious that the media were not willing to accept the story as reported out of Japan but insisted on confirmation from US sources, particularly since it was Japan (according to the United States government) which had recorded and initially translated the conversations. US spokesmen originally stated that the interceptions had to be translated from Russian to Japanese to English; it was unclear whether the US had original recordings of its own, or whether the government relied on the recordings made by the Japanese and did their own English translations. According to Japanese Defense Agency officials, "more than half" of the data released on September 1 by George Shultz came from Japanese intelligence sources. See: Sam Jameson, "Disclosures on Soviet Pilots Costly to Japan's Security," *Los Angeles Times*, September 19, 1983, Part I, pp. 1, 15 (p. 15).

[18]Michael Getler, *Washington Post*, September 2, 1983, p. A17. Getler's resolution of the confirmation problem indicates that the print media use an attribution standard similar to that of the networks. Doug Feaver told us that the *Washington Post* has a "two-source rule" and that it is the reporter's responsibility to decide when he has two independent sources and when he has the same ultimate source through two different conduits. Feaver was one of *Post* editors who dealt with the Watergate revelations. Whenever no source of the information is identified at all, he said, the *Post* always has gotten independent confirmation. Further, the phrasing 'a source said' always means <u>one unnamed source</u> and the paper "will always soften the lead in this instance." Feaver was interviewed May 27, 1986.

[19]Interview with Jack Reynolds, June 18, 1986. In 1983 he was the NBC News Pentagon Correspondent. Reynolds reaffirmed this account on two subsequent occasions.

[20]Interview with George Wilson, June 3, 1986.

[21]Getler, *Washington Post*, September 2, 1983. See the discussion in Chapter Two.

[22]*ABC NEWS, THIS WEEK WITH DAVID BRINKLEY* [transcript], September 4, 1983, p. 11.

[23]FBIS, *Daily Report. Japan*, September 6, 1983 [OWO60407 Tokyo KYODO in English 0327 GMT 6 Sep 83].

[24]*Mainichi Daily News*, September 6, 1983. Gotoda, speaking at a hastily summoned press conference, was faced with "persistent press questioning" [cited by Johnson, *Shootdown*, p. 169]. Johnson comments, "It is doubtful if Mr Gotoda realized what a huge cat he was letting out of the bag. . . ."

[25]FBIS, *Daily Report. Japan*, September 6, 1983 [OWO60536 Tokyo KYODO in English 0522 GMT 6 Sep 83]. Although reports of the ground-to-air conversations and alleged excerpts from the transcript had been circulating in Tokyo for five days, this was the first government denial of the existence of that recording. On the 7th, AFP reported that Shinji Yazaki had reiterated the Japanese government denial. See: FBIS, *Daily Report. Japan*, September 7, 1983, p. C1 [OWO70319 Hong Kong AFP in English 0138 GMT 7 Sep 83]. Yazaki maintained this position in 1985, when an organization comprised of the families of Japanese victims petitioned their government to release all relevant tape recordings. See: *Asahi Evening News*, "Gov't Refuses to Release Tape of KAL Jet Shooting Incident," January 16, 1985, p. 1 [cited by Pearson, *KAL 007: The Cover-Up*, p. 322].

[26]Steven Weisman, *The New York Times*, September 8, 1983, p. A12.

[27]According to Rohmer, the pilot transcripts released by American and Japanese authorities were monitored by the Rescue Co-ordination Center of the Japanese Ministry of Transport (pp. 125-29). This center had a voice-activated recorder which constantly monitored "every communications frequency used by the Soviets in controlling their fighters." Rohmer also comments on a so-called "second tape," which has never been released in any form:

> According to undisclosed military sources, three such sets of communications were monitored. Apparently this was done by the military who, with their facilities at Wakkanai and elsewhere, could reasonably have been expected to have set up a system for monitoring not only transmissions from Soviet pilots to the ground, but ground-to-air instructions as well. In addition to the three two-way conversations between the ground and the aircraft, the Japanese facilities also monitored Soviet orders in dispatching eight ships to the area in the Sea of Japan near Moneron Island, thirty nautical miles off the southwestern Sakhalin coast, where the 747 had probably gone down (p. 129).

This undisclosed second tape is the ground-to-air interchange.

[28]Sam Jameson, *Los Angeles Times*, September 19, 1983, Part I, pp. 1, 15 (p. 15).

[29]Johnson, *Shootdown*, p. 171.

[30]Robin Morgan and Patrick Forman, "The airliner: not such a cold-blooded kill," *The Sunday Times*, September 11, 1983, p. 18. [Emphasis in the original.]

[31]*Newsweek* 's story bordered on the irresponsible. The magazine stated that "a Japanese listening post heard the pilot discuss the contact [with KAL 007] with his ground control" (p. 16). In the next paragraph, the article declared:

> The fighter pilot trailed his target for 14 minutes before the attack—and ra-dioed full recognition that his missiles were locked on a civilian commercial aircraft. The fatal shot itself appeared to be no accident: according to reported transcripts published in Japan, every move was carefully orchestrated by ground controllers.
>
> The pilot was ordered to take aim at the target. He replied that he had taken aim. The controller ordered him to fire. Pilot: 'The target is destroyed. I am breaking off attack.' [emphasis added]

This is the only known repetition of the report that the fighter pilot acknowledged the civilian status of the 'target', an account that is empirically refuted by the pilot transcript. Although the magazine reportedly "went to bed" more than a week before the cover date, and, therefore, prior to American and Japanese denials of the existence of the ground control transcript, there should have been time to confirm the story. A close reading of the quotation supports this judgment: the final comment of the Soviet pilot—"The target is destroyed. I am breaking off attack"—almost exactly duplicates the official translation, which was not released prior to September 5. While ABC, on September 3, had reported "Missile fired, target destroyed," *Newsweek* was the only outlet to report the exact wording. And they were the only one to include the statement "I am breaking off attack." These facts imply either that the newsmagazine found someone who would talk or, more likely, that the story was rewritten after the transcripts had been made public. The text in *Newsweek* contains none of the tentativeness of the other US media accounts. Their version is an interesting blend of fact and fiction, a practice one would have hoped the newsmagazines had abandoned long ago.

Nevertheless, the magazine certainly treats the existence of the ground-to-air tape as genuine. Midway through the article, the account states: "Fourteen minutes later, with approval from the ground, he [the Soviet pilot] fired" (p. 19).

[32]Carolyn Smith told us government officials have been known to call and deny stories that had been aired by the network.

[33]According to an Associated Press story, Japanese Foreign Ministry sources said that releasing the tape of the Soviet fighter pilots "had led to a two-thirds reduction of information on Soviet military transmissions because the Soviets changed frequencies and

started coding." See: "Airplane Missing Near Sakhalin May Be a Soviet Airliner," *Tallahassee Democrat*, May 17, 1985, p. 6A.

[34] Anthony Sampson, "What Happened to Flight 007?" *Parade Magazine*, April 22, 1984, p. 12.

[35] Philip Taubman, *The New York Times*, September 3, 1983, p. A6; George C. Wilson, *Washington Post*, September 2, 1983, p. A15. Such interceptions, achieved by monitoring different Soviet communications networks, would themselves probably not contain the ground-to-air conversations.

[36] See, for example, Wilson, *Washington Post*, September 2, 1983, p. A15. In addition, Hersh derogated such reports as "spurious" and flatly denied the existence of any intercepted instructions from Soviet ground dispatchers, stating about such accounts, "The line between fact and fiction . . . had been erased" (p. 113).

[37] Hersh writes: "Soviet aircraft had been alerted in anticipation of a routine . . . reconnaissance mission, code-named Burning Wind, whose early-morning flight from the American air base at Kadena, Okinawa, passed just east of Sakhalin en route to its normal patrol in the Sea of Okhotsk" (p. 56). One of the purposes of such flights is to confirm that the Soviets have not switched broadcast frequencies. Hersh claims this flight was cancelled. We believe Hersh is incorrect.

[38] For example, Navy P-3 aircraft on submarine detection missions near Soviet territorial waters routinely listen to Soviet ground stations as a precautionary measure.

[39] In this regard, one should not ignore Japanese capabilities, not all of which are coordinated with US intelligence activities. In particular, it is known that Japan has a small number of "dedicated" ELINT platforms--that is, aircraft specifically equipped to monitor electronic emissions--but it is not known if any of these craft were deployed in the area of Sakhalin that night.

[40] Historically it has been true that the government would not prosecute suspected spies within the intelligence establishment because of the information about sources and methods that must be revealed in open court in order to obtain a conviction. The Pelton trial in 1986 was a noteworthy exception. On the other hand, when the government threatens journalists with prosecution, the issue always involves US intelligence assets, not information, except insofar as the information itself reveals the source. See: Eleanor Randolph, "Casey Warns Writers, Publishers About Putting Secrets in Books," *Washington Post*, June 26, 1986, p. A11.

CHAPTER FOUR

THE KAL TAPES

> [I]t is imperative to secure original
> materials.... Otherwise accepted historical
> "facts" may turn out to be traps for
> the unwary.
> —*Carey Joynt and Percy Corbett*

In levelling the charge of murder against the Soviet Union, US officials described a two-and-a-half hour period of actions in the air and on the ground. References were made to "reflected Soviet radar data" and flight dispatcher messages both on Kamchatka Peninsula and Sakhalin Island. American representatives alluded to other intelligence intercepts (apparently from locations in and around Moscow, or near the Soviet border with China, where Beijing has allowed the Americans to install listening posts) that shed further light on the deliberative procedures within the Soviet military command structure.

But the only evidence actually released was a tape recording of the Soviet pilots—particularly one identified as 805—who participated in the final interception over Sakhalin that concluded with the destruction of KAL 007. The pilots spoke in Russian, of course, which was an unfortunate circumstance for Western commentators—governmental and private—who rushed to analyze Soviet actions on the basis of the tape recording's presumed contents. Most of the published commentary based on this tape has been hopelessly muddled.

As a prelude to discussions of both the Soviet propaganda campaign and the claims of Western conspiratists, we undertake in this chapter to provide an accurate recitation of the meaning of the Russian, comments regarding the accuracy of the two authorized translations[1] that have been distributed, and an assessment of the manner in which the facts of the intercept—as recorded by Japanese military intelligence—have been distorted. Such distortion, we suspect, was both witting (when promulgated by the Soviet Union) and unwitting (when highly speculative and overly imaginative interpretations have been proffered in the writings of the conspiratists).

An ancillary issue, which will be addressed more directly in later chapters, is the whole matter of factual accuracy. In the empirical studies that follow, we propose three avenues of criticism of both the propagandist and the conspiratist:

1. Structure of discourse—to expose the rhetor's *Weltanschauung*;

2. Techniques of argumentation—to situate rhetorical examples along a persuasion/coercion axis;

3. Factual accuracy and relevance—to judge the evidentiary value of the data adduced in support of arguments.[2]

Factual accuracy may seem at first glance to be a shallow notion, but it can play a significant role whenever the rhetorical topic involves complex scientific or technical subjects such as arms control, AIDS, Chernobyl, or KAL. The simple truth is that in its domestic propaganda the Soviet Union places little or no value on factual accuracy as that term is understood in the West.[3] Perhaps it is just ethnocentric bias, but Americans do not seem shocked by such a state of affairs, nor, accordingly, is much credence placed in Soviet pronouncements.

An altogether different relationship obtains, however, between the Western citizen (at least, the American variety thereof) and the 'free' Western press (at least, the English speaking and writing media). The difference is a presumption of accurate reporting, regardless of political, social, or philosophical bias; indeed, responsible Western journalism is expected to announce its bias beforehand. Even when the media are severely criticized, at issue is the editorial selection of stories and facts, or (it is claimed) the slanted viewpoint that colors analysis and interpretation. It is well known that the set of all factual information that might be adduced in public argument is never presented by any single rhetor, who purposely selects for use in the framing of arguments that subset of facts deemed to be most persuasive. Nevertheless, one can reasonably expect the facts so chosen to be "true facts." Thus, it is a salient and damning critique to say someone has gotten the facts wrong.

Technological or specialized topics pose unique problems for the average information consumer. One is almost tempted to draw an analogy to the Soviet counterpart in that there are few, if any, means of independent corroboration available to a reader. Of necessity, on technical issues at least, the reader grants the writer an ethos of expertise conferred by the very fact of publication. As we shall see, the writer must stray a long way before confronting the danger of forfeiting that ethos.[4]

Some questions are quite basic: Is it proper to "win" a public argument with bad evidence? Further, is it not an effective form of analysis to challenge the accuracy or the relevance of data adduced as evidence? This is certainly an accepted method of criticism in other fields, *e.g.* history and the precise sciences. There are those, of course, who would reject such a criterion, arguing that only effects are the legitimate objects of rhetorical criticism. But we would counter that such is the case only when, in Fisher's words, the rhetor is "being reasonable," when the rhetoric is "non-manipulative, bilateral, deliberative, and attentive to data."[5] The underlying assumption made by Fisher is one of good will on the part of rhetorical opponents. Such rhetors

> will have employed special knowledge of the issues, both procedural and evaluative, that they apply in the given case; they will have informed themselves of relevant data, assessed the arguments that can be made for and against the decision, weighed the values that impinge on the matter, and decided to adopt a position that satisfies the tests of coherence and fidelity. In advocating their position, they will exhibit reasonableness... (pp. 118-19).

Fisher admits, however, that "in autocratic communities and societies...the nature and rules of 'coherence' and the limits of 'fidelity' are circumscribed."[6]

The conspiratists who converged on the KAL disaster do not, by and large, meet rigorous tests of accuracy or evidentiary validity. This is a serious charge, we realize, one that must itself be supported rigorously. To begin with, none of the important KAL conspiratists has a technical or linguistic background, although their arguments rely heavily on technical and linguistic evidence. Oliver Clubb, R. W. Johnson, and Sugwon Kang are all political scientists; David Pearson is a graduate student in sociology; P. Q. Mann is an advertising executive. None of these individuals knows Russian (among all the KAL investigators only Alexander Dallin is a sovietologist).

This is not necessarily debilitating, if knowledgeable consultants are utilized. Unfortunately, critics with specific technical expertise have castigated the level of such expertise evidenced in the writings of the conspiratists. In a discussion of Johnson's *Shootdown*, Philip Klass has said, "I've never read a book so filled with errors." A Navy specialist who participated in the search for the airliner's black box told us that Johnson's description of the recovery attempt relies on simplification and "half-truths."[7] Of David Pearson, James Oberg has written:

> Pearson delivers an avalanche of technical and military terminology which gives a good appearance of true expertise. But ... [he] repeatedly makes the most elementary technical errors in his evident eagerness to appear to prove his ... case.[8]

Oberg also authored a rejoinder which was printed by *Defence Attaché* after Korean Air Lines sued the magazine for publishing the P.Q. Mann article; he wrote, "I believe that careful, precise analysis can show that neither of [Mann's pivotal] claims has any validity."[9] Australian journalist Murray Sayle has described one claim made in *The Nation* as "another technological illiteracy."[10] And Frederic Golden, science editor of *Time*, offered the following pithy summary: "If the conspiracy theorists want to be believed, they will have to do better than rely on flat-earth physics."[11]

One aspect of the KAL story in which the present authors claim expertise is the analysis and explication of the tape transcript which records the comments of Soviet fighter pilots during the 49-minute interception, the so-called air-to-ground tape.[12] Speculation surrounding a US role in the tragedy has led to numerous attempts to substantiate the basic Soviet position—the spy plane theory—charging the US with complicity and a reckless disregard for human life. Central to all such theories is the extent to which the Soviet version is believable. Since they have released virtually no data about the events of August 31/ September 1, 1983, the best available data are contained in the KAL Tapes. In this discussion, we will address the various claims for which linguistic data are adduced. The primary issues concerning these tapes are:

1. How accurate are the two authorized translations?

2. What do the original Russian tapes reveal about:

   (a) KAL 007's external lights;

   (b) Soviet attempts to contact KAL 007 by radio on the 121.5 MHz emergency [Mayday] frequency;

(c) Soviet attempts to attract KAL 007's attention by firing warning shots?

3. Based on the above information, did the Soviet fighters follow accepted ICAO procedures in attempting a non-lethal interception of the Korean jetliner?

In fact, almost none of the Soviet account is substantiated in the Russian transcript (nor in the English translations, for that matter).

Before analyzing the evidence of the air-to-ground transcripts, however, mention should be made of a critical limitation of all transcripts: by reducing speech sound to graphemes, a transcript eliminates meaningful signals such as inflection, loudness, and tone, thereby creating a truly mediated communication. In a crisis situation or, later, in the hands of an imaginative writer, the ambiguity generated by the loss of these suprasegmental meaning elements can lead to incorrect interpretation of data. Hersh described the problem as it relates to the KAL Tapes:

> "Those of us in the SIGINT [signals intelligence] business know how fragile SIGINT is," one officer explained. "You've got to listen to (the tape) carefully and go over translations."
> One example of misunderstanding, cited later by a number of intelligence officers, revolved around the phrase, "The target is destroyed." The SU-15 interceptor pilot was overheard making that statement—widely depicted as a cry of triumph—at the moment his missile impacted.... To a communications expert, "The target is destroyed" means that an enemy interception—whether real or simulated—has been brought to a successful end. "We hear it twenty times a day in training," one Electronic Security Command officer explained.... [T]he SU-15 pilot may indeed have been exultant when his missile struck the aircraft, but concluding as much because he said "The target is destroyed" is based on faulty and incomplete knowledge...."[13]

Johnson committed a major blunder by failing to heed the SIGINT officer's warning to listen to the tape (or have someone who understands Russian listen to the tape for him). Early in his analysis, Johnson juxtaposed transcripts of two interchanges: KAL talking to Tokyo air traffic control and SU-15 reporting to its dispatcher.[14] At 18:23:05 the Soviet pilot requests "Say again." Johnson speculates that the Soviet flight dispatcher has relayed KAL 007's ATC status report to the SU-15 pilot, who supposedly manifests utter disbelief. This makes for very good drama, but it is pure fiction. The actual Russian tape recording does not support this interpretation. What <u>can</u> be heard from the pilot is a routine, unemotional request that a command be repeated, one of six such instances during the interception.

Given the manner in which these transcripts were to be utilized, it is doubly unfortunate that the two authorized translations do not always agree. Some of the differences are trivial, such as the fact that the ICAO version does not include a translation of the expletive "Yolki-palki," which the US translates as "Fiddlesticks!".[15] A more significant difference is the fact that the ICAO does not mention cannon fire from the interceptor, whereas the revised US version contains this passage:

> **18:20:49**[16] Daiu ocheredi iz pushek.
>
> US I am firing cannon bursts.[17]

On the whole, the US translation accords quite well with the Russian text that has been released. There are several instances, however, where the US version randomly interchanges the noun *"target"* and the pronoun *"it"* (without reference to the actual Russian) when the Soviet pilots mention the Korean jetliner. The ICAO translation is more consistent in this regard.

One of these instances occurred in the translation of an important passage; it has fueled a totally unfounded controversy regarding whether or not KAL 007's air navigation lights (called ANOs after the Russian term) were lit throughout its flight or off, as the Soviet government contends. In the disputed passage, the Soviet pilot says:

> **18:10:51** A ponial. Ona s migalkoi idet, s migalkoi.
>
> MKL Roger. She (it) is flying with [its] flasher [on], with [its] flasher [on].
>
> US Roger. (The target's strobe) light is blinking.
>
> ICAO Roger. Target is flying with strobe light. With strobe light.[18]

Kang[19] and R. W. Johnson both claim that it is impossible to tell which aircraft is being described as flying with lights on—KAL 007 itself, the SU-15 that destroyed the jetliner, or another Soviet aircraft—

and castigate the American position expressed at the UN by Ambassador Kirkpatrick.[20] Pearson, discussing Soviet confusion when they had scrambled interceptors two hours earlier over Kamchatka Peninsula, makes the following statement:

> If K.A.L. 007 was flying with its air navigation lights (ANOs) on at that time, the Soviet fighters should have seen it in the clear sky at 33,000 feet from as little as twenty miles away. That they did not suggests the airliner's ANOs were not on.[21]

Based on this misapprehension, Pearson incorrectly interprets the Soviet pilot to be saying later (over Sakhalin in this 18:10:51 passage) that he has turned on his own lights as the first step in the intercept procedure. Both Kang and Johnson agree with David Pearson's contention.

Linguistic evidence proves that these claims are wrong. There can be no doubt: the Soviet fighter pilot clearly states that the Korean airliner had its running lights on. When referring to KAL 007, all four Soviet pilots consistently use the feminine pronoun ona *("she/it")* because the Russian word tsel' *"target"* is grammatically feminine. By way of contrast, when referring to their aircraft or to one another, the Soviet pilots always use grammatically masculine forms, including the pronoun on *("he/it")*. Such masculine forms occur no fewer than nineteen times during the fifty minutes of taped comments. Thus, there is no question that in using ona, the Soviet pilot was referring to KAL 007 and not to himself or any Soviet plane.

Accordingly, Pearson's conclusion that the Soviet pilot first observed the target's ANOs at 18:21:35 (a full eleven minutes later, and only five minutes before the airliner was destroyed) is wrong.[22] But since he never checked the Russian,[23] he can't tell this. Therefore, his subsequent conclusion also is a total misrepresentation:

> It appears the pilot of K.A.L. 007, realizing he was being intercepted, turned on his lights as a signal that he would comply with the instructions of the [Soviet fighter] (p. 120).

Because he is wrong here, Pearson provides no evidence in this article that the KAL pilot knew he was being intercepted and, consequently, no reason to believe that he took evasive action except the word of the Soviet government. The Soviets have continuously asserted that the airliner was running without lights, but that is a patent lie. Quite the opposite interpretation is supported by the *ICAO REPORT* itself:

> The information in the USSR preliminary report states that the aircraft lights were 'off'. This contradicted the monitored air-to-ground communications (p. 43).

Among all the carefully worded and non-judgmental statements in the *ICAO REPORT*, this flat assertion of Soviet duplicity stands out.

The Soviet government also has claimed that its fighters attempted to contact KAL 007 by radio, as part of careful attempts at non-lethal interception, both over Kamchatka and Sakhalin. The air-to-ground tape does not cover the Kamchatka interception;[24] it does, however, provide testimony regarding the Sakhalin interception. The two authorized translations disagree on one line in a manner that the conspiratists have utilized to advantage:

18:13:26	A tsel' na zapros ne otvechaet.
US	The target isn't responding to IFF. (Identification/Friend or Foe)
ICAO	The target isn't responding to the call.

Pearson does not investigate possible reasons for this disagreement in order to develop a basis for selecting one version over the other; rather, he only speculates (p. 120) what "facts" might be inferred assuming first that the US translation is correct and then assuming that the ICAO translation is correct.

But zapros has the technical meaning *radar interrogation utilizing a transponder* (zaproschik-otvetchik), that is, an IFF radar inquiry. In the context of a fighter pilot talking to his ground controller about a potential enemy aircraft, this is certainly the most likely meaning of zapros.[25] Taken out of context, of course, the Russian statement is potentially ambiguous. Zapros has a colloquial meaning of verbal inquiry, and there is a slight possibility the pilot might have used the word in that sense. This ambiguity is heightened by the transcript at 18:17:49 and 18:17:58, where two different verbs are used in the specific context of voice inquiry. One of these verbs (zaprashivat') is morphologically related to zapros and zaproschik; the other verb is sprashivat'.

Still, given the actual situation, there is virtually no chance (in our judgment and that of a professional translator with over two decades of military intelligence experience) that the pilot's intended meaning was anything other than IFF. Indeed, as early as 1963, in the *First Supplement to AGARD Aeronautical Multilingual Dictionary,* published by Pergamon Press "for and on the behalf of ADVISORY GROUP FOR AERONAUTICAL RESEARCH AND DEVELOP MENT/NORTH ATLANTIC TREATY ORGANIZATION," one finds the following entry:

> **interrogation,** *noun, radar.* The act of sending forth radar pulses to trigger a *transponder* and receive answering signals; the radar pulses so sent. Also called a "challenge" (p. 116).

Alongside the French, German, Spanish, Greek, Italian, Dutch, and Turkish equivalents, one finds <u>zapros</u> listed for Russian. The 1980 edition of this manual contains the following definition:

> **interrogation.** In an SSR or IFF system, the act of transmitting a signal to the target or object to be interrogated (p. 245).

What, then, is one to make of Kang's assertion that "the problem with Mrs. Kirkpatrick's analysis is that the Soviet pilot never said anything of the sort"—meaning "The target isn't responding to IFF"—or, further:

> Could it be that the pilot was referring to some radio message he had attempted, without success, on the emergency frequency? All we know for certain is that he did not say "IFF" in his report to ground control (pp. 36-37).

Given the facts as we have outlined them, it is clear that this is an unsupportable statement. In lieu of analysis, however, Kang (pp. 36-37) implies, not for the first time, that CIA involvement in handling the KAL Tapes has tainted their evidentiary value. Johnson does likewise:

> It is known that before the tapes were handed over to Charles Wick's USIA (and thence to Mrs Kirkpatrick) their actual translation was effected by the CIA and it seems not impossible, to put it mildly, that there was an element of positive disinformation involved in the transcript so theatrically produced at the UN (p. 166).

We should point out that many US officials (particularly UN ambassadors Lichenstein and Kirkpatrick) had uttered vigorous protestations that the tape contains no indication the SU-15 pilot attempted to make voice contact with KAL 007. But any such attempt would of necessity not be reflected there, since the Soviet pilot would be required to transmit on 121.5 MHz, the international hailing frequency: the intercepted conversations, of course, took place on another frequency. Nevertheless, given the nature of the conversations, some subsequent reference to a call would have been heard on the air-to-ground frequency. It seems clear, then, that no verbal call was made and that it is not true Soviet personnel employed the 121.5 MHz channel.[26]

Another issue that sparked controversy between the superpowers was the Soviet claim that the crew of KAL 007 had ignored numerous, almost constant Soviet attempts to signal it in the air. A critical factor in the argument is evaluation of the cannon bursts fired by Major Kas'min, pilot of the SU-15 (#805) that destroyed the Korean jetliner. The Soviet government said the cannon bursts were warning shots, containing visible tracer rounds, that constituted the last attempt to signal 007 after the jetliner had ignored wing waggling (pokachivanie s kryla na krylo) and the flashing of lights.[27] It was further claimed by Ogarkov that the tracer shells were "clearly seen by the second pilot,... who during that period, at that moment, reported to the command post that he observed the four bursts of tracer shells along the path of the intruder aircraft."

These claims are refuted by the transcripts. At 18:19:02, pilot 805 states: "I am closing on the target." While there is no indication of how close he is at this point, a minute and a half later, at 18:20:22, he states: "(I) need to approach it (closer)." In seven seconds (18:20:30), 805 radios, "I'm approaching the target." **It is at this point** (18:20:49), that 805 tells ground control, "I am firing cannon bursts." Evidently, 805 is still well behind the aircraft: **more than half a minute after firing his cannon**, at 18:21:24, he states: "Yes. I'm approaching the target, I'm going in closer," and eleven seconds later (18:21:35) observes that he is now within two kilometers of the "target." In another 45 seconds (18:22:17) the 805 pilot is moving in front of the target and 25 seconds after that (18:22:42) finds himself abeam of the airliner, then drops back into an attack position (18:22:55 and 18:23:37). Note that it is 88 seconds after the tracer shells are fired, rather than before, that the 805 pilot makes any attempt to approach the target in a manner which might be visible to the Korean crew. Indeed, US analysts are not entirely convinced that these cannon bursts were not an attempt to fire on the airliner. Given the point at which the cannon fire occurs in the interception sequence, it is difficult to come to any other conclusion.[28] Moreover, there is no indication anywhere in the transcripts of a report to ground control by the second interceptor that he saw the tracer shells: this claim is a pure fabrication.

As to the wing-waggling and the flashing of lights, not only is there no evidence in the transcripts that these activities ever occurred, there simply was not time between the cannon bursts and the actual shoot-down for such elaborate interception efforts. The entire span of time between the 805 pilot's statement, "I am approaching the target, I am going in closer," and his falling back covers a **minute and a half**, from 18:21:24 to 18:22:55. At 18:23:37, the pilot announces that he has dropped back into an attack position and will fire rockets; three minutes later the target is destroyed. The *ICAO REPORT* [p. 43] concluded, "There was no evidence that complete visual identification procedures were employed." The *ANC REPORT* [pp. 13-14] contained an even more forceful statement disputing the Soviet claim:

> [T]he transcript ... gives no clear indication that the intercepting aircraft had taken up a position "within view of the pilot of the intercepted aircraft" or "to enable the pilot of the latter aircraft to see the visual signals given" as recommended.... This has been highlighted because ... it is of paramount importance for the interceptor aircraft to ensure that it attracts the attention of the pilot-in-command of the civil aircraft.

A unique perspective on the alleged interception sequence has been provided to us by Harold Ewing, the 747 pilot whose reconstruction of possible cockpit actions constituted a significant portion of *"The Target Is Destroyed"*. In a widely ranging conversation[29] Ewing described the sensation of flying behind a 747 jumbo jet. Even at a distance of six miles, the airplane "looks huge," Ewing said. When 805 pilot Major Kas'min reported closing to within two kilometers (1.24 miles), KAL 007 would have "filled his windscreen." Under these circumstances, all changes in relative motion or position would be magnified in the perception of the SU-15 pilot.[30] If one assumes that Major Kas'min was relying primarily on his vision—not his instrumentation—at such apparent close range, and that he would have had no experience whatsoever tailing such a large aircraft, then it is easy to imagine that he could believe himself to be situated only two kilometers behind 007 when in fact he might have been much farther away. (Recall that it took 88 seconds after firing his cannon for the swift interceptor to overtake the airliner.) That being the case, he could very well have been trying to shoot down the jetliner at 18:20:49 when he reported, "I am firing cannon bursts." In this speculative scenario, Major Kas'min would have misjudged his range, failing to destroy KAL 007 because he was trailing the jumbo jet by more than two miles—the effective limit of his cannon fire.[31] In this context, an otherwise mysterious passage takes on a perfectly reasonable, if chilling, meaning:

18:23:37	Seichas ia rakety poprobuiu.
MKL	<u>Now</u> I will try my rockets.
US	Now I will try rockets.[32]
ICAO	Now I will try a rocket.

The most likely explanation for saying "now" at this juncture is that an initial attempt to bring down the airplane using cannon had been ineffective.

Ewing's extrapolation is just that—an extrapolation. But it certainly is plausible, and it accords with the testimony provided by the KAL Tapes. Supported by external evidence, analysis of the air-to-ground messages leads to the following conclusions, which we accept as a true representation of events:

(1) Major Kas'min did not refer to KAL 007 as anything but "the target" and "she {it}";

(2) KAL 007 was flying with its ANOs burning, so that it would have been clearly visible in the night sky;

(3) No attempt to contact KAL 007 by radio was carried out, but an electronic IFF inquiry from the SU-15 demonstrated that the target did not belong to the Soviet military;

(4) Any non-lethal interception attempt was performed in a cursory manner, at best, and—except for the IFF challenge—probably wasn't performed at all. Certainly none of the claimed wing waggling or flashing of signal lights is confirmed by the SU-15 pilot, who diligently reported his every action during the interception.

Throughout Part One we have demonstrated the extent to which American officials selectively presented evidence in support of the allegation that Soviet military leaders knowingly ordered the destruction of a civilian airliner. We have just seen that the arguments presented by many of the prominent conspiratists depend upon evidence, the authenticity of which is particularly doubtful.[33] In Part Two of this study we will demonstrate the extent to which Soviet authorities simply invented a story that, they hoped, would prove acceptable to their citizens. The linguistic analysis offered in this chapter raises a profound, troubling issue for contemporary rhetorical criticism: to what extent (if, indeed, at all) does the role of critic extend beyond a simple explanation of how argumentation persuades to consideration of the purposes for which one engages in public argument or the ethical characterization of argument structure and evidence as it is employed in any specific instance.

To historians and historians of science who have been nurtured by Western traditions, the answer to this issue seems self-evident. Joynt and Corbett have discussed the matter in great depth as it relates to international conflict, and they have stated the historical perspective succinctly: "The crucial problem which confronts us ... has to do with the accuracy of the data.... Respect for the facts is the hallmark of science and in the case of world politics this means historical facts."[34]

This issue is less clear-cut among contemporary theorists of rhetorical criticism. In fact, without question, prevailing opinion holds not only that many people will be persuaded by the art and the ethos of the speaker, rather than by the facts of a case (the KAL incident provides an excellent example), but also that assessing the validity of evidence is not a proper function of the critic. "Facts aren't important—no one is persuaded by facts," we are told. From this it follows that expertise is to be scorned, for only experts can understand the arguments of other experts and argue against them successfully. Many would exclude the expert from the process altogether, because it is persuasion of the common citizen that matters above all, and the common citizen is incapable of arguing with the expert.

Joynt and Corbett view "a very detailed examination of the primary data" as the *sine qua non* of research. They emphasize "the importance of securing the original text" and warn of the pitfalls that await those who would ignore this advice.[35] Applying this standard to the Russian language data available in the taped comments of the Soviet fighter pilots, however, it is evident that the Soviet Union distorted the truth, the United States ignored it when this suited political purpose, and the conspiratists were incapable either of discerning it or evaluating it. And it is regrettably true that neither truth nor reason has reigned throughout public discussions of the Korean airliner. Equally true—and equally regrettable—is the fact that many rhetorical scholars would remain unconcerned by this situation.

NOTES

[1]These are (a) the revised official US version disseminated September 11, 1983 and (b) the ICAO version, dated December 30, 1983, disseminated as Appendix D of its final report on the incident. Except as noted, all translations in this chapter follow the revised US version. According to Hersh (private communication), NSA transcribers continued to refine the tape transcript through late 1985, but no further changes were ever announced.

[2]This factor has also been called the "Truth Criterion."

[3]See Chapter Five for a discussion of some philosophical and political reasons why this is true.

[4]We depend on the very same situation, of course, expecting the reader to accept as accurate the following discussion of Russian, but knowing full well that few will be able to discern any errors we may commit.

[5]Walter R. Fisher, "Assessing Narrative Fidelity: The Logic of Good Reasons," Chapter Five in Walter R. Fisher, *Human Communication as Narration: Toward a Philosophy of Reason, Value, and Action* (Columbia: University of South Carolina Press, 1987), 105-123, p. 117.

[6]Fisher, "Assessing Narrative Fidelity," p. 121.

[7]Klass, who is now retired, served for many years as Senior Avionics Editor of *Aviation Week & Space Technology*. Both of these assessments were reported in our review of *Shootdown* . See: "007—Conspiracy or Accident?", *Commonweal*, September 12, 1986, 472-73.

[8]Oberg is a spaceflight operations engineer at the Johnson Space Center near Houston and a noted science writer. See: "Sense and Nonsense: A Reader's Guide to the KE007 Massacre," *American Spectator*, October 1985, 36-39.

[9]James E. Oberg, "Sakhalin: sense and nonsense," *Defence Attaché*, 1985: 1 (January/ February), 37-47, p. 37.

[10]Sayle, "A Conspiracy of Coincidence," p. 51. Sayle was awarded the British "Magazine Writer of the Year" award in 1985 for his articles on the KAL tragedy.

[11]*Discover*, December 1984, p. 8.

[12]Hersh (p. 264) and Maertens (p. 26), two of the anti-conspiratists, have cited a paper of ours which subsequently appeared in print (slightly modified) as part of "Corres-

pondence." See: Michael K. Launer, Marilyn J. Young, & Sugwon Kang, *Bulletin of Concerned Asian Scholars*, **18**: 3 (July-September, 1986), 67-71. The present chapter extends the analysis of that study. We will use the term "KAL Tapes" throughout this chapter to refer only to the pilots' portion of the intercepted communications. Sugwon Kang has publicly stated that the conclusions he originally drew on the basis of the linguistic evidence revealed by the KAL Tapes were largely in error.

[13]Hersh, p. 75. Hersh continues, aptly, "and simply may not be correct." This is a veiled way of saying, "and is wrong in this instance" without explicitly revealing that he has discussed this transcript with the transcribers; but elsewhere in the book there are indications (*i.e.*, p. 61) that Hersh was shown (or had described to him) the updated NSA transcript. See our review article concerning this book in *Washington Book Review*, **2**:1 (January 1987), 9-11.

[14]Johnson, *Shootdown*, pp. 22-24.

[15]Given the variants "Oh, fuck!", "Holy shit!", and "Oh, my God!", which we provided, Hersh chose the last (p. 166). According to Paul Turner of the National Transportation Safety Board, "Just before an event occurs, somebody generally says, 'Oh, shit.' I see that more, perhaps, than I see any two words. You sit right there with them and you'd say the same thing." Quoted in the "Outlook" section of the *Washington Post*, September 9, 1984. See, also: Michael K. Launer, "Yolki-palki!—Fiddlesticks or Fir Trees," *No Uncertain Terms*, Summer 1987 (2: 2), 4-6. Those who read Russian will find of interest: V. Voinovich, "Yolki-palki," *Novoe russkoe slovo*, October 28, 1983, p. 3.

[16]A time frame may be helpful. The first transmission on the transcript occurred at 17:56:58 GMT (2:6:58 am local time), the last at 18:46:09. The deadly missiles were fired at 18:26:20; two seconds later the Soviet pilot announced, "The target has been destroyed."

[17]Of course, this constituted one of the corrections made by NSA transcribers after the tape was played at the September 6, 1983 United Nations Security Council meeting. We will return to this passage below. There is no explanation why the ICAO translation omitted this passage; although it is not clear exactly when that translation was done, it had to be later than September 11.

[18]According to both the *ICAO REPORT* (p. 31) and the *ANC REPORT* (p. 12), KAL 007 was equipped with a revolving red light on its undercarriage, rather than a strobe.

[19]Kang, "Flight 007: Was There Foul Play?"

[20]Kang (p. 37) wrote, "I fail to see any evidence in this Russian-language transcript issued by the Press Office of the State Department to support the contention that in these critical statements the pilot was talking about lights on the intruding aircraft, although such a possibility cannot be ruled out. Just as likely, given the sequence of the pilot's remarks, is that he was talking about lights atop his own Su-15 fighter that he

had been instructed to switch on." Johnson (*Shootdown*, p. 166) wrote, "There is simply no way of knowing—*pace* Mrs. Kirkpatrick—whether the Soviet pilot had been referring to 007's lights, his own or those of another of the Soviet fighters."

[21] Pearson, "K.A.L. 007: What the U.S. Knew And When We Knew It," p. 118.

[22] Kang (p. 38) tentatively supports this suggestion.

[23] Telephone interview, December 1984.

[24] A search and rescue satellite (SARSAT) was in position over Kamchatka to hear any transmissions that might have been made on the emergency channel. According to the *ANC REPORT* (p. 9), "There is no record or other information of any calls on 121.5 MHz having been heard by any civil or military ground unit or by other aircraft within VHF [very high frequency] range of the intercepting aircraft, or any record of such transmissions having been received via the . . . SARSAT . . . system." Duane Freer of the ANC staff in Montreal has stated that the 121.5 MHz frequency was monitored during the Sakhalin interception and that no voice call was made by the Soviet pilot. See: Todd Leventhal, "FOCUS: The Korean Airliner Shootdown: One Year Later," Voice of America Special Report #4-0877, August 30, 1984.

[25] According to both the ICAO general report and the technical report of its Air Navigation Commission, KAL 007 carried Secondary Surveillance Radar (SSR), not IFF. Moreover, even if an airplane were equipped with IFF—and if the mechanism were turned on, which is not always the case—then an electronic response would be sent automatically, and a pilot would not necessarily be aware that such an inquiry had taken place. In any event, there exist complex technical reasons to believe that Soviet jet fighters cannot trigger the transponders carried by Western civilian aircraft.

[26] Moreover, pilots using the emergency frequency are required by standard ICAO procedures, to which the USSR is signatory, to make such calls in English. There has been no indication in the many Soviet media interviews with the pilot who shot down KAL 007 that he speaks English. Granting this constitutes only inferential support for the ICAO position, it is nonetheless obvious that the Soviet government would have gone out of its way to demonstrate the pilot's ability to speak English.

[27] Kang accepts this contention uncritically: "Even if the crew [of the Korean jet] had not noticed anything unusual outside while the Su-15 was shooting off fireworks parallel to 007's flight path . . . " (p. 42).

[28] Rohmer has no doubts about this: "In my opinion, when the Soviet fighter pilot fired his cannon he was attempting to destroy the Boeing 747 and had been ordered to do so by his ground control" (p. 84). It is possible, however, that Major Kas'min was just testing his cannon.

[29] Telephone interview, September 30, 1986.

[30]To understand Ewing's point you only need recall the sensation of sitting at a stop light and having the vehicle next to you begin inching forward: it may feel as though your car has rolled backward instead. Whether the interceptor sped up, say, or KAL slowed down, it would have the same visual effect in the environment of a night sky that had no background to provide a point of orientation.

[31]In this scenario, the tracer bullets would have fallen to earth unseen by the South Korean crew.

[32]The plural form "rockets" is another of the corrections to the US transcript that were made public on September 11, 1983.

[33]This is one of several issues that will be addressed in Part Three.

[34]Joynt and Corbett, "Rival Explanations in International Relations," Chapter Nine in *Theory and Reality in World Politics*. They caution, however, that the scientific approach "is not and can never be a substitute for historical explanation" (pp. 115-116).

[35]Joynt and Corbett, p. 139 [n. 28].

PART TWO

THE SOVIET UNION

COMMUNICATION IN SOVIET SOCIETY

In this chapter we attempt to describe important factors that impinge upon the nature of information and public communication within Soviet society and to provide a general overview of Soviet foreign relations in the 1970s and early 1980s. Our goal is to provide some understanding of the communication environment that had been developed over the course of the Soviet era and to portray the contemporary political milieu within which the Korean airliner controversy ran its course.

Because of the nature of news in the United States, the average American probably has little appreciation for the role of news and the media in the Soviet Union or similar societies, and (since most discourse today is mediated) little comprehension of the role that rhetoric plays in the dissemination of information there. However, when discussing communication in Soviet society, one postulate underlies all other considerations—that is the very notion of information, which is perceived as the inextricable bonding of fact to interpretation. Adams, quoting Grebnev, states that the political role of the Soviet newspaper as "tribune for the propagandist and agitator," "disseminator of political information," and "weapon of communist building" is well known.[1] Evseev has commented: "The press, television, radio, oral propaganda, and agitation must ... assist the Soviet citizen in orienting himself correctly in domestic life and in international events."[2]

In such a system, news is the equivalent of public oratory. Matuz has commented, "A [Soviet] newscast is not a mirror, but a magnifying glass."[3] One might successfully argue that in the United States, at least, while the media may be the means for presenting rhetoric to the public, the news is not itself rhetorical (there are those who would disagree). By way of contrast, however, we would maintain that in authoritarian[4] systems (such as the existing system within the Soviet Union) the news itself is rhetoric. News is presented not for its own sake, but as proof that the postulates of the socialist state are correct. The reasons for this "spoon-feeding" of the masses are intrinsic to Soviet Marxist philosophy. As Kenez notes,

> The Socialists believed that in Marxism they possessed an instrument that allowed them to analyze the process of history.

They and they alone had access to 'true knowledge.' The task of
the revolutionaries, therefore, was not to search for knowledge,
for that was already achieved. Their duty was instead to bring the
fruits of Marxist analysis to the proletariat.[5]

One suspects that this is the case in most deductive systems, where all
knowledge must proceed from first premises and only one universal
explanation can be true.[6] And Soviet rhetoric, reflecting such a Platonic
system, must stem from universal principles, moving towards greater
wisdom and contributing to the goal of perfecting the communist state.
Meisel has written:

Nothing has a greater effect on the way in which the media deal
with crises than the character of the political regime.... The most
fundamental distinction here is that between a totalitarian system in which the media are closely controlled and a pluralist
one, where they are given a substantial degree of freedom.
There are gradations of freedom and constraint, of course,
within each of these modal types, but the importance of the
quintessential difference between the two cannot be exaggerated.[7]

It is important to realize that suppression of alien ideas and outside
information in Russia was not initiated by the communists and is not
a uniquely Soviet phenomenon. Censorship was practiced by the czars
and had been part of the fabric of Russian life long before the Revolution.

Since the end of the seventeenth century ... Russian rulers have
displayed a consistently ambivalent attitude toward things foreign. They covet Western technology and know-how, but are
uneasy with Western values and ideas.... Ideas of any kind are
elusive, but the government has always taken the position that
control of at least their written expression must be attempted
nonetheless.... The continuity of the Russian attitude is especially striking in the case of foreign publications.... [Today the]
regime has changed but the concern remains the same. It is important to recognize this continuity—the Soviet censorship is
rooted deeply in prerevolutionary Russia.[8]

When Lenin closed down all hostile newspapers in 1918, his task was
made much easier by the lack of a tradition of a free press.

Much has changed in the Soviet Union since then, particularly with
respect to the technology of communication, and Soviet ideologists

have declared that society has progressed beyond the dictatorship of the proletariat to a stage called "mature" or "developed" socialism.[9] Vladimir Shlapentokh, a sociologist and recent immigrant to the US, states that Soviet society has moved away from "the stage of mass repression and strong ideology."[10]

> The current phase of Soviet development is characterized by relatively mild political repression.... In the post-Stalin period, the disappearance of mass repression has drastically altered the nature of life in Soviet society. This is especially true with respect to the young, who ... have been brought up in an atmosphere that does not know mass arrests and all-pervasive fear.[11]

But remarkably little of Lenin's theory of communication has been modified over the course of time.[12] The ideological foundation was laid down prior to World War I by Lenin himself: "[I]t was none other than V. I. Lenin who conceived the theory of a new type of Party, and of the role of the press in its creation and development."[13] His primary goal was to proselytize a new social order among imperial Russia's impoverished, superstitious, intensely religious, and largely illiterate peasantry: for this reason he stressed the importance of 'agitation'— oral, face-to-face instruction.[14]

After the October revolution, additional goals assumed critical importance—consolidating power and legitimizing the new government. World War I had not yet come to an end, but the Bolshevik leadership had repudiated Kerensky's commitment to continue fighting. Grzybowski has described how

> [t]he most imminent danger to the existence of the new revolutionary regime came from the West, where the continued advance of the armies of the Central Powers was threatening the very base of the Bolshevik power. In this situation propaganda was the only weapon the new regime had and the only technique of social and governmental action with which it was familiar.[15]

Under the circumstances, the "Soviet regime was the first in the world with the task and opportunity to build an entire press network."[16] What was unprecedented in Lenin's approach was his concept of utilizing the press for propaganda, transforming it into an "instrument of the dictatorship of the proletariat."[17] Remington would concur that much of Lenin's genius consisted in his profound understanding of political communication, a lesson learned from Marx: "[T]he key to the possibility for the 'great man' to dominate the development of a new ideology lies in his ability to transcend the contemporary modes of communication."[18] One of the first decrees of the Council of People's Commissars—the Sovnarkom—was Lenin's Decree on the Press, which stated that the press was a more dangerous weapon in the hands of class enemies than either bombs or machine guns. In Evseev's words:

> Measures were subsequently taken to liquidate bourgeois publications that spoke out against the new order and in favor of reestablishing the old system. Two decades after the Great October socialist revolution—when the exploiting classes had been totally eradicated and the victory of socialism had been assured—only then could the 1936 Constitution of the USSR guarantee free speech, freedom of the press, [and] freedom of assembly.... [19]

Lenin's beliefs were shaped not only by his reading of Marx and Engels, but by personal observation, as well. Imperial Russia's "governing style was centralized, bureaucratic and authoritarian.... The scope of government was unusually broad: it extended not only to those spheres of life in which other governments of the time were active, such as public order and taxation, but also into economic entrepreneurship and control, religion and morals, and the detailed administration of justice."[20] As Friedgut has commented,

> Almost the entire experience of the Russian Communists as a conspiratorial group within the autocratic czarist state served to confirm in their eyes Engels' characterization of the repressive and administrative apparatuses of the state as class-dominated structures whose raison d'etre was the strangling of social change.[21]

The results of Lenin's efforts bore fruit in the Second Conference of Journalists in May 1919. Kenez describes the results of that meeting:

> [I]n the developing system there could be no such profession as journalism but simply a party function for publishing newspapers. The press would have no other task than to spread and advertise the policies and decisions of the Party.... The Party... wanted no mediators between its policies and the publicizing of those policies.[22]

Obviously, the press was not expected to debate the advantages and disadvantages of alternative policies; indeed, it was forbidden to do so. Rather, by embodying Party ideology, the press would "define the terms of political discourse and establish the limits of the public sphere."[23] In other words, the press was destined to became an extension of the propaganda efforts of the new government, a function which has changed little over the years.[24] Hazan, describing Soviet activities in the Third World, has stated flatly: "Falsehood is an integral part of Soviet propaganda."[25] This was the essential message of Yuri Gudim-Levkovich, a Soviet immigrant, who in 1956 described what it was like to be a journalist in Stalinist Russia. "You must remember," he said, "that lying is the professional duty of every Soviet editor and newspaperman. I know this from my own experience."[26]

In 1962 Edward Crankshaw described Khrushchev's conception of the press:

In his eyes, in the eyes of all party leaders, the press has no other function than this "educative" one. Education, in this sense, means telling people what to think, printing what you want them to know, suppressing what you don't want them to know, and, generally, manipulating the truth in the supposed interests of the regime.[27]

This goal was never fully realized, of course, not even under Stalin. Nevertheless, modern Soviet society remains "a community in which control, totalism and personalization are the principal characteristics," one dominated by the "needless and crude intrusion of political values into private life," where "party control is ... a norm of Soviet life."[28] For example, White comments on the importance accorded 'visual agitation'—posters, slogans, etc.—that are "designed to reinforce the party's efforts at the place of work, in public parks and town squares, on major buildings and elsewhere":

The original emphasis of such measures was upon the citizen's place of work and public places generally; but since the early 1960s, and especially since the introduction of the five-day week in 1967, it has been increasingly recognised that this will tend to leave housewives, pensioners, and the very young outside the ambit of the party's propaganda, together with employed members of the labour force on their days off. The organization of political work in residential areas has accordingly received a higher priority in recent years, and it forms an important part of the responsibilities of the local party Department of Agitation and Propaganda.[29]

The centrality of all socialization policies was officially reaffirmed in 1976:

> The Communist Party ... has developed ... a coordinated system of measures designed to intensify the Party's influence in all spheres of society.... A significant role ... has been assigned to improving the activity of propaganda and mass-information organs, which exert a tremendous daily influence on the course of the economy, development of science and the arts, and on all societal life.[30]

The effort has been sufficiently successful over time that even today's *Pravda* is very close to the Lenin ideal. It bears little resemblance to the typical Western newspaper, something that is impossible to discern unless one reads Russian. As Barghoorn has written:

> It is difficult for a foreigner without a good knowledge of Russian to acquaint himself in depth and perspective with the content of the Soviet press. In part this is because content analyses and other essential specific studies have so far been scarce.[31]

Consequently, most Americans impose their own expectations and experiences, perceptions that are reinforced by Western media, which tend to reprint or comment on Soviet domestic news of international import or international news reported in the Soviet press. This practice gives a false picture of Soviet newspapers, which, in reality, report very little "hard news" of any kind.

In order to eliminate this misconception, it might be helpful to describe Soviet newspapers, all of which follow a standard format. To begin with, the major national dailies are either four or six pages long, with one edition per week extended to eight pages. Most of the space is taken up by editorials, government notices, and exhortative feature stories about outstanding metal workers, collective farm milkmaids, or second lieutenants in far-off outposts [the stereotypical girl-meets-tractor success stories]. The back page consists of sports features [usually about the national teams, international chess tournaments, and the A-League soccer or ice hockey results]; TV schedules; weather; and, in *Krasnaia zvezda*, an occasional obituary about a leading military officer.

Each newspaper reserves one page for international reports (two on the days the paper is expanded to eight pages). Nearly always, a portion of this space is devoted to quotes from the "fraternal" (*i.e.*, socialist) press in support of Soviet policies or initiatives. *Krasnaia zvezda* occasionally publishes quasi-technical articles on new Western weapons, aircraft, or radar systems—following *Aviation Week & Space Technology* or, sometimes, the publicity releases of US manufacturers. *Izvestiia* devotes the right hand column of its international page to short fillers (new findings by Western anthropologists or archeologists would be a typical subject). Both *Izvestiia* and *Pravda* carry substantial (1500-2500 word) feature essays on a variety of negative aspects of life in the United States: topics included here are race relations, hunger in America, the homeless, etc. Occasionally one finds, for example, a story from Rio de Janiero on the unfavorable reaction of South American audiences to performances by the hard rock group "KISS" or the notorious piece that recently claimed the AIDS virus was developed by the CIA at the Ft. Detrick biological warfare laboratories in Frederick, MD— in this instance, the TASS correspondent got the name of the facility wrong, calling it Ft. Derrick.

This leaves little space for anything an American would recognize as news. Many stories covered by the Western press are considered inappropriate for the Soviet press. There used to be a list of topics— including crime, drugs, occupational injuries, pay and special privileges for athletes—that could not be discussed under any circumstances.[32] To Robert Kaiser, an American journalist who wrote about his experiences as a correspondent in the USSR, this "indifference to news" was the most striking aspect of Soviet newspapers. Kaiser estimated that "[r]eports on events that occurred the day before, at home or abroad, take up only a small fraction of a Soviet paper, perhaps 15 percent."[33] In fact, even most of the hard news stories in a typical daily edition are written more than twenty-four hours in advance of publication; an editor's principal task each morning is that of correcting page proofs of the next day's paper. While American media place a premium on timeliness, Soviet media place the premium on 'correctness of interpretation': nothing is printed without the express approval of higher authorities. Although neither system necessarily encourages accuracy, Soviet media needn't worry about being 'scooped'; there is no competition for news sources or stories.

Another consequence of the "educative" function of all media in the USSR is to retard the flow of information severely. Hollander states:

> The most important quality of the Soviet newscast is "purposefulness".... Although news should be as up-to-date as possible most of the time, it should not convey spontaneity, and recounting of happenings should never supercede the reporting of historically more basic events.... News is a part of the overall plan and always relates to a particular policy which is currently being emphasized.[34]

This instrumentalist view of the media dictates that the state control not only the content, but also the timing of information dissemination.[35] Hollander believes it is the greater importance of history, as compared to happenings, that explains delays in Soviet reportage of significant political developments.[36] Kaiser has offered the opinion that the "length of time it takes *Pravda* to react to an event can be an indication of its importance—or the confusion it causes inside the Soviet leadership,"[37] and cites the instance, in 1972, when Egyptian President Anwar el-Sadat expelled over 10,000 Soviet 'advisors':

> *Pravda*'s first reaction was silence. After a delay of more than 24 hours, the Soviet papers published an official announcement that the Soviet troops stationed in Egypt were coming home by mutual Soviet-Egyptian agreement because they had completed their mission.[38]

There were similar silences when President Nixon mined Haiphong harbor in North Vietnam and when the nuclear reactor at Chernobyl was ripped by explosions.

In the instant case, the first mention of Korean Air Lines 007 appeared in *Pravda* and *Izvestiia* on September 2, 1983 (the "continued its flight in the direction of the Sea of Japan" story). On the 3rd, *Pravda* printed a story in which authorities maintained that the airliner had not responded to signals or efforts to assist it in landing at a Soviet airfield; the government "regretted" the loss of life. The Soviets did not admit shooting the plane down ("terminating the flight") until a TV announcement on September 6. One thing should be obvious: there is no Soviet equivalent of a fast-breaking news story.

The Chernobyl incident is particularly instructive regarding the approach Soviet media take to rapidly developing events. On Saturday morning, April 26, 1986, as the No. 4 nuclear reactor was spewing radioactivity into the Soviet air, *Pravda* published a TASS story, datelined Washington, April 25th, reporting that after a month of "covering up," the Pentagon was "forced to admit" that in March a "serious accident" had occurred aboard the Poseidon nuclear submarine USS Nathaniel Green, which was on patrol in the Irish Sea. The incident, it was stated, was "fraught with the danger of radioactive contamination of the coastal waters of several European countries." On May 3, exactly one week later, both *Pravda* and *Izvestiia* cited a *Washington Post* story about the USS Atlanta, a nuclear sub which had gone aground in the Straits of Gibraltar. Military spokesmen "were quick to assure [reporters] that no emission of radioactive materials had occurred." Further details concerning the Nathaniel Green were also provided.

On May 4, both newspapers reported a KLAS-TV (Las Vegas) story concerning the accidental destruction of $70 million worth of electronic equipment during the most recent "Mighty Oak" underground nuclear test. *Pravda* called the accident "the latest in a series of incidents at the Ranier Mesa nuclear test site." *Krasnaia zvezda,* which also carried the "Mighty Oak" story on May 4, had run a report of French nuclear testing on Tuesday, April 29.

Although the timing of *Pravda's* first article was surely coincidental—and, in retrospect, quite ironic—publishing the remaining stories constituted part of a curiously subtle propaganda campaign aimed at Soviet readership. For it was only on April 28, two days after the accident, that the first, four-sentence reference to Chernobyl appeared in *Izvestiia,* while neither *Pravda* nor *Krasnaia zvezda* mentioned the event until Tuesday, the 29th. Indeed, throughout the first week, these three national Soviet newspapers carried fewer than thirty column inches on the worst nuclear power disaster in history; by way of contrast, Western dailies had been printing that much or more every day. In fact, it was only on May 14th that Chernobyl got pushed off the front page of the *Washington Post*; in comparison, much of the sparse Soviet coverage during the first two weeks had been buried in a corner of an inside page under the innocuous-sounding title "From the USSR Council of Ministers."

The Soviet government announcement about Chernobyl that appeared in the morning edition of *Izvestiia* on Monday, April 28 was virtually identical to the first public statement that had been read over Soviet television the preceding evening. There were no further media statements until the following night, when *Vremia* broadcast the next terse announcement. The highest Soviet authorities would have had to approve that original release on Sunday prior to 9:00 p.m. [Moscow time]. Not only were no reporters sent to cover this "story," which was one of the most significant events in recent times, but a full twenty-four hours elapsed before the Soviet public officially learned more than it had already heard on Sunday night. It is difficult to imagine a system of news reporting more diametrically opposed to Western traditions.

The differences between Soviet and American journalistic practice are fundamental. In an interview long after the Korean airliner story had receded into memory, *Washington Post* reporter Douglas Feaver described the role of American media at any point while reporting a fast breaking story as one of presenting "the truth as it appears at that time." Feaver's colleague George Wilson also described his work during those tumultuous first days of September, 1983. His job, Wilson said, was simply to report the story: "I wasn't doing history." Notwithstanding Wilson's disclaimer, these personal comments by respected American newsmen accord quite closely with Joynt and Corbett's description of the "actual practices of historians in the ongoing search for adequate accounts of events": "At any given moment the set of facts and hypotheses is an approximation of the truth in the light of available evidence." Such a "coherence account" of historical events "is a function of available evidence and is subject to modification as understanding and inquiry proceed."[39]

In Western practice, a sharp distinction must be drawn between fact and analysis. On the other hand, Soviet theorists would contend that news reporting in their country emphasizes creation of a deep understanding of any event in the light of communist ideology and prevailing policy goals.

> The strength of the state resides in the enhanced consciousness of the masses; it is strong when the masses know everything, when they can evaluate everything and can approach everything consciously. In this regard, the instruments of mass communication play an exceptionally important role, informing the population on a broad range of problems and providing them with the correct interpretation.... In bringing to life the theoretical postulates of the classics of Marxism-Leninism, our Party has always and at every stage of history openly and directly provided an interpretation of events as they occur.... [40]

To classical Soviet ideological theorists all communication is public, and all public communication is political. Murty expressed this concept succinctly: "Strictly controlling all educational, information, communication, and social processes, the [ideological] strategists will be able to build up desired predispositions [among the citizenry]."[41]

In order to fully comprehend how fundamental the interconnection is between the notions of public communication and political indoctrination in Soviet society, one need only ponder the implications of the following anecdotal evidence. In 1984 a two-volume collection of essays on current US foreign policy was published under the imprimatur of the Soviet Academy of Sciences. One of the studies bears a title that translates literally as "Propaganda in the Service of Foreign Policy," but in the English-language table of contents at the back of the volume this article is listed as "Mass Media and Foreign Policy."[42] Not surprisingly, Berzin and Davydov depict Radio Free Europe and Radio Liberty as "blatant instruments of 'psychological warfare' ... preaching the most vicious anti-communism." The United States Information Agency is correctly described as the "most significant specialized organization in the US charged with directly and systematically carrying out the ideological struggle and propaganda in the international arena."[43] In addition, however, the authors list *National Geographic* as an influential element of the US "private sector ideological business."[44] The message is clear: if it's public, it's political.

Properly understood, the Marxist dialectic can interpret virtually any activity as propaganda. Academician Georgi Arbatov, Director of the Academy of Sciences Institute of the USA and Canada, is one of the most visible Soviet spokespersons in the West and, perhaps, the leading Soviet Americanist.[45] In a book surveying the history of propaganda in world affairs, Arbatov called the Marshall Plan, the Alliance for Progress, and the Peace Corps "patently propagandistic."[46] In the same study, Arbatov recounted Heilbroner's description of Standard Oil's Venezuela operations:

> [I]n an effort to offset the revolutionary movement and the rapid spread of anti-Yankee feeling [Standard Oil] increased the [payments] from its profits to the country's budget, raised the salaries for Venezuelans, moved local specialists into executive posts and began training them so that "some day" when the company "steps out" they should be able to take over the management.[47]

Other sources cited by Arbatov describe "a similar picture of the overseas practices of American firms and of their efforts to indoctrinate their local staffs in an anti-communist spirit."[48] Doubtless these efforts are perceived in the West as quite the opposite—as unexpectedly enlightened and far-seeing policies, rather than the blatant exploitation one normally expects from a powerful multi-national corporation.

Not surprisingly, the attempt to control knowledge is not limited to the news media; it is all-encompassing. Indeed, the Soviet Union supports professional propagandists, as well as a vast network of occasional public speakers—totalling perhaps as many as three million individuals—whose function it is to interpret both historical and current events in terms of prevailing domestic and foreign policy at meetings of factory workers, students, or neighborhood groups.[49] Kaiser has concluded that, as a consequence of these various activities, "Soviet authorities have managed to destroy the history of their own country. Because history has been rewritten so often, people cannot keep up with the latest version."[50] Occasionally, Soviet attempts at information control have been so crude as to provoke laughter from Western observers. One of the most notorious cases is detailed by Choldin:

> It should be noted that [Czarist] Russia ... had a tradition of excision; as early as 1750 foreigners living in Saint Petersburg had been ordered to deliver certain publications in German and other languages to the authorities to have objectionable pages cut out.... The Soviets have devised more effective techniques, and excision is for the most part no longer necessary. They simply reprint the offending page to their specifications. Occasionally, however, an item in a published work becomes an embarrassment and the old technique is used again. A case in point from the Stalinist period is the article on Lavrentii Pavlovich Beria, chief of Stalin's secret police, in the second (1949) edition of the *Bol'shaia sovetskaia entsiklopediia* (Large Soviet Encyclopedia).[51] After Stalin's death, when Beria fell from power and was executed, the editors of the BSE sent a notice to all subscribers, domestic and foreign, instructing them to remove the offending pages (including the full-page portrait of Beria) and to replace them with pictures of the Bering Sea, the contiguous article.[52]

Friedberg has noted that during the Khrushchev era "some of the more blatant ideologically inspired falsifications of history" were exposed or more or less openly challenged." From that point onward, in Friedberg's opinion, "outright falsifications of the historical record became rarer, but discreet silences and half-truths often replaced them."[53] In fact, falsifications have not become more rare, as our analysis of the Soviet campaign over the Korean airliner will demonstrate. Indeed, the legacy of Khrushchev himself became a victim of the system. Cohen has written:

> Few political leaders have been less honored for the good they achieved than Nikita Khrushchev, who led the Soviet Union out of the terror-ridden wasteland of Stalinism. Overthrown by the political elite on October 14, 1964, his entire career was excised from official histories. No Soviet obituary marked his death ... seven years later. And today, Khrushchev is the only former supreme leader about whom nothing candidly favorable can be published in the Soviet Union.[54]

What <u>has</u> changed, compared to earlier periods, is the level of sophistication often exemplified by Soviet propaganda. Except in crisis situations, such as that presented by KAL 007, Soviet propagandists have become less crude in their manipulation of facts.

Friedberg believes that studying Soviet media—and, for that matter, literature and the arts, as well—"reveal[s] the extent to which the government is successful in its efforts to isolate the population from the rest of the world and to restrict the impact of the outside world upon its citizens, especially the various elites." As will be demonstrated, one of the salient effects of the KAL disaster was the manner in which Soviet media treatment of the incident reflected the penetration of external ideas. Still, it remains true, as was stated more than a decade ago by Vitali Kobysh, then *Izvestiia*'s London correspondent, that Soviet readers usually cannot verify factual information presented in their media, so that they cannot verify the interpretations offered them.[55] Most recently, in his historic broadcasts from the Soviet Union, Phil Donohue observed, "The [Soviet] state has deprived [the people] of the information they need to be self-critical."[56]

What, if anything, restrains this governmental impulse to control information and to manage the public perception of reality? In the West the press often serves this function—the Andersons, Woodwards, Bernsteins, and Hershes, to name only a few of the most prominent investigative reporters. Even the conspiratists evolved from the same spirit of investigative journalism and 'loyal opposition.'[57] Within the Soviet Union certain constraints have been imposed recently by the startling appearance of ideological or political disputes on the pages of Soviet newspapers—a growing trend in the Gorbachev era, particularly after Chernobyl, as economic and public policy debates have been afforded greater publicity. Nevertheless, it remains true that no equivalent institutional or societal checks exist in Soviet society, although samizdat (underground) publishing[58] and the recently disbanded Helsinki Watch group have made heart-rending efforts. In reality, however, the most significant countervailing force upon the Soviet leadership has always been imposed from the West in the form of transnational broadcasting.

Most of the elements in the KAL controversy—the various actors and the forums in which they appeared—are well recognized and easily identified. One, however, is invisible to and barely known by Americans: the group of radio stations sponsored by Western governments, stations which broadcast into Eastern Europe and the Soviet Union. Included here are the BBC, West Germany's Deutsche Welle, and three stations supported by the United States—Voice of America (VOA), Radio Free Europe (RFE), and Radio Liberty (RL). The American radio stations played a significant role in this international argument, enabling the United States government to present its version of the incident to people behind the Iron Curtain.

VOA (or, 'The Voice,' as insiders commonly refer to it) was chartered immediately after Pearl Harbor.[59] Today it is the largest single component of the United States Information Agency (USIA), broadcasting news, commentary and entertainment (particularly American jazz) around the world.

RFE and RL were established at the outset of the Cold War, ostensibly as private non-profit corporations: RFE began in 1949 as the National Committee for a Free Europe; RL originated in 1951 as Radio Liberation, established under the auspices of the American Committee for Freedom for the Peoples of the USSR, Inc.—Amcomlib, for short. In truth, for about twenty years both stations were secretly funded by the CIA,[60] a fact that the Soviet Union never fails to stress. Today they exist as RFE/RL, Inc. and are administered openly by the Board for International Broadcasting.[61] The original goal of each organization was to support research and to provide general intelligence; they also were conceived as a way to provide employment to many well-educated but otherwise unemployable refugees who fled Eastern Europe at the conclusion of World War II.[62] Although both organizations now engage exclusively in broadcasting, this function was almost an accidental outgrowth of their original purposes.

VOA and RFE/RL have different goals:

VOA is recognized as the official radio voice of the United States Government. Like all other USIA activities, it gives a preponderant emphasis to American developments. VOA programming contains relatively little information about internal developments in its audience countries.

   RFE and RL programming ... gives citizens of the communist countries information on conditions, attitudes, and trends within their own countries and on international developments as they relate to the special interests of the listeners.[63]

RFE/RL is seen as "a surrogate free press for the captive peoples."[64] Hale describes their function as one of providing "an alternative Home Service in the target areas."[65] Jon Lodeesen, Director of US Operations for RFE/RL, has stated that much of their programming is designed to supplement and counter the information that appears in specific home media outlets. As Lodeesen expressed it recently, RFE/RL often says, in effect, "On such-and-such a program you were told such-and-such. But did you know...?" VOA, on the other hand, resembles in its news broadcasting nothing so much as a wire-service of the air. Dispatches are typically short, often consisting of official statements by government spokespersons and agencies; reports are updated continuously throughout the day. In addition, VOA broadcasts longer programs that resemble television news magazine segments.

In September, 1983 VOA and RFE/RL coverage of the KAL disaster played to the worst fears of the Soviet establishment by continuously and insistently challenging the regime's control of information. Because radio "is the only unstoppable medium in mass communications"[66] it is capable of "reach[ing], and in a sense ... creat[ing], a public opinion which questions the single-minded assumptions of governments claiming a monopoly of the source of news and information."[67] KAL is a perfect case in point. According to Sam Lyon, RFE/RL Director of Broadcast Analysis in Munich, W. Germany:

The initial treatment in 1983 by RL's Russian service of the KAL shoot-down was extensive, involving 153 minutes of first-run feature time (27 items, 9 percent of total first-run features) during the first five days following the event (September 1-5) and from September 1 to October 8, 1560 minutes of first-run features (news coverage on the first five days absorbed 43 percent of newscast time).[68]

Accordingly, through the facilities of the transnational radio broadcast stations maintained by the United States government, the official, semi-official, and general news treatment of KAL available to Americans and other Westerners was presented to the citizens of Soviet bloc nations.

No one, least of all officials at USIA, would claim that the version presented was unbiased, because "propaganda is what international radio is all about."[69] But much that was unfavorable to the official position of the United States government was broadcast by VOA and RFE/RL. True, VOA always provided the appropriate State Department or White House 'spin,' but it did transmit information concerning such factors as the RC-135 which was patrolling in its 'mission orbit' off the coast of Kamchatka peninsula prior to KAL 007's first incursion into Soviet territory. In 1984, it even carried stories on official US reaction to the spy-theory articles published by David Pearson and P.Q. Mann.[70]

US transnational broadcasting did challenge the Soviet government's claim to correctness and infallibility in this, as in other events. The Soviet sense of losing control over information undoubtedly began long before the KAL tragedy, as troops posted to foreign occupation zones began to return home with knowledge and experiences that potentially confirmed the counter-programming of Western radio. [Some observers estimate that the 1968 invasion of Czechoslovakia was a watershed.] Nonetheless, because of the magnitude of the issue, KAL seems to have had a permanent effect on Soviet information policy. It is our belief that the KAL tragedy contributed to—indeed, was perhaps the initial impetus for—a reassessment which ultimately resulted in the policy now known as glasnost'. [See Chapter Ten.]

We have already alluded to the requirement, in Soviet terms, that the news reflect significant policy goals of the state. As those goals change over time, one would expect similar shifts in news coverage. That this is exactly what happened in the case of the Korean airliner is apparent if one compares treatment of the disaster with coverage of a similar event—the 1973 destruction of a Libyan passenger airliner over the Sinai Peninsula by the Israeli Air Force.[71] The Israeli action was described as an "act of piracy," a "crime against humanity and the norms of international law," and an inexcusable violation of international rights. It was compared in a radio broadcast to "four bandits attacking a blind man who had lost his way and was without a guide." A Soviet lawyer, speaking on another radio broadcast, said, "International codes consider the passenger airline to be a peaceful civilian target and in no circumstances can it be the object of a surprise attack.... [C]ivilians must be protected and must not be the target of attacks, even if people involved in military operations are among them."

As can be seen, Soviet opportunism regarding the two disasters was a match for that of the American government, which had chosen to interpret the Israeli action as a tragic wartime accident. [See Chapter One.] The reasons for such dissimilar treatment of similar events must be obvious. During the 1973 Yom Kippur War, Soviet military and diplomatic might was aligned with the Arab states. In 1983, the Soviet Union's primary foreign policy initiative was directed at stopping the impending deployment of US missiles in Europe. Even if the United States government had not taken advantage of the KAL disaster to vilify the Soviet Union, it is reasonable to expect that the Soviet interpretation of whatever international situation arose would have been designed to promote its major foreign policy objectives. Under the additional pressure of world opinion, it probably was impossible for the public reaction of the Soviet government to have been any different.[72]

In order to place the Soviet response to KAL in historical perspective, it may be useful to review briefly the changes that had occurred in their foreign policy objectives over the preceding several years.[73] The primary difficulty, of course, was the collapse of detente. From the Soviet point of view, in fact, no such deterioration should have been possible. Legvold cites an article by Arbatov published in 1973 in the authoritative journal *Kommunist* as evidence that Soviet leaders "were taking it for granted" that detente "flowed from a major structural change," that they expected this change to last and develop.[74] One can find indications at least as late as 1978 that Soviet ideologists believed detente to be a never-ending reality. In a book that bears all the hallmarks of an authoritative, expert statement of current ideology, reference is made to "imperialism's ultimate historical fate and the historically irreversible nature of changes in the correlation of forces in the world arena."[75]

Detente is said to have arisen, to paraphrase various Soviet ideologists, from a "deepening crisis" of imperialist foreign policy, the real facts of a newly developing "correlation of forces" on the international scene, and from a more realistic US assessment of the chances that it could achieve worldwide hegemony. What this actually meant is: the US was faced with substantial internal dissent and rising budgetary problems because of the war in Vietnam, and the Soviet Union's growing nuclear arsenal had eliminated a previously existing arms imbalance favoring America, so the US was forced to accept the Soviet Union as a player of equal importance internationally.[76] Bialer has described what each superpower basically hoped to gain from detente:

> The Americans assumed that they could moderate both Soviet arms spending and Soviet behavior through the creation of a web of arms control and cultural, political and economic relations. The Soviets understood detente as the final recognition by the United States of the Soviet Union's achievement of strategic parity. Furthermore, the Soviets assumed that this military parity could be translated into global political parity with the United States.[77]

But the Soviets wanted more, in Bialer's opinion:

> [T]hey believed that while detente required a freeze on existing spheres of influence in Europe, it left the Soviet Union the right to expand in an unrestricted manner, through the use of its own or proxy military forces, into those areas of the world outside the superpowers' spheres of influence.[78]

In practice this meant supporting indigenous insurgencies in Central America and elsewhere, sending Cuban forces to Angola, and, finally, directly intervening in Afghanistan. Arbatov stated this position to the West quite adamantly:

> While waging an active ... struggle for detente ... the Soviet Union and other socialist countries did not, nor could they, pledge themselves to guarantee the preservation of the social status quo in the world, to stop the processes of class and national liberation struggle unfolding in keeping with the objective laws of historical development. ... And we reject the assertions that support for the peoples fighting against colonial oppression violates ... the principle of non-interference in the affairs of other states and the respect for their independence and sovereignty. ... [F]oreign aggressors are *already* interfering in the affairs of [Angola]. ... Therefore solidarity with ... the just cause of liberation of peoples from the colonial yoke does not constitute interference in the internal affairs of other countries.[79]

Both sides concur that detente came to an end during the late 1970s,[80] but there have been differences of opinion concerning the causes for detente's failure. The American side holds that Afghanistan was the last straw. Arbatov has claimed that "detente was undermined by the shift in U.S. foreign policy in the late 1970s and the early 1980s."[81] Bialer believes, however, that the American side finally "recognized that if detente did not curtail Soviet military spending and limit Soviet expansionist drives in the Third World, then it made little sense to continue with it"; moreover, he feels, misperceptions on the part of both superpowers finally undermined the process of detente: "It was these two basically different concepts of detente that accounted for the mutual lack of consciousness of how one's own actions affect those of the other."[82] It is Legvold's opinion, apparently, that the Soviets should bear most of the blame:

> Detente ultimately could not be insulated from Soviet loyalty to the national liberation struggle, and the Soviet Union's inability or unwillingness to understand this, more than any other factor, dealt detente a mortal blow.[83]

It seems that Soviet leaders fell prey to a situation Wilensky had described in the late 1960s:

> "[F]acts, arguments, and propaganda directed at friends and enemies alike ... can be self-convincing.... Many a leader becomes captive of the rhetoric he customarily presents.... If supplying the symbols that guide executive action is "window dressing," it is the kind of display that tells what is in the store.[84]

That is to say, the Brezhnev government truly may have come to believe that the United States, under Presidents Nixon and Carter, had embarked on the course of detente—and then maintained that policy in the face of obviously provocative Soviet initiatives in the Third World—out of necessity rather than choice. And that, further, such a belief may have emboldened the Soviets to the point of failing to recognize the limits within which the Americans would tolerate such activities—indeed, failing to recognize even the very existence of such limits.[85]

Soviet difficulties were compounded when Ronald Reagan triumphed in the 1980 national elections. Not only did the shrillness of anti-Soviet rhetoric increase dramatically, but it became obvious that reliance on military power would become the cornerstone of American foreign policy. Legvold capsulized the Soviet dilemma: "[T]he international setting ... shows serious signs of reverting to old forms.... American globalism is not contracting, but reviving."[86] In his view, Brezhnev and his inner circle of advisors decided to "gamble" that the Americans could not back up their words with deeds, "even though the Reagan administration took its rhetoric seriously and intended to do something about it."[87]

An indispensable element of the planned US military build-up was the deployment of cruise and Pershing II missiles in Western Europe. But in order to achieve this goal the Reagan Administration would need to secure permission from America's NATO allies. Some of those countries faced serious difficulty in gaining the support of public opinion: particularly doubtful was West Germany's ability to gain legislative approval in the face of strong opposition by the Greens Party, an environmental group deeply committed to fighting both nuclear arms and atomic power generation.

Obviously, impeding this planned US expansion became a critical foreign policy goal for the Soviet Union, because it presented a direct challenge to several essential elements of state security. First and foremost, even in czarist times Western Europe occupied a central position in national security considerations. Hamburg has called Europe "the linchpin of Soviet strategy," noting that "[d]rawing these countries away from dependence on the United States has been a central Soviet objective."[88] On a more visceral level, it would be foolish to ignore the salience of World War II and Nazi aggression in Soviet national consciousness—no informed observer should be surprised by the sincerity or the depth of Soviet "concerns about the West Germans and the anxiety that they might acquire nuclear weapons."[89] Brown has commented upon this essential element of political culture in the Soviet Union:

> There is a constant reinforcement of such feelings in the 'official political culture'. It is not surprising that party leaders and propagandists lay such constant stress on the 'Great Patriotic War' in their conscious political socialization efforts, since there is no other shared experience with which they can so instantly achieve a rapport with their listeners or readers.[90]

The Soviet Union's diplomatic problem was compounded by the continuing deterioration of its relationships with the United States, primarily due to the growing Soviet involvement in Afghanistan and the heightened unrest in Poland. Both of these situations also had an adverse effect on public opinion on the Continent, including relations between the USSR and the communist parties in various European countries.[91] But Soviet foreign policy planners developed a creative solution, one that involved de-emphasizing the importance of the United States in its policy considerations. Legvold had, in fact, suggested that Soviet leaders might face the "choice between a U.S.-centered policy and a decentralized policy." Rather than "tying all other relationships to their relationship with the United States ... [they] could concentrate on repairing their position with the remaining major power centers."[92] Bialer believes that early in the 80s the Soviets had initiated an attempt "to uncouple its deteriorating relations with the United States from its detente with Europe. This desire to exploit the fissures in the Western alliance constitutes the cornerstone of ... Soviet foreign policy [after the invasion of Afghanistan]."[93] Arbatov expressed the thrust of Soviet efforts in the following manner:

> [O]ne can spend ... billions of dollars more on the military build-up, but this will be of no avail.... Reagan's course has forced enormous masses of people to think seriously about the problems of war and peace. The public in Western Europe and now in the United States itself has sensed the existence and growth of the nuclear threat more sharply than ever before. The changed political and psychological climate on both sides of the Atlantic has led to an increased opposition to the policy of intensified military buildup and confrontation.[94]

In the same set of interviews, Arbatov strongly rejected the notion that much of the Western European opposition was fomented by Soviet propaganda, although there seems to be no real doubt that organizations such as the World Peace Council, with strong ties to Soviet interests, have participated along with independent indigenous groups in West Germany and Great Britain. In any event, Bialer suggested that if the Soviet Union were successful in "exploiting the pacifistic and antinuclear trends that have become so prominent among European leftists and youth," it might be successful in its attempts to revitalize detente with Western Europe. Should that happen, the United States might face "insurmountable obstacles in the path of the deployment of new U.S.-controlled theater nuclear weapons in Europe." In the extreme, such a situation might even "slow the upgrading of NATO conventional forces."[95]

Judging by the size and intensity of anti-war and anti-nuclear demonstrations throughout Europe during the summer of 1983, and the well coordinated Peace Offensive that was scheduled for the fall of that year, it appeared that Soviet efforts—or, at least, Soviet hopes— were on the verge of fulfillment. But it was precisely at this juncture that KAL was destroyed. Once again, it seemed, the Russians had demonstrated their well known predilection for 'shooting themselves in the foot.'[96] Time would tell whether the hoped for detente with Western Europe would also fall victim to the actions of Soviet PVO forces.

CHAPTER FIVE

NOTES

[1]Jan S. Adams, "Critical Letters to the Soviet Press: An Increasingly Important Public Forum," in Donald E. Schulz and Jan S. Adams, eds., *Political Participation in Communist Systems*, Pergamon Policy Studies on International Politics (New York: Pergamon, 1981), 108-37, p. 108. See: A. V. Grebnev, "Gazeta, organizatsiia raboty redaktsii" [*The Newspaper: The Organization of Editorial Operations*] (Moscow, 1974), p. 6.

[2]V. S. Evseev, "Partiinoe vozdeistvie pressy" [*The Influence of the Press in Support of the Party*] (Moscow: Izdatel'stvo politicheskoi literatury, 1980), p. 18.

[3]See: Rose Matuz, "TV News in the Framework of Television Political Programmes," *Radio and Television*, 2 (1963), 3-6 [cited in Hollander].

[4]The term 'authoritarian' has been chosen to avoid the negative connotations of police-state repression that have accrued to the word 'totalitarian.' We would prefer the initial meaning of totalitarian, which is reflected in this statement: "The USSR is commonly perceived as totalitarian, in the sense that politics infuses the entire social and economic life of the nation." See: D. Richard Little, "Bureaucracy and Participation in the Soviet Union," in Schulz and Adams, 79-107, p. 92.

[5]Kenez, p. 5.

[6]Michael Calvin McGee and Martha Anne Martin, "Public Knowledge and Ideological Argumentation," *Communication Monographs*, 50 (1983), 47-65, p. 53.

[7]John Meisel, "Communications and Crisis: A Preliminary Mapping," in Daniel Frei, ed., *Managing International Crises* (Beverly Hills: Sage Publications, 1982), 61-75, p. 66.

[8]Marianna Tax Choldin, *A Fence Around the Empire. Russian Censorship of Western Ideas Under the Tsars*, Duke Press Policy Studies (Durham: Duke University Press, 1985), pp. 1-2. As Friedberg has wryly commented, all the Soviet government wants is "a fire that will not burn." See: Maurice Friedberg, "Cultural and Intellectual Life," in Robert F. Byrnes, ed., *After Brezhnev: Sources of Soviet Conduct in the 1980s* (Bloomington: Indiana University Press, 1983), 250-89, p. 251.

[9] Leonid I. Brezhnev made the official declaration in a 1967 speech entitled "Socialism's Fifty Years of Great Triumphs." See: Evseev, p. 15.

[10]Vladimir Shlapentokh, *Soviet Public Opinion and Ideology. Mythology and Pragmatism in Interaction* (New York: Praeger, 1986), p. 153.

[11]Shlapentokh, pp. 116, 137. In Stalinist times children were encouraged to inform upon their own parents. One such child, Pavlik Morozov, was turned into a social hero in 1932 by Soviet propagandists after relatives killed him for denouncing his father to the authorities. The official image of this child has been modified over time, significantly de-glamorizing his actions. (See: Shlapentokh, 52-54; and Felicity Barringer, "Changing Times Turn Tables On a 'Saint' of the Stalin Era," *The New York Times*, March 21, 1988, pp. 1, 8). Nonetheless, until sometime after Khrushchev's 1956 secret speech exposed the Stalinist cult of personality "the situation in the USSR was such that most people were fearful of sharing their opinions with others, even members of their families. . . . The fear of informers still plays an important role in social life, but it no longer extends to members of one's family or friends" (Shlapentokh, 43-44). Brown believes that Western political scientists underestimate the continuing importance of Stalin in contemporary Soviet society. See: Archie Brown, "Soviet Political Culture through Soviet Eyes," in Archie Brown, ed., *Political Culture and Communist Studies* (London: Macmillan, 1984), 100-114, pp. 102-103.

[12]In 1964, Butler described *The Art of Oratory*, his translation of a Soviet treatise on rhetoric published in Moscow by the State Publishing House of Political Literature, 1959. This study has two drawbacks: it is nearly a quarter-century old and it is not a study of rhetoric-in-action. However, it does provide useful insights into the Soviet concept of rhetoric and the linkage between those notions and Marxist-Leninist doctrine. See: Jack H. Butler, "Russian Rhetoric: A Discipline Manipulated By Communism," *Quarterly Journal of Speech*, 50:3 (October 1964), 229-39. For a treatment of speech communication in East Germany, see: Michael McGuire and Lothar Berger, "Speech in the Marxist State," *Communication Education*, 28:3 (July 1979), 169-78.

[13]Evseev, p. 8.

[14] This, too, represented a continuation of past practice. Czarist government was based upon a society "in which there was a strong tradition of group solidarity ... [and] a greater degree of reliance upon face-to-face relations than upon anonymous procedures. " See: Stephen White, *Political Culture and Soviet Politics* (London: Macmillan, 1979), p. 64.

[15]Kazimierz Grzybowski, "Propaganda and the Soviet Concept of World Public Order," in Clark C. Havighurst, ed. *International Control of Propaganda* (Dobbs Ferry, NY: Oceana, 1967), 41-67, p. 41. Emphasis added.

[16]Kenez, p. 226.

[17]Kenez, p. 49.

[18]Thomas Remington, *The Origin of Ideology* (Pittsburgh: University of Pittsburgh, University Center for International Studies, 1974), p. 9.

[19]Evseev, p. 41. Dialectical reasoning can produce this sort of rhetoric, which Hugo has classified as 'cant'—"a mode of expression, or a cast of thought, of which the effect . . .

is to create a discrepancy between the natural meaning of words and their practical significance, a discrepancy even more dangerous when, as often happens, the speaker is as much misled as his audience." See: Hugo, p. 19.

[20]White, *Political Culture and Soviet Politics*, p. 64. It can be seen that in many ways the Revolution entailed a continuation of the existing patterns of governance. White stated this conclusion most explicitly in a 1980 lecture presented at Garmisch-Partenkirchen, FRG. A revised version was published as "Soviet Political Culture Reassessed," in Brown, ed., *Political Culture and Communist Studies*, 62-99. In this article, one reads, "My own conclusion . . . is that the element of continuity is very important" throughout Soviet history (p. 91).

[21]Theodore H. Friedgut, *Political Participation in the USSR* (Princeton: Princeton University Press, 1979), p. 33.

[22]Kenez, p. 48.

[23]Kenez, p. 233.

[24]The "basic function" of Soviet media "remains essentially that conceived by Lenin: They are the Party's instruments of intensive overt, explicit political socialization or indoctrination." See: Gayle Durham Hollander, *Soviet Political Indoctrination: Developments in Mass Media and Propaganda Since Stalin* (New York: Praeger, 1972), p. 21; see, also: Adams, p. 108.

[25]Baruch A. Hazan, *Soviet Propaganda: A Case Study of the Middle East Conflict* (New Brunswick, NJ: Transaction Books, 1976), p. 230.

[26]"The Soviet's Lie About Censorship," *U. S. News & World Report*, January 13, 1956, 68-76, p. 74. Most Americans would find this statement both extreme and biased, the bitter attack of a disaffected former citizen. Yet, thirty years later, Shlapentokh could point to a 1984 book on ethics that "chose not to mention" such qualities as "tolerance, honesty, pride, self-respect, or sincerity." Further, in his experience, "when Soviet analysts address issues of personal ethics, they usually rarely discuss lying." Shlapentokh cites another textbook on ethics for teenagers that failed to mention honesty among almost seventy moral virtues. "Even Soviet ideologists, who routinely display the ability to ignore elements of Soviet reality, seem to experience difficulty in attacking lies, which are an integral part of everyday social functioning." But he points to a "daring" 1980 Soviet film, *Autumn Marathon*, which

> vividly depicted how lying is a part of Soviet life. Of course, the director could not explicitly focus on lying, but his allusions were sufficient for sophisticated Soviet filmgoers, and he was able to convey the real atmosphere in Soviet society.

Indeed, when Yuri Andropov assumed power, he was faced with "almost total corruption and deception" in Soviet society, while "widespread practices of nepotism,

127

bribery, and other forms of corruption . . . [have] particularly angered the younger generations." (Shlapentokh, pp. 22, 169, 150).

[27]Edward Crankshaw, "Case History of an Unfree Press," *New York Times Magazine,* December 2, 1962, pp. 35, 134-135. When Soviet ideologists speak of the need for raising the level of political culture among the citizenry today, they are advocating a continuation of this educative function. See: Brown, "Soviet Political Culture through Soviet Eyes," pp. 103-110, and the works cited therein.

[28]Friedgut, p. 303 ff.

[29]White, *Political Culture and Soviet Politics,* p. 81.

[30]"XXV s"ezd Kommunisticheskoi partii Sovetskogo Soiuza. Stenograficheskii otchet" [*The 25th Congress of the Communist Party of the Soviet Union. Verbatim Transcript*], vol. l, p. 104. Quoted by Evseev, p. 18.

[31]Frederick C. Barghoorn, *Politics in the USSR,* 2nd ed., The Little, Brown Series in Comparative Politics (Boston: Little, Brown, 1972), p. 158. See also: Wilbur Schramm, ed., *One Day in the World's Press* (Stanford: Stanford University Press, 1959) [discussed by Barghoorn, pp. 158-61].

[32]Mickiewicz, pp. 53-54.

[33]Robert G. Kaiser, *Russia: The People and the Power* (New York: Atheneum, 1976), p. 217. See, also: Mickiewicz. Another, less sympathetic, description of Soviet journalistic practices is contained in: Leonid Vladimirov, "Problems of the Soviet Journalist," in *The Conflict of INFORMATION—'Detente,' Freedom & Constraint,* Conflict Studies No. 56 (April 1975), 3-10.

[34]Hollander, p. 106. In the case of the Korean airliner, the overriding foreign policy goal of the Soviet Union in September 1983—as it had been for quite some time—was to keep the United States from deploying its cruise and Pershing II missiles in West Germany [See Chapter Six]. As will be demonstrated in the following chapter, Soviet propagandists attempted to deflect the international furor evoked by the shootdown and continue the campaign against America's Euromissiles.

[35]Nearly thirty years ago the International Press Institute acknowledged that within the Soviet press establishment "control is exercised . . . by systematic planning." See: *The Press in Authoritarian Countries* (Zurich: International Press Institute, 1959), Survey No. 5, p. 28 ff. [Cited in B. S. Murty, *Propaganda and World Public Order. The Legal Regulation of the Ideological Instrument of Coercion* (New Haven: Yale University Press, 1968), p. 40.]

[36]Hollander, p. 106 ff.

[37]Kaiser, p. 225.

[38]Kaiser, pp. 225-26. See also Kaiser's Chapter Six, "True or False," especially pp. 255-57.

[39]Joynt and Corbett, pp. 105-106. As far as journalism is concerned, of course, the attention given to modifications depends on timing. Nothing is as ignored as "old news". A common and recurring complaint against American media is the tendency to "bury" corrections and modifications in the back pages among the advertisements and obituaries.

[40]Evseev, pp. 18, 69. Emphasis added.

[41]Murty, p. 61.

[42]L. B. Berzin and Yu. P. Davydov, "Propaganda na sluzhbe vneshnei politiki," in Trofimenko, ed., "Sovremennaia vneshniaia politika SShA" [Current U.S. Foreign Policy], vol. 2, 91-112.

[43]Berzin and Davydov, pp. 102, 97. Ever since inception of "The Voices," the Soviet Union has carried on a continuous campaign against their activities. Opposition has been registered both in domestic media and in the international arena, particularly at the United Nations.

[44]Berzin and Davydov, p. 103. The Trofimenko collection was not designed for a mass readership: only 5600 copies were printed, a sure sign in the USSR that a specialist audience was being addressed. Given the sponsoring organization, the book should be considered an authoritative source of prevailing doctrine.

[45]Ebon devotes a separate chapter to this fascinating individual. Martin Ebon, *The Soviet Propaganda Machine* (New York: McGraw-Hill, 1987) See: Georgi A. Arbatov and Willem Oltmans, *The Soviet Viewpoint* (New York: Dodd, Mead, 1983).

[46]Georgi Arbatov, *The War of Ideas in Contemporary International Relations*, David Skvirsky, trans. (Moscow: Progress Publishers, 1973), p. 218 [original title: "Ideologicheskaia bor'ba v sovremennykh mezhdunarodnykh otnosheniiakh"].

[47]Arbatov, *The War of Ideas*, pp. 204-205. See: Robert L. Heilbroner, *The Worldly Philosophers* (New York: Simon & Schuster, 1962), 2nd ed., p. 209.

[48]Arbatov, *The War of Ideas*, p. 205.

[49]This so-called 'agitation' apparatus—a nationwide effort coordinated at the Central Committee level of the Communist Party—has been described by Thomas Remington, *Soviet Public Opinion and the Effectiveness of Party Ideological Work*, The Carl Beck Papers in Russian and East European Studies, No. 204 (Pittsburgh: University of Pittsburgh, Russian and East European Studies Program, 1983); and by V. G. Baikova, "Ideologicheskaia rabota KPSS v usloviiakh razvitogo sotsializma" [*CPSU Ideological Work under Developed Socialism*] (Moscow: Mysl', 1977). Recent studies

have cast doubts upon the effectiveness of this activity. See: Shlapentokh, 99-112; White, *Political Culture and Soviet Politics,* especially Chapters Four and Six; and G. T. Zhuravlev, "Sotsiologicheskie issledovaniia èffektivnosti ideologicheskoi raboty" [*Sociological Investigations into the Effectiveness of Ideological Work*] (Moscow: Mysl', 1980). The jargon term agitprop subsumes both agitation and propaganda.

[50]Kaiser, p. 259. The piquancy of this remark remains undiminished today. In the spring of 1988 American historians Stephen Cohen and Robert Daniels were invited to the Soviet Union to speak about the excesses of Stalinist times and particularly about individuals such as Nikolai Bukharin, a non-person for over fifty years. Nevertheless, as one Associate Press story indicates, "Many important episodes of Soviet history remain outside the bounds of official scholarship." The AP reports, "Even now, the rewriting of history is directed by central Communist Party authorities." See: "Preserving the past confronts today's Soviets," *Tallahassee Democrat,* April 17, 1988, pp. 1B, 7B.

[51]As an aside, we would like to comment on Choldin's translation of this title. The *Bol'shaia sovetskaia entsiklopediia* is, indeed, large: It encompasses 30-plus volumes with annual supplements, somewhat akin to the *Encyclopedia Brittanica.* But *Bol'shaia* in the title refers more to the existence of the *Malaia sovetskaia entsiklopediia,* a shorter version. [In the same vein, there exist the *Bol'shoi* and the *Malyi* theaters, differentiated by the size of the halls and their seating capacities.] One might translate the encyclopedia titles as *The [Great] Soviet Encyclopedia* and *The Condensed Soviet Encyclopedia.* Our point is that ludicrous translations—which one can read nearly every day in *The New York Times* or the *Washington Post*—trivialize the sense of the original. By extension, we believe, they make it difficult for Americans to take the originators seriously. In any event, such translations of Soviet political statements render argument analysis difficult and content analysis impossible, thereby decreasing the likelihood of meaningful contributions from communication specialists.

[52]Choldin, p. 31. This event is also reported by Ebon, p. 19. As Ebon commented, this step was taken in order to "eliminate [Beria] from historical memory." One of the present authors, M. Launer, remembers seeing the substitute pages stapled to the original text, which, of course, his university library had neglected to cut out of the encyclopedia.

[53]Friedberg, pp. 255, 257. Most Americans are shocked when they learn of such occurrences, but Soviet specialists tend to take them for granted.

[54]Cohen, p. 47. This text comes from a column that first appeared in *The Nation,* October 20, 1984. In early 1988 two remarkable articles in the Soviet press invalidated Cohen's observation. First, *Nedelia* —the Sunday supplement to *Izvestiia* —published an exposé of Lavrenti Beria, the sadistic head of Stalin's secret police, in which the sons of both Khrushchev and Anastas Mikoyan recounted stories told to them by their late fathers. Then, in April the bi-weekly *Literaturnaia gazeta* devoted a full page to an article—indisputably approved by Mikhail Gorbachev himself—excoriating Stalin and praising Khrushchev effusively. See: Nikolai Zhusenin, "Beriia," *Nedelia,*

February 12-18, 1988, pp. 11-12; and Fëdor Burlatskii, "Kakoi sotsialism nuzhen narodu" ["What Kind of Socialism Do the People Need?"], *Literaturnaia gazeta*, April 20, 1988, p. 2.

[55]Vladimirov, p. 3. In this regard, Butler has written: "Soviet speakers may well consider themselves as honest purveyors of the truth. They may actually believe or simply accept the validity of their cause, for the validity is confirmed by every definition available to them" (p. 239). According to Ebon (p. 303), Kobysh now occupies a major position in the Central Committee's International Information Department, which is generally accepted to be the originator of most Soviet international disinformation, including outright forgeries.

[56]Gary Lee, "Donohue's Russian Revelations," *Washington Post*, February 7, 1987, p. C11. As Kaiser commented, "When lies are accepted as readily as the truth—and that is just what happens in the Soviet Union—then the distinction between them inevitably begins to disappear" (p. 248).

[57]The Soviet Union, of course, is not unique in its control of information. Nor would we suggest that one encounters no managed news in the United States. Recent events—the Cuban missile crisis, Watergate, and the Iran-Contra affair—put the lie to this notion and lead one to wonder just how much of the news is managed on a day-to-day basis. Moreover, as Meisel has noted, "No country has a free press in the absolute sense, and restrictions can take forms other than governmental control" (p. 66).

[58]For a description of samizdat, see Mark Hopkins, *Russia's Underground Press* (New York: Praeger, 1983).

[59]Julian Hale, *Radio Power. Propaganda and International Broadcasting* (Philadelphia: Temple University Press, 1975), p. 32.

[60]Not even Congress was aware of this fact prior to 1967. See: Sig Mickelson, *America's Other Voice. The Story of Radio Free Europe and Radio Liberty* (New York: Praeger, 1983), p. 1.

[61]B.I.B. is supposed to have no secret functions, but access to its offices in Washington, DC, is controlled by the kind of cipher lock one finds in the Pentagon, at CIA headquarters in Langley, VA, and at NSA facilities at Ft. Meade, MD.

[62]Mickelson comments: "The two corporations were born out of a curious blend of charitable motives and a desperately felt need in government circles for developing new sources of intelligence concerning Communist intentions in Central and Western Europe" (p. 2).

[63]Presidential Study Commission on International Broadcasting, *The Right to Know* (Washington: U. S. Government Printing Office, 1973), p. 42. [Cited in Hale, p. 39.]

[64]Mickelson, p. vii. Also: "it might be described as all-talk radio" (p. 3).

[65]Hale, p. xiv.

[66]Hale, p. ix.

[67]Hale, pp. xii-xiii. Note, however, this comment: "Radio propaganda is also a conservative force in that listeners for the most part tune in only to the stations that carry the message they want to hear" (p. xvii).

[68]We are grateful to Mr. Lyon, who provided this information by Telex, 23 January 1987, per our request to Jon Lodeesen.

[69]Hale, p. xviii.

[70]One must keep in mind that VOA, in particular, wasn't dogmatic about being even-handed. For instance, although the RC-135 reconnaissance aircraft was prominently mentioned on September 4, 1983 (the day the information became available) and on the 5th, it essentially disappeared from that point onward, despite being a bone of contention between the Soviet Union and the US government.

The lead stories on the 6th were the UN Security Council meeting where Ambassador Jeane Kirkpatrick played the tape recording of Soviet pilots and the Soviet Union's admission that its forces had indeed destroyed the Korean airliner. There is only one mention of the reconnaissance plane: Soviet Ambassador Oleg Troyanovsky told the Security Council that if the RC-135 had not been directing KAL 007's actions it could have warned the passenger aircraft. See: Voice of America, CN-068, September 6, 1983, [13:07:28]. The next mention of the RC-135 in VOA materials was a single reference in a twenty-minute show broadcast on the occasion of the first anniversary of the tragedy. See below, Chapter Seven.

On August 16, 1984, USIA wired to all United States Information Service (USIS) offices, which are housed in American embassies around the globe, a twelve-page document entitled "THE DEATH OF KAL 007: 'THIS APPALLING AND WANTON MISDEED' (Chronology: Soviet shootdown and world reaction)". This document, designated POL405, recounts events through publication of the *ICAO REPORT* in December, 1983. It was designed to give cultural attachés factual information and policy guidance in handling the upcoming KAL anniversary. Nowhere in the text is the RC-135 mentioned.

[71]The discussion which follows quotes directly from a news release entitled "Moscow's Reactions to Prior Downings of Civilian Aircraft Reveal Blatant Double Standards," *Press Reports on Soviet Affairs*, September 22, 1983. These reports are issued by the Advanced International Studies Institute (Washington) in association with The University of Miami. Soviet sources for all statements are published in the news release.

[72]Of course, no bureaucracy (including the Soviet government) can completely control the behavior of all actors who might represent it. As Jervis has commented,

what is of most importance for international relations is that decision-makers generally overestimate the degree to which their opposite numbers have the information and power to impose their desires on all parts of their own governments. The state's behavior is usually seen as centrally controlled rather than as the independent actions of actors trying to further their own interests and their partial and biased conceptions of the national interest. . . .

See: *Perception and Misperception*, p. 324. This comment seems to be particularly relevant to the Soviet state in the Gorbachev era.

[73] The following overview of Soviet foreign policy goals does not pretend to completeness. It reflects readings of studies by both Soviet and Western specialists and is intended to provide general background information. For more detailed discussions, the reader is directed to sources mentioned in those studies and in our bibliography.

[74] Robert Legvold, "The 26th Party Congress and Soviet Foreign Policy," in Seweryn Bialer and Thane Gustafson, eds., *Russia at the Crossroads: The 26th Congress of the CPSU* (London: George Allen & Unwin, 1982), 156-77, p. 162. See: G. Arbatov, "O Sovetsko-amerikanskikh otnosheniiakh" ["On Soviet-American Relations"], "Kommunist" [*Communist*], #3 (February 1973), p. 101-113.

[75] D. Nikolaev, "Informatsiia v sisteme mezhdunarodnykh otnoshenii. Organizatsiia i funktsionirovanie informatsionnykh organov vneshnepoliticheskogo mekhanizma SShA" [*Information in International Relations. The Organization and Operations of Information Agencies within the US Foreign Policy Establishment*] (Moscow: Mezhdunarodnye otnosheniia, 1978), p. 171. Primary concern here is devoted to computerized information management and foreign policy forecasting. The author discusses the compilation of top secret US National Intelligence Estimates, as well as the use and abuse of intelligence information by Presidents Kennedy, Johnson, and Nixon. The book, only 4000 copies of which were published, gives evidence of surprising depth of knowledge on the part of its author, who is well versed in English and had access to a very broad range of sources.

[76] Arbatov develops the Soviet position in *Soviet-American Relations: Progress and Problems* (Moscow: Novosti Press Agency, 1976), where he discusses "the far-reaching objective changes that have occurred in the world and in the United States" (p. 27). See, also: Nikolaev, pp. 10, 47, 166.

[77] Seweryn Bialer, "The International and Internal Contexts of the 26th Party Congress," in Bialer and Gustafson, eds., 7-38, p. 12.

[78] Bialer, p. 12.

[79] Arbatov, *Soviet-American Relations*, pp. 16-18. Emphasis in original. See also: V. F. Petrovskii, "Amerikanskaia vneshne-politicheskaia mysl'" [*American Foreign Policy Thinking*], (Moscow: Mezhdunarodnaia otnosheniia, 1976), pp. 177-80.

[80] In 1981 Arbatov assessed the situation in these terms: "[O]ne has to face the fact that the overall international situation has deteriorated seriously over the last several years." See: Arbatov and Oltmans, p. 1.

[81] Arbatov and Oltmans, p. 2. Of course, this position is inconsistent with previous assertions of historical inevitability. Such assertions were simply ignored, never reinterpreted.

[82] Bialer, p. 12.

[83] Legvold, p. 164.

[84] Wilensky, pp. 23-24.

[85] If perceptions of Soviet and American leaders could be so incommensurate on an issue as fundamental as detente when both sides had the political will to cooperate, perhaps one should not be surprised when the same phenomenon occurred, under the less favorable circumstances obtaining in late 1983, on an issue such as the destruction of the Korean airliner, which was less crucial to long-term superpower relations.

[86] Earlier we cited the opinion of both Gaddis ("The Rise, Fall and Future of Detente") and Tucker ("The Role of Defense in the Foreign Policy of the Reagan Administration") that America's military posture had virtually replaced diplomacy as the cornerstone of international relations.

[87] Legvold, pp. 164, 167.

[88] Roger Hamburg, "Political and Strategic Factors in Soviet Relations with the West: Soviet Perceptions," in Roger E. Kanet, ed., *Soviet Foreign Policy in the 1980s* (New York: Praeger, 1982), 197-230, pp. 198, 200.

[89] Hamburg, p. 205.

[90] Brown, "Soviet Political Culture through Soviet Eyes," p. 103.

[91] See: Joan Barth Urban, "The West European Communist Challenge to Soviet Foreign Policy," in Kanet, ed., *Soviet Foreign Policy in the 1980s*, 171-93.

[92] Legvold, pp. 170-71.

[93] Bialer, p. 16.

[94] Arbatov and Oltmans, pp. 83-84.

[95] Bialer, pp. 16, 17.

[96]One assessment of the Soviet Union's self-inflicted political damage utilized a soccer metaphor—kicking the ball into your own net (score one for the Americans). See: Peter Calvocoressi, "How Russia hit an 'own goal,'" *Sunday Times*, September 11, 1983, p. 16.

CHAPTER SIX

THE MANY GUISES OF TRUTH
(THE SOVIET VERSION)

Bureaucracies are seldom prepared to handle the public relations aspects of extraordinary crisis situations. Two recent cases in point have been provided by Three Mile Island and the chemical disaster at Union Carbide's plant in Bhopal, India. Governments are no exception, and their problems are compounded by recognition that a simple statement of fact is unlikely to address the perceived needs or opportunities inherent in the political ramifications of any crisis. In the case of the Korean airliner, the perceived Soviet need was extreme; for, no matter how contrived the American sense of crisis may have been, the Soviet crisis was real indeed.

Given what is known about Soviet information policy and decision-making procedures, it is not surprising that the immediate response to the furor stemming from the destruction of KAL Flight 007 was one of silence, then denials of any knowledge or actions by Soviet forces other than tracking the plane. The day following the tragedy, with the US making accusations of murder and the world clamoring for information, the Soviet government released a 90-word statement describing an attempted interception which concluded with the "unidentified" aircraft continuing its flight toward the Sea of Japan. With this, the Soviet Union began a massive campaign[1] of disinformation designed to obfuscate its action.

Although this may seem to be an overly judgmental opinion from which to begin a discussion of the Soviet reaction to US accusations, it is shared by Dallin, a respected observer who has been praised in the West by pro- and anti-conspiracy advocates alike. Dallin described the "handling of the episode" in the following manner:

> a characteristic syndrome of stonewalling, buckpassing, withholding and fabricating evidence, *lakirovka* [GLOSSING THINGS OVER-mkl], and what is commonly known as *vran'io* [PREVARICATING-mkl]—an enthusiastic, at times cavalier, at times excessively imaginative manipulation of the truth.... [T]hese traits do appear to be sufficiently pronounced, widespread, and significant in the Soviet Union to identify them

as relevant to the behavior of the actors in the Korean jetliner drama.[2]

In this chapter we will examine the Soviet propaganda campaign, isolating the primary arguments, the forms of proof, and the rhetorical strategies used by officials of the USSR and by the Soviet media. We begin with a statement of the basic goals—both strategic and tactical— that impinged upon the Soviet rhetorical campaign and sketch briefly the development of the Soviet position in broad outlines. After this overview will come a discussion of specific major themes that recurred throughout most public statements regarding the causes and consequences of the airliner's intrusion into Soviet airspace. Finally, the evidence brought to bear on the Soviet Union's fundamental allegation—that the South Korean jet was participating in an espionage mission sponsored by the United States—will be subjected to close analysis from both a rhetorical and a factual point of view.

Throughout this discussion one should bear in mind the fact that little specific information about the internal operations of the Soviet government or military is ever made public there. [Indeed, a US Foreign Broadcast Information Service analysis of the Soviet response to KAL remarked on the unusual extent of public comment by Soviet officials with regard to military and security procedures.][3] It is difficult for Americans—who routinely encounter news stories about the latest military hardware, read magazine articles exposing supposedly secret military operations around the globe, and listen to members of Congress annually debating the size of the Defense Department budget— to comprehend the information vacuum that exists in the USSR concerning such matters. The overwhelming amount of official discussion regarding KAL demonstrated to Soviet citizens the significance that the government attached to ensuring proper interpretation of the event: even the response of oral agitators throughout the country was organized almost immediately.[4] In this sense, the accuracy or inaccuracy of Soviet statements was not as significant as the very fact of such statements. Still, public ignorance about such information allowed Soviet propagandists to fabricate a response with impunity, confident that their citizenry had virtually no independent means of verification.[5]

As we have observed, the Soviet government said little of a substantive nature until September 6, when it first officially admitted having shot down the airplane. [Although typical, this situation was particularly remarkable given the attention the tragedy was receiving in the West.] The Soviets did not reveal a coherent position on the issue until their full-blown propaganda campaign was launched September 9, 1983, when Marshal Nikolai Ogarkov, Chief of Staff of the Soviet armed forces, led a rare press conference, allegedly to answer the world's questions about Soviet actions during the incident.

What was most significant about this press conference was that it took place at all. Only slightly less noteworthy is the fact that the press conference was conducted by a top-ranking military officer: as noted, the first direct domestic statement regarding the tragedy made in the Soviet Union by a political official occurred on September 28 (fully four weeks after the fact) when Soviet Premier Yuri Andropov included three paragraphs on US adventures such as KAL within a long statement decrying the dangers of American plans to deploy cruise missiles in Western Europe.[6]

The Ogarkov press conference was clearly intended for domestic as well as foreign consumption, illustrating the two audiences that Soviet planners had to contend with. On the one hand were the non-communist nations, outraged by what they perceived as an act of wanton disregard for human life. But far more critical was the Soviet domestic audience,[7] to which one must add the Warsaw Pact nations, other Soviet allies, and members of the Western European communist parties. The Soviet government televised 75 minutes of this two-hour press conference domestically and highlighted it in their news broadcasts (the televised version, which was taped and not live, omitted most of the question-and-answer period).

In our opinion, this unprecedented action demonstrates that the primary goal of Soviet propagandists was to convince leading elements among their own citizenry of the correctness of Soviet actions. This was true, in part, because citizen-perceived leadership infallibility has always played a fundamental role in Soviet governmental self-legitimation.[8] Furthermore, as Murty has commented, "[I]n times of ... insecurity, belief in the infallibility of the leaders, and identification with them, will give relief from anxieties and also strengthen identification with the leaders."[9] One of the curious contradictions within any society is the fact that intellectuals and other elites constitute the groups most likely to pay attention to the mass media and least likely to trust the information presented.[10] In this regard, Friedgut has observed that "[m]uch of the social control function exercised in the USSR is aimed at suppression of nonconformism among intelligentsia groups."[11] Noting that "the intellectuals are the most active critics of the system," Shlapentokh comments on the "ambivalent" attitude of the leadership toward "intellectuals in view of their contradictory role in socialist society."[12] Thus it is not surprising that information provided by Shlapentokh allows an observer to conclude that the legitimation function of Soviet propaganda increases sharply during a crisis and that, concomitantly, the amount of practical information also rises dramatically.[13]

Analysis of Soviet media reveals that, aside from the press conference, essentially the entire campaign was directed primarily to this domestic audience, including the allies, and only secondarily towards foreign consumption.[14] Nevertheless, the government could not be indifferent to the effect that adverse reaction worldwide might have on important foreign policy initiatives. Of primary importance, of course, was the effort to halt US emplacement of nuclear missiles in West Germany. Of lower priority, but not unrelated to this issue, were general efforts to limit US development of advanced military systems—including the MX missile.

Indeed, an important line of argument was developed over the first half of September to promote exactly that theme. This progression involved successive reinterpretations of the KAL flight—in US parlance, the application of an appropriate governmental 'spin.' According to the scant information released on the 2nd, no serious incident had even occurred. Rather, "an aircraft of unknown origin had entered Soviet airspace," Soviet Air Defense fighters had "attempted to render aid" to the plane, but the "intruder" ignored "the fighters' signals and warnings and continued its flight in the direction of the Sea of Japan" [TASS, *Pravda*, 2 Sep, p. 5]. The next day it was acknowledged that a South Korean aircraft had disappeared, and the US was raising a "ruckus" [shumikha] over the incident, even though US government statements proved that "American intelligence personnel had followed the flight as attentively as possible throughout its duration." Obviously, the incident was "a planned action." However, "TASS was authorized to express condolences regarding the casualties, but resolutely condemns those who, whether consciously or through criminal negligence, had allowed lives to be lost and were now trying to exploit the event for obscene political purposes" [TASS, *Pravda*, 3 Sep, p. 4]. As noted earlier, on the 4th *Pravda* cited an Australian newspaper account which speculated that KAL 007 might have been mistaken for a US "spyplane" ["The Provocateurs Cover Their Tracks,"*Pravda*, 4 Sep, p. 5].

On the 6th, two signed articles gave testimony to the next stage in the development of this line. Vitali Korionov quoted former NSA Director Bobby R. Inman: "This incident will make it much easier to achieve unity between the US and Western Europe on the need to take extreme measures in the area of security." Korionov commented that the goal of the American action was obvious:

Having purposely driven negotiations on limiting nuclear weapons in Europe into a dead end while endeavoring by whatever means necessary to deploy American 'Pershings' and cruise missiles, the US president is trying to heap all blame for the breakdown in negotiations on the Soviet Union. ["A Policy of Subverting Peace," *Pravda*, 6 Sep, p. 4].

V. Zakharov claimed that KAL was an

intentional, planned action with far-reaching political and military goals.... This devilish game was played consciously, without taking into account possible loss of human life. [The US] was apparently counting on demonstrating the possibility of carrying out unhindered intelligence flights over Soviet territory in the guise of civilian aircraft and, in case of failure, on turning it into an excuse for slanderous accusations against the Soviet Union ["What's Hiding Behind the 'Incident,'" *Pravda*, 6 Sep, p. 4].

The culmination of this strategy came one week later in an article by Vladimir Simonov entitled "Seven Days in September" [*Literaturnaia gazeta*, 14 Sep, p. 9]. Simonov suggested that the whole affair might have been a deliberate provocation designed to entrap the Soviet Union's PVO into destroying the South Korean intruder.

The Western intelligence agencies and those American officials who sent Flight 007 to its destruction must answer for the death of the passengers. Better than anyone else, the instigators of the espionage operation knew how it might end.
Perhaps they even wanted such an end?
Horrible thought. But it haunts me relentlessly as I re-read the paragraphs of President Reagan's speech delivered—no, dramatically performed—in front of the cameras on September 5.[15]

Thus, in a matter of days, the destruction of KAL 007 was transformed rhetorically from a non-event to an event that might have been an accident, but might have been intentional; to a planned spy mission; to a spy mission with the secondary motive of embarrassing the Soviet Union should military action be taken against the aircraft; to a provocation intentionally designed to trap the Soviet Union into destroying a passenger plane—so that the US could orchestrate such a furor worldwide that West Germany would be unable to resist US military demands. The culmination, of course, was Andropov's September 28 policy pronouncement.

> Even if someone had illusions as to the possible evolution for the better in the policy of the present American Administration, the latest developments have dispelled them. For the sake of its imperial ambitions it is going so far that one begins to doubt whether it has any brakes preventing it from crossing the mark before which any sober-minded person would stop.
>
> The sophisticated provocation masterminded by the United States special services with the use of a South Korean plane is an example of extreme adventurism in politics. We have elucidated the factual aspect of the action thoroughly and authentically. The guilt of its organizers, no matter how hard they may dodge and what false versions they may put forward, has been proved.
>
> The Soviet leadership expressed regret over the loss of human life resulting from that unprecedented, criminal subversion. It is on the conscience of those who ... masterminded and carried out the provocation, who literally on the following day hastily pushed through Congress colossal military spending and are now rubbing their hands with pleasure.[16]

These, then, were the two strategic goals of Soviet propagandists: (1) to maintain the image of the government as infallible leaders of the country;[17] and (2) stop the deployment of US Euromissiles, particularly in West Germany. The tactics that were employed in order to accomplish these strategic purposes entailed convincing the domestic audience that actions taken by PVO personnel were correct and justified. What was required was a means for evaluating events in light of communist ideology and prevailing policy—putting an interpretive 'spin' onto a factual problem and, thereby, exculpating the government in the process. The solution was to parcel out bits of information and misinformation as "more and more facts come to light every day" confirming the nefarious American plot. This might create the impression that an ongoing investigation was systematically unraveling the secret mission.

This rhetorical campaign developed three main themes: 1) KAL 007 flew over Soviet territory on an intelligence mission; 2) the Soviet Union was justified in shooting it down; and 3) the United States, particularly President Reagan, was exploiting the incident to its own political and military ends. The first two themes received almost equal play in news releases primarily intended for domestic audiences (those originally released in Russian) and those clearly intended for foreign audiences (originally released in languages other than Russian).

The notion that Reagan was using this incident to advance his budgetary priorities and reactionary policies received the most attention in Russian language material obviously intended for domestic consumption; this theme was not emphasized in the international arena.[18] The military aspect of this third theme focused mainly on the US defense budget, deployment of US weapons in Europe, and the proximity of the shootdown to East-West arms limitation talks in Geneva. Soviet commentators maintained that the Reagan Administration was stirring up "anti-Soviet hysteria" in order to gain an advantage with Congress, NATO, and in the disarmament talks. For this segment of the Soviet campaign the rhetorical style was hyperbolic and appeared calculated to remind the Soviet people that it was, as always, 'us against the world.' Such an approach served to bolster the spy plane theory that was to become the centerpiece of the Soviet effort.

Having finally admitted shooting down the airliner, the Soviets quickly attempted to prove that their military was justified in taking the action it did. Over the next three days legal experts appeared in print and were interviewed on radio. On the one hand, they cited Soviet law, international law, and ICAO rules regarding interception of intruding aircraft.[19] Various commentators asked, rhetorically, what the United States would do if a foreign jet were to wander into the airspace over Los Alamos and were to behave as the Soviets claimed the Korean airliner had. Officials and commentators repeatedly declared that the Soviet Union, like any other sovereign nation, was entitled to defend its airspace and would continue to do so.[20]

Justification of their actions, however, rested only partly on a technical legal position; judging from the amount of air time and newspaper space devoted to the subject, the Soviets relied primarily on their contention that the jetliner had flown over the Soviet Union on an intelligence mission planned and executed by the United States. It was in focusing on this fundamental theme of the propaganda campaign—

the allegation that KAL 007 was a spy plane—that Soviet officials and commentators most frequently resorted to dezinformatsia.[21]

The spy plane charge was developed around three main arguments: (1) the plane could not have strayed accidentally; (2) the airliner could have been warned by American and Japanese air traffic control; and (3) the behavior of the aircraft proved conclusively that it was hostile. Each of these arguments will be treated in turn.

CLAIM #1: KAL COULD NOT HAVE STRAYED ACCIDENTALLY

Soviet officials and the Soviet press were adamant that the aircraft could not have strayed accidentally into restricted airspace. A great deal of attention was given to the sophisticated, redundant navigation systems aboard the jetliner. For example, on September 5, *Pravda* quoted an Alitalia pilot familiar with the inertial navigation system (INS) of the Boeing 747:

> Let us listen, for example, to the opinions of Italian pilot C. Petrosellini, who captained such a plane for 11 years. "Leaving aside emotions and taking the purely technical aspects of the matter, the possibility of that type of plane leaving its assigned course, particularly for a long period, is absolutely out of the question," the pilot points out. The flight is constantly monitored by three computers which, in turn, check one another. Moreover, these computers are linked to the autopilot, and the captain can precisely determine the airliner's coordinates at any moment. "The possibility of an accident or breakdown of this monitoring system is absolutely out of the question," C. Petrosellini stresses.[22]

In a similar vein, on September 7, 1983, Soviet commentator A. Palladin wrote in *Izvestiia*:

> [A]ccording to *The New York Times* this type of aircraft is run by electronic equipment which has never let pilots down and which can't let them down because it is triply redundant. Consequently, only the person seated at the controls or those who deliberately fed distorted parameters for the usual route into the onboard computers could have taken the Boeing 747 five hundred kilometers off course deep into Soviet airspace.

The author of this passage paints a black and white scenario in which only two possibilities exist: either the navigation system failed

144

or the 'error' was no error, but was deliberately planned. Since the navigation system could not fail, the only possible explanation is a deliberate act. The false dilemma depicted in this excerpt is characteristic of the basic Soviet argument.[23] This selection also illustrates another characteristic of their rhetoric, which will be discussed more fully in Chapter Seven: a tendency to quote the foreign press to bolster one's own arguments.

Palladin is not the only Soviet commentator to express the view that the jetliner's navigation system was infallible. Similar remarks appeared in *Krasnaia zvezda* the next day, September 8:

Who sent this aircraft, outfitted with the most sophisticated equipment that would <u>rule out the slightest possibility of its</u> "losing its bearings" or "<u>straying" into Soviet airspace,</u> and for what purpose did they do this?

Following the Russian proverb, **POVTOREN'E—MAT' UCHEN'JA** ("repetition is the mother of learning"), *Izvestiia* printed another article with the same theme on September 9:

The first thing that comes to mind is a problem with the navigational equipment or, similarly, malfunction in the computer that controls the automatic pilot. However, as knowledgeable people confirm, both hypotheses are extremely unlikely in the case of a Boeing 747.[24]

At this point, *Izvestiia* reprinted the Petrosellini quotation from the September 5 issue of *Pravda* thereby illustrating still another characteristic of Soviet propaganda: repetition of material which originally appeared in another Soviet forum. This tactic also is explored more fully below.

There is no reason to assume that the Soviet writers would know of the data collected by NASA and the FAA, statistics which show how often airliners equipped with triple navigation systems identical to that installed in KAL 007 have flown significantly off course over the North Atlantic.[25] Nor is there any reason to assume that either the Soviet writers or their audience have any experience with computers. Undoubtedly, this lack of knowledge contributes to the mystique of technology, which makes the false dilemmas used by these writers plausible. But computers can and do fail, and the article ignores the possibility of human error other than misprogramming.[26]

Of course, it also suits the Soviet Union's purpose to tout the reliability of computers, particularly those on board the Korean airliner. Non-conspiratorial explanations such as those suggested by Sayle, Hersh, and other investigators would not fit the world view espoused by the Soviet propagandists. Given the need to reinforce the infallibility of their government's actions, deliberate misprogramming of the computers on a civilian aircraft, in order to obtain military intelligence, makes a much better story.

The Soviets also stressed the 'waypoint' reporting required of all airliners flying the North Pacific routes. This idea was propounded initially by Marshal Ogarkov in his September 9 press conference:

> [T]his international route has been provided with modern technological means for air traffic safety. Approximately 12,000 aircraft fly there annually. The US is responsible for air traffic control along this international route from Alaska to Kamchatka; the Japanese are responsible beyond that point. Special checkpoints (NEBI, NEEVI, NIPPI, etc.) have been established along the way. Scheduled flights are <u>required to fix their position over each one of them</u> and report to ground control, which should <u>strictly monitor their passage</u>. One asks: Given the <u>absence of such waypoint reports</u> from the South Korean aircraft and, more importantly, the <u>absence of the plane itself</u>, why didn't American personnel sound an alarm immediately? So far no answer has been provided for this question either.

This point was repeated three days later, September 12, in an interview of General-polkovnik Moskvitelev, Commander of Aviation of the USSR air defense forces, conducted on the Moscow Domestic Television show *I Serve the Soviet Union*. General Moskvitelev offered the following assessment:

> The aircraft has <u>five radios</u> set to various assigned frequencies and communications channels. Finally, as I have already indicated, it has a mapping radar which provides the pilot with a complete picture of the terrain over which he is flying; moreover, this was highly contrastive terrain. Its route was supposed to be over the ocean, but <u>they were flying over land the entire time</u>.
> The crew was required to communicate with ground stations, and, once it deviated from its assigned course, <u>US or Japanese controllers should have informed their Soviet counterparts that</u>

this was a civilian aircraft with passengers on board. But this wasn't done, even though there was more than enough time.

Both of these passages demonstrate seemingly extensive knowledge about the guidance systems on board the KAL plane, and about the route; at the same time, they reveal a lack of knowledge, whether feigned or real, about the reporting system on NOPAC Route 20. Way-points are arbitrary locations over open water approximately forty fly-ing minutes apart.[27] The reporting system does not require the pilot to compute his position at each location. Rather, those coordinates are programmed into the INS computer while the aircraft is still on the ground, and the computer alerts the co-pilot when the plane is sup-posed to be approaching one of the check-points; he then radios arrival at the point, reports other technical data, and estimates time of arrival at the next waypoint. As a matter of practice, these positions are not recalculated because the INS usually is incredibly accurate. Neverthe-less, the citation of massive amounts of information, particularly information which cannot be verified by auditors, has been identified as one of the hallmarks of conspiratist rhetoric.[28]

Unless KAL was a spy plane, the co-pilot would naturally assume that the waypoint had been reached when the alert light came on. With no reason to believe that the INS was incorrectly programmed, he would radio his position report. And air traffic controllers, who were receiving the reports at approximately the correct times, would have no cause for alarm.[29]

To assume otherwise would imply that the air traffic control has the plane on radar at all times. That is patently untrue, and Soviet officials should know that. The problem with the long Pacific routes is that the plane is not observable on radar for 2200 miles: from the point it passed "out of Anchorage radar coverage there was no other [civilian] radar available for monitoring the aircraft's flight until it approached Japan."[30] Indeed, that is the reason for the check-points. Yet, in justi-fying their actions, officials and commentators in the USSR alleged that the opposite was the case. Marshal Ogarkov claimed, in his September 9 press conference:

By the time our radar systems had picked it up at a point 800 km northeast of Petropavlovsk-Kamchatsky, it had already veered about 500 km off course. But during all this time the flight was within radar range of American air traffic control and the US air defense system.

At a later point in the press conference, an unidentified Soviet official commented:

Why, if this was an ordinary passenger flight, didn't the American civil aviation service, which monitors flights in its zone, sound the alarm as soon as the aircraft had left its assigned path and headed for Soviet territory? It is impossible that they knew nothing about this.

On occasion, these same spokesmen seem to confuse civilian and military radar in the region. It should be noted that Soviet practice does not make the same distinctions between civilian and military radar that other governments make (and, interestingly, neither does their "Law on the USSR State Border," which, contrary to ICAO regulations, treats military and civilian aircraft identically). Nevertheless, in the attempt to prove their point, the Soviets move back and forth between the civilian and military tracking capabilities of the United States indiscriminately.[31] The fact of the matter is, the truth in this instance is irrelevant; it serves the Soviet official purpose to confuse the issue and to claim the airliner was under continuous radar observation. Given our understanding of Soviet public knowledge, such a claim probably has salience for the domestic audience.

Soviet commentators were no doubt aided on this point by Secretary of State George Shultz's failure to make clear the type of information in the possession of the US. In his September 1 statement, made only hours after the tragedy, Secretary Shultz spoke repeatedly of what the US "knew" about the incident (which appeared to be a great deal), thus giving the impression that the information was gained from real-time monitoring of Soviet activity. Subsequently, to be sure, the US government has steadfastly denied that any monitoring was done in real time; these denials came too late to be convincing.[32]

CLAIM #2: KAL COULD HAVE BEEN WARNED

The Soviets also refer to powerful US radar and intelligence installations in the Kamchatka-Sakhalin region to 'prove' their second major argument: that the pilot of the jetliner could have been warned by the US or Japan. Marshal Ogarkov concludes the passage quoted above:

[A]nd what about the US air defense system? They could not possibly either "lose" the aircraft or fail to notice such a huge deviation from its assigned route. Such a possibility must be ruled out. So the question arises: Why didn't they correct the aircraft's course if this was an ordinary scheduled flight?

Ogarkov was continuing a prevalent theme. We have already quoted portions of an article by political observer A. Bovin, which had appeared in *Izvestiia* the preceding day, September 8:

> Occasionally one hears the following reply: the portion of the route along the Soviet border lies beyond the range of ATC radar. But here is what the *Washington Post* reports: "The Federal Aviation Administration and the US Department of Defense had an agreement, whereby long range military radar in Alaska would be used to verify that passenger aircraft were not off course when they left Alaska and began the long flight along the Soviet border. Federal Aviation Administration officials reported that a similar agreement exists between Japanese civil aviation authorities and the Japanese armed forces." Consequently, there were people who could have helped the "straying" aircraft.

The conclusion drawn in this passage does not follow from the *Washington Post*'s information. The agreement referred to in this statement only provided for determining whether passenger aircraft were on course at the beginning of the flight across the Pacific.[33] As a matter of fact, US military radar at King Salmon, Alaska did register KAL's course deviation, although this information was not officially reported to the air traffic controllers at Anchorage.[34] In any event, the military's responsibility would have ended once the plane left its radar coverage, approximately 175-200 miles from the Alaskan mainland. Bovin's use of the term 'long-range' (s bol'shim radiusom deistviia) in the quoted passage implies coverage over the entire route, and thus plays on the ignorance of his readers. However, by the time the airliner entered Soviet airspace, any military responsibility for its progress was long past (assuming, of course, it was not a spy plane). At the other end, Japanese air traffic control never had the airliner on radar; and the Japanese military did not have time to determine that they were "seeing" KAL 007 on their radar at Wakkanai before the "blip" disappeared from the screen.[35]

Two days earlier, O. Pilyugin, writing in *Krasnaia zvezda*, quoted *The New York Times* regarding US surveillance installations in the Western Pacific. He then concluded:

All of these details ... are cited here solely to reinforce the question now being asked by many politicians, public figures, experts, and the press: Why didn't US and Japanese air traffic controllers, who followed the South Korean aircraft throughout its entire flight, warn the crew that they were violating the airspace of the USSR?

Regarding the RC-135, known to be in the vicinity, Pilyugin wrote,

If it was doing its job, the RC-135, with its powerful electronic equipment, could not have failed to notify a civilian aircraft and Japanese ATC of an accidental incursion into the airspace of the USSR.

The casual observer cannot appreciate the extent to which this whole propaganda campaign was fabricated without knowing that the Soviet government had made no serious mention of the RC-135 prior to September 6. However, after Congressman Wright told the whole world about it, they began to recoup their public relations losses at home.[36]

The Soviet position assumes monitoring in real time, which, the US press pointed out in their descriptions of the RC-135, is not the function of the reconnaissance plane[37] or the surveillance stations in the Pacific. Most of the information is taped and relayed to NSA headquarters in Maryland, where it is analyzed at a later time.[38] In its intelligence gathering function, the RC-135, and, to some extent, the land-based surveillance installations, resemble nothing so much as a Great White Shark, gathering in everything that falls within its programmed parameters.

Since their own system does not distinguish civilian from military radar, it is not surprising that the Soviets would fail to consider such a distinction in their interpretation of American actions. [Moreover, it is difficult to accept claims that US military installations could not "see" the airliner or take action to warn it, even at three o'clock in the morning.] The manner in which the Soviets take rhetorical advantage of this blurring of function is apparent in the movement back and forth between the two kinds of radar installations, illustrated by the following passage from the September 9 press conference. The speaker was not identified.

The U.S. chargé d'affaires in Moscow, in his first contact with the Soviet Ministry of Foreign Affairs, alluded to the fact that radar contact with the plane had been maintained until the very end. Despite giving the correct approximate time and location of the aircraft's disappearance, he declared at the same time that radio contact was lost at a point nearly 600 km away from the actual place where the aircraft disappeared.

The US, of course, claimed that the data was not collected in real time and, thus, had to be reconstructed. This conforms with what is publicly admitted about the *modus operandi* of the RC-135 and US military tracking stations in the region. The last comment cited above reflects the fact that the Japanese air traffic controllers initially thought the airliner was on course, based on the position report radioed in at NIPPI, and thus, when it became apparent that the aircraft had disappeared, assumed it had gone down in the Pacific Ocean somewhere along Route 20.

Incidentally, this section of the press conference contains an interesting assertion on the part of Soviet officials. The speaker in the passage above claims that ten hours went by, and "it was only then that an Assistant Secretary of State in Washington and the US chargé d'affaires ad interim in Moscow almost simultaneously inquired if we knew anything about the aircraft's fate." At yet another point in the press conference, Georgi Kornienko, First Deputy Minister of Foreign Affairs stated in part:

There exist communications between Tokyo and Khabarovsk on a fixed shortwave frequency, and Tokyo ATC is linked to Moscow by telegraph. So there are more than enough communications channels, but Japanese personnel did not utilize any of them to make any kind of report or inquiry about the flight of this aircraft. The question arises: Why weren't these channels employed even when—as they could plainly see—this aircraft suddenly disappeared from Japanese radar screens in the vicinity of Sakhalin?

This claim is absolutely refuted by published transcripts of ATC communications between Japan, the US, and the Soviet Union.[39] At 21:05 on August 31, less than two hours after KAL 007 was last heard from and at the beginning of the distress phase, a message was relayed to the Khabarovsk rescue coordination center and the Khabarovsk aeronautical fixed station. Then there was a delay, occasioned by the fact that the Japanese ATC thought the airliner had gone down along its prescribed route; however, a message requesting information was sent to Khabarovsk and Irkutsk (ATC) and Moscow Civil Aviation Authority at 02:02 a.m. on September 1, seven hours after the last communication with KAL 007. No reply was received and several subsequent messages were sent.

Nevertheless, the scenario as painted by Soviet commentators and in the Ogarkov press conference—a flight straying 500 km off course over the airspace of the USSR while it was being monitored by US civilian and military radar, and no one even bothered to call either the South Korean pilot or Soviet officials—enabled the Soviets to don a cloak of righteous indignation. Thus, they might appear to their civilian populace as not only justified, but, indeed, as the victims of this wanton act of provocation and disregard for human life.

CLAIM #3: KAL 007 WAS A SPY PLANE

It is clear that the overriding goal of the Soviet propagandists was to shift the blame for the shootdown from the USSR to the United States. The *piece de resistance* in this effort was their third argument: KAL 007 was in the airspace of the USSR on an intelligence mission planned and executed by the CIA. Soviet political analysts and commentators focused on this issue, recounting every incident of US planes overflying the territory of the USSR, beginning with the U-2 in 1960.[40] They reminded their audiences of a previous incursion by another Korean airliner, KAL 902 in 1978, when, they claimed, the Korean pilot attempted to evade the Soviet interceptors and was forced to land only after being fired upon. Comparisons between this incident and KAL 007 were drawn and commented upon.

The 'evidence' that the jetliner was on a spy mission occupied more column inches in the Soviet press and more air time on Soviet television and radio than any other aspect of the incident. Although a variety of charges surfaced in Soviet media, the spy theory revolves around three alleged behaviors of the airliner: (1) it altered course to fly over sensitive military areas on Sakhalin Island; (2) it failed to acknowledge all attempts to contact it or attract its attention; and (3) it was flying without lights.

Regarding the first of these points, little is actually known. One technical explanation for any apparent alteration is offered in the *ICAO REPORT* and by Sayle: it could be an anomaly in the radar track caused by the approach of an aircraft to a position almost directly above the radar installation following its course.[41] In any event, no clear evidence of such a course change is to be found in the transcripts of the Soviet fighter pilots talking to their ground control. And none of the governments involved has ever provided actual radar data.

An early map of KAL's route that appeared in Soviet newspapers (September 3) clearly depicted a course alteration over Sakhalin; in retrospect, it appears that this map represents the first positive step toward the formation of a coherent Soviet position—an evasion attempt would certainly reflect conscious response by the KAL 007 crew. But the notion of planned course changes, including allegations that KAL 007 rendezvoused with the RC-135 prior to its first intrusion into Soviet territory, was conceived fairly late in the propaganda process.

Ogarkov made much of this contention, showing a definite change of course over Sakhalin on the huge map used as a back drop to the press conference. Aside from fervent US denials of authenticity—which one can hardly take at face value because they are obviously self serving—two facts support the independent conclusion that Ogarkov's map, and the charges it supposedly substantiates, were fabricated. First of all, KAL's course as described by the SU-15 fighter pilot is fully 60 degrees different than the maneuver claimed by Ogarkov.[42] Ogarkov was also contradicted on this score less than two weeks later when a map published in the Soviet press depicted the airliner's route with no exaggerated turn over Sakhalin; in fact, the track on this map nearly duplicates the flight path depicted on September 6th at the Emergency Session of the United Nations Security Council. Second, in order to forestall any possibility that US intelligence could demonstrate KAL had already left Soviet territory prior to its destruction, Ogarkov's map also contained a false time for the shooting: it showed 1824 GMT, two minutes earlier than the time indicated on the voice-activated tape of Soviet fighter pilots.[43]

Allegations that the airliner was flying with its ANOs turned off, and that it failed to acknowledge Soviet attempts to contact it, are treated much more extensively. The Soviets maintained from the beginning that KAL 007 did not acknowledge any of their attempts to communicate with it. This, they claim, was the primary basis for their assumption that it was a hostile intruder. In contrast, US analysts concluded that there was no indication that the airline crew had any idea they were being intercepted. The *ICAO REPORT* (p. 56) agreed.

In propounding their spy plane theory, the Soviets go to great lengths to stress the extensive procedures used to make contact with and/or to attract the attention of the intruder. They first employed this strategy in the TASS statement of September 3: "Soviet air defense aircraft were scrambled. On several occasions they tried to establish contact using generally accepted signals.... However, the intruder ignored all this."

As time passed, the descriptions of the actions of the interceptor pilots became more detailed. In a September 4 Radio Moscow interview, subsequently published in revised form in *Izvestiia, Pravda*, and *Krasnaia zvezda*, General Romanov detailed the procedures used:

> This means, first and foremost, establishing radio contact with the intruder on the 121.5 MHz emergency frequency using the standard call signal, then repeating that call on the other emergency frequency. But <u>despite all his attempts</u>, the Soviet pilot couldn't make radio contact with the intruder, since the intruder's crew would not respond to the radio signals. Then the pilot resorted to <u>visual signals, i.e. maneuvering his aircraft: rocking from wing to wing</u>. In addition, our interceptor was flying with its lights on, <u>flashing them in order to draw the intruder's attention</u>. But neither rocking his wings nor flashing his lights produced the desired result.

These detailed descriptions were reiterated at the September 9 press conference: "Measures were taken by the aircraft, drawing close and dipping their wings and signalling with their lights."

The Soviets further claimed that, failing to attract the plane's attention by other means, the first intercepting aircraft (the SU-15 pilot, identified in the transcripts as 805) "gave four bursts of tracer shells from his cannon. This was clearly seen by <u>the second pilot</u>,... who during that period, at that moment, <u>reported to the command post that he observed the four bursts of tracer shells</u> along the path of the intruder aircraft."

As was demonstrated in Chapter Four, these claims of elaborate interception attempts are refuted by the transcripts of the Soviet fighter pilots. In contrast to the transcripts, Soviet commentators gave the impression that the attempts at interception, including visual contact with the intruding aircraft, continued for the entire two-hour overflight. On September 8, an article in *Izvestiia* reported: "[T]he attempts to make contact with the plane—by waggling wings and flashing lights—went on for two hours." Ogarkov stated on September 9: "[W]e were busy with this aircraft for two hours." At the same press conference, an unidentified speaker commented, "For two hours we struggled, in essence, to make the aircraft land...." There is no evidence of this in the transcripts, which cover the entire forty-nine minute period of the interception over Sakhalin. But the statement recalls an earlier claim that KAL had been flying over land continuously for these two hours, when in fact most of that time it had been flying over the international waters of the Sea of Okhotsk, which separates the Kamchatka Peninsula from Sakhalin Island. The Soviets made no effort to intercept the airliner during this period.

Concerning the first interception attempt over Kamchatka, Boris Reznik reported in his September 12 *Izvestiia* article, "How It Was":

> Our pilots demonstrated restraint and coolness in carrying out their assignment to intercept the target in flight. <u>Several times they had to come very close to the intruder in order to draw attention to themselves</u>. At night, in <u>poor visibility</u>, this entailed great risk.

The Soviet government asserted as much in its presentation to the ICAO investigative team. In section 2.12.2 of the *ICAO REPORT*, one finds:

> When overflying Kamchatka Peninsula, KE007 was intercepted by fighter aircraft of the USSR Air Defense Command for the purpose of identifying and compelling the aircraft to land at an aerodrome in USSR territory in accordance with the laws of the USSR. The interim report from the Soviet Accident Investigation Commission stated:
>
> <u>"The intruder aircraft was flying with its navigation and strobe lights switched off</u> and the cabin lights extinguished. The Air Defence fighters <u>flew up to the aeroplane, flashed their lights on and off and rocked their wings</u>. The aeroplane did not react to the fighter signals or the <u>interrogations transmitted on the international emergency frequency of 121.5 MHz from both the ground and the air</u>, but continued its flight and departed in the direction of the Sea of Okhotsk." (p. 41)

Despite these affirmations, however, US intelligence officials contend that the interceptors over Kamchatka never came closer than twenty miles to the Korean airliner.[44]

155

In several instances, some of them quoted above, Soviet officials and commentators claimed that both ground control and the interceptor pilots had attempted to contact the airliner on the emergency frequency of 121.5 MHz. Yet, as the ICAO indicated, there is no clear indication in the transcripts that such an attempt was made. More importantly, the Air Navigation Commission stated in their report that no calls on 121.5 MHz were picked up by the various stations that monitor that frequency nor by the Search and Rescue Satellite System (SARSAT), which also monitors the emergency channel.[45]

In their attempts to demonstrate the lengths to which the air defense command went to properly intercept the Korean plane, Soviet spokesmen often contradicted themselves. For example, with respect to the tracer bullets, Marshal Ogarkov maintained that the cannon bursts were fired along the flight path of the intruder. During his television interview, the 805 pilot contradicts this claim himself: "The second thing is that I fired four bursts of tracer shells right across his nose. At night they are visible many kilometers away. And this was right next to him. I dipped my wings...." (emphasis added). Interesting, but patently untrue. The pilot also contradicts the reports he had made during the interception: "[T]he aircraft was in total darkness. Even on the side of the dark area of the sky there were no signs of any illumination on the aircraft." Obviously, even at this late date, there was little coordination of the propaganda effort.[46]

Asked how the Soviet radar operators and pilots could mistake a Boeing 747 for an RC-135, Marshal Ogarkov responded, "The distance between [KAL 007 and the fighter] was such that it was difficult to discern these differences." Ogarkov ignored all of the alleged approaches made to signal the airliner. Indeed, the *ICAO REPORT* (p. 43) concluded, "[V]isual identification [procedures] should have resulted in a recognition of the type of aircraft involved as well as the civilian airline markings."

The Soviet claim that they were unable to identify KAL 007 as a civilian airliner rests on their allegation that the plane was flying without navigation lights. This, too, is a position they took from the beginning: "In violation of international regulations, the plane flew without navigation lights...."[47] In his September 4 interview, General Romanov had maintained: "The aircraft was flying without lights...." According to the "Soviet Government Statement" released late on the evening of September 6 and published or broadcast via all major Soviet media, "when they terminated the flight of the intruder, the Soviet pilots could not know that it was a civilian aircraft. It was <u>flying without navigation lights,</u> in the dead of night, <u>under conditions of poor visibility.</u>" Another *Pravda* article printed September 8 made a similar statement: "The measures taken were even more justified because the outline of the aircraft, <u>which was flying with its navigation lights extinguished</u> and which made no attempt to communicate [with our fighters], looks very much like an American RC-135 spy plane." Marshal Ogarkov reiterated the claim September 9: "<u>The Soviet aircraft did not see the lights of the Korean aircraft....</u>"

As has been demonstrated, the arguments propounded by the Soviet government simply are not supported by the evidence found in the KAL Tapes. At 18:10:51, pilot 805 reports, "Roger, the (target's strobe) light is blinking." At 18:18:34, one hears, "The ANOs are burning. The (strobe) light is flashing." At 18:21:35, 805 reiterates, "The target's (strobe) light is blinking."[48]

At one point, when a reporter asked why the transcripts refer to the Soviet pilots as having noted the flashing of lights on the target plane, Marshal Ogarkov responded, "I can comment on that. <u>The second aircraft,</u> which was following behind the first Soviet aircraft, <u>saw these lights on the first aircraft and reported this to ground control.</u>" This statement, too, is simply untrue.

In several instances, the Soviets allege a similarity in appearance between the Boeing 747 and the RC-135, a modified Boeing 707. In an interview on Moscow Domestic Television, September 10, General Moskvitelev made the following claim:

> The RC-135 reconnaissance aircraft and the Boeing 747 passenger aircraft are <u>sister ships.</u> They have the <u>same shape and dimensions,</u> and the <u>same flight speed,</u> as well. In the air <u>they can be distinguished only during daylight,</u> visually, and at close range. It's absolutely impossible for a pilot to do this at night.

A similar argument was made by Boris Reznik in his September 12 *Izvestiia* article "How It Was":

> The interceptor assumed a parallel course. Through the canopy of his cockpit the pilot saw the big, dark silhouette of an aircraft very similar in outline to an American RC-135 reconnaissance aircraft.... Along with military specialists we looked at photographs and drawings of these aircraft. An RC-135 has the same

swept-back wings as a Boeing, the same shape, and its engines are slung from pylons in the same way. In addition, their technical capabilities are nearly identical.

This last passage is internally contradictory. If Soviet pilots had gotten close enough (as had been claimed in previously quoted material) to see the "big, dark silhouette" and had positioned themselves to perform risky intercept approaches, they were close enough to see the characteristic hump of the Boeing 747, a type of aircraft used almost exclusively for civilian purposes.[49] They should also have noted its considerably larger size.[50]

Viktor Belenko, a former Soviet pilot and training instructor for MiG fighters and the SU-15, has stated that Soviet personnel do not receive training in aircraft identification and could not be expected to recognize the physical difference between an RC-135 and a Boeing 747, much less a 707 (of which the RC is a structural variant).[51]

Nevertheless, even without close visual identification, it is difficult to imagine that the Soviet PVO ground personnel seriously believed that the airliner was an RC-135, regardless of what else they might have thought it was. Soviet radar operators routinely track RC-135's in their mission orbits off the coasts of Kamchatka and Sakhalin and should be familiar with their flight characteristics. Indeed, they probably rely on those flight characteristics to identify the RC-135's on their radar screens.[52] The RC-135 moves more slowly than an airliner, particularly while on a mission, and generally flies in a figure-eight pattern. Moreover, once the SU-15 pilot reported seeing the jetliner's lights, it should have been obvious that the airplane was not a military craft.[53]

The primary reason the interceptor pilot did not verbally identify the airliner as such was either because he never was close enough or because identification was not his purpose. To the extent that, from the very beginning of their radar contact with KAL 007, the Soviets regarded it as a hostile intruder on an intelligence mission, the latter reason is probably the accurate one. This notion is further supported by the fact that the 805 pilot probably did get within two kilometers of the airliner, at one point was probably in front of it for a brief period, and then was abeam (flying parallel with it; the Russian incorporates the meaning of 'neck-and-neck', as in a horse race)[54]—again for a brief period. This should have been sufficient to reveal the distinctive characteristics of the 747, even in a 40% moonlit sky. (The Soviets make much of the cloud cover and the darkness of that night; however, at its altitude of 33,000-35,000 feet, the airliner was probably above the clouds, with the moon almost half full).[55] The comments of the Soviet pilots during their television interview, quoted above, indicate that, on one side, at least, the airliner was not in darkness.[56]

Thus, it is difficult to conclude that the alleged confusion of KAL 007 with the RC-135 was anything other than a convenient rhetorical device, taking advantage of the fact that the Soviet population could not corroborate or refute the information they were receiving.[57] We have been able to determine from Voice of America transcripts that in its broadcasts to the Soviet Union the station repeatedly mentioned the presence of the RC-135 on September 4 and 5, but not at all thereafter. Accordingly, it is highly probable that Western broadcasting failed to provide the factual information that might have refuted Soviet disinformation on this important point. This is significant because to a great extent the credibility of all Soviet domestic propaganda regarding the KAL incident depends on the alleged rendezvous.[58]

SUMMATION

There is little doubt in the minds of most Western experts that the Soviets did, in fact, regard the KAL plane as a reconnaissance aircraft on some sort of intelligence mission.[59] Having acted on this assumption, Soviet officials were, in all likelihood, unprepared for the vehemence of the world-wide reaction. They may have also been startled to learn that there were 269 people aboard. This might account for the fact that prior to the Ogarkov press conference they never told their population how many had died.[60] These two factors—the Western public outcry and the actual number of deaths—undoubtedly created a rhetorical situation in which justification of the attack was imperative. Soviet officials assumed an air of righteous indignation and a tone of injury, and, after a period of 'stonewalling,' undertook a full-scale campaign of propaganda and disinformation. The preceding discussion has set forth some of the more flagrant instances of <u>dezinformatsia</u>: the discounting of all possibilities for accidental overflight; the deliberate confusion of civilian and military radar functions and capabilities; the false claim that the airliner was flying without lights; the exaggeration of what was, at best, an abbreviated attempt at non-lethal interception; and, finally, the confusion of the Boeing 747 with the smaller, slower RC-135.

People in the Soviet Union know much more about the West than Westerners know about them. In large part, this is due to the greater openness of Western societies. However, that very openness makes it difficult to understand how the Soviet officials thought they could "sell" their story to indignant non-communist nations. It seems only logical (as analysis confirms) that the propaganda campaign would be aimed primarily at their own domestic audience, since no average Soviet citizen could know how much of the information being provided was false. Any Westerners who could be convinced put them that much ahead. Indeed, the Soviet Union did make points with some: the P.Q. Mann article in *Defence Attaché* and the David Pearson article in *The Nation* appear to accept much of the Soviet version of events.

In mounting their propaganda campaign, the Soviets relied on a number of techniques, some of which are familiar to Western sovietologists. A frequent tactic is the use of unanswered questions, which appear in a number of the passages quoted above. Sometimes the questions are grouped together, as in this selection from a September 7 article in *Krasnaia zvezda*:

> Reagan has failed to respond to the questions that must be answered by those who sent the spyplane into Soviet airspace. Why did it veer 500 km off course and stay off course for two and a half hours? Why, <u>once it saw the Soviet fighters</u>, didn't it leave Soviet airspace or land at a prescribed location? Why was it <u>flying without identification lights</u>? Why did it <u>make such an effort to penetrate secret areas</u>? And, finally, why didn't the <u>United States</u>, which <u>was monitoring the flight</u>, intercede during this time?

The fact that the questions are not answered is, of course, the proof that the airliner was on an intelligence mission. This is a tactic frequently used by Western conspiratists, particularly the radical right.

Sometimes the questions are presented in a sequence, separated by commentary, as illustrated by this example from a Moscow television broadcast of September 6:

> First question: Why was the aircraft flying on an incorrect course over Soviet territory? It was a Boeing 747 whose navigation equipment made it <u>technologically impossible to get lost</u>. So say Western pilots who have flown on this aircraft. <u>There was malicious intent and the President must know this</u>, or at least admit it; but he keeps silent.

Second question: Why was the aircraft's course not corrected on instructions from the ground? <u>US and Japanese air traffic controllers had the flight under continuous observation</u>. Why didn't they correct it? <u>Here, too, there was malicious intent, and the President must know this</u>, or at least admit it; but he keeps silent....

Sixth question: Why were no attempts made to contact the Soviet side? It is easy to pick up a telephone and call Moscow. <u>There was sufficient time—two and one-half hours. And the President surely knows this</u>, but he keeps silent.

This selection represents still another rhetorical device frequently used by the Soviets—repetition. The repetition of the statements about President Reagan is an obvious persuasive technique; each reiteration makes the silence more ominous. The same can be said for the device as a governing strategy; these questions do not vary much from article to article, commentary to commentary, and with each restatement the lack of response becomes more pronounced.[61]

Soviet spokesmen not only repeated questions addressed to the United States, they also recounted their own version of events, with increasing embellishment. A favorite technique of the Soviet press is the reporting, as news, of a story, interview, or commentary which appeared in another forum. Occasionally, a Soviet journal reprinted its own stories and commentaries, usually a day or so later, often as part of another story. For example, on September 4, General Semion Romanov (Chief of Staff of the Air Defense Forces) was interviewed for Radio Moscow by V. Ostrovsky, political observer for Novosti Press Agency. This interview was published as an article with Romanov's by-line in *Pravda* on September 5, under the title, "Political Provocation with Long-Range Goals". On September 6, both *Izvestiia* and *Krasnaia zvezda* published a modified version of the interview under the title, "Provocation with Long-Range Goals"; Radio Moscow broadcast a news item in which the interview was quoted; and Ostrovsky published a column in *Krasnaia zvezda* based on that same interview. As is often the case with Western conspiratists, these repetitions gain credibility both with the auditor and with the rhetor: the repeated items often become the 'proof' of further arguments.[62]

The Soviets frequently published the same text with differing titles in three or four newspapers. In those instances, *Pravda* or *Izvestiia* would print the fullest version, with the remaining national dailies deleting one or two internal paragraphs. The cumulative effect of such redundancy is one of profound *déjà vu*.

Items appearing in the Western press which could be used to bolster the Soviet position were also frequent targets for repetition. Obviously, close attention was paid to US newspapers such as *The New York Times* and the *Washington Post*; any material potentially damaging to the US position was reprinted as evidence of the validity of Soviet claims.[63] Here, too, Soviet commentators are preying on the ignorance of their audience, since Soviet citizens do not have direct access to Western media. The reprinting of so many items from foreign sources, a relatively new tactic in the USSR, underscores the emphasis placed on persuading the domestic audience: Soviet claims—which might be discounted by a skeptical citizenry—were being supported by outsiders, making them more compelling.[64]

Other Soviet propagandists took their cues directly from the Western press. A clear example is provided by Soviet treatment of the RC-135 revelation, which was described above. Initial reaction on September 6th consisted solely of Western reports: *Pravda* quoted CBS, a Moscow television newscast quoted Congressman James Wright, and another newscast quoted UPI quoting the US Secretary of Defense. Only later was Soviet "domestic" information provided. That evening, the government finally announced that the PVO had observed an RC-135 off the coast of Kamchatka. Subsequently, Soviet officials even claimed to have scrambled a fighter to monitor the activities of that aircraft.[65] During the September 9 press conference, Marshal Ogarkov declared for the first time that the RC-135 had rendezvoused with KAL 007, flying in tandem with the Korean plane for some minutes prior to the first intrusion.

We have mentioned that Soviet propagandists tend to repeat information which has appeared previously in their own media accounts. The most flagrant instances of anti-Soviet aggression, from Nazi stormtroopers to the U-2 flight of Gary Francis Powers, have a timelessness uncommon in the West. A curious blend of these factors can be seen in a group of four articles published on October 5, 1983.[66] All four are datelined Paris and contain nearly identical text; all cite a news dispatch in *Jeune Afrique*; all talk about the destruction of a Libyan passenger jet by Israeli Air Force jet fighters. The effect created by the articles is astonishing. The Korean airliner had already receded in importance in the press, particularly after publication of Andropov's September 28 policy address. One's first impression, while reading the lead paragraph, is "Not again—not twice in the span of a month." Only in the second or third paragraph does any of these articles mention the fact that this event had occurred a decade earlier.

What becomes obvious from close scrutiny of Soviet statements during the first two weeks following the destruction of KAL 007 is the reactive nature of their propaganda effort. After saying little of substance for five days, and being battered by world opinion, they began to organize a counterattack centered around an incredible public relations gift from the US—acknowledgement of the presence of an American reconnaissance plane near the path of the jetliner. Then, just as the Soviets appeared to be making progress, the UN Security Council heard the revelations of the tape transcripts, with their damning evidence. It was primarily to overcome the impact of the tape that the Soviet government held their press conference, the sheer novelty of which lent credibility to Ogarkov's remarks, both abroad and at home.

In the weeks that followed, further elaborations were conceived. Air Force Marshal Kirsanov claimed that the flight of KAL 007 was coordinated with the passage of US spy satellites and was supervised by US astronauts on the space shuttle "Challenger," aloft at the time.[67] Subsequently, the Soviet government had to deal with the ICAO investigation. Soviet authorities reacted by withholding vital information on some issues and blatantly lying in response to other questions.

Such tactics were, no doubt, a necessary stratagem, as the Soviets presented little evidence of their own. With the exception of the interviews of the fighter pilots (which contained inaccuracies refuted by their own words), most Soviet media commentary on the shootdown of KAL 007 consisted of variations on the basic Soviet position. On nearly every substantive point, propagandists embellished the Soviet version in successive stages. However, despite the frequent claims of "new information coming to light almost daily,"[68] no hard evidence was ever presented. The progressive fabrications give the impression that an ongoing investigation continued to produce more and more information. Indeed, Ogarkov claimed that his preliminary statement was based on a thorough investigation of data available in Moscow and the Soviet Far East, but not a single supported fact was ever adduced by Soviet officials.[69] Even the "huge map" displayed at the press conference was a reconstruction and not a radar trace. Ogarkov himself remarked, "We see no need to provide any proof for what is completely obvious."

DISCUSSION

In the preceding chapter, we discussed the nature of public knowledge in the USSR, suggesting that, because of government control of the flow of information, there exists an official public knowledge, which predominates over the culturally based form more nearly like that of the Western democracies. Underneath the official truth, of course, lies an unofficial public knowledge, based on memories of both Russian and Soviet history, the current relationship of the citizen to the state, and information coming from various unofficial sources: word-of-mouth, transnational broadcasts, and the underground press.[70] On one level, however, Soviet citizens 'know' only what the state tells them: official government statements, including those appearing as news stories in the media, seldom have taken unofficial public knowledge into account.

We have commented that Soviet rhetoric, in its traditional form, appears to be a Platonic system, based on first premises and universal truths, as interpreted by the state—what has been termed a 'deductive system.'[71] All rhetoric must stem from these truths, moving always towards greater wisdom, contributing to the goal of the perfection of the communist state. To this end the Soviet press "seeks not to bring out base impulses or to cater to corrupting weaknesses, ... but rather to point out roles and models for imitation or avoidance."[72] In such a system, to borrow from Kneupper, "subservience to a pre-given truth ... ultimately makes rhetoric a merely didactic (some would say even a totalitarian) instrument."[73] Certainly, conventional Soviet discourse appears to fit this model: rhetoric serves as an instrument for control rather than for development of the individual. In Moran's words, the "concept of control may be the single most important difference between communication and pseudocommunication."[74] Thus, the rhetoric, when coupled with restrictions on information flow, is situated at the noncommunicative end of the continuum from persuasion to coercion.

There are many ways in which Soviet discourse on the subject of KAL 007 reflects past practices. Most obvious, of course, is the long official silence, which allowed the state to respond to the rhetorical situation by interpreting the destruction of a civilian airliner within the matrix of communist ideology and prevailing policy. Once the presence of the RC-135 had been revealed, no time was lost in attempting to shift the blame for the tragedy. Korean Air Lines Flight 007 became part of the imperialist struggle against the progressive forces of Marxism-Leninism.

Essentially, the USSR had fallen back on a time-tested argument. That it should have done so is not at all surprising, because exigencies of the moment do not often allow the luxury of careful consideration of new policy options, nor do they provide the best environment for the critical assessment of one's own belief system or preconceptions. Anything else, in fact, would normally increase the cognitive dissonance of political actors—an extremely unlikely eventuality in a reactive situation such as that faced by the Soviet Union.[75] Once an action has been undertaken, the natural response of the actor is justification, not analysis. Moreover, in a crisis situation only such a response—one that accurately takes into account political culture (public knowledge)—is most likely to strike a sympathetic chord within a polity. One should not be surprised, therefore, that the thematics underlying the Soviet response to Western charges sounded so familiar.

It is generally recognized that Soviet society has an ambivalent attitude toward the West, particularly the United States. A deep-seated, traditional fear of outsiders mingles with curiosity; a desire for progress is entangled in distrust of things foreign. The exemplars of rhetoric examined in this study indicate that the government trades on these mixed feelings: accusations against the United States are juxtaposed with quotations from American media that support the Soviet position; the technological mastery of the US is used as a rationale for charges of spying.

As we have claimed, KAL presented an anomaly to the Soviet propagandists, since it was a factual, rather than an interpretive incident: the condemnation of the USSR abroad and the questions raised at home stemmed from the act, not from perceptions of its meaning. Thus, a primary consideration was finding a means to place the destruction of the airliner into a scenario which could be interpreted by the application of communist doctrine. The spy-plane theory met this requirement. However, since the Soviet government had no direct or indirect proof that the airliner was engaged in an espionage mission, it had to rely on circumstantial evidence and an inductive argument structure.

If a case could be made that the navigation system which guides normal commercial flights is infallible, then it would be impossible for the aircraft to have strayed because of technological failure. Likewise, if convincing evidence could be adduced to demonstrate that the US was in a position to warn the airliner, then the probability of KAL 007 being a spy flight would be increased; hence, the action of the PVO could be justified, alleviating the culpability of the USSR. The arguments chain together in a manner that allows the persuasive force of one to augment the persuasive force of the other two. In adopting the conspiratist argument as the centerpiece of its case, the USSR resorted to tactics familiar to students of conspiracy theory in the West—an indication, perhaps, that conspiratist discourse is, truly, a rhetorical genre.[76]

It is symptomatic of the traditional Soviet rhetorical system that the effectiveness of these associative arguments depends on a paucity of information from competing sources and on the ignorance of the audience. The tactic is also designed to blunt the effectiveness of any alternate sources of knowledge, a topic addressed more fully below.

In that regard, the treatment of the KAL disaster also appears to represent something of an anomaly in Soviet rhetoric. A number of factors contribute to this impression. The Soviet government ultimately admitted not only to the shootdown, but also to the loss of life, an unusual circumstance in itself. The resultant propaganda campaign focused on the domestic audience, and included a Western-style press conference. [The fact that the question-and-answer portion was edited for the print media and not reported at all on television should not obscure the fact that the press conference was a unique event in the Soviet Union.] The media reported (indirectly and selectively, to be sure, but reported nonetheless) revelations emanating from the United States, such as the presence of the RC-135.[77] Finally, on a number of occasions the government appeared to be responding directly to information coming into the Soviet Union from outside sources.

Nevertheless, the argument can be made that these were merely tactics in the grander strategy of winning the propaganda war among the audiences that counted most—communist party members in Western Europe, the Soviet Union's Warsaw Pact allies, and, at home, the Soviet citizenry, especially the intellectuals and Party elite. The very uniqueness of these tactics, which itself testifies to the gravity of the situation as perceived by the Soviet leadership, would contribute heavily to the credibility of the overall government position. Dallin commented that "maintaining the façade of infallibility vis-à-vis it own population" had become an "overriding priority" of the leadership.[78] As McClosky and Turner point out:

> The 'infallibility' of Marxist-Leninist doctrine is the ultimate source of all Soviet legitimacy, the justification for the dictatorship and for the suppression of competing beliefs and opinions.[79]

Faced with a public relations fiasco at home and abroad, the Soviet government had to take drastic measures in order to preserve the domestic façade of infallibility. The propaganda effort had to parry charges from the accuser states and give the appearance of forthrightness. Again, this is indicative of the fact that the Soviet propaganda campaign remained essentially coercive, for it subverted the rational processes by which most individuals arrive at a determination of sociopolitical truth. The words of McClosky and Turner echo those of Ogarkov: "If the 'truth' is finally and incontestably known, why permit it to be challenged by opinions which must of necessity be false or dangerous?"[80]

CHAPTER SIX

NOTES

[1]It is safe to say that no single event in the post-World War II era had occasioned a propaganda barrage in the print media equalling the Soviet response to the KAL crisis. For instance, *Krasnaia zvezda* increased its propaganda about the United States 21% in September, 1983. Sixty-two percent of the publication's coverage of the US during that month concerned KAL 007. See: Organization of the Joint Chiefs of Staff. Special Operations Division, *KRASNAYA ZVEZDA. Soviet News and Propaganda Analysis,* 3:9 (September 1983). During the same month *Pravda* published a total of 68 items relating to KAL, 47 of these between September 6th and 18th. NB: In this chapter citations of Soviet newspapers will be included in the text.

[2]Dallin, *Black Box,* p. 83.

[3]FBIS, *The Public Soviet Response to the KAL Incident* [Analysis Report FB 83-10041], p. 5.

[4]No commentator has emphasized how remarkable it was for the Soviets to concentrate so much attention on domestic propaganda in the aftermath of the Korean airliner shootdown; only Dallin even highlights the fact at all. Citing a French news dispatch [Alain Jacob, "Circonstances atténuantes?", *Le Monde,* September 10, 1983], Dallin states: "Apparently within days, party members were being summoned to meetings to be briefed on the whole affair; . . . three days after the incident a confidential memorandum was sent out from Moscow to higher party organizations around the country explaining what had occurred." See: *Black Box,* pp. 90-91.

[5]Mickiewicz has observed that the primary topics discussed by the central newspapers are those about which "readers have no independent knowledge or experience. . . . The very lack of alternative information sources has inflated the prestige of the central press. . . " (p. 47).

[6]Andropov's statement was read over radio and television, then published on the front page of all Soviet daily newspapers the next day.

[7]Even Dallin, who has little interest in the Soviet media campaign itself, views this emphasis as significant in determining the official government reaction. See: *Black Box,* p. 88.

[8]Dallin (*Black Box,* p. 89) speaks of "maintaining the facade of infallibility vis-à-vis its own population" as an "overriding [Soviet] priority"; Shlapentokh mentions "the importance of stability and the appearance of infallibility in the official public ideology" (p. 40). As Thomas Kane, professor and pundit, has often observed, "Superpowers never have to say they're sorry."

[9]Murty, p. 23.

[10]See the citations in Remington, *Soviet Public Opinion*, pp. 15-16.

[11]Friedgut, p. 323. See also: Samuel P. Huntington, "Social and Institutional Dynamics of One-Party Systems," in Samuel P. Huntington and Clement H. Moore, eds., *Authoritarian Politics in Modern Society* (New York: Basic Books, 1970), 3-47, p. 32.

[12]Shlapentokh, p. 91.

[13]Shlapentokh, pp. 95-97.

[14]But it is worth noting here that, in some sense, anything published in the Soviet press could be construed as aimed at both foreign and domestic audiences; TASS often provided translations to Western reporters. In any event, Soviet authorities knew that most, if not all, of the material would be picked up by Western journalists working in the Soviet Union.

[15]As described below in Chapter Seven, this tentative suggestion became, on the first anniversary, an established 'fact' in the Soviet interpretation of events. "The Reagan Administration knew perfectly well that the inflammatory flight of the Boeing would be terminated, but the White House resorted to it in cold blood. . . ." See: Iu. Bandura, "Provokatory u pozornogo stolba" ["Provocateurs in the Stocks"], *Izvestiia*, August 31, 1984, p. 5.

[16]*Pravda*, September 28, 1983; *The New York Times*, September 29, 1983 [quoted by Dallin, *Black Box*, p. 99].

[17]Nearly every commentator has noted the unusual circumstance that it was military officials who provided most of the personnel engaged in public explanations of the military actions taken and justification of the Soviet position with regard to US complicity. The reasons propounded have been various and, predominantly, incorrect. In our opinion, the simplest answer is best: all high-ranking government officials who might have stepped forward were also high-ranking Party officials, and it was imperative that the Party be insulated from whatever adverse reaction could not be avoided by activating the agitprop apparatus. Given the tenuous relationship that had developed in the '70s and '80s between the CPSU and communist parties throughout the world, such considerations were important on the international, as well as domestic, stage.

[18]For example, treatment of the KAL incident in *Moscow News*, Novosti Press Agency's foreign language weekly, was almost perfunctory. Aside from translations of the September 6 "Soviet Government Statement" (*MN*, No. 37, September 18-24, 1983, pp. 1, 3), in which the shootdown was first acknowledged, an edited version of Ogarkov's September 9 press conference (*MN*, No. 38, September 25—October 2, 1983, pp. 1, 3), and

Gromyko's September 7 speech in Madrid (*MN*, Supplement to No. 38), only one article was printed. "Seven questions to the President" (*MN*, No. 37, pp. 1, 3) stated:

[T]he incident politically benefits only those who strive to aggravate international tensions.

No wonder the President capitalized 110 per cent on what happened in order to justify and confirm his line in beefing up arms.

Even the time seems to have been specially chosen: it happened at the dawn of International Peace Day, on the eve of the "hot autumn" in the antiwar movement, not long before the meeting of ministers of foreign affairs in Madrid, not long before resumption of the Geneva talks on nuclear arms in Europe. . . .

Ambassador Troyanovsky's response to Ambassador Kirkpatrick's charges September 6 at the United Nations and these comments, in a publication virtually unknown to Americans, constitute almost the entire Soviet commentary in the United States on the president's opportunism.

[19]Dallin lists several sources concerning the relevant legal issues. See: *Black Box* , pp. 118-119 [n. 31]. For another perspective, see: Farooq Hassan, "A Legal Analysis of the Shooting of Korean Airlines Flight 007 by the Soviet Union," *Journal of Air Law and Commerce*, 49:3 (1984), 555-88.

[20]In particular, this defense was offered by Foreign Minister Andrei Gromyko both in public addresses and in a private meeting with US Secretary of State George Shultz, which took place during the international human rights conference held in Madrid during the second week of September. Gromyko's remarks, the only ones attributed to a Soviet political official prior to September 28, were covered by the press in both the United States and the Soviet Union.

[21]Citations used in this discussion were drawn from the following Soviet materials: articles in *Izvestiia, Krasnaia zvezda, Literaturnaia gazeta,* and *Pravda;* transcripts of programs on Moscow Domestic Service (radio) and Moscow Domestic Television Service; and Russian and English language releases by TASS. Transcripts from the electronic media were provided by Jon Lodeesen.

[22]Emphasis added. Throughout this chapter we have underlined passages which are either untrue or misleading or which assume *a priori* that KAL was a spyplane (that is, are circular in their argumentation).

[23]The false dilemma appears to be a trademark of conspiratist argument. See: Marilyn J. Young, *The Conspiracy Theory of History as Radical Argument: The John Birch Society and Students for a Democratic Society*, Diss. University of Pittsburgh, 1974 (Ann Arbor: UMI, 1975). On the rhetorical use of the false dilemma, see: Part three, below.

[24]The hedging remark "extremely unlikely" (ves'ma neveroiatny) was unique in all Soviet commentary on the Korean airliner.

[25] This point is also made by Murray Sayle, "A Conspiracy of Coincidence." See: "Statement of William D. Reynard, Manager, Aviation Safety Reporting System, [NASA]" in "Aircraft Navigation Technology and Errors," Hearings before the Subcommittee on Transportation, Aviation, and Materials of the Committee on Science and Technology, U.S. House of Representatives, 19 September 1983 (pp. 3-19). Reynard testified that among 22,429 voluntary incident reports filed during a 5 1/2 year period, 954 concerned "navigational anomalies," of which 623 were caused solely by crew error. The remaining 331 incidents included both "simple mechanical breakdown [and] operational failures precipitated by actions of the flight crew" (p. 4). Of these, 21 involved navigational systems identical to the one installed on 007. The greatest deviation from course was 250 nautical miles (compared to KAL's 310+ miles off track), but it occurred on an American carrier flying a route system with significantly better flight safeguards—particularly, so-called "exit gate" radar at each landfall to ensure that aircraft are on course when they start their over-water passage (p. 11). Nonetheless, Reynard testified, the data "support the conclusion that errors caused by onboard navigation equipment are uncommon events, bordering on the rare" (p. 4).

[26] A number of possibilities are discussed at length by Sayle, Dallin, and Hersh, who suggest theories of accidental deviation from the prescribed route. [Dallin ultimately concluded that the espionage scenario was the most reasonable.] A variant non-accidental theory is expressed by Rohmer, who argues the Korean pilot purposefully flew the fatal route to save fuel. Richard Witkin reported that Capt. Park Yong Man, the pilot of KAL 015, claimed in a Korean language interview published in the December 1986 issue of Seoul's Chosun Review, that the pilot of KAL 007 knew his INS had been misprogrammed but tried to fly to Seoul anyway in order to avoid severe punishment from company executives. See: Richard Witkin,"Korean Pilot Offers New Theory on Downed Plane," The New York Times, December 28, 1986, p. 8; John Burgess, "KAL Punishment Policy Cited In 007 Disaster," The Guardian, January 11, 1987, p. 17; and Cho Kap Che, "KAL007: Choihu eui Mokkyukja" ["The Last Witness"], Chosun Review [Seoul, South Korea], December 1986.

[27] Sayle, "A Conspiracy of Coincidence," p. 46.

[28] See: Hofstadter, p. 37; and Earl G. Creps III, The Conspiracy Argument as Rhetorical Genre, Diss. Northwestern University, 1980 (Ann Arbor: UMI, 1981), p. 45.

[29] Rohmer (p. 74) points out that the Japanese air control center at Tokyo had accepted as correct KAL 007's report that it had passed the NIPPI waypoint. There was no reason to believe otherwise, since there was no civilian radar coverage of the aircraft either at NIPPI or at the NOKKA waypoint. However, when the 747 reported passing NIPPI, out over the Pacific, at 17:07 GMT, it was actually flying over Kamchatka, 250 nautical miles to the northwest.

[30] Maertens, p. 27.

[31] According to Hersh (pp. 60-64 et passim) the extensive U.S. military radar and radio network did pick up the flight of KAL 007, as well as remarks of the Soviet interceptor

pilots, in real time; but it was impossible for the technicians to know the airplane was not Soviet, or the interception live and not a Soviet early morning training exercise. See also: Philip Taubman, *The New York Times*, September 14, 1983, p. A 12.

[32]Hersh claims that the whole event was actually monitored by an American serviceman stationed at Wakkanai on Hokkaido, but he had no idea that what he was listening to was an actual interception until the plane had already been hit by Soviet rockets (pp. 60-62).

[33]*ICAO REPORT*, p. 39.

[34]There now seems to be no doubt that military radar data was available in the Anchorage air traffic control room. See: Pearson, *KAL 007: The Cover-Up*, 308-311 *et passim*.

[35]Rohmer, pp. 74-75. See, also: Douglas Feaver, "Dangers of Violating Soviet Airspace Well-Known to Pilots," *Washington Post*, September 2, 1983, p. A8.

[36]See Chapter Two. A map published in *Pravda*, September 20, 1983, and a similar map provided to the ICAO investigating team, placed varying numbers of RC-135s in different (and incorrect) positions. See: Oberg, "Sakhalin: Sense and Nonsense," p. 41.

[37]Sayle, who is not alone in claiming this, wrote that RC-135s "are not radar-carrying aircraft." See: "A Conspiracy of Coincidence," p. 52. A different opinion is offered by Bernard and Eskelson. For obvious safety reasons, the RC-135s in which Bernard and Eskelson flew along the coast of Vietnam did contain radar that would allow the crew to anticipate the approach of enemy aircraft

[38]See: Hersh, pp. 4, 37-38, and Chapter 5, especially p. 42; and Jeffrey Richelson, *American Espionage and the Soviet Target* (New York: William Morrow, 1987), p. 94 and Chapter 9, especially pp. 223-224.

[39]*ICAO REPORT*, Appendix E.

[40]The most recent incursions had occurred during joint maneuvers by American and Japanese forces in the Spring, 1983. A flight of Navy jets reportedly penetrated Soviet airspace over the Kurile Islands, along which runs the correct Route 20 that KAL 007 should have been following. According to Howard Blum, convicted spy John Walker passed documents to the Soviet Union indicating that this incident was an intentional provocation. A review of this book states that "a State Department source told several reporters in a background briefing that the incident was caused by a navigation error," but that Blum had been told by a source at NSA that "[we] burned them in the overflight" during fleet exercises. See: Howard Blum, *I Pledge Allegiance. The True Story of the Walkers: An American Spy Family* (New York: Simon & Schuster, 1987); and Tom Burgess, "Book says Walker action encouraged KAL shooting," *San Diego Union*, October 24, 1987, p. A-2.

[41]*ICAO REPORT*, p. 43; Sayle, "A Conspiracy of Coincidence," p. 52. The well known phenomenon involved is called the "slant effect." An aircraft six miles high will still be six miles away from the radar site even when directly overhead; this distance shows up on the two-dimensional radar screen as a curved line, even though the aircraft continues to fly in a straight line.

[42]Rohmer, pp. 85-88. The SU-15 pilot, Major Vasili Kas'min, was interviewed on Soviet television (September 10, 1983) and in *Krasnaia zvezda* (Col. V. Filatov, "Letel samolet iz Ankoridzha" ["An Airplane Flew From Anchorage"], September 13, 1983, p. 3).

[43]1826 GMT is accepted without question as correct by all other individuals, governments, and investigative bodies. Aside from making this one change, the Soviet government never challenged the time, either. Perhaps the change was prompted by VOA newcasts that suggested the airliner had been shot down "as it emerged from restricted Soviet airspace" [CN-063 (September 4, 1983) and follow-ups]. Our analysis has shown that Soviet officials take great cognizance of such newscasts. It is important to realize in this regard that a commercial jetliner flying at normal cruising speed [520-540 knots] would cross all of Sakhalin Island in less than ten minutes.

[44]See: David Shribman, *The New York Times*, October 7, 1983, p. A10; and Pearson, "K.A.L. 007: What the U.S. Knew and When We Knew It," p. 118.

[45]*ANC REPORT*, p. 9.

[46]Senior Pentagon and State Department officials reportedly were surprised at the "hesitant, self-contradictory, hastily improvised" Soviet propaganda effort. See: Walter S. Mossberg, "Soviet Military, Civilian Leaders Clash Over Downed KAL Plane, U.S. Contends," *Wall Street Journal*, September 27, 1983, p. 38.

[47]TASS Statement of September 3, 1983.

[48]Wording of the revised US transcript released September 11, 1983.

[49]Of course, Air Force One and the airborne command center used by the Strategic Air Command are among the exceptions to this statement.

[50]Johnson and Kang both deride the contention that the SU-15 pilot could not tell that KAL 007 was a passenger aircraft.

[51]Interview with Todd Leventhal, USIA, February 10, 1987. According to Leventhal, Belenko also denied that SU-15 fighters are equipped with the radio transmitters needed to enter into voice contact with non-Soviet aircraft; that is, they could not have called KAL 007 on the 121.5 MHz international hailing frequency. This statement, however, has been disputed both by the Soviet government and by some US authorities.

[52]We agree with Michael Westlake: "It is possible but hard to believe that Soviet ground-based air-defense radar systems are so deficient in signal-processing that they cannot identify an individual type of aircraft's radar 'signature.'" See: "On Course for Disaster," *Far Eastern Economic Review*, October 13, 1983, p. 32. This judgment is so intuitively obvious that Westlake is quoted by both Dallin and Sayle.

[53]According to Steven Weisman: "[A]dministration officials cited the existence of the flashing lights . . . as ample evidence for the Russians to understand that the plane was a civilian aircraft. These officials noted that military or reconnaissance aircraft use no lights. . . ." See: *The New York Times*, September 5, 1983, p. A6. Another fact seldom mentioned is that RC-135s do not have any windows.

[54]Sayle remarks that the aircraft were flying at the same altitude, as well, but American intelligence analysts who deal with such matters have told us that na traverse ('abeam') does not necessarily imply this, although usually it would be true.

[55]"ICAO checks with aircraft reports and with weather satellite photographs showed that the weather was CAVU—ceiling and visibility unlimited, with underlying clouds a few thousand meters below." See: Oberg, "Sakhalin: Sense and Nonsense," p. 41.

[56]Shortly after the incident occurred, some US officials believed it quite possible that the pilot of the SU-15 did not realize KAL 007 was a civilian passenger plane. See: *The New York Times* of September 5, 1983, p. A1; and September 18, 1983, pp. A16, A17. But also see note 53.

[57]Many commentators have claimed initial Soviet confusion over the aircraft, as evidenced by the fact that KAL 007 was initially identified by radar operators on Kamchatka as an RC-135, then as an unidentified aircraft. It is a mistake, however, to read too much into these assertions: we have been told by US military personnel that the Soviets routinely identify all unidentified aircraft—both military and civilian—as RCs when first sighted on radar. This behavior follows good military procedure accepted the world over: unidentified aircraft are presumed hostile until proven otherwise.

[58]In addition, there was virtually no coverage of the actual contents of the air-to-ground tape. Neither USIA nor VOA officials seem to believe that failure to monitor Soviet information media impedes the mission of the station, although it would appear that cues as to needed emphases might be gleaned thereby. As we have mentioned, RFE/RL performs such monitoring on a routine basis.

[59]See: *The New York Times*, September 5, 1983, p. 1; September 18, 1983, pp. 16, 17; and October 7, 1983, p. 10.

[60]Remember that this kind of information is not released even under normal circumstances. Although conditions are changing, it has been true that Soviet media would not

carry stories about Aeroflot crashes or other disasters; in some instances even families of the dead are not informed.

[61]Dallin has noted the uniformity of the questions and the frequency with which this tactic was utilized as clear evidence of the coordinated, planned Soviet responses via all channels of mass communication.

[62]See Part Three.

[63]Compare the results obtained in a recent study of press behavior in East Germany during the period 1983-84:

> A particular vulnerability of the Western press to propaganda exploitation is its convention of covering "both sides of the story." There is thus almost always a critical perspective that can be quoted accurately, if out of context. . . . These highly significant findings leave little doubt that <u>Neues Deutschland</u> systematically employs a wide range of foreign news media citations to reinforce the persuasiveness of its unitary, highly ideological perspective on world events.

See: Randall L. Bytwerk and Stuart J. Bullion, "In Others' Words: Foreign News Media Citations in <u>Neues Deutschland</u>," paper presented to the 1985 annual convention of the Association for Education in Journalism and Mass Communication, Memphis TN (August 1985).

[64]White, citing data provided by Hollander, states that fewer than one in five readers of *Izvestiia* bothers to read its articles on propaganda themes. He continues:

> The Soviet reader, moreover, tends generally to take a somewhat sceptical view even of those parts of his daily paper which he does in fact consult. Interviews with emigres, for instance, have established that the Soviet media are generally regarded as unreliable in factual matters and interpretation. . . .

See: White, *Political Culture and Soviet Politics*, pp. 139-40; and Hollander, pp. 62-69, 168, 181-83.

[65]In this connection, see also: Rohmer, pp. 106-107. Rohmer's discussion, while basically unexceptionable, is slightly muddled because he has translated kontrolirovat' as 'to control' rather than 'to monitor'. This error probably stems from the *Moscow News* translation "Soviet Government Statement" (*MN*, No. 37, September 18-24, 1983, pp. 1, 3): "Several Soviet interceptor planes were made airborne. One of them controlled the activities of the US RC-135 plane" (p. 1).

[66]"Air Pirates," *Izvestiia*, p. 5; "The US Manipulates Information," *Krasnaia zvezda*, p. 3; "Washington's Short Memory," *Komsomol'skaia pravda*, p. 5; and "Hypocrites," *Sovetskaia Rossiia*, p. 5 [all published October 5, 1983].

[67]The Kirsanov allegation, which formed the cornerstone of P.Q. Mann's charges published in *Defence Attaché* and which was repeated by other conspiratists, elicited a

rare direct response from VOA. An editorial broadcast two days later said, "[T]his outright lie is only one of the latest in a sequence of distorted reports and allegations which are designed to shift the blame away from the Soviet officials who ordered Flight 007 shot out of the sky." ["Murkier Still," VOA editorial 0-0715, September 22, 1983.]

[68]Similar claims were being repeated even three years later. See Chapter Seven.

[69] There is no reason to believe such evidence actually exists. Hersh relates the details of a fascinating interview he held in Moscow with Marshal Ogarkov and Deputy Foreign Minister Georgi Kornienko, at which time he received "explicit acknowledgement that [the Soviet] government, for all of its public finger-pointing, had no evidence of American involvement in the flight path of the Korean airliner" (p. 191).

[70]White comments that in Soviet society "there appears to be a greater degree of reliance upon word-of-mouth communication and even rumour than would be the case in most western countries." See: *Political Culture and Soviet Politics*, p. 140.

[71]McGee and Martin, p. 53.

[72]Mickiewicz, p. 53.

[73]Kneupper, p. 184. If, on the other hand, the universal truths or first principles of the system are false, then what is left is a Sophistic system, Platonic in form only.

[74]Moran, p. 185. In discussing pseudocommunication, Moran points out (p. 187) that the message sender attempts to control both the information flow and the methods of analysis available to the receiver.

[75]See: Jervis, *Perception and Misperception*, pp. 382-406.

[76]See below, Chapter Eight.

[77]It should be noted that Soviet media did not report either the demonstration of the tape or the ensuing UN debate. The existence of the tape, which had been mentioned almost casually in a newspaper report on September 4, was later reported indirectly after the US issued corrections to the transcript corroborating Soviet claims of having fired warning shots [See Chapter Two]. Soviet reportage of the September 6, 1983 Security Council session was limited to a charge that the United States had extended its "unrestrained anti-Soviet campaign" to the floor of the UN. Ambassador Oleg Troyanovsky was quoted as having responded to the allegations:

> All the facts show that the spy plane's route and the nature of its flight were not accidental. The facts of the matter indicate with total clarity who bears responsibility for the loss of the South Korean aircraft, and who gambled with people's lives, [making them] the latest victims of the "Cold War," the protagonist and apologist for which is the current American Administration. [*Pravda*, September 8, 1983, 2nd edition, p. 5; underlined

words were deleted when the text was repeated in *Pravda*, September 9, 1983, 1st edition, p. 5.]

[78]Dallin, *Black Box*, p. 89.

[79]Herbert McClosky and John E. Turner, *The Soviet Dictatorship*, (New York: McGraw Hill, 1960). [Quoted in Butler, p. 239.]

[80]Butler, p. 239.

THE DENOUEMENT

As we have observed earlier, Yuri Andropov's statement on September 28, 1983, marked the culmination of predictable internal processes: this was the final, authoritative interpretation issued by the highest societal body, the Politburo. Although the 'party line' had become quite clear earlier in the month, leaders of <u>agitprop</u> sessions[1] in the various enterprises and collectives of the country could now definitively link the KAL 007 provocation to the arms race and to capitalist preparations for war with the progressive forces of socialism. These Western imperialist goals necessitated that the United States find a way of forcing its NATO allies to accept deployment of new intermediate range Pershing and cruise missiles in Western Europe. Hence, the KAL provocation. The Soviet interpretation of the incident had progressed in a month's time from

a non-event...

to possibly an accident...

to a planned spy mission...

to a spy mission with the secondary motive of embarrassing the Soviet Union should action be taken against the aircraft...

to a provocation designed to entrap the defensive forces of the Soviet Union into destroying the Korean intruder so as to create the public furor that would virtually force West Germany to capitulate to US demands.

Kremlinologists find nothing amiss in this progression. Just as there is no fast-breaking news story in the Soviet system, equally so the interpretation of any international incident is refined in successive stages at progressively higher levels of the bureaucracy. Evidently, the Soviets were quite taken aback by two factors important during the early days of the KAL controversy. First, political leaders there apparently were upset that Shultz and Reagan revealed US knowledge of Soviet interceptor conversations before Moscow had received transcripts from its own Far East PVO command. Second, given the slowness with which analysis and interpretation rises through the Soviet bureaucracy (at least in terms of public acknowledgement) mid-level Soviet bureaucrats seemed stunned that President Reagan could 'go public' as quickly as he did.[2] In fact, a rumor within US diplomatic circles—one given considerable credence by experienced American observers—describes Soviet indignation at the 'planned' nature of the KAL intrusion as largely genuine. Operative here is a phenomenon known as mirror imaging[3] or projection. This Soviet perception was the result of a technology gap and differences in societal custom. In a comparable situation the Soviet leadership could not under any circumstances have obtained such precise information so quickly; accordingly, no response could have been developed with such rapidity unless it had, in fact, been planned in advance. The Soviets were not chagrined that the US secretary of state should have made the first announcement (which did surprise American observers); it was the president's statement only 24 hours after the fact that troubled them.[4]

In contrast, the Soviet bureaucracy ground through its normal procedures at its usual pace, ultimately reaching the point where the KAL issue could finally be placed 'in storage,' ready for use at suitable moments in the future.[5] The whole incident had become part of official Soviet public knowledge, part of the institutional (system) memory. But that was not the end of the story. For one of the most fascinating aspects of Soviet political communication is the manner in which incidents tend to resurface over time. Such is the topic of this chapter.

Soviet press coverage, and to a lesser extent TV coverage as well, continued sporadically through the middle of October,[6] when Euromissiles, arms negotiations, and the US invasion of Grenada[7] supplanted KAL as topics of official interest. Then the KAL controversy disappeared completely until December, when it resurfaced in response to a Voice of America broadcast. In dispatches dated the 8th, 12th, 13th and 20th, VOA mentioned the United Nations' *ICAO REPORT*. In its first story, VOA announced the imminent release of the report and the conclusion it was expected to contain—that KAL had strayed over Soviet territory "probably because of a navigation error." The Voice commented:

> The Soviet Union says the Korean Air Lines plane must have entered Soviet space intentionally, because no well-trained crew could have made such a mistake in navigation. The results of a Soviet investigation of the incident have not been released.[8]

In each succeeding dispatch, VOA countered the substance of the Soviet position. For example:

Portions of the report ... indicated the KAL aircraft strayed over Soviet airspace because of mistakes the crew made in programming the flight computer. That conclusion would undercut Soviet allegations that the Korean airliner was on a spy mission.[9]

[Federal Aviation Administration Director J. Lynn] Helms told reporters the inquiry clearly indicated the pilot of the aircraft never knew he was lost.[10]

After the *ANC REPORT* was released in February, 1984, VOA transmitted a more detailed account of the ICAO's findings:

An International Civil Aviation Organization panel says the Soviet Union has not justified its downing of a South Korean airliner last September.

The I.C.A.O. Commission concluded that the Soviet pilot did not follow proper procedures for intercepting a civilian aircraft. [OPT] It said there was no indication the pilot made his plane visible to the jetliner, and no evidence the Korean crew knew it was being intercepted.

The panel also concluded there is no indication the Soviets attempted to contact the Korean plane by radio, as Moscow claimed, and no evidence to support Soviet charges the plane was on a spy mission....[11]

The release of the *ICAO REPORT* was greeted by silence from Soviet authorities.[12] But on December 11, 1983 (three days after the first VOA mention of the report and two days before its official release), *Sovetskaiia Rossiia* published, under the rubric "A Reader Is Interested," a column by A. Peshcherin entitled "Spy Behind The Clouds," ostensibly responding to a request for information concerning "US aerial and space reconnaissance and its provocations against our country" that the letter writer believed "might be of interest to many readers."[13] Peshcherin's response covers forty years of US reconnaissance and spying—culminating with the KAL 007 spy flight that, he claimed, was coordinated with military ships at sea, reconnaissance aircraft, ground stations, and spy satellites. The lead paragraph exemplifies a typical Soviet rhetorical tactic employed earlier in the propaganda campaign:

Aerial espionage was not discovered by the ruling circles of the USA; it was borrowed by them from the arsenal of the Third Reich. The Nuremburg Trials exposed the Nazis. The term 'aerial espionage' first appeared in the pages of the world press on 30 November 1945, and mankind learned of previously unknown methods for violating the sanctity of airspace.[14]

Shortly thereafter references to KAL 007 appeared once again in the Soviet press. In its January 18, 1984, edition the weekly magazine *Literaturnaia gazeta* published a slightly abridged translation of an article that had appeared in *The Guardian*, R. W. Johnson's "007: Licence to kill?" A banner headline in one-inch type proclaimed **VELIKII OB-MAN**—THE BIG LIE. We have elsewhere described the Johnson article as an "unsubstantiated claim that intelligence requirements, combined with the hope of derailing the Western European peace movement, led the CIA to provoke a violent Soviet action."[15]

Also in January, 1984, *Aviatsiia i kosmonavtika* published an oblique allusion to policy changes that had been adopted in the aftermath of a high-level Soviet appraisal of the performance of its Far East Theatre forces. Air Force General S. Golubev called for increased discipline and responsibility on the part of both air and ground personnel in emergency situations. In a lengthy introduction Golubev wrote that the "imperialist predators," the American "nuclear maniacs," instigated hundreds of provocations each year. KAL was specifically mentioned. While praising the bravery of Soviet PVO forces, the General conceded that they

> cannot avoid the problem concerning the responsibility of those who must decide to scramble a crew and, if necessary, to open fire.... The commander, the senior officer, must not delay in making a decision. After all, every second is precious if the enemy is not to be allowed to get away unpunished.... [T]he situation in the air can develop in such a way that the final decision must be made by the pilot himself. For instance, to compel the intruder to land at the nearest airfield. Acting in strict accordance with established rules, he must do everything possible to make the intruder aircraft land. And if the crew [of the intruder] does not comply, to take decisive measures. Mature, independent actions are an important indicator of the military fitness [required] of a warrior in the air.

In Soviet terms, this article constituted a serious criticism of the manner in which the Korean airliner incident had been handled by the front-line troops involved in the interceptions over Kamchatka and Sakhalin and by the various levels of command on the ground. It is as close as the Soviet government had come to admitting what is now generally conceded by US intelligence personnel—the pilot of the SU-15 that destroyed KAL 007 was not ordered to, and in fact did not, complete identification of the aircraft before attacking. Information to this effect had already been broadcast into the Soviet Union by Voice of America on October 7, 1983:

> The U.S. State Department says the Soviet pilot who shot down a South Korean airliner more than a month ago should have determined it was a civilian plane. A spokesman said Soviet air defense personnel failed to fulfill their obligations under international law to identify the aircraft and give it an effective warning. The spokesman was commenting on a report in *The New York Times* saying the Soviets probably did not know the seven-forty-seven jumbo jet was a commercial airliner. The report said some U.S. intelligence experts had determined the Soviet pilot was below and behind the airliner and never alongside of it. Therefore, the report said, the pilot could not have positively identified the plane.[16]

A VOA follow-up report that same evening clarified the position of the United States:

> The U.S. State Department said Friday there are no mitigating circumstances in the Soviet attack of the Korean airliner. This, after a newspaper report said U.S. intelligence analysts have concluded Soviet jet pilots were probably not aware they were tracking a civilian aircraft.
>
> The State Department spokesman said under international law the Soviet Union had a responsibility to correctly identify the aircraft. Two-hundred-sixty-nine people were killed in the crash September first.
>
> *The New York Times* newspaper reported Friday U.S. intelligence analysts have concluded the Soviet pilots believed they were chasing an American reconnaissance plane, and the pilot who fired the fatal rocket was behind and below the Boeing seven-forty-seven so he could not make a correct identification.
>
> At the same time reports said the Soviet Union has been shaking up its Far Eastern Air Defense Command because of the incident. Sources said Soviet leaders are upset by the apparent confusion over the identity of the aircraft and the fact it penetrated Soviet airspace for more than two hours before it was caught by Soviet interceptors.[17]

KAL receded into the background once more. Then, on June 16, 1984, a respected British journal, *Defence Attaché*, published "Reassessing the Sakhalin Incident," attributed to P. Q. Mann, the pseudonym of a London public relations executive named Anthony Devereux.[18] The article—containing a map modeled on the one that had appeared in *Pravda* in conjunction with Marshal Kirsanov's September 20, 1983, essay—adhered fairly closely to the line of argument propounded in the Soviet press. In particular, Mann claimed, the Space Shuttle "Challenger" had played a role as controller of the intrusion by KAL 007, which was coordinated with overflights of a US spy satellite.[19] This article was the first major Western attempt to demonstrate US complicity in KAL 007's fate. It received world-wide attention. Western technical experts, in particular, questioned the author's competence.[20]

On the morning of June 18, VOA aired its first KAL story in nearly four months. Secretary of Defense Caspar Weinberger was quoted as complaining that P. Q. Mann "apparently picked up lock, stock, and barrel the total set of lies the Soviet Union published."[21] The Soviets, Weinberger said, had been "trying desperately to hide the fact they murdered the 269 people aboard the plane without the slightest provocation whatever."[22] Later that day, VOA correspondent John Roberts reported Weinberger's off-hand dismissal of *Defence Attaché* as "this British magazine, whatever it is, I've never heard of it...."[23]

The Mann 'revelations' were accorded full exposure in the Soviet press. *Krasnaia zvezda* carried a brief publication announcement on June 17. Between June 19-22, every major national daily carried at least one descriptive article, with *Pravda* running three.[24] A full translation of the *Defence Attaché* text was published in *Za rubezhom*, a weekly review of foreign affairs, under the heading "The Article Which Created The Stir."[25]

These articles share certain common characteristics. All but the last story consist of TASS wire service reports originating in major foreign centers: Washington, London, Tokyo, Paris, West Berlin. All quote a variety of individuals and publications criticizing the US;[26] the Soviet military has receded into its accustomed anonymity, and there are no references to specific Soviet sources. Caspar Weinberger is actually quoted in *Pravda* (June 21) as alleging that the *Defence Attaché* article contained no new information and that in general "it repeated the Soviet version" of the incident. To this the *Pravda* writer responded, "It was not the Soviet version that the magazine repeated, but facts which run counter to the phony (lzhivaia) US version that the airliner wound up in the airspace of the USSR 'by mistake.'"

New elements were added to the Soviet compendium of evidence: two weeks prior to its destruction KAL 007, it is claimed, spent two days at a US Air Force base in Anchorage—presumably, Elmendorf—being outfitted with spy equipment.[27] And the litany of US Far Eastern assets brought to bear on the provocation is said to have included aircraft of the "6981st and 6920th radar jamming squadrons."[28] The three articles published on June 20 contain a report of an independent study by two Socialist deputies of the Japanese parliament purportedly demonstrating that Japanese Defense Agency personnel participated in the spy mission.

Two other factors merit comment. First, much of the stridency of September had disappeared. Ten months had passed since the actual event, tempers had cooled, and KAL had been absent from Soviet press reports for quite a while. Thus it is not surprising that the *ad hominem* attacks upon President Reagan, so vigorously advanced in September, had been replaced in June by references to "Washington," "the Reagan Administration" and "the United States." All references to planning and coordination of the spy flight were tied to "US intelligence." Although terms such as "cold blooded" do appear in these texts, one also encounters, in the lead of the final article, the expression "tragic incident."

This group of articles seems to form a komplekt, a set, which mirrors typical Soviet methodology. Just as Andropov's September 28, 1983, position paper summed up a month-long campaign, so the final story in this komplekt—the only one not datelined to a foreign city—presents a fairly complete recitation of the official Soviet position, thus reinforcing and reaffirming the correct interpretation to be preserved in the consciousness of the people, in the Soviet storehouse of public knowledge. Accordingly, the less strident tone evident in these articles should be interpreted as a softening in the official rhetorical stance regarding the incident, an attempt to lay matters to rest.

There was a resurgence of KAL material in the Soviet press in August, 1984, perhaps reflecting the fact that a spate of books, articles, and television specials had appeared in the West to mark the first anniversary of the tragedy. Early in the month, Soviet commentators reported spy plane scenarios written by John Keppel, Akio Yamakawa, and David Pearson.[29] Then, during the period August 24—September 5, there appeared in the Soviet press a total of twenty-three KAL articles and one report alleging US spy flights over North Korea. This press coverage contained some new assertions along with much that is repetitive of earlier propaganda.

The most significant piece of new information appeared in "The Truth is Stronger Than Lies" by *Pravda's* political commentator Vsevolod Ovchinnikov.[30] Recalling the 1978 incident involving KAL 902, he wrote:

> Passengers on board saw with their own eyes that despite the insistent signals from Soviet interceptors, the South Korean crew attempted to continue the flight, and only after warning shots [were fired] did it obey the order to land.

Ovchinnikov failed to mention that these warning shots sheared off much of the airliner's left wing, killing two passengers and wounding two more.[31]

Earlier we detailed many Soviet statements in the aftermath of the 1983 disaster which claimed that the cannon bursts reported by Major Kas'min were "tracers" (<u>trassery</u>, <u>trassiruiushchiesia snariady</u>), the intended impression being that such cannon bursts could not have lethal effect. This is untrue, of course. Interestingly, the September 1984 edition of *Aviatsiia i kosmonavtika* contains an article on fighter-bomber crew training entitled "Tracers Hit Their Target."[32]

In the context of the international furor regarding whether or not Soviet pilots had fulfilled requirements to signal KAL 007, Ovchinnikov's statement amounts to a tacit admission by the Soviet government that the "cannon bursts" mentioned by the SU-15 pilot were not intended for any purpose other than attack.

Ovchinnikov mentions and dismisses purported Western explanations for 007's supposed forty-minute delay in taking off from Anchorage: "pilot error,"[33] cited earlier, and bad weather.[34] He even repeated Marshal Kirsanov's old charge that the delay was required to coordinate KAL 007 with scheduled overflights of Soviet territory by US spy satellites.[35]

Also apparent in these first-anniversary articles are some reflections of the original rhetoric. Accusations of American lying are contained in nearly identical *Izvestiia* and *Krasnaiia zvezda* articles.[36] *Ad hominem* attacks on President Reagan, missing in the June articles, reappear occasionally.[37] It must be stated, however, that the overall tone of these Soviet articles remains more measured and less strident than the tone encountered in September, 1983.

One theme reaches its apotheosis in these anniversary articles: the idea that the KAL passengers were deliberately and purposely sacrificed to produce the maximum anti-Soviet reaction throughout the world. As stated above, the first hint of this assertion had appeared September 14, 1983, in a *Literaturnaiia gazeta* article bearing the intriguing title "Seven Days in September."[38] On August 31, 1984, columnist Iu. Bandura wrote:

> You can't say it any clearer than this: the British journal [*Defence Attaché*] comes to the conclusion that Washington knowingly condemned the people to death in order to achieve the aims of the flight.

In the same column, Bandura quotes from an article by A. Yamakawa published in the Japanese publication *Gundzi minron:*

> The Reagan Administration knew perfectly well that the inflammatory [provokatsionnyi] flight of the Boeing 747 would be terminated, but the White House resorted to it in cold blood in order to gain, above and beyond the "fruits" of the espionage, the opportunity to mount a massive propaganda campaign against the USSR.

Reagan's goals, Bandura claimed, were to intensify the Cold War and to prepare for a "hot" one.[39] Ovchinnikov called the flight a "no lose move"—"If the military aspect of the operation didn't succeed, then its failure would become the pretext for an anti-Soviet campaign."[40]

As has been explained, public communication in the Soviet Union has come to reflect the external characteristics, the 'trappings,' of argumentation as practiced in the West. One of the most obvious similarities is the attempt to support allegations with sourced quotations and commentary. In this regard, certain characteristics of these anniversary articles in the Soviet press warrant comment. Of the twenty-seven KAL-related articles published between August 6—September 5, 1984, only the bylined Bandura and Ovchinnikov commentaries (which appeared August 31 in *Izvestiia* and *Pravda*, respectively) were something other than TASS wire-service stories from foreign cities. As usual, only foreign sources are cited—Western technical specialists, various print and electronic media, and, most prominently, the conspiratists themselves.

Soviet citation practices are always fascinating to a Western reader. On the one hand, it is rare for the Soviets to use 'veiled attribution' of non-Soviet sources—individuals are named. Conversely, the individuals named usually are quite obscure—e.g., R. Khardzher (Harger?), "a former intelligence officer in the U.S. Air Force"[41] who "took part in USAF reconnaissance flights over Vietnam"[42] (this individual is unknown in the West, whereas Bernard and Eskelson did achieve widespread notoriety); and Alex Braun, then editor of *Microwave Systems News*, who claims that the US Navy actually recovered KAL 007's flight recorder from the Sea of Japan.

Media citations also fit the same pattern. Amid references to *Il Messaggero* (Rome), *Diario-16* (Madrid), *Daily Telegraph* (London), and *USA Today*—even *People's World*, the organ of the CPUSA, is a recognized entity—there are references to obscure publications such as *Unsere Zeit* and *Deutsche Volkszeitung-Tat*, newspapers that German natives teaching German language and literature in US universities would have extreme difficulty identifying or characterizing.[43] In the Soviet press, it seems, all sources are equivalent.

There is one regard in which Soviet propagandists behave like Western conspiratists: When they encounter a printed statement that agrees with their position they accept it as corroboration regardless of its evidentiary value. And if the statement is quoted elsewhere, this is taken as confirmation. Indeed, in both world views, repetition serves as validation. Allegations become fact, irrefutable evidence (neoproverzhimye uliki in Soviet jargon).[44]

The identification of individuals in Soviet media manifests certain interesting characteristics. Some people are described in a matter-of-fact manner by profession or title. For instance, Robert Allardyce, a colleague of John Keppel and David Pearson, is "an American engineer."[45] Major General Richard Rohmer is "former Chief of the Canadian Air Force Reserve."[46] Bernard and Eskelson are "former members [sotrudniki][47] of American electronic intelligence forces"[48] who "served on these reconnaissance aircraft during the Vietnam years."[49] Other persons are identified in a variety of ways. For instance, John Keppel, a retired State Department employee who served for some time in Moscow, is referred to in the Soviet press as a:

(1) former State Department officer [sotrudnik] (*Pravda* August 6; *Izvestiia*, August 29)

(2) prominent American expert (*Pravda*, August 6)

(3) former American diplomat (*Krasnaia zvezda*, August 24, quoting *Il Messaggero*)

(4) former American diplomat who has worked in the past in the State Department and the CIA (*Pravda* September 2)

(5) former employee [sotrudnik] of the State Department Office of Reconnaissance and Scientific Research (*Sovetskaia Rossiia*, September 4)

Not every State Department employee is a "diplomat." Keppel's "prominence," if not his expertise, was certainly open to question. Notice, too, the casual reference to 'diplomats' who work for the CIA.

When a source is deemed particularly useful, the Soviet press is wont to enhance that source's prestige. It is clear that references to David Pearson follow this pattern. As noted, Pearson is a graduate student—specifically, a **doctoral candidate**[50]—in the Sociology Department at Yale. He was identified as such by *The Nation*:

David Pearson is a **Ph.D. candidate** in sociology at Yale University.... Pearson's **doctoral dissertation** has to do with the Defense Department's little-known World Wide Military Command and Control System....

and by VOA:

The writer is a Yale **graduate student** specializing in the study of the U.S. worldwide military command and control system....[51]

The Soviet press cited Pearson on ten occasions in the period August 11—September 4, 1984. He was referred to or identified as a:

(1) specialist in US military command and control systems from Yale University (*Pravda*, August 11)

(2) **doctor of philosophy** from Yale University (*Pravda*, August 18)

(3) scholar [uchënyi][52] (*Pravda*, August 18)

(4) prominent American specialist in military communications systems (*Za rubezhom*, August 24-30, in its editorial introduction to a translation of the Pearson article, p. 17)

(5) Yale University scientific researcher [nauchnyi sotrudnik], who has painstakingly studied data concerning the incident (*Izvestiia*, August 30; *Krasnaia zvezda*, August 30; *Pravda*, August 30)

(6) specialist in military command and control systems from Yale University (TASS interview, *Krasnaia zvezda*, August 31)

The TASS interviewer said:

(7) An article published in the August issue (*sic*) of the American magazine *The Nation* can serve as an example of articles on this topic intended for the serious reader. Its author, David Pearson, has devoted his **doctoral dissertation** to military systems of communication and control; he examines the "Sakhalin incident" as a specialist in this field.

(8) Yale University scientific researcher [nauchnyi sotrudnik] studying Pentagon communications systems (*Sovetskaia Rossiia*, September 1)

(9) "Western experts, in particular ... David Pearson" (TASS quoting *Stern*, *Pravda*, September 1)

A September 4 article in *Sovetskaia Rossiia* said:

(10) Pearson is a rather well known figure in the US. At Yale University he is engaged in the study of systems of communication among the country's command centers.

Since David Pearson has not completed and defended his dissertation, in Soviet parlance he is correctly termed an aspirant 'graduate student'. Thus, prestige enhancement is obvious. But the translations provided actually underplay the buildup given Pearson, because the expressions that we have chosen to use, **doctoral dissertation** and **doctor of philosophy**, do not mean in English what their verbatim equivalents mean to a Russian. The Soviet correlates of our Ph.D. dissertation and degree are called kandidatskaia dissertatsiia and kandikat nauk—literally 'candidate's dissertation' and 'candidate of science'. A Soviet doktorskaia dissertatsiia is written and defended only by mature, eminent scholars, usually late in their careers. Obtaining the title doktor nauk is a crowning achievement in one's career, superseded only by election to the Academy of Sciences and winning the Nobel Prize. The nearest English equivalent title is probably 'Distinguished Professor'; occupying an endowed chair would also be similar.

Pearson, then, has been elevated in the Soviet press from a graduate student to a distinguished and "rather well known" senior scholar. But he himself has never claimed to be what he is not. Inasmuch as Pearson, who is a young man, was interviewed by a TASS correspondent, there can be no real question concerning interlanguage difficulties— such a disparity would certainly have emerged in the course of any conversation. As always, of course, no Soviet reader could fathom the level of distortion exemplified here. What is fascinating, though, is the Soviet establishment's perceived need to engage in such reputation building.

Of equal, if not greater, significance are Soviet references to two Japanese individuals, Akio Takahasi[53] and Akio Yamakawa.[54] Takahasi is a mysterious pseudonym. According to Thomas Maertens of the US State Department, the US attempted, without success, to identify the actual author of *President's Crime*. Maertens believed that the book might be a Soviet fabrication, although, he said, no evidence has been developed that would either confirm or deny that idea. Sayle, however, states that much of the text "originated in Russian, with Novosti and other branches of Soviet officialdom more than helpful to the author while the work was in manuscript, and even before."[55]

Yamakawa is another story altogether. Maertens[56] and three officials with present or former connections to USIA, CIA, or the National Security Council have stated unequivocally that Yamakawa is a Soviet 'agent of influence'.[57] This was learned when Stanislav Levchenko, a KGB disinformation specialist who defected to the United States in 1979,[58] admitted to being Yamakawa's control in Tokyo. Yamakawa is identified in *Krasnaia zvezda* as a "prominent Japanese military expert and journalist." *Izvestiia* called him "a prominent Japanese expert on military issues." Yamakawa is said to have associated the KAL incident with America's "global 'secret war'". He is also quoted as having claimed that the CIA, Pentagon, and State Department have at their disposal "a network of professional intelligence officers in various countries" whose job it is to "plant false stories in the media."[59] According to Yamakawa, all the documentary evidence concerning KAL released by Washington "was fabricated or censored by the CIA." Earlier cited commentaries claiming Washington intended that the KAL passengers die were also attributed to Yamakawa.

The breadth of Soviet coverage devoted to KAL at this first anniversary seems incommensurate with Western programming (via

RL and VOA), hence not directly a response to such external stimuli. Reasons for this disparity may include the wealth of such attractive propagandistic reporting that emanated from foreign media sources during the month of August and the expectation that US attempts to capitalize on the upcoming anniversary would exceed the efforts actually expended.

According to the information provided us by Radio Liberty in Munich, that station's coverage of the anniversary, while fairly extensive, consisted mostly of reruns of year-old material: it amounted to 169 total minutes of feature programming "a week before and a week after the anniversary"—*i.e.*, essentially coextensive with the bulk of Soviet reporting, which saw twenty-three articles published in the period August 24—September 5, 1984.

Voice of America broadcast very little material around the first anniversary because, as a Reuter wire-service story reported from Seoul, an unidentified American official expected Western statements to be "rather restrained." A South Korean Foreign Ministry official said, "The Korean government is trying hard to keep this incident unpoliticized."[60] The report stated that the anniversary, it was expected, would "pass in Washington and Seoul on a low key in contrast to the angry words and outpouring of grief" a year earlier.[61]

VOA did broadcast an editorial on September 1, 1984,[62] and two separate reports of a high-level background briefing by a "senior State Department official."[63] This briefing contained the admission that "perhaps the Soviets did think it was on an intelligence mission." [Although such a statement represented a softening of the United States' position, it was of little practical value to the Soviet side and had no discernable effect on the latter's propaganda effort at the time.] The official did term the Soviet response "bizarre, but characteristic." However, he also expressed the "personal view" that "it's uncertain as to whether the Soviets had positively identified this as a civilian airliner. I think the problem is that they did not make the positive identification that they should have made and that as a result of which they would not have shot it down." This measured comment contrasts vividly with a snide VOA editorial broadcast December 18, 1983, which described the event as a "massacre of innocents" and called the proposition that the Soviet government would not have shot down the aircraft had they known it was a civilian airliner "a questionable assumption at best."[64]

VOA did produce one hard-hitting show for the 1984 anniversary.[65] It contained the assertion by Duane Freer, Director of the ICAO Air Navigation Commission in Montreal, directly refuting Soviet claims that they followed accepted intercept procedures:

> The International Emergency Frequency, on which they said they had attempted to contact Korean zero-zero-seven—there were other aircraft in the air who were monitoring the frequency; there were other ships at sea presumably monitoring it. Unfortunately, there is no evidence of any flight or ship at sea or anyone else who heard any such broadcast on the emergency frequency.

Freer and Donald Segner, Associate Administrator of the FAA, criticized the USSR for failure to cooperate with ICAO. Segner attributed the ICAO censure of the Soviet Union to the latter's unwillingness to provide the UN body with requested data.

U.S. Assistant Secretary of State Richard Burt also blasted the Soviet government for its "really preposterous" behavior immediately following the shootdown. In addition, Herbert Romerstein, a USIA official and a leading American specialist on disinformation, flatly called the Soviets liars:

> [Romerstein] At first they believed that we could not prove that they shot the plane down.... After the United States released the actual transmissions of the Soviet plane,... then Soviet disinformation took on a new phase and they began pretending that the K-A-L was a spy plane....

> [Host] Romerstein says that lying is the basic technique of disinformation and that the Soviets believe that if they repeat their lies long enough, even the most simple truths can be obscured.

> [Romerstein] The tradition in Soviet disinformation is: when faced with a serious problem, lie. And if one lie doesn't work, then some others are thought up. It's the technique of using the lie and repeating it over and over again so that by the time people begin thinking about the issue, they have heard the false story so many times that it has an impact on their thinking.

It was a very unyielding broadcast.

At this point, the story almost ends. Enough, it seems, was enough. The Korean airliner controversy disappeared just as abruptly as it had burst into world wide prominence. On the second anniversary American treatment was perfunctory. Radio Liberty broadcast time devoted to KAL 007 amounted to only ten minutes; Voice of America did no special shows and read only one editorial, which didn't even mention KAL until its third paragraph.

And, except for a single story on September 1, 1985,[66] the Soviets ignored it altogether until April, 1986, when it was mentioned by General N. I. Moskvitelev. In an interview commemorating National PVO Day, Moskvitelev cited the KAL incident as a "specific example of the reliability of our air defense system."[67] A month later *Pravda* cited a May 7, 1986, United Press International (UPI) wire story that named Larry Porter, an air disaster consultant from Spokane WA, and John Keppel. They had participated in the first of a series of nationwide press conferences organized by The Fund for Constitutional Government, during which it was claimed that the United States had doctored the air-to-ground tape of Soviet pilots and certain air traffic control (ATC) tapes made in Japan.[68]

This allegation was published only once. It seems surprising that the Soviet Union did not make more of such an inflammatory charge, which, if true, would constitute convincing circumstantial evidence that Soviet spy allegations had been correct. Moreover, when R. W. Johnson's *Shootdown* was published simultaneously in Great Britain and the United States during the month of June, it alleged US complicity in an intelligence mission, engendering tremendous controversy. That, too, was virtually ignored. Johnson's 1984 article in *The Guardian* had been translated and published in its entirety, but his book was discussed in only one Soviet article.[69] Despite several US television programs broadcast at the time,[70] *Shootdown* was almost totally ignored by both Soviet and American propagandists. Perhaps this general lack of attention to 'revelations' about the Korean airliner can be attributed to the impact of the developing tragedy at Chernobyl, which had occurred only six weeks earlier.

On August 2, 1986, *Izvestiia* published a dispatch from Tokyo stating that a Japanese weekly containing a "sensational article about new facts concerning Flight 007" sold out in a matter of hours. "A former high-ranking official" of the military "who would not allow his name to be used for reasons of safety" told the magazine that the KAL crew transmitted nothing but "FALSE DATA" to ground controllers and lied about its altitude to Japanese air traffic control. On the basis of this information, the official concluded, "There is every reason to believe that Flight 007 was carrying out a well planned spy mission."[71] That conclusion was probably the most guarded statement published by the Soviet press in the three years that had passed since the airliner had been shot down.

In mid-August, a TASS news release announced implementation of Soviet-American-Japanese accords regarding emergency contact among civilian ATC centers; this North Pacific Air Safety Agreement was prompted by the 1983 disaster, but KAL wasn't mentioned in the TASS story.[72] In addition, a Tokyo speech by American lawyer Melvin Belli was quoted by *Pravda*.[73] *Izvestiia* carried stories concerning the victims' families [September 2] and more "new facts" attributed to a Japanese newspaper [September 3]. On the 6th and 7th, *Krasnaia zvezda* printed two stories about US radar capabilities in the Pacific; neither article specifically mentioned the KAL incident, however. The second

Izvestiia story is significant primarily because it contains a neW allegation: that the KAL pilot had ordered some cargo unloaded in Anchorage. This is the only other Soviet reference to *Shootdown*.[74] It was obvious that neither side could be bothered with one more spy story.

In our opinion, everybody wanted the KAL story to go away. And it probably would have, were it not for the publication of Seymour Hersh's *"The Target Is Destroyed"*.[75] The Voice of America took cognizance of the renewed American interest, decided to broadcast a hardline editorial marking the third anniversary,[76] and made a big mistake. In the midst of this text, which—like all VOA editorials—was translated into every one of the station's broadcast languages, there appeared the following statement:

> The Soviets have a new story this year. They now admit 007 was not a spy plane, but say they didn't know that at the time, so they shot it down.

The Soviet government had made no such admission. We interviewed the author of this editorial and learned that there was no basis in fact for this 'new' Soviet position other than rumors of private admissions made to visiting Americans during "walks in the woods, you know how that is." The editorial writer also referred us to statements in Hersh's TV interviews that neither Marshal Ogarkov nor Deputy Foreign Minister Kornienko had any evidence of KAL's spy mission.

When we informed an official in USIA's Office of Policy Planning of our discovery, that official became upset—VOA editorials are subjected to close pre-broadcast scrutiny, but this gaffe had not been caught.

Soviet reaction was angry and, by Soviet standards, immediate. During the September 1, 1986 telecast of *Vremia*, a sharp rejoinder was read by commentator Genrikh Borovik, the newscaster who three years earlier had conjured up the vision of Nazi stormtroopers pushing women and children ahead of them. Borovik's response said, in part:

> I did not plan to say anything, either in the press or on tele-vision, on the occasion of the 3d anniversary of this tragedy, a tragedy which was used for propaganda, considering, as many others around the world do, that the gist of what happened 3 years ago is today quite clear. However, the other day Voice of America presented the world with a statement which, as it was said, reflects the point of view of the U.S. Government, and I was again surprised at the shamelessness of those who have this point of view and those who reflect it. I will quote several para-graphs....
> There is falsehood in every sentence. The Soviet statements were not taken back by the Soviet authorities and were not refuted by anyone. Moreover, every day gives them ever more authoritative confirmation from various sources....[77]

A VOA internal memorandum cites the Borovik commentary as evi-dence that Soviet authorities attach great significance to countering VOA's message: "Regardless of the hostile content, such a *Vremya* segment cannot but create (or enhance) interest in our broadcasts." Nevertheless, the memorandum acknowledged, "even TV watchers sympathetic to the VOA must be wondering what is fact and what is fancy in Borovik's tirade"; it was suggested that broadcasting a KAL update might be a good idea.

VOA did just that. Todd Leventhal, who had written the FOCUS program commemorating the first anniversary, was assigned to pro-duce another retrospective emphasizing the publication of *"The Target Is Destroyed"*.[78] In contrast to the earlier program, this FOCUS concen-trated on technical, not political, issues. The tone of this broadcast was much more objective than the first, although its content was not any more favorable to the Soviet position. Among the persons interviewed were: Viktor Belenko, Harold Ewing, Philip Klass, Thomas Maertens,

James Oberg, and Seymour Hersh. Both *Shootdown* and" *The Target Is Destroyed*"were discussed during the program.

Again the Soviet propagandists reacted sharply. Three days later *Krasnaia zvezda* published its rebuttal,[79] which has proven to be the last antagonistic thrust in this prolonged battle of words. According to the Russian text, the stimulus for this article was a story that had appeared in the September 1, 1986, edition of *U.S. News & World Report*.[80] But, judging by the timing and content of the Soviet rejoinder, there is no question that the true impetus was Todd Leventhal's FOCUS program, which had just been broadcast by the Voice of America.

This *Krasnaia zvezda* article is perhaps the best piece of creative writing produced over the entire three year period. We present it in its entirety:

The primary spy establishment in the USA—the CIA—is diligently covering its tracks. Tracks of the monstrous crime committed on September 1, 1983, when a Boeing 747 operated by the South Korean airline company KAL flew from the USA into Soviet airspace on a spy mission. The CIA chose the famous American journalist Seymour Hersh as the mouthpiece for its new fabrications concerning this anti-Soviet provocation.

The CIA knew that for more than two years Hersh had been gathering facts about the ill-fated flight in order to write a book. So he became the object of a certain amount of 'attention.' The chief of the US spy establishment himself, W[illiam] Casey, telephoned him. Moreover, according to *U.S. News & World Report*, the CIA head even provided Hersh access to what was termed "supersecret data obtained by American electronic intelligence in the Far East." As a result, the CIA chief deigned to "personally approve" what appeared in the pages of Hersh's book *"The Target Is Destroyed"*.

Now Western media have hurriedly, but with noteworthy uniformity, written about the sensational nature of this 'work.' It purports to demonstrate a "neutral" version of the tragedy that occurred three years ago; Hersh declares that "no one is to blame" for the death of the Boeing 747 passengers. It was merely "the result of errors." In the words of *U.S. News & World Report*, it was Casey who spoon fed these notions to the author of the book.

There is no doubt that highly placed administration officials in Washington are completely happy with this new 'interpretation' of the events of September 1, 1983. They expect this publication will conceal the truth more securely in a pile of false data from the bottomless pit of the CIA archives.

Washington has never conceived of achieving its imperialist pretensions to world supremacy without global espionage.

It is well known that prior to the launch of the first American spy satellites the CIA's top-priority 'technical means' for carrying out strategic aerial reconnaissance were U-2 airplanes. As *Newsweek* wrote on April 2, 1979, CIA director A[llen] Dulles was "ecstatic over photos taken during high altitude U-2 flights over the USSR."

According to directive 10/2 of the US National Security Council, such secret activity was supposed to be carried out in a manner that would make it impossible to prove government complicity. "One of the cornerstones of the plan" D[wight] Eisenhower recalled about the U-2 problem in his memoirs, "was the decision that this airplane would self-destruct should there be unforeseen circumstances, and the pilot would perish." Only extreme circumstances (the May 1, 1960, capture of the American saboteur G[ary] Powers and his confession) forced the United States government to accept responsibility for its deeds. It also bore responsibility for the fact that, to the satisfaction of 'hawks' in Washington, the "U-2 incident" ruined the imminent summit meeting among leaders of the USSR, USA, England, and France, [which would have been] so important for the cause of peace on the planet.

And the outcome, more than two decades later, of the latest aerial espionage operation against the Soviet Union is well known. But the CIA is trying to convince people with its new version of events that responsibility is borne by no one. For if they admitted this premeditated act, the guilty parties would have to answer not only for 'tickling' the Soviet line of defense in the Far East, but also for the abrupt deterioration of Soviet-American relations provoked by Washington.

Many indisputable facts attest that all of this was the result of a monstrous criminal act by the intelligence services of the USA. For example, the array of aerial and satellite 'special technical means' brought to bear on the September 1, 1983, provocation speaks for itself. This includes not only the South Korean 747 purposely sent deep into the USSR, but also the US RC-135 electronic reconnaissance aircraft located in the vicinity, as well as the American spy satellite 1982-41C. And not the least significant role in this incident was played by US, Japanese, and South Korean radar installations. These are the true facts. And no number of clever fabrications can conceal them.[81]

For the record, Manning's *USN&WR* story contained only one reference to the CIA and its director, William Casey: "Hersh's book ... has attracted most attention, both because of his credentials as an investigator of Washington's secrets and because of CIA Director William Casey's concerns about his revelations."

It is instructive to look at the broad outlines of Soviet press treatment of the Korean airliner three years after the event. Overall, the tone had softened considerably following the second anniversary, and in all likelihood would have remained so had it not been for the direct assault to Soviet credibility contained in the August 31, 1986, VOA editorial. After Borovik's sharp response the next day, moreover, there were clear indications that Soviet propagandists wanted to revert to a less confrontational stance.[82] Of course, this did not entail forgetting about KAL; rather, the change was manifested in a reversion to the tactics of indirection. On September 13, *Krasnaia zvezda* published an article entitled "The DC-9 Affair: Will the Truth Be Known?"[83] The text, which runs for about twenty column inches, begins dramatically:

A flash, an explosion—and a DC-9 passenger airliner of the Italian airline "Itavia" crashed into the sea. The disaster swept away 81 lives. The time of this action—June 27, 1980; the place—Ustica Island, near Sicily.

The text of this article goes on to charge that Italian forces participating with NATO military exercises had shot the plane down, and that the Italian government had classified all relevant information in order to conceal the truth. Following an analysis of Italy's growing militarization, the article concludes with this paragraph:

One cannot fail to notice something else. The Italian DC-9 airplane disaster automatically brings to mind events surrounding the South Korean Boeing 747, which intruded into Soviet airspace three years ago for the purpose of espionage. There are those in the West who would like to revive that failed anti-Soviet slander campaign. It is noteworthy that in both instances the true causes of the tragedies have been carefully hidden from people.

Despite the thinly veiled reference to Hersh's new book and the VOA editorial, one is struck by the lack of vituperative language in Batyrev's column. Still, this text is most remarkable because it is so obviously intentional: absent any new information or analogous occurrence, a six-year old event cannot be newsworthy in any meaningful sense. But the rhetorical purpose behind publishing the column becomes apparent from the anachronistic lead sentence of the concluding paragraph: by resurrecting Western military complicity in the DC-9 deaths, an analogy can be drawn to KAL—which obviously is the point of the whole exercise. The lesson is clear: the Soviet Union is not the only country whose military had shot down a passenger plane in peacetime. No mention is made here of the 1973 Libyan plane that Israel destroyed, but Batyrev's column reminds one of the series of articles published in October 1983 about that tragedy. It is also reminiscent of the *tu quoque* articles about nuclear accidents in the West published immediately after the explosions at Chernobyl.

Of course, no one in the Soviet Union could predict that just four days later VOA would broadcast the Todd Leventhal "FOCUS" program, which was viewed as a continuation of the VOA attack and which therefore required a rebuttal. Nevertheless, the KAL propaganda war nearly came to an end with that exchange. Soviet propagandists ignored the incident completely for several months, only to resurrect it again in May, 1987. At that time, *Krasnaia zvezda* reprinted under the title "Disinformation—A US Specialty" an article that had been published in Paris and attributed to one Schofield Coryell.[84] The article surveys US attempts to spread disinformation—defined as "the fabrication of lies and their distribution for governmental purposes"— regarding Libya (prior to the 1986 US air strikes), the "Bulgarian connection" to the assassination attempt upon the life of Pope John Paul, in the Middle East, and in Nicaragua. Four paragraphs are devoted to the Korean airliner.

Charging that "the Reagan Administration used the incident to the greatest extent possible for propaganda purposes," the author claims that the essence of the American campaign was the notion that the deaths of 269 passengers "supposedly was an unforeseen opportunity to incite anti-Soviet feeling both in the United States and in Western Europe." Other elements in the US position included the fact that the aircraft was civilian, and that "the Russians had shot it down intentionally" (<u>russkie umyshlenno sbili ego</u>). Such direct factual statements are rare throughout all of the Soviet treatment of KAL. Indeed, as far as can be determined, this is only the second mention of the exact number of deaths to appear in official Soviet commentary, the other instance having been the Ogarkov press conference on September 9, 1983. In addition, *"The Target Is Destroyed"* comes in for unlikely praise. Whereas nine months earlier Hersh had been vilified as "the mouthpiece for ... new [CIA] fabrications concerning this anti-Soviet provocation," now his "revelations" (<u>razoblacheniia</u>) have proven that the "[American] government version was a lie."

Yet this article is remarkable not only for what it says: equally remarkable are the things unsaid. There is no mention of the CIA or the NSA; the flight of the airliner is not called "intentional," nor is any of the standard jargon employed—no "provocation," "ruckus," or "long reaching goals" are alleged.[85]

Following publication of this translated French article, the Korean airliner again receded into the background until the fourth anniversary—September 1, 1987. At that time an article in *Krasnaia zvezda* stated that "reactionary circles" in the United States were using the anniversary "to stage all sorts of anti-Soviet orgies."[86] The ideological thrust of the article was two-fold: to reinforce the established interpretation—that the deaths were intentional—and to equate the United States with Nazi Germany:

> The U.S. special services quite deliberately assigned the main task in this spy mission to the passenger plane. The calculation was highly cynical. If the crew performed its mission, the Pentagon would receive important intelligence data about the Soviet Armed Forces. If the Boeing was shot down, it would provide an excuse for an anti-Soviet campaign....
> That is why the U.S. special services sent a passenger plane on a spy flight, making people the hostages of their provocation. They behaved just like those who drove peaceful inhabitants onto minefields.[87]

Coming as it did after a long silence, this column was somewhat unexpected. Moreover, if the Soviet Union was going to publish such a hard-line statement on the occasion of the fourth anniversary, it is surprising that it would completely ignore the publication of David Pearson's book, which espouses a position the Soviets would certainly want to endorse and disseminate. That is exactly what happened, however. Of course, it is possible that some sort of response was expected from the government of the United States. But no official of the

American government made any statement, and the anniversary passed virtually unnoticed in the West. Even Pearson's book elicited almost no critical comment.

The final salvo in this battle was launched in January, 1988. Congressman Lee H. Hamilton, Chairman of the Committee on Foreign Affairs of the US House of Representatives, released declassified documents indicating that Seymour Hersh was correct: the American government had ignored the absence of hard evidence when it charged that the Soviet Union with knowingly destroying a civilian airliner.[88] The Soviet Union registered this information with a domestic radio broadcast that charged the United States with utilizing "a torrent of slander and accusations" in "attempts to distort our history." Nonetheless, the overall tenor of this commentary was fairly conciliatory: it was noted that the West was manifesting signs "of interpreting the image of the Soviet Union in a different manner"; moreover, nowhere in this latest discussion of the tragic events of August 31/September 1, 1983, can one discern any intimation that the Korean airliner had been engaged in an espionage mission.[89]

This survey of Soviet propaganda spanning four years demonstrates the fluctuations that can be manifested in the interpretation of an important international event. There seems to be no question that the official Soviet position regarding the Korean airliner and its role in an American spy mission has been extremely malleable: when it served the government's purpose, its rhetorical tone could be indignant, unyielding, and vituperative; equally, when the political situation had changed, Soviet propaganda was modified to keep pace. The facility with which propagandists shifted from one mode to the other is further testimony to the subservient position of public communication within this authoritarian system. Initially, of course, it was imperative to create a rhetorical totem—America's Korean airliner provocation. Once that had been accomplished, however, once the event had been assigned its place in the official history of US-Soviet relations, in Soviet public knowledge, so that the totem could be trotted out whenever it suited official purpose, then particular fluctuations in the rhetorical trappings could be utilized to emphasize current political priorities.

Given the tactical shifts which have occurred recently in Soviet domestic and foreign policy, it is probably not accidental that since the summer of 1986 nearly every printed reference to the Korean airliner in Soviet media has appeared on the pages of *Krasnaia zvezda*, the military's daily newspaper. For this is the audience that must be reached with the most salient propaganda message. As tension on the international scene has receded in the past few years, it has been expedient to reduce the shrillness of Soviet rhetoric both at home and a-broad. Thus, it appears, the Soviet government has adopted the methodology of intermittently reinforcing its official interpretation of the event with language that is less confrontational, while reserving its harsher rhetorical tone for those occasions when it has been deemed necessary to rebut (or forestall?) continued American attacks on the legitimacy of Soviet actions. It is in this final development that one sees most clearly the predominance of domestic over international political considerations throughout Soviet treatment of KAL Flight 007.

CHAPTER SEVEN

NOTES

[1] According to RFE-RL research, 62% of Soviet citizens interviewed mentioned agitprop meetings as a source of information regarding KAL, making this the most frequently cited source. Soviet television, Western radio, and Soviet radio were approximately equal, whereas, unexpectedly, only 19% of respondents specifically mentioned the Soviet press. See RFE-RL, *The Korean Airline Incident: Western Radio and Soviet Perceptions,* Soviet Area Audience and Opinion Research Report AR 4-84 (April 1984), p. 5.

[2] By way of contrast, American journalists had chided the president for trying to salvage his Labor Day vacation. It was reliably reported, as noted above, that the president had to be convinced to return to Washington earlier than planned in order not to appear derelict in duty or insensitive to the tragedy. For details, see: Kadell, pp. 136-38, *et passim*; and Speakes, pp. 120-21.

[3] Kenneth Boulding, "National Images and International Systems," *Journal of Conflict Resolution,* 3 (1959), 120-31. Cited in: Farrell Corcoran, "The Bear in the Back Yard: Myth, Ideology, and Victimage Ritual in Soviet Funerals," *Communication Monographs,* 50 (December 1983), 305-20, p. 320.

[4] These complaints stem directly from Soviet officials in Moscow (private communication).

[5] Americans have a similar 'storehouse of knowledge' about the Soviets, consisting primarily of numerous alleged treaty violations which are brought up each time a new accord with the Soviets is proposed. In addition, of course, are the Soviet actions in Hungary, Czechoslovakia, Berlin, Cuba, Poland, Afghanistan, KAL 902, and now KAL 007 and Chernobyl. As Ralph K. White put it: "We Americans know well the many things the Soviets have done that have angered us." Ralph K. White, *Fearful Warriors: A Psychological Profile of U.S.-Soviet Relations* (New York: Free Press, 1984), 164.

[6] One of the latest articles was "Razoblachenie Izhi" ["Unmasking the Lies"], a *Krasnaia zvezda* story published October 16, 1983, which reported that a British TV broadcast called the American version of events "false from beginning to end." Four Americans were cited, T. Kaplan (identified as the *Boston Globe'* s military commentator), Charles Jones (identified as a representative of the Information Center on Military Problems in Washington), and Tom Bernard and T. Edward Eskelson (former US reconnaissance officers during the Vietnam era whose OpEd piece in the *Denver Post* [September 13, 1983, p. 3B] had first called into question the truth of the United States government's position). On October 21, 1983, *Sovetskaia Rossia* published

"Elektronnaia pautina" ["Electronic Web"], p. 5, which discussed US surveillance assets in the Northwest Pacific.

[7]*Pravda* actually predicted the Grenada attack, reporting the deployment of US vessels in the Caribbean. This is ironic, since the US military, fearful of another media blitz such as had preceded and accompanied the ill-fated Bay of Pigs invasion, prohibited journalists from accompanying the American forces into battle.

[8]Voice of America, CN-057, December 8, 1983 [no time indicated].

[9]Voice of America, CN-051, December 13, 1983 [10:57:47].

[10]Voice of America, CN-075, December 14, 1983 [no time indicated].

[11]Voice of America, CN-062, February 28, 1984 [10:35:58].

[12]As far as we have been able to determine the only reference to the *ICAO REPORT* in Soviet print media appeared in *Komsomol'skaia pravda*, August 24, 1984, p. 3. In an article entitled "Reis 007—shpionskaia aktsiia TsRU" ["Flight 007—A CIA Spy Action"], John Keppel is quoted as having characterized the conclusions contained in the *ICAO REPORT* as "criminal with respect to the victims of the catastrophe" and "a crude attempt to deceive world opinion." It states, incorrectly, that ICAO attributed a 40-minute delay in KAL 007's takeoff from Anchorage to "pilot error" (netochnoe pilotirovanie).

[13]On the importance of letters to newspapers within Soviet society see: Alex Inkeles, *Public Opinion in Soviet Russia: A Study in Mass Persuasion* (Cambridge: Harvard University Press, 1950); Alex Inkeles and H. Kent Geiger, "Critical Letters to the Soviet Press," in Alex Inkeles, ed., *Social Change in Soviet Russia* (Harvard University Press, 1968), 291-324; Alex Inkeles and Raymond Bauer, *The Soviet Citizen* (New York: Atheneum, 1968); and Adams, who compared her 1977 data with the results obtained in 1947 by Inkeles and Geiger. Adams found that "Soviet citizens feel freer than in the past to voice their personal grievances" but that, despite significant change in Soviet society over the intervening thirty years, characteristics of letter writing revealed a "relative lack of change" (pp. 119, 130). Adams concluded that "the system of tight political control over the expression of [self-criticism], though operating today with a less heavy hand than in the past, is, to an astonishing degree, the same system that existed in the terrible postwar years of Stalin's tyranny" (p. 131).

[14]A. Peshcherin, "Shpion za oblakami" ["Spy Behind the Clouds"], *Sovetskaia Rossiia*, December 11, 1983, p. 5.

[15]*The Guardian*, December 17, 1983, p. 15. See our review of Johnson's book *Shootdown*. For Johnson's reaction to the Soviet translation of his 1983 article, see pp. xiii-xiv in *Shootdown*.

[16]Voice of America, CN-086, October 7, 1983 [15:05:07]. The article cited in this report is: David Shribman, "U.S. Experts Say Soviet Didn't See Jet Was Civilian," *The New York Times*, October 7, 1983, pp. A1, A10.

[17]Voice of America, CN-122, October 7, 1983 [21:38:39]. See also: Richard Halloran, "Soviet Is Said to Shake Up Far East Air Command," *The New York Times*, October 8, 1983, p. L3.

[18]See: Voice of America, American Viewpoints #85-17, April 29, 1985. Reporters: Robert Arnold and Peter Fedynsky; and Pearson, *KAL 007: The Cover-Up*, p. 284.

[19]In August 1984, the airline company sued *Defence Attaché* for libel. That Fall an out of court settlement was reached, whereby KAL received a "substantial" amount of money, an apology in open court, and the promise of a published retraction. See: *The New York Times*, November 20, 1984, p. A5; and *Time*, December 3, 1984, p. 47. Along with the retraction the magazine printed a detailed technical rebuttal of Mann's (and Kirsanov's) arguments. (See: Oberg, "Sakhalin: Sense and Nonsense") Oberg is a recognized expert on the technology that Challenger and KAL 007 allegedly used to communicate with one another, but his analysis was derogated in pro-conspiracy writings. The conspiratists subsequently claimed that no money changed hands and that the magazine agreed to settle only because it could not afford to lose a huge damage suit. Editor R. Pengelley was, of course, constrained from commenting further. See: Johnson, *Shootdown*, pp. 153-59; and Pearson, *KAL 007: The Cover-Up*, pp. 288-90.

[20]Frederic Golden's "flat-earth physics" rejoinder cited earlier was aimed at David Pearson and P. Q. Mann. Pearson contends that Oberg, Golden, and other writers in *Time*, the *Washington Times*, and *U.S. News & World Report*, were simply echoing "the official line" espoused by Assistant Secretary of State Richard Burt. See: Pearson, *KAL 007: The Cover-Up*, p. 296.

[21]Herbert Romerstein, Senior Policy Officer and Coordinator on Soviet Active Measures at USIA, specifically cautioned us, in a July 1986 interview, against reading more into some circumstances than was warranted by verifiable fact. Specifically, Romerstein said there was absolutely no evidence of Soviet participation in the appearance of "Reassessing the Sakhalin Incident." That did not stop VOA from ascribing the article to Soviet active measures: in their April 29, 1985 "American Viewpoints" program, Robert Arnold and Peter Fedynsky interviewed former CIA officer Donald Jameson, who called the Mann article part of a "definite Soviet effort to manipulate Western public opinion" and a "classic example of Soviet disinformation." For evidence of possible Soviet complicity, see also: James E. Oberg, "The Sky's No Limit to Disinformation," *Air Force Magazine*, March 1986, 52-56.

[22]Voice of America, CN-033, June 18, 1984 [09:45:32].

[23]Voice of America, NEB-030, Correspondent Report 2-8189, June 18, 1984 [12:15:24].

[24]This set of articles included:

"On a Spy Mission," *Krasnaia zvezda*, June 17, p. 3;
"When Secrets Become Clear," *Pravda*, June 19, p. 5;
"Criminals and Their Accomplices," *Sovetskaia Rossiia*, June 20, p. 5;
"It Has Boomeranged," *Pravda*, June 20, p. 5;
"The Provocateurs Miscalculated," *Krasnaia zvezda*, June 20, p. 3;
"Covering Up Their Tracks," *Pravda*, June 21, p. 5;
"Caught Red-Handed," *Komsomol'skaia pravda*, June 22, p. 3;
"The Amount of Evidence Has Increased," *Izvestiia*, June 22, p. 4.

Much of the text of the three articles published June 20 is identical; similarly, the June 21 *Pravda* article and the June 22 *Komsomol'skaia pravda* article come from the same wire-service dispatch. Typically, different titles are utilized, but the repetition is intended to reinforce the impression received by any reader who encounters more than one item.

[25]"Pereotsenka sakhalinskogo intsidenta," *Za rubezhom* [*Beyond the Border*], 1984, No. 27 (29 June—5 July), pp. 10-11.

[26]The individuals are all named, but with the exception of James Bamford (author of *The Puzzle Palace*), Tom Bernard, and T. Edward Eskelson, they are surely unknown to a Soviet audience. Among the many persons cited, these three, along with Ralph McGehee (author of *Deadly Deceits: My Twenty-Five Years in the CIA)* and Kenneth Lawrence (sp?), are former US intelligence officers.

[27]"Kogda tainoe stanovitsia iavnym" ["When Secrets Become Clear"], *Pravda*, June 19, p. 5. Sometime later it would be claimed that Andrews AFB [which is located outside of Washington, DC] was the place where 007 was outfitted with cameras. This rumor was widespread in the US, as well.

[28]"Ulik stalo bol'she" ["The Amount of Evidence Has Increased"], *Izvestiia*, June 22, p. 4. According to Reed Irvine of "Accuracy In Media," the first public allegation of possible US jamming appeared in a publication called *Counterspy*. (See: Voice of America, American Viewpoints #85-17, April 29, 1985.) *Izvestiia* did not cite any source for this information, stating it as established fact. The two squadrons are actually part of the USAF Electronic Security Command, which collects ELINT for NSA. It was in the 6920th on Hokkaido that Major Kas'min was overheard saying, "The target has been destroyed." [See: Hersh, pp. 10, 61.] The 6981st, based at Elmendorf AFB, is the unit which monitored Soviet radar operators on Kamchatka. See also: Jeffrey Richelson, *American Espionage and the Soviet Target* (New York: William Morrow, 1987), pp. 204-221.

[29]These stories appeared in *Pravda* (August 6/11/18, 1984) and *Krasnaia zvezda* (August 7, 1984). An otherwise unrelated article in *Izvestiia* (August 17, 1984), "Sdelano v TsRU" ["Made in the CIA"], listed the KAL incident among other CIA operations-- the Bay of Pigs invasion and the deaths of Patrice Lumumba and Salvador Allende.

[30]"Pravda sil'nee lzhi" ["The Truth is Stronger than Lies"], *Pravda*, August 31, 1984, p. 4.

[31]An accurate, thorough description of the 1978 incident appears in Oberg, "Sakhalin: Sense and Nonsense."

[32]"Trassery b'iut po tseli" ["Tracers Hit Their Target"], *Aviatsiia i kosmonavtika*, September 1984, 42-43.

[33]*Komsomol'skaia pravda*, August 24, 1984, p. 3.

[34]*Pravda*, September 4, 1984, p. 5.

[35]In fact, winds aloft in the Pacific that night were so favorable that estimated flying time to Korea was reduced by forty minutes. Take off was scheduled so that KAL 007 would arrive in Seoul at 6:00 am local time, when the customs office began its daily operations. According to the *ICAO REPORT*, this was standard KAL procedure—Flight 007 never had a fixed takeoff time. See: *ICAO REPORT*, pp. 4-5.

[36]"Vykruchivaiutsia" ["Twisting and Turning"], *Izvestiia*, August 30, 1984, p. 5; and A. Liutyi, "Otvetstvennost' nesut SShA" ["The USA Bears Responsibility"], *Krasnaia zvezda*, August 30, 1984, p. 3.

[37]"Umyshlennaia provokatsiia" ["Malicious Provocation"], *Pravda*, August 27, 1984, p. 5; "Eto byl zagovor" ["It Was a Conspiracy"], *Pravda*, September 4, 1984, p. 5.

[38]Vladimir Simonov, "Sem' dnei v sentiabre," *Literaturnaia gazeta*, September 14, 1983, p. 9.

[39]Iu. Bandura, "Provokatory u pozornogo stolba" ["Provocateurs in the Stocks"], *Izvestiia*, August 31, 1984, p. 5.

[40]"Pravda sil'nee lzhi" ["The Truth is Stronger than Lies"], *Pravda*, August 31, 1984, p. 4. This "no lose" terminology first appeared in: General-polkovnik artillerii E. Iurasov, "Zven'ia odnoi tsepi" ["Links in the Same Chain"], *Krasnaia zvezda*, October 4, 1983, p. 3. It was this article that belatedly claimed, five years after the fact, that the 1978 flight of KAL 902 had also been coordinated with US spy satellites. Like the September 20, 1983 Kirsanov article concerning Flight 007, Iurasov's contained a map--this one completely fabricated--showing the overflight of US satellites alleged to have participated in KAL 902's intrusion. No such maps had been published in 1978.

[41]*Izvestiia*, p. 5; *Pravda*, p. 5; *Krasnaia zvezda*, p. 3 [all August 30, 1984].

[42]*Sovetskaia Rossiia*, September 1, 1984, p. 5.

[43]One individual queried holds a *Vordiplom* from the university in Mainz: Ms. Katinka Fischer of Tallahassee FL, who did not recognize either title, was an undergraduate journalism major.

[44]For example, in *KAL 007: The Cover-Up* (pp. 216, 219), Pearson cites Kang as the source of so-called "correct translations" of incorrect passages in the revised US transcript of the air-to-ground tape. One of these passages involves "the call" [See Chapter Four]. But Kang stated in a telephone interview that he accepted allegations and statements of facticity that had first appeared in Pearson's own article, "K.A.L. 007: What the U.S. Knew and When We Knew It." Kang has admitted in print that he "was expressly endorsing David Pearson's argument." See: Launer, Young, & Kang, p. 70. By quoting Yamagawa, Bandura was repeating Soviet disinformation: see below.

[45]*Sovetskaia Rossiia*, September 2, 1984, p. 5.

[46]*Krasnaia zvezda*, September 2, 1984, p. 3.

[47]The Russian noun sotrudnik means 'skilled, white-collar employee whose job is mental, not physical, requiring intelligence and training.'

[48]*Pravda*, August 26, 1984, p. 5; and *Izvestiia*, August 29, 1984, p. 5.

[49]*Sovetskaia Rossiia*, September 2, 1984, p. 5; and *Krasnaia zvezda*, September 2, 1984, p. 3.

[50]Emphasis has been added in the citations which follow.

[51]Voice of America, CN-081, August 8, 1984 [11:01:38]. This report substituted "specializing in" for CN-072's "with extensive study of" [10:38:22].

[52]*The Nation* was not above building up its new celebrity, either: "It is appropriate that a scholar whose areas of concentration are complex organizations and communication, rather than a member of the traditional press, . . . should be the one to break this extraordinary story" (p. 105).

[53]Mentioned by Ovchinnikov [*Pravda*, August 31, 1984, p. 4].

[54]"Tainaiia voina Vashingtona" ["Washington's Secret War"], *Krasnaia zvezda*, August 7, 1984, p. 3; Also mentioned by Bandura [*Izvestiia*, August 31, 1984, p. 5].

[55]Murray Sayle, "Shooting on suspicion: the final secrets of KE007," unpublished manuscript, p. 2. Sayle, who lives in Japan, sought out and interviewed a man who claims to be the author. Although "ignorant as a schoolboy about aviation," Akio Takahasi "displays an academician's knowledge of the dates and texts of Soviet laws relevant to his subject." Sayle continues: "Whoever may have compiled the rest of the book, this chapter reads unmistakably as Soviet arguing with Soviet, with Takahasi playing, rather in the manner of *Roshomon*, the role of medium" (p. 5). Sayle believes

that the purpose of the book was to set forth Soviet arguments regarding the legality of the shooting. In his opinion, the intention all along was to translate the book into Russian—if he is correct, the book would constitute another instance of <u>dezinformatsiia,</u> with Soviet propagandists deciding that a foreign source would increase the credibility of information that might be received skeptically if published without such authority.

[56]Maertens, p. 30.

[57]An agent of influence "covertly inject[s] Soviet views into governmental, political, journalistic, business, labor, and academic circles of a foreign country. To accomplish this objective, KGB officers develop relationships with key figures from these influential circles who are willing to collaborate (wittingly or unwittingly) on matters of mutual interest. . . . In those cases in which the agent is a journalist, the connection with [Soviet] covert propaganda operations is apparent." See: Richard H. Shultz and Roy Godson, *DEZINFORMATSIA. Active Measures in Soviet Strategy* (McLean, VA: Pergamon-Brassey's, 1984), pp. 32-33.

[58]L. Jameson, p. 24.

[59]One could term this *tu quoque, i.e.,* "the pot calling the kettle black."

[60]The Reuter correspondent pointed out that this statement meant the South Koreans were trying to repair relations with the Soviet Union so that the Eastern bloc nations would not boycott the 1988 Summer Olympics in Seoul as they had boycotted the 1984 Games in Los Angeles.

[61]Granville Watts, "Year After KAL Disaster Mystery Remains on Why Plane Strayed," Reuter, Seoul, South Korea, August 29, 1984.

[62]Voice of America, Editorial 0-1057, "Memory and Resolve," September 1, 1984.

[63]Voice of America, Correspondent Report 2-1605 [NEB-036], "KAL 007-One Year Later," [Reporter: Lee Hall]; and Russell Dybvik [USIA diplomatic correspondent], "KAL 007 Tragedy Must Never Be Repeated," August 28, 1984.

[64]Voice of America, Editorial 0-0800, "An Impartial Report," December 18, 1983.

[65]Voice of America, Special Report #4-0877, "FOCUS: The Korean Airliner Shootdown: One Year Later," August 30, 1984 [Reporter: Todd Leventhal]. VOA also broadcast, beginning August 31, 1984, a shorter version of this report as a CLOSE-UP with the same title.

[66]"Zaplanirovannaia shpionskaia missiia" ["A Planned Spy Mission"], *Pravda,* September 1, 1985, p. 5.

[67] Yuri Ivashchenko, "Shchit otechestva," *Nedelia,* April 7-13, 1986, p. 6 [translated as "The Fatherland's Shield," *Soviet Press Selected Translations.* Current News Special Edition, No. 1528, December 30, 1986, 181-86].

[68] "Zaplanirovannaia aktsiia" ["A Planned Action"], *Pravda,* May 9, 1986, p. 5.

[69] "Podopleka provokatsii" ["The Real Truth about the Provocation"], *Krasnaia zvezda,* June 13, 1986, p. 3.

[70] Johnson appeared on *Nightline* (ABC) [June 10, 1986], *Good Morning America* (ABC) [June 11, 1986], and *Crossfire* (CNN) [June 12, 1986].

[71] "Reis 007: Tainoe stanovitsia iavnym" ["Flight 007: What Was Secret Becomes Clear"], *Izvestiia,* August 2, 1986, p. 1.

[72] FBIS, "Joint U.S.-Japan Air Traffic Agreement Praised," *Daily Report. Soviet Union,* August 18, 1986, CC8.

[73] "Videozapis' razoblachaet," *Pravda,* August 17, 1986, p. 5.

[74] This charge is levelled in *Shootdown,* pp. 6-8; Johnson further alleges that the captain of KAL 007 took on unneeded extra fuel. These assertions have been analyzed by Harold Ewing, who has determined that they are without basis in fact. See: Hersh, pp. 196-98.

[75] Prior to publication of the book, a long excerpt appeared in *Atlantic Monthly,* September 1986, 47-69. Hersh's book generated widespread interest in the print media and occasioned more television segments, some of which featured relatives of KAL victims, on *Nightline* (ABC) [August 25, 1986], *The Larry King Show* (CNN) [September 2, 1986], and *Donohue* (syndicated) [September 16, 1986].

[76] Voice of America, Editorial 0-2069, "KAL 007: Three Years Later" [August 31, 1986].

[77] FBIS, "Commentary Discusses Downing of KAL Airliner," *Daily Report. Soviet Union,* September 4, 1986, C 1.

[78] Voice of America, Special Report #4-1948, "FOCUS: The Korean Airliner Shootdown Revisited," September 17, 1986 [Reporter: Todd Leventhal]. VOA also broadcast, beginning September 18, 1984, a shorter version of this report as a CLOSE-UP with the same title. The present authors were interviewed for these Special Reports, but that material was not included in the broadcast versions.

[79] Podpolkovnik Iu. Borin, "Zametaiut sledy" ["Covering Its Tracks"], *Krasnaia zvezda,* September 21, 1986, p. 3.

[80]Robert A. Manning, "A Chase for the Elusive KAL Story," *U.S. News & World Report*, September 1, 1986, p. 69. Manning discusses the Johnson and Hersh books, as well as "[David] Pearson's forthcoming book."

[81]On an ironic note, Hersh reported that during a May, 1984, interview Ogarkov and Kornienko revealed that they expected him to find evidence to support the Soviets' spy-plane theory. Hersh wrote:

> Kornienko [told] me why I had been invited to Moscow: he and Ogarkov had agreed to my visa in the hope that they could persuade me, as a journalist, to investigate the Central Intelligence Agency's role in the shootdown. Taken aback, but realizing that the two senior Soviet officials were serious, I asked Kornienko with a laugh whether he was trying to be my editor. His response came in English: 'Your assignment is to find that it was an intruder.' The Deputy Foreign Minister added that the American public would never accept the shootdown as a rational act on the Soviets' part unless it could be proved that the overflight of sensitive military installations was deliberate. I could not decide which was more surprising—his faith in the American First Amendment or the explicit acknowledgment that his government, for all of its public finger-pointing, had no evidence of American involvement in the flight path of the Korean airliner.

Seymour M. Hersh, "The Target is Destroyed," as excerpted in *The Atlantic Monthly*, September 1986, pp. 47-48.

[82]One can speculate that Mr. Gorbachev's consolidation of power, improving relations with the United States, and continuing preoccupation with Chernobyl may all have played a role in this development.

[83]S. Batyrev, "Delo DC-9: Stanet li izvestna istina?", *Krasnaia zvezda*, September 13, 1986, p. 5.

[84]"Dezinformatsiia—spetsial'nost' SShA," *Krasnaia zvezda*, May 23, 1987, p. 5. The article was reprinted "with minor deletions."

[85]James Oberg has pointed out that this article appeared just a week before the young German, Matthias Rust, flew his Cessna unimpeded all the way to Red Square in Moscow. "Did Koldunov or any of his pilots read it?" he asks (private communication).

[86]*Krasnaia zvezda*, September 1, 1987, p. 3.

[87]A. Gol'ts, "Rejoinder: Like Driving People Onto Minefields. . . ." [FBIS, *Daily Report. Soviet Union*, September 22, 1987, p. 34: PM150831].

[88]See: *Hartford Courant*, January 13, 1988, pp. Al, A9: and *San Diego Union*, January 14, 1988, p. A-14.

[89]FBIS, *Daily Report. Soviet Union*, January 14, 1988, pp. 13-14 [LD140001 Moscow Domestic Service in Russian 1600 GMT 13 Jan 88].

PART THREE

THE CONSPIRATISTS

CONSPIRACY THEORY AS ARGUMENT

> Conspiracy is as natural as breathing. And
> since the struggles for advantage nearly al-
> ways have a rhetorical strain, we believe that
> systematic contemplation of them forces it-
> self upon the student of rhetoric.
> —*Kenneth Burke*

As the propaganda war waged by the Reagan Administration began to fall under its own weight, it was not surprising that significant numbers of Americans began to wonder if the US government were directly involved in the fate of KAL 007. Almost immediately, conspiracy theories began to develop. Consequently we turn our attention in Part III to the rhetorical problem posed by the conspiratist argument. In the present chapter we will explore the genre of conspiratist rhetoric, focusing primarily on treatments by communication scholars. In Chapter Nine, we examine the article which most prominently alleged a conspiratorial role for KAL 007; allegations presented in this article, which serves as an exemplar of mainstream conspiracy theories, are compared to the official position of the American government.

Conspiracy theories have been a recurrent theme in the United States: American history is rife with such charges, some justified, some not. All are perpetuated by those who believe that social and political phenomena have identifiable and isolable causes. In short, conspiracy theory "is the view that an explanation of a social phenomenon consists in the discovery of the man or groups who are interested in the occurrence of this phenomenon ... and who have planned and conspired to bring it about."[1] Early targets for the conspiracy charge in America tended to be religious or allegedly anti-religious groups: the Masons, the Catholics, the Illuminati, the Jacobins, the Jews (the infamous "Protocols of the Learned Elders of Zion"). More recent victims of the allegations are less personal: monopolists, international financiers, imperialists, the establishment, and, of course, the communists. Bunzel remarked twenty years ago on the epistemic character of conspiratist rhetoric, "the persistent cries of conspiracy are not just a right-wing phenomenon, but a reflection of the pervasiveness of this way of

217

looking at things."[2] Creps, noting that conspiracy allegations are essentially rhetorical in nature, demonstrates that the argument constitutes a genre of rhetorical discourse, in other words, an interaction of situation with form or style.[3]

In the years since 1963, when Hofstadter first introduced the notion of "paranoid style," it has become increasingly apparent that extremist elements on the left or right are not the only ones who avail themselves of conspiracy as an explanatory vehicle. Goodnight and Poulakos identify the assassination of John F. Kennedy as a kind of watershed, a 'landmark' instance when the conspiratist's finger was turned back on American society's most frequent purveyor of the conspiracy hypothesis, the radical right.[4] The shift became more pronounced as conspiracy charges were leveled against the "military-industrial complex" (Vietnam) and the US government itself (Watergate). Not unscathed were industrial giants with no direct connection to the military effort; crusaders such as Ralph Nader took advantage of the mood of the country to expose abuses by automobile manufacturers, oil companies, and pharmaceutical houses. Gradually, "the 'paranoid style' moved away from ideological extremes to the mainstream of political life."[5] To the extent that individuals and organizations as disparate as Nader, Woodward and Bernstein, Ronald Reagan, and Soviet propagandists have had recourse to this tactic, it must be accorded greater status as a recognized and viable instrument of both intra- and intercultural discourse. While not all texts that allege conspiracy fall into the genre of conspiratist argument, developing a means for analyzing this type of argumentation assumes greater importance as conspiracy claims become an element not only of radical discourse, but of mainstream politics as well. The Korean airliner disaster is a case in point.

Recent literature provides some insight into the rhetorical nature and persuasive power of conspiratist interpretations of political situations. For example, Goodnight and Poulakos provide a useful explanation of how conspiracy theories are integrated into social history once they have become accepted by society.

> Conspiracy awareness usually begins following the appearance of an unusual event: an illegal act, an accident, a significant mistake with important consequences. The event draws interest because it represents a human tragedy, or alternatively, a comic departure from the normal course of public affairs.[6]

Typically, such events are surrounded by ambiguous, conflicting, and/or highly technical information. In any event, once an event has occurred, a normalizing process begins, with explanations and assessments. Goodnight and Poulakos argue that the more dramatic the event, the greater the haste to place it in perspective; whence the origin of the inevitable loose ends. Jervis observes that these more dramatic cases prompt closer scrutiny and become fertile ground for skeptics:

> Because it is rare that all the facts are consistent with the same conclusion, the closer one looks at the details of a case the greater the chance that some of them will contradict the accepted explanation. So it is not surprising that in cases that attract a lot of attention—such as political assassinations—many people are dissatisfied with the official account. The trouble with their objections is not so much that they imply the existence of conspiracies, but that they fail to appreciate that even the correct explanation will not be able to tie up neatly all the loose ends.[7]

Real life, unfortunately, contains random events that have no cosmic meaning and, thus, no tidy explanation.[8] But for some individuals or groups, the prevailing explanations will never suffice: "Either there is not enough evidence to warrant claims of certainty or no amount of evidence will do." When this occurs, there is a search for an alternative explanation.

> Old evidence may now be seen as less conclusive than once thought, perhaps even as false. When inconsistencies in proof are adduced, and when those in charge of defending the commonly accepted interpretation only reiterate previous explanations, suspicions grow. Interest in the initial event is compounded with interest in the perceived attempt to thwart the search for truth.[9]

Zarefsky, on the other hand, has considered a more general problem: elaborating the social circumstances and establishing the techniques of argumentation that help make conspiratist arguments credible to moderates as well as zealots. He notes that "conspiracy arguments become widely accepted when they explain an otherwise ambiguous evil and a pattern of anomalies"; moreover, it is precisely "when a large number of (anomalous) events occurs, and the anomalies seem to have a pattern, [that] the search for an explanation intensifies."[10]

Many of Zarefsky's "propositions" depend upon the debate-oriented context that he addressed in his article; they have less applicability to a situation that may actually be more common, where the "debate" is more or less one-sided: a charge is leveled, but the alleged conspirator makes little or no effort to confront the argument at all. However, Zarefsky's most disturbing conclusion has particular relevance to the rhetorical power of any conspiratist argument: "Inferences are a more persuasive form of evidence than documents."[11] The importance of this finding derives from its relation to the particular method of proof identified with the conspiratist argument.

Hofstadter first noted the scholarly pedantry of paranoid literature: "[T]he entire right-wing movement of our time is a parade of experts, study groups, monographs, footnotes and bibliographies."[12] Enormous energy is expended trying to provide "elaborate documentation of the links between The Plot and most of the history of civilization."[13] Yet the final product is "a veritable jungle of interlocking evidence and assertion."[14] Ultimately, it is inference that is the staple of the cabalist argument, for the vast corpus of evidence is merely "careful preparation for the big leap from the undeniable to the unbelievable."[15] What distinguishes the paranoid style is the "curious leap in imagination that is always made at some critical point in the recital of events."[16]

This strategy places minimal argumentative burdens on the conspiratist:

> While the claim of evil intrigue may be oppressive for the accused, the rhetor who launches the indictment can do so easily.... This is not to say that any allegation of a plot is automatically believed but that the threshold level of plausibility for conspiracy theories is quite low.[17]

Ironically, these minimal proof burdens "are often accompanied by enormous quantities of supporting quotations, references, and other scholarly paraphernalia."[18] The impact of this strategy of inference lies not in the preponderance of evidence, however, but in its enthymematic structure. Zarefsky attributes Lincoln's success to an inherent characteristic of the enthymeme: "the audience participated ... in reasoning through his inferences."[19]

Similarly, Warnick indicates that Fisher's notion of the narrative paradigm[20] may provide insight into the description of some conspiracies (such as the "Prince of Evil," the Nazi explanation of Germany's problems).[21] As with the enthymeme, part of the strength of the narrative paradigm derives from the participation of the auditor in validating the account—testing it against what is already known or believed.

While such literature has been useful in describing conspiratist rhetoric, it has often been lacking in evaluative force. For instance, Goodnight and Poulakos, in their explication of conspiratist rhetoric, suggest only a REALITY/FANTASY dichotomy: "If claims of a conspiracy are vindicated, then the rhetoric of the conspirators is revealed to be nothing more than the perpetuation of fantasy."[22] From this point of view, one has only the result of the struggle by which to judge the efficacy of the protagonists, and history, as we well know, is written by the victorious. That is to say, rhetorical fantasy is defined by social acceptance.[23] Indeed, certain implicit assumptions vitiate the extent to which one can generalize from Goodnight and Poulakos. They argue from the *a posteriori* vantage point of knowing that the Watergate conspiracy actually existed and was exposed (Nixon and his forces lost the battle for belief in their version of the truth—now labeled fantasy in the Goodnight/Poulakos schema). Had society judged events differently, Woodward and Bernstein would be the place-holders for a fantasy-theme.

One needs to add, of course, that if the conspiratists are not believed—since one cannot prove a negative, one cannot disprove the existence of a conspiracy—the same "fantasy" characterization must be applied to their rhetoric. Surely there are instances—the whole experience of the Army-McCarthy hearings, for one—in which the 'knowledge' of the conspiratists was proven false (again, in the public mind, because the conspiratists are never totally without foundation for their beliefs, or they would not have been taken seriously to begin with).[24]

FOUNDATIONS OF A CONSPIRATIST RHETORIC

It is precisely in the case of narratives which make "too much sense" that the critic is not well served by abandoning the conventions of formal and informal logic.[25] Moreover, as Rowland has observed, narrative fidelity and probability (Fisher's criteria for determining how well a story coheres, or makes sense internally) "must test not merely the story, but the story in relation to the world."[26] Warnick's essay underscores this point:

A narrative such as Hitler's is invidiously persuasive precisely because of its narrative fidelity.... The narrative in *Mein Kampf* provides a convenient mode for responding to any questions or

221

issues that those who are not "true believers" might want to raise.[27]

However, when a 'reality check' is applied via narrative fidelity and narrative probability, it becomes "essentially equivalent to the tests of evidence and reasoning that are traditionally applied to public argument."[28]

The example Warnick has chosen is fortuitous. It illustrates the "self-sealing" nature of conspiratist argument,[29] and in so doing, it underscores the necessity for rhetorical critics to involve themselves in the discussion of ways to appropriately praise or blame a given argument. This is especially true if Zarefsky is correct in observing that conspiratist argument has become a staple of American politics. Such an undertaking gains new urgency if Bunzel is correct in his warning that political paranoia threatens democracies precisely because of its tendency toward authoritarianism.

Nevertheless, as we have stated, in some situations a charge of conspiracy is most likely proper; in some it is not; and in some cases not enough of the evidence necessary to render a judgment is available. The Reality/Fantasy distinction mentioned above merely describes outcomes that are assigned to competing views as determined by public argument. The focus of the present analysis, however, is specifically the nature of any discourse which alleges conspiracy, irrespective of that final outcome.

When one considers such discourse, a good starting point is the generic nature of conspiratist rhetoric. Campbell and Jamieson have remarked that a generic perspective "requires careful textual analysis ... [and] heightens an awareness of the interrelationship between substantive and stylistic elements in discourse."[30] Likewise, one might consider the conspiratist's own value system: "A rhetor's *Weltanschauung* manifests itself not only in the premises he assumes but also in his structuring of arguments, his rhetorical tone, his use of language and in the types of evidence he educes."[31] Indeed, the very nature of the data can contribute to the plausibility of an alleged conspiracy: complex scientific, technical, and linguistic evidence is central to any discussion—including charges of conspiracy—in cases such as the Korean airliner disaster. (It is possible that the inherent plausibility of conspiracy may be enhanced by the highly technical nature of some incidents.)[32] Although the public may be swayed by the ethos or verbal skills of a rhetor to accept such evidence at face value, it must be pertinent to any critical judgment to assess the factual accuracy and evidentiary relevance of all specialized data brought to bear on a public issue.[33] Thus, one can assess the world view of the conspiratist—the ideological ground on which the charge of conspiracy rests—by examining the rhetorical use of quasi-logical argument, the perceived stylistic use of language, and the technical nature of the educed evidence.[34]

Hofstadter described the paranoid style as an essentially "subversive" style of political rhetoric, one which Fisher identifies as "an anti-ethos rhetoric; that is, it invariably is an attempt to undermine the credibility of some person, idea, or institution.... Typical of this approach to subversion are those attacks on authority that allege the existence of a conspiracy...."[35] Creps defines the substance of conspiratist rhetoric as its "proposition[al], thematic, logical, and evidential content."[36] Two characteristics of this type of rhetoric are: (a) the "strictly dichotomous view of morality" it evinces; and (b) the closed system of analysis, offering a "deductive, causal claim," which is formed by its arguments.[37] This evidentiary methodology is particularly significant, because conspiratist rhetoric characteristically employs the false dilemma (a dissociative construct that imposes upon the auditor a binary choice). Associative strategies frequently employed by the conspiratist include guilt by association, reliance on circular and *post hoc* reasoning, and a variant of the 'Halo Effect' which we term 'Lesser Facts, Greater Facts' (the use of trivial detail to imply knowledge of more important issues). Each of these associative/dissociative techniques functions effectively within the narrative structure of conspiratist argument. Perelman and Olbrechts-Tyteca explain association as a rhetorical tactic in which

> two terms are presented as if their insertion into the same class went without saying, and [as a result] there is a formation of a class ad hoc through the union of the two terms on a plane of equality.... [E]lements placed side by side ... to form a class ... react on each other in the [auditor's] mind, and it is because of this that the technique assumes its argumentative value.[38]

The ambiguity and implicitness of its claims—the implicative character of story-telling structure—enables narrative to account for seemingly discrepant facts.[39] Ambiguity becomes manifest as parataxis, the argument form which is characterized by an "absence of precise connection between [its] parts.... The [auditor] is left free to imagine ... a relationship that by its very lack of precision assumes a mysterious, magical character...."[40] In this manner, associations/dissociations are asserted as if they were already proven fact, thus allowing the power of inference to work. Parataxis "leaves greater freedom, and does not appear to wish to impose a particular viewpoint"; in contrast, hypotaxis, "the argumentative construction par excellence," stems from "well-constructed legal reasoning." But parataxis can be misleading, and it is from this absence of formal argumentation that narration derives its persuasiveness. Parataxis, then, is one characteristic which allows for—indeed, creates—the self-sealing attribute observed by Zarefsky and others. Warnick provides an excellent example: "If those skeptical of Hitler's account pointed out the existence of Jewish workers not conforming to his stereotype, his response would be 'that is one more indication of the cunning with which the Jewish plot is being engineered'."[41]

The characteristics of the conspiratist argument function together to produce a rhetoric that is coercive. One of the goals of such rhetoric is polarization. Fisher contends that it is the critic's function to identify such motives in rhetorical discourse:

> Rhetorical communication is as much grounded in motives as it is in situation.... It would seem useful to try to describe the strategy and tactics, the characteristics of discourse and its presentation.... The concern of the rhetorical critic should be to discern the motive operative in a rhetorical situation....[42]

Fisher identifies the motive of subversion as entailing "an anti-ethos rhetoric; that is, it invariably is an attempt to undermine the credibility of some person, idea, or institution." According to Fisher, conspiratist rhetoric exemplifies the subversive motive.[43] Murty illustrates this point by describing the difference between persuasion and coercion:

> A persuasive process may be defined as one which leaves for the person whose opinions, attitudes, or behavior are sought to be influenced a number of alternatives with expectations of high gains and low cost. A coercive process is one in which few such alternatives are left and the available ones are attended with expectations of high cost and low gains.[44]

Andrews posits a continuum of rhetorical action in which "rhetoric becomes less persuasive and more coercive to the extent that it limits the viable alternatives open to receivers of communication."[45] He notes that "[Griffin] sees a rhetorical action as being 'coercive rather than persuasive' when it is 'essentially non-rational'...."[46] We would argue that coercion need not entail the use or threat of physical force:

rhetoric can itself be coercive. Since a goal of the conspiratist is the narrowing of alternative interpretations of events, language in the service of conspiracy tends toward the coercive. Even the traditional view of coercion recognizes this basic form of the argument, for "the proposition ultimately addressed in coercive situations is this: to do as invited is reasonable because failure to do so is certain to result in dangerous consequences for you."[47] Certainly this epitomizes the dilemma form. The conspiratist simply argues that the "dangerous consequences" are world domination by the Soviet Union or a similar enemy. This familiar-sounding argument is used, as well, by mainstream politicians seeking election or passage of a pet proposal. Indeed, the false dilemma is easily recognized as a familiar tactic of political rhetoric.

Similarly, because an auditor is constrained to choose between two carefully selected alternatives, employing the false dilemma as a rhetorical tactic also serves to delimit choices artificially; hence, the false dilemma is a form of linguistic coercion, because it polarizes the alternatives purportedly available to decision-makers. The tendency for conspiratist rhetors to polarize their audiences is not new. Raum and Measell pointed out in their study of George Wallace that "Asch ... identified Father Coughlin's penchant for reducing 'all social alternatives to two mutually exclusive categories' ..."[48] Relying on Black's notion of the copula, Raum and Measell observe that the most basic copula tactic is the establishing of artificial dichotomies, for

it is upon these that other tactics ... depend. The tactic itself is most explicit; the speaker openly states that only two alternatives can be chosen by the auditor on a given issue.... It is the reduction of a many-faceted situation to two diametrically opposed alternatives that creates polarization.[49]

Zarefsky posited the importance of polarization to the acceptance of the conspiratist claim:

Conspiracy arguments become generally accepted when polarizing positions helps to resolve ambiguity.... [T]he argument transforms the situation into one presenting a clear-cut choice of alternatives. The conspiracy argument goes beyond more general forms of challenging an opponent's *ethos* because of its focus on what is *secret* as a basis for inducing polarization.[50]

The rhetorical critic must vigorously resist all attempts to restrict public discourse in this manner, not only as a matter of principle, but for tactical reasons as well. As a tactical matter, defending established 'ground rules' of public discourse is imperative to "avoid getting trapped in someone else's definition of [a] situation."[51]

The false dilemmas produced by these tactics are simplistic—which is both their virtue and their vice. Nixon's Air Force Academy speech (June 4, 1969) demonstrates that mainstream politics is not immune to such dichotomous thinking,[52] as does Reagan's statement concerning the destruction of KAL 007: "I speak for ... people everywhere who cherish civilized values in protesting the Soviet attack on an unarmed civilian passenger plane."[53]

Hence, it follows that the <u>conscious use of false dilemma</u> (or other logical fallacies) <u>as a rhetorical tactic distorts the communicative nature of the rhetorical act, transforming it from persuasion to coercion.</u> Furthermore, coercion thrives in the medium of narration precisely because of the absence of formal argumentation.

Accordingly, the central task of critical analysis analysis must rest in determining the extent to which the conspiratist *Weltanschauung* and the coercive nature of conspiratist rhetoric interact to delimit the rhetorical choices of the populace, thus intensifying polarization. The "objects" of analysis are those textual elements which project the ideology of the rhetor, and the techniques of subversion employed to convey that ideology. If the critic can utilize the immanent structural characteristics of a rhetorical text to demonstrate the presence of a *Weltanschauung* that is consistent with the ideology described above, one of the cornerstones of conspiratist rhetoric shall have been uncovered. In addition, the deductive, causal claim described by Creps can be evaluated on its own terms: Are the purported facts accurate and relevant? That is, what is the quality of the conspiratist's evidence? If it can be demonstrated that the conspiratist employs false dilemmas or other flawed tactics to <u>establish</u> consistency, to claim causality where only anomaly logically resides—and if it is claimed that a conspiracy is the causal factor—then it is proper for the critic to focus attention on the nature of those fallacies. For it is this tactic that allows the inferential leap so characteristic of conspiratist rhetoric. Even Lincoln drew his inferences from Douglas' actions or inactions, reinterpreting "ambiguous or even seemingly trivial events to make them fit into a larger pattern."[54] When such devices adumbrate within a well constructed text, a spurious sort of narrative plausibility may be created.

Perelman and Olbrechts-Tyteca state that the primary requirement of argumentation is that it provide "the means of obtaining the adherence of the audience through variations in the way of expressing thought."[55] Accordingly, the form of a discourse must not be separated from its substance, nor should stylistic structures be studied "independently of the purpose they must achieve in the argumentation."[56] Such analysis makes it "possible to track down [i.e., to discern the motive for] the choice of a particular form."[57]

Only through textual analysis is it possible to distinguish conspiratist rhetoric from, e.g. careful investigative journalism. In fact, comparison to Hersh's reportage of the My Lai cover-up or Woodward and Bernstein's seminal articles on Watergate is instructive. Such writing differs from conspiratist argumentation in nearly all respects, save the basic similarity as subversive rhetoric (in Fisher's sense of the term). These reporters were required by their newspapers to meet very rigorous tests of evidence and reasoning. For instance, editors at the *Washington Post* placed exceptional strictures on Woodward and Bernstein, demanding confirmation of every factual assertion by two independent sources. According to Doug Feaver, every Watergate story was cleared by a special editorial committee: Woodward and Bernstein were required to detail their investigative procedures and lead the editors through the reasoning process by which the writers had arrived at each new conclusion.[58] Due to the explosiveness of the revelations and the power of the presidency, *Post* editors displayed extreme caution throughout the long investigation. Even so, had it not been for Alexander Butterfield's fortuitous revelation of the existence of President Nixon's personal tape recordings, it is doubtful that many people would have believed the conspiracy allegations—allegations Woodward and Bernstein themselves reluctantly came to accept as true.

We contend that the task for the critic of conspiratist narrative may rightly include the application of universal criteria in assessing that rhetor's motives, particularly if those criteria are applied to evidence found within the conspiratist narrative itself. Warnick correctly argues that the internal coherence of a text, its narrative probability, "is inadequate for the judgment of narrative used rhetorically" and, further, that it "cannot function as the sole means for ... assessing [a] text's adequacy as the response to a rhetorical situation."[59] In part this is true because "the primary goal of a rhetorical narrative is to advocate something beyond itself";[60] because the "claim supported by a rhetorical narrative must be articulated outside of the narration";[61] because, simply stated, rhetoric attempts to persuade. Hence, the rhetor who utilizes narrative in order to achieve the goal of promulgating a particular *Weltanschauung* may be held accountable by the critic for the value criteria which underlie that vision. Yet, as Warnick cautions, "Fisher's studies of narrative used rhetorically do not reveal value criteria external to the critic's own value system."[62]

One may view a conspiratist, *e.g.* David Pearson, as the 'critic' of 'narrative used rhetorically,' *e.g.* the United States government's explanation of the KAL incident. [Thus, those who would comment on conspiratist literature become, in effect, the critic's critic.] From this point of view, one can see in Pearson a critic with no external criteria other than his own moral values. However, to the extent that Pearson (functioning as the 'rhetor' who propounds his own 'narrative used rhetorically') advocates a particular *Weltanschauung,* one may also judge that his narrative constitutes "a mask for ulterior motives."[63] In analyzing Pearson's 1984 essay as a case study of conspiratist rhetoric, we shall examine the evidence adduced on behalf of this specific conspiracy claim and shall demonstrate that, while factually and logically inadequate as proof, the text nonetheless artfully creates its own version of reality—one which is seductive to the non-critical reader.

NOTES

[1] Karl Popper, "Prediction and Prophecy in the Social Sciences," in Patrick Gardiner, ed., *Theories of History* (New York: The Free Press, 1959), p. 281. A standard question in Soviet media discussions of any international incident is: Komu èto vygodno? 'Who comes out ahead?' This was stated explicitly in *Moscow News* ("Seven questions to the President," September 18-24, 1983, p. 3): "7. Lastly, the main question when seeking the truth in any matter—who profits from all this?" Throughout this controversy Soviet domestic media continuously raised the issue. Typical is the following passage in an article by political observer Vitali Korionov ("Politika diversii protiv mira" ["A Policy of Sabotaging Peace"], *Pravda*, September 6, 1983, p. 4):

> A question comes to mind: for what purpose was this latest provocation against the USSR carried out? The answer is obvious—this provocation is one more link in a chain of other provocations that the White House has been carrying out for several years to inflame the international situation.

Ultimately, of course, the claimed goal is deployment of American missiles on the European continent.

[2] John H. Bunzel, *Anti-Politics in America*, (New York: Vintage Books, 1967), p. 51. See, also: Young, p. 17.

[3] Creps is specifically concerned with the "ways in which [conspiratist] discourse operates to resolve the rhetorical problem posed by evil" (p. 5). Nevertheless, most of his discussion and many of his findings are applicable to the entire genre of conspiratist rhetoric. See, also: Campbell and Jamieson, p. 21.

[4] G. Thomas Goodnight and John Poulakos, "Conspiracy Rhetoric: From Pragmatism to Fantasy in Public Discourse," *Western Journal of Speech Communication*, 45 (Fall 1981), 299-316, p. 299.

[5] Goodnight and Poulakos, p. 299.

[6] Goodnight and Poulakos, p. 302.

[7] Jervis, *Perception and Misperception*, p. 158.

[8] In contrast, conspiracy rhetoric seems to appeal to the same aesthetic sense as the detective or mystery novel, where no event is random. Thus, otherwise unimportant events on page 7, such as dogs that don't bark or hungover butlers, will undoubtedly prove to be significant on page 227.

[9] Goodnight and Poulakos, p. 303.

[10]Zarefsky, "Conspiracy Argument," p. 72.

[11]Zarefsky, "Conspiracy Argument," p. 74.

[12]Hofstadter, p. 37.

[13]Creps, p. 45. For a recent example, see A. Ralph Epperson, *The Unseen Hand: An Introduction to the Conspiratorial View of History*, (Tucson: Publius Press, 1985). The jacket blurb touts this 600-page book as "a compact overview of the conspiratorial forces that have shaped the major world events of the past 300 years."

[14]Creps, p. 45.

[15]Hofstadter, p. 38.

[16]Hofstadter, p. 37.

[17]Creps, p. 4.

[18]Creps, p. 217 [n. 14].

[19]Zarefsky, "Conspiracy Argument," p. 75.

[20]Walter R. Fisher, "Narration as a Human Communication Paradigm: The Case of Public Moral Argument,"*Communication Monographs*, **51**:1 (March 1984), 1-22. See also: Walter R. Fisher, "The Narrative Paradigm: An Elaboration,"*Communication Monographs*, **52**:4 (December 1985), 347-67.

[21]Barbara Warnick, "The Narrative Paradigm: Another Story,"*Quarterly Journal of Speech*, **73** (1987), 172-82, p. 176.

[22]Goodnight and Poulakos, p. 301. It should be noted that Goodnight and Poulakos use the term "fantasy"in a manner slightly different from that of Bormann, the originator of the fantasy theme notion for rhetorical analysis. Bormann's conception of the term derives from his study of small group processes and is more nearly that of the social scientist, who studies the "chaining out"of group fantasies; the term is not intended to imply the fanciful or mythical, although critics feel this line is sometimes blurred in Bormann's own work. Goodnight and Poulakos, on the other hand, appear to apply the term "fantasy"more in its colloquial meaning, similar to a "fairy tale." See: Ernest G. Bormann, "Fantasy and Rhetorical Vision: The Rhetorical Criticism of Social Reality,"*Quarterly Journal of Speech*, **58**:4 (December 1972), 396-407.

[23]The Soviets have been doing this for decades, rewriting history to suit current ideological need. For a recent discussion, see: "Preserving the past confronts today's Soviets," *Tallahassee Democrat*, April 17, 1988, 1B, 7B. Closer to home, one can cite the Johnson Administration's fabrication of the Gulf of Tonkin incident, and its subsequent

unmasking, as indicative of the pervasive nature of the urge to utilize the "creation of truth"for rhetorical purposes.

[24]Young, p. 5.

[25]Warnick, p. 176.

[26]Robert C. Rowland, "Narrative: Mode of Discourse or Paradigm?"*Communication Monographs*, 54:3 (September 1987), 264-75, p. 270.

[27]Warnick, pp. 176-77.

[28]Rowland, p. 270.

[29]Zarefsky, "Conspiracy Argument," p. 72.

[30]Campbell and Jamieson, p. 21.

[31]Jamieson, "The Rhetorical Manifestations of *Weltanschauung*," pp. 4-5.

[32]In the modern world, lack of technical expertise often leads to feelings of helplessness. In such environments, it has been found, rumor abounds. Conspiracy theories would also seem likely to flourish in this atmosphere. [See: Jervis, *Perception and Misperception*, pp. 372-78.] Neuman suggested that part of the appeal of the conspiracy theory is its ability to explain an "out-of-control"world. [See: Franz Neuman, *The Democratic and the Authoritarian State* (Glencoe, IL: Free Press, 1957), p. 279.] This notion has face validity and, if true, it predicts the movement of conspiracy claims into the mainstream. Indeed, one might expect such rhetoric to increase as the world becomes more complex. The growth of technology has rendered negligible the average person's ability to grapple with the policy questions that must be answered by the electorate. This problem is similar to the one faced by citizens in authoritarian societies: the absence of a means for verifying information.

[33]See: Barnet Baskerville, "The Illusion of Proof,"*Western Speech*, 25:4 (Fall 1961), 236-42.

[34]For a discussion of quasi-logical forms, see Chaim Perelman and L. Olbrechts-Tyteca, *The New Rhetoric: A Treatise on Argumentation*, John Wilkinson and Purcell Weaver, trans. (Notre Dame: University of Notre Dame Press, 1969), pp. 193-260.

[35]Fisher, "A Motive View," p. 138.

[36]Creps, p. 16. This definition would seem to be too narrow because it ignores important stylistic considerations. Such matters of style are integral to the effect (*i.e.,* the persuasiveness) achieved by discourse and are best elucidated by textual criticism. See below.

[37]Creps, p. 96.

[38]Perelman and Olbrechts-Tyteca, p. 129.

[39]Warnick, p. 176.

[40]Perelman and Olbrechts-Tyteca, p. 157 ff.

[41]Warnick, p. 176.

[42]Fisher, "A Motive View, " pp. 132, 139.

[43]Fisher, "A Motive View," p. 138.

[44]Murty, p. 28.

[45]Andrews, p. 10.

[46]Andrews, p. 10.

[47]Parke G. Burgess, p. 68.

[48]Richard D. Raum and James S. Measell, "Wallace and His Ways: A Study of the Rhetorical Genre of Polarization,"*Central States Speech Journal,* 25:1 (Spring 1974), 28-35, pp. 28-29.

[49]Raum and Measell, p. 31.

[50]Zarefsky, "Conspiracy Argument," p. 73. Emphasis in original.

[51]Richard L. Merritt, "Improbable Events and Expectable Behavior,"Chapter Five in Frei, ed., *Managing International Crises,* 77-86, p. 84.

[52]Windt, p. 249. See also: Robert P. Newman, "Under The Veneer: Nixon's Vietnam Speech of November 3, 1969,"*Quarterly Journal of Speech,* 56:2 (April 1970), 168-78.

[53]*COMPILATION,* p. 2.

[54]Zarefsky, "Conspiracy Argument," p. 74.

[55]Perelman and Olbrechts-Tyteca, p. 163.

[56]Perelman and Olbrechts-Tyteca, p. 142.

[57]Perelman and Olbrechts-Tyteca, p. 143.

[58]Interview with Doug Feaver, May 1986. For an elaboration, see Chapter Three, note 18.

[59]Warnick, pp. 177, 178. See, also: Shlapentokh, pp. 22, 36; and Bitzer, "The Rhetorical Situation."

[60]Warnick, p. 178.

[61]John Lucaites and Celeste Condit, "Reconstructing Narrative Theory: A Functional Perspective,"*Journal of Communication*, 35:4 (Autumn 1985), 90-108, p. 101.

[62]Warnick, p. 180.

[63]Fisher, "Elaboration," p. 364. This statement might also apply, *ipso facto*, to the position maintained by the United States government.

CONSPIRATIST RHETORIC AND KAL 007

Beginning in December, 1983, a number of articles appearing in the West claimed to demonstrate US culpability in the shootdown of KAL 007.[1] One of these was "KAL 007: What the U.S. Knew and When We Knew It," by David Pearson, published in *The Nation* on the eve of the first anniversary of the tragedy.[2] Like the others, Pearson's analysis is an attempt to substantiate the spy-plane theory, thus implicating the US government in the destruction of the airliner. Not only did *The Nation* highlight this article in a national advertising campaign just prior to the 1984 presidential election,[3] but the unanswered questions raised by Pearson caught the attention of such syndicated columnists as Tom Wicker of *The New York Times*.[4]

Pearson's essay is an excellent example of how one artful construction of a story can be transformed into evidence of a conspiracy. It is important because, of all the studies that advance the hypothesis of an American role in the KAL tragedy, none has gained greater notoriety and none has influenced other investigators more. In the opinion of Murray Sayle, a veteran journalist whose reportage on KAL won great praise in England, that article in *The Nation* was the "serious authority" relied on by Oliver Clubb and "many another conspiracy enthusiast." The most recent addition to the list of adherents was Oxford political scientist R. W. Johnson, who used much of Pearson's material to support his own version of the conspiracy theory in *Shootdown: KAL 007 and the American Connection*.

In the *Nation* article, Pearson contended that the United States government knew (or should have known) the situation into which KAL 007 had placed itself; the US government, on the other hand, has consistently maintained that KAL was an "unarmed civilian aircraft" which had innocently strayed over Soviet territory unbeknownst to anyone, including the crew.[5] As Sayle observed, "Pearson ... has faced the choice between accident and conspiracy, and he gives us the heaviest possible nudge in the direction of conspiracy."[6]

Pearson's article is also important in that it demonstrates the potential rhetorical power of the conspiratist argument in focusing and directing public debate. Not only has his interpretation heavily influenced journalistic understanding of the tragedy,[7] there is evidence that this interpretation has had a noticeable impact on public perceptions.[8] Indeed, the conspiracy notions surrounding the tragedy of KAL 007 have not dissipated. In June 1986, a nationwide survey found that fully 25% of Americans still believed that the civilian airliner was on an espionage mission.[9]

Pearson enjoyed a brief celebrity: he was frequently interviewed on US radio; he appeared on ABC's *Nightline* and NBC's *Today Show*; and, of course, the Soviet press quoted him extensively, once describing him as a "rather well known scholar at Yale University." His subsequent efforts on the KAL story have been supported financially by both The Nation Institute and The Fund For Constitutional Government.[10]

When Seymour Hersh published *"The Target is Destroyed"* in 1986, many thought Pearson's argument had been laid to rest. This notion, however, was belied by the publication of Pearson's own book, *KAL 007:The Cover-up (Why the True Story Has Never Been Told)*, on the fourth anniversary of the shootdown. Indeed, Pearson's position has changed little over the intervening years: while he has retreated from some of the claims which demonstrated his lack of technical expertise, he now charges that a continuing US cover-up has prevented the American public from learning the truth about this tragedy.

Fisher contends that in a democratic system all stories compete for acceptance and are judged on their cohesion, that is, according to their ability to make sense of a situation. It is this interaction which creates discourse. Indeed, the explanatory power of Fisher's narrative paradigm depends on the claimed ability of all stories to compete equally.[11] But in this instance the government was operating at a disadvantage in the unfolding rhetorical drama. The Reagan administration's propaganda campaign occurred at the intersection of political and security interests; the sensitive nature of much of the information surrounding the destruction of KAL 007 left the US government with an incomplete story to tell, for—as we have seen—there are limits to the government's willingness to disclose highly classified information, no matter how strongly felt are the beliefs that might be substantiated. Due to this circumstance, and Pearson's persuasive account of the incident, at least some segments of the American public perceive the official US position as a fabrication, a fantasy in the Goodnight and Poulakos dichotomy.[12]

The void created by the Reagan administration's natural unwilling-ness to release all of its classified information did more than simply enhance the credibility of conspiratists such as Pearson; it also closed off discourse, thus violating the notion of competing stories. Accord-ingly, in a situation such as this, where one party to a controversy can-not speak freely, Fisher's notion of narrative fidelity cannot serve as a final barometer of integrity. To be sure, the US government did much to foster the unbelievability of its own position, giving added support to the embryonic conspiratist argument, and establishing a context in which the conspiracy notion could flourish.[13]

In short, although the Soviet Union had committed an act for which there seemed to be no ostensible provocation, no possible justi-fication, blunders in the United States persuasive effort had instilled a reasonable doubt (see Chapter Three). Still, this merely created an opportunity for conspiratists by establishing a field of battle; initially the odds of winning such a battle still were stacked in favor of the chal-lenged authority. In a pluralistic society it is inevitable that this process involve public address and conflicting attempts at persuasion: a strug-gle emerges with both sides competing for the public's belief. What is at stake is public acceptance and public perception of reality.[14] We are pri-marily interested here in positioning the notion of conspiracy in a con-text that includes all possible elements of the rhetorical matrix—the al-leged conspirators, the rhetors charging conspiracy, and the public fo-rums in which the battle of persuasion is waged.

In Chapter Two, we referred to the importance of public knowledge as an intrinsic part of the warranting process for public discourse in pluralistic societies. The presence of conspiracy interpretations of po-litical and social events validates the notion that Bitzer's public is "historically situated" and "divisible rather than necessarily unitary."[15] This perspective enables the critic to explain the persistence of extrem-ist (or, more generally, minority) beliefs within a larger polity, while describing the very essence of public address (the struggle between competing points of view to win assent from all or most auditors) within the narrow context of conspiratist rhetoric. Consequently, one cannot define the social reality of public knowledge uniquely, as this may differ for different 'publics.' Indeed, some people will doggedly maintain belief in even the most palpably false allegations.

It seems intuitively obvious, moreover, that the warranting process within an authoritarian society such as the Soviet Union is quite different from that in a pluralistic society. There was little likelihood, for example, that anyone residing within the Soviet Union could refute state allegations (and effectively counter them in public).[16] The Soviet government is truly the highest source of the definition of reality within that system: in one instance described earlier, Soviet propagandists simply made up nonexistent quotes, attributed to *U.S. News & World Report,* purporting to indicate that CIA Director William Casey had "spoon fed" classified information to Seymour Hersh and personally approved the contents of *"The Target Is Destroyed".*[17]

What we have, then, are interactive reality levels. Social reality—the judgment within each segment of any specific society—is dependent upon rhetorical reality, and all real world outcomes are determined by the relative effectiveness of rhetorical visions that compete to interpret events and define truth. The socio-political outcome of a struggle for belief represents the projection of an 'objective' set of facts through a prism of persuasive rhetoric; thus, perceived reality may be in a constant state of flux. Of course, when considering an international incident such as the 1983 Korean airliner disaster, it is probable that the set of social realities is greater than one, hence there may be more than one victorious stand.

Accordingly, in the analysis that follows, we attempt to assess the communicative factors operating in "KAL 007: What the U.S. Knew and When We Knew It," factors which successfully convinced many Americans that their government deserved at least some of the blame for the fate of Korean Air Lines Flight 007. Our primary concern here is to analyze the internal dynamic of one particular text alleging conspiracy. Because of the significance of technical evidence in Pearson's argument structure, we examine the extent to which there exists independent confirmation or refutation of specific charges, the use to which this rhetor puts such independent confirmation, and the manner in which he deals with seemingly discrepant evidence. This effort requires that a judgment be rendered concerning the extent to which claimed anomalies are indeed anomalous.

Nevertheless, our interest is focused primarily on rhetorical reality: How did this conspiratist marshal his arguments? If Pearson's article makes the type of deductive, causal claim described by Creps, how might one evaluate the components of that claim? How might one evaluate the technical and linguistic assertions underlying the claim? How do stylistic choices within the conspiratist text themselves support the rhetor's arguments? How do all of these elements come together to create a convincing narrative?

ESTABLISHING A RHETORICAL WORLD VIEW

An examination of David Pearson's article reveals four underlying themes, or leitmotifs, which he uses to establish a frame of reference for the reader. These themes are intertwined in the introductory section entitled "A Predictable Event," and run throughout the text. Thus, they serve a rhetorical function by providing a skeletal structure on which the author's arguments are assembled. They simultaneously provide the reader with 'relevant' history to make sense of the story the author is telling.[18]

The first theme concerns the timing of recurrent intrusions by US planes into Soviet airspace *vis-à-vis* sensitive East-West negotiations. The author cites six instances of intrusions by US military aircraft, most importantly the U-2 in 1960; of these six, two are shown to have occurred at diplomatically "sensitive" moments. He then juxtaposes the downing of another Korean Air Lines jet (#902) in 1978, thereby equating KAL 902 to the military overflights. However, this connection is established not on the basis of any evidence, but by temporal correlation to external events: "As with the earlier incidents, the downing of KAL 902 happened at a sensitive moment..." (p. 106).[19] Jervis has commented on the tendency to assume causality, which this passage illustrates:

> Men are also hesitant to believe that actions affecting them and occurring in rapid sequence could have occurred by coincidence.... Although modern men know of coincidences, psychologists have noted that it is nevertheless true that "when two events are appropriately coincidental in time, space, and sequence, an unavoidable and indivisible experience of causality occurs."[20]

Pearson's association of these conjunctions in time uses a bit of linguistic sleight of hand, of course, since "as with the earlier incidents" implies "as with all the earlier incidents"—a contention that is never demonstrated. More importantly, the passage creates in the mind of the reader an association between the 1978 Korean Air Lines flight and earlier military overflights of Soviet territory. Further, the description of the flight of KAL 902 implies similarities with the alleged events surrounding KAL 007 in 1983: KAL 902 was 1000 miles off course, overflew Soviet military installations, took evasive action when inter-

239

cepted, and, ultimately, was forced to land after being struck by Soviet air defense missiles. Pearson appears to suggest that KAL 007, KAL 902, and the military planes were all of a piece—purposeful aerial surveillance of the Soviet Union—and, therefore, shooting down one was no different than shooting down the others.[21]

The second theme (still drawing on the earlier overflights of Soviet territory), is his observation that the US has usually cited radio or navigational difficulties as the cause of incursions into Soviet airspace, even when the intruder craft took evasive action (p. 107). One may presume, of course, that the US government is reluctant to admit spying on the Soviets, but the author implies that whenever navigational and radio difficulties are mentioned as causes of overflights, spying has occurred.[22] Thus, if the reader can be convinced that, "From the very beginning, KAL 007 was not a normal flight" (p. 107), any claims of navigational problems will reinforce that impression.

Pearson is particularly adept at using expository prose to further the associative power of his narrative, exploiting for conscious effect the tendencies inherent in grammar. Certain words have a subtle logical force, and, as Stankiewicz has written, "every part of speech and every grammatical category can be utilized as a poetic device."[23] Take, for instance, the following passage, where the word **although** establishes an antithetical relationship between the information contained in the subordinate clause and the information transmitted by the main clause:

> Although two people died and others were injured, the only explanations ever offered for [KAL 902's] deviation from course were equipment failure and navigational difficulties (p. 106).

Pearson is obviously implying here that claims of equipment failure and navigational difficulties are not sufficient explanation of instances resulting in loss of life—that such instances must have a deeper, more ominous explanation or lives would not have been lost. Once again, linguistic choices result in exculpating the Soviet Union, or at least mitigating its guilt.

An uncritical reader might thus be swayed by the *post hoc* assertion that navigational problems constitute proof of deliberate spying. It is significant in the present context, however, that narrative structure alone provides the driving force behind whatever plausibility may reside in this assertion. Indeed, the association of disparate ideas in the course of story telling is the foremost device utilized by the conspiratist to create the self-sealing argument that is required to proselytize for his ideology.

Pearson introduces his third leitmotif when, in discussing the interceptions of previous intruders, he emphasizes the care with which Soviet pilots follow accepted procedures, opening fire only when all other methods fail.[24] Thus, he attempts to establish the credibility of the Soviet claim that their air defense personnel used proper procedures of identification, interrogation, and interception in the case of KAL 007 as well.[25]

The author's fourth and final theme is the most disturbing, particularly with respect to the fate of KAL 007. He notes the number of US military personnel who have lost their lives during aerial intelligence-gathering missions over Soviet bloc countries and concludes that the United States places a very high priority on penetrating Soviet airspace for intelligence-gathering purposes, "sometimes at the expense of human life" (p. 107). This is the last statement before, "That is the context in which the tragedy of Flight 007 must be understood" (p. 107).

Accordingly, there can be no doubt about the writer's intent in his extended introduction, starting with the section title itself. He has established for the reader a rhetorical world with two characteristics: a lack of concern for human life on the part of US officials, coupled with a strict adherence to life-preserving procedures on the part of Soviet officials. The overriding impression created is that of a Soviet government concerned only with defending its sovereign territory against the aggressive intrusions of the United States. In this authorial world, not unlike that of the 007 spy novels,[26] it would not be hard to imagine a government callously sending defenseless civilians to their deaths in the futile pursuit of intelligence goals, a scenario in which the tragedy of KAL 007 would indeed be "a predictable event."

In constructing this world view, the author offers no direct proof to support the version of history in which he grounds his argument; rather, he builds his case almost entirely on suggestion and the structural device of narrative position, allowing inference to substitute for evidence. In other words, Pearson uses the tactic of association to establish the narrative fidelity of his story. As Fisher observes, it is the power of association which makes stories function—as the individual tests the story against that which he or she already 'knows.'[27] The difficulty lies in determining if the claimed association is legitimate. In the case of the *Nation* article, for example, by carefully juxtaposing elements of his narration the author creates functional identity between a civilian airliner operated by a South Korean corporation and military reconnaissance aircraft operated by the United States government. Lacking documentation, the entire fabric of this narrative depends on guilt by association. The reader is invited to participate in the discourse by developing the *post hoc ergo propter hoc* enthymeme for himself.

An allied tactic is another variant of the "Halo Effect," one which might be defined for our purposes as 'acquittal by association.' For example, in the *Nation* article Pearson argues: (a) The Soviets were correct about the location of the mission orbit of the US reconnaissance plane, an RC-135, that was in the area; (b) They were correct about the point at which KAL 007 entered Soviet airspace; therefore, (c) The Soviets must also be correct about the RC-135 making a second loop outside its mission orbit in order to rendezvous with KAL 007 (p. 111).[28] The author has confirming evidence to support his analysis on the first two points:

> U.S. officials have acknowledged that the RC-135 was off the northeast coast of Kamchatka Peninsula at the time KAL 007 approached Soviet territory.... [I]n both Soviet and U.S. accounts the jetliner did not actually penetrate Soviet airspace until it was over Kamchatka.... So KAL must have ... penetrated Soviet airspace almost exactly where the Soviets claim... (p. 107).

Unfortunately, no evidence whatsoever is presented in support of the existence of the second loop. Pearson apparently bases this charge solely on the Soviet allegation made by Ogarkov on September 9, 1983. Ten days later Kirsanov amplified these charges in a front-page article in *Pravda*, indicting Reagan and alleging that Flight 007 was coordinated with US spy satellites.[29] Michael Dobbs, a *Washington Post* Foreign Service reporter, commented the next day (September 20), "As in the case of previous Soviet statements on the airliner incident, no documentary evidence was provided [by the Soviets] to support these charges."[30]

Nevertheless, the effect in the 1984 *Nation* article is to create an aura of legitimacy for the entire Soviet version of events, including the completely unsubstantiated 'double loop' theory.

LOGICAL FORM AS A RHETORICAL TACTIC

In the introduction to Part III, we suggested that a rhetor's use of logical structure provides one of the keys to understanding *Weltanschauung*, and, hence, to judging ideology. Thus, a component of the proposed methodology for evaluating the intellectual rigor of mainstream conspiratists must be the analysis of reasoning. Perelman and Olbrechts-Tyteca have defined as "quasi-logical" those arguments which "claim to be similar to the formal reasoning of logic or mathematics.... Since there are formal proofs of recognized validity, quasi-logical arguments derive their persuasive strength from their similarity with these well-established modes of reasoning."[31]

One often reads conspiratist literature with the vague impression that the case is made through logical flaws, but seldom is the reader in a position to undertake a formal analysis. Applying such techniques to the *Nation* article confirms this impression: in addition to more traditional rhetorical strategies, Pearson often uses logical fallacy to substitute for evidence and reasoned argument. The overriding flaw is that the entire article amounts to a false dilemma: because the US allegedly had the technical capability to monitor the airliner, failure to do so means one of two things—either this was a major intelligence breakdown on the part of the US military or the US actually did know what was going on and is covering it up. The author argues, in effect, that US monitoring capabilities are so extensive that the first scenario is impossible.[32] Thus, it must be the case that the US is hiding something. And if the government is hiding something, it must be true either that officials decided to take advantage of an accidental situation or that they planned the entire operation.

> The most charitable interpretation is that U.S. military and intelligence agencies suffered an extraordinary series of human and technical failures which allowed the airliner to proceed on its deviant course.... However, a much more likely and frightening possibility is that a conscious policy decision was made by the U.S. government ... to risk the lives of 269 innocent people on the assumptions that an extraordinary opportunity for gleaning intelligence information should not be missed and that the Soviets would not dare shoot down a civilian airliner (p. 106).

The article assumes that the US military had the technical capability to track KAL 007 throughout the course of its flight; that any such equipment should have been employed in this fashion; that if it wasn't, this in and of itself constitutes a failure. One is presented here a conundrum on the order of "Have you stopped beating your wife?" But the position depends on points which the author never establishes: that the capability exists; that the equipment, if technically capable of such monitoring, was normally employed for this purpose; that the monitoring, if done, was done in 'real time' (which is necessary if the tragedy were to be averted); and that those watching were aware of what was happening.[33] Thus, many steps are omitted from the overall argument. Hiding those gaps are masses of sometimes irrelevant technical detail and many logical fallacies.

For example, an instance of false cause occurs in the analysis of the route of the RC-135, the US reconnaissance aircraft that was on station near Kamchatka at the time. The Soviets allege that the RC-135 performed a control function in an espionage operation, that both it and the Korean airliner changed course in order to rendezvous just of the coast of Kamchatka. In Pearson's words, "That [extra] loop [in the route of the RC-135] ... may have been an anomaly undertaken to bring the aircraft into close proximity to KAL 007" (p. 110).

We have already indicated that the only evidence extant for this 'double loop' theory is the map (not actual recorded radar data) displayed by the Soviets at their press conference.[34] Of course, the existence of this loop is essential to proving the allegation that the RC-135 was involved in this event, and a role for the RC-135 is crucial to the conspiracy theory. Despite the absence of any hard data,[35] Pearson assumes this Soviet allegation to be true throughout the remainder of the article, justifying this position in part because the US government has refused to release any information concerning the reconnaissance plane's mission orbit:

> Why would the United States consider that information sensitive? Because the time during which the two aircraft were in closest proximity was about a half hour before KAL 007 first entered Soviet airspace—plenty of time to warn the jetliner, call ground stations, or notify higher authorities (p. 111).

In this instance of the 'post hoc' fallacy, it is useful to test the negative syllogism ('if not B, then not A'), yielding the following:

> If (and only if) KAL 007 had not penetrated Soviet airspace 30 minutes after the airliner and the RC-135 were in closest proximity to one another, then the US government would not

consider information concerning the mission orbit of the RC-135 sensitive.

For that statement to be true, reconnaissance routes would have to be public knowledge or, at least, non-classified information at other times. This is obviously not the case, since it is highly unlikely that the US government is willing to make such information public under any but the most unusual circumstances.

This passage also represents another use of the false dilemma, for the reader is presented with a binary choice: either the RC-135 was involved in the "spy mission" or the US would release the pertinent information about its route.

CIRCULAR REASONING: ASSUMING THE CONCLUSION

The strategy of false cause tends to impute conscious behavior when, in fact, none may exist. Most people know that the mere occurrence of two events in a time sequence in no way implies a causal relationship between them, even though there may be some other relationship. However, 'post hoc' fallacies will work as a strategy when the alleged relationship can be made to <u>appear</u> reasonable.[36] Thus, it is the associative power of narrative that allows circular reasoning to succeed. For example, if there were a conspiracy involving the CIA, the National Security Agency, and Korean Air Lines, the United States government certainly would want to hide the fact of a rendezvous between KAL 007 and any reconnaissance plane that was supervising its actions. In this instance, however, the false cause depends on an unproven assumption and the argument becomes circular: that is, the explanation makes sense only if one assumes *a priori* the existence of a conspiracy and the need to cover it up; yet the refusal to reveal classified information is used as proof of the conspiracy (an illustration of the self-sealing nature of conspiratist argument).

Pearson's explanation of US reluctance to discuss its reconnaissance activities is not atypical. The fabric of much of the argumentation in his article follows the same formula of assuming conclusions which need to be proven. For instance, one finds the rendezvous accepted as fact in the following passage explaining why the Soviet air defense forces "had trouble figuring out what the intruder was":

Because of the complex flight path of the reconnaissance aircraft, its convergence with the flight path of KAL 007, the airliner's reported change of altitude at the moment of convergence and its changed course shortly thereafter, it is not difficult to imagine at least some confusion (p. 118).

Although stated as fact by Pearson and by the Soviets, these allegations are specifically left 'open' by the ICAO: "No evidence was available to either support or refute the contradictory information from the USSR and the United States concerning the proximity of KE007 and the reconnaissance aircraft."[37] Of course, the general reader, not having access to this report, is left at the mercy of the author's interpretation of the two conflicting versions.

The conspiracy theory for which Pearson so eloquently argues depends absolutely on two of his allegations: that the airliner was under surveillance by the United States and that the KAL pilot took evasive action. Unless the flight of KAL 007 was monitored, the alleged "intelligence bonanza" could not materialize. As mentioned above, the author bases his analysis of the technical capabilities of US military intelligence radar installations in the Western Pacific on unwarranted assumptions supported by seemingly relevant, but insufficient, evidence. For instance, he cites James Canan's statement that the huge phased-array radar known as Cobra Dane is "so powerful it can spot a baseball at a range of 2000 miles out in space" (p. 116), supposedly placing Kamchatka and Sakhalin well within its range. This may be arithmetically true, but the conclusion is unwarranted because Cobra Dane can see that far only in line-of-sight (*i.e.*, out into space). Both Kamchatka and Sakhalin are beyond the horizon from Shemya Island in the Aleutians, where Cobra Dane is situated, and, therefore, inaccessible even to such extraordinary equipment. Once again, Pearson depends on the rhetorical strategy of "Lesser Facts, Greater Facts," and the reader is in no position to evaluate the accuracy or significance of this information.[38]

Similar errors can be found in the author's analysis of the recorded comments of Soviet interceptor pilots, which he uses to support his allegations of evasive maneuvers by the Korean pilot.[39] Pearson incorrectly concludes that the ANOs were not on (p. 118), and based on this misapprehension, incorrectly interprets the Soviet pilot to be saying later, over Sakhalin, that he has turned on his own lights as the first step in the intercept procedures (pp. 119-120). Accordingly, Pearson has no evidence that the pilot of KAL 007 knew he was being intercepted and, therefore, no independent reason to believe that he took evasive action, except the word of the Soviet government.[40]

But it is essential to the conspiracy theory that the pilot have taken evasive action, for if he did not there is no evidence to demonstrate he was aware of his true location, or of the Soviet interception.[41] Indeed, according to the *ANC REPORT*, "[a]vailable information suggests that the flight crew of KE007 was not aware of any of the interceptions reported by the USSR.... [There was] no reference to any visual or radio contact by KE007 with intercepting aircraft."[42] Pearson, however, ignores this when he claims KAL 007 changed course again and took evasive maneuvers over Sakhalin, moves which are not easily explained as "human error" (p. 122). "[W]hich leaves us with the most persuasive theory: that the airliner made a deliberate, carefully planned intrusion into Soviet territory with the knowledge of U.S. military and intelligence agencies..." (p. 122).

Unfortunately, a majority of the allegations in this article, and particularly this last one, are actually unsubstantiated. The writer nevertheless assumes their validity and employs them as premises in later arguments, substituting repetition for proof. The most obvious instance, involving the Cobra Dane radar, was detailed above: the writer claims that the US military not only could, but indeed did, track the plane in real time throughout its flight. The question is not even whether the US possesses undisclosed means for accomplishing what Pearson claims, but rather that he has presented absolutely no evidence to that effect and doesn't even predict, *à la* other conspiratists, that such a revelation is imminent.

At another point in the *Nation* article, in a discussion concerning variant US and ICAO translations of a crucial line in the transcript, the author writes:

At 1813:16, the pilot of the SU-15 replied to another instruction from ground control. "Roger," he said. Ten seconds later, according to the U.S. translation of the transmissions, the pilot reported back to ground control, "The target isn't responding to I.F.F. (Identification/Friend or Foe)." If I.F.F., a military procedure, was used, it is clear the Russians believed they were dealing with a hostile military aircraft. But in its final report, the I.C.A.O. team investigating the incident translated that message, "The target isn't responding to the call." "The call" might refer to an attempt to contact KAL 007 on the international hailing frequencies of 121.5 or 243.0 [MHz]....

If the I.C.A.O. translation is correct, the Soviet pilot may well have used the international hailing frequency in accordance with accepted interception procedures. **Yet** the transcripts show no response from KAL 007 (p. 120).[43] (emphasis added)

Fleshing out Pearson's reasoning, we arrive at the following: (1) If the ICAO translation is correct, the Soviet pilot may have used the International Hailing Frequency. (2) If the Soviet pilot used the International Hailing Frequency, KAL 007 should have responded. (3) KAL did not respond. CONCLUSION DESIRED: KAL 007 was being evasive.

It is the word **yet** that colors the entire passage, because there would be no false reasoning without it:[44] if one were to substitute **in any event**—an equally pedestrian connector—the statement would become one of co-occurrence, coincidence, rather than causality. But claims of causality are essential to vindicate the conspiratist's stance: for it is precisely 'coincidences' that have no credibility within this world view. Jervis remarks on the general lack of credibility accorded accidental occurrences:

> Accidents, chance and lack of coordination are rarely given their due by contemporary observers. Instead, they suspect that well-laid plans give events a coherence they would otherwise lack.... Men are also hesitant to believe that actions ... occurring in rapid sequence could have occurred by coincidence.[45]

The attractiveness of this appeal is its deductive logic, which "can transform all data into indisputable 'evidence.'"[46]

Most importantly, Pearson can't prove that the International Hailing Frequency was, in fact, used. Indeed, as demonstrated earlier, all evidence is to the contrary.[47] The difficulty with this argument is its ambiguity: the "evidence" on which the author relies is hypothetical. The most likely scenario is that **zapros,** the Russian term in the transcript, is used in its military meaning, which is 'IFF.' Paraphrasing Toulmin, the most this warrant will authorize in the movement from data to claim is an ambiguous "may have been taking evasive action".[48]

Thus, the conclusion that KAL 007 engaged in evasive maneuvers does not follow from the "evidence" presented. Clearly it would have been in the airliner's interest to respond, identifying itself as a civilian plane with passengers aboard, particularly if, as the Soviets allege, a civilian aircraft was specifically chosen as a "cover" for the spy operation to ensure safety. The obvious conclusion must be that the 'call' was not a verbal inquiry made on the 121.5 MHz International Hailing Frequency, rather than that KAL 007 wished to avoid identification.

248

Nevertheless, the hypothetical nature of Pearson's claim is soon lost in his attempt to demonstrate that the Soviet pilot was following established intercept procedures.[49] Failure to succeed in this effort would undermine one of his four leitmotifs. In addition, since a voice call on 121.5 MHz is a *requirement* of those procedures, Pearson's entire argument would be vitiated if it could be demonstrated that no such call was made.[50]

LESSER FACTS, GREATER FACTS: IN THE ABSENCE OF PROOF

In public argument, the lack of direct proof often leads a proponent of a pet hypothesis to adopt an associative tactic one might call "Lesser Facts, Greater Facts." In using this technique, the rhetor accumulates a multitude of tangentially relevant details in order to give the impression that he knows more than is actually proved—enabling him to overclaim his evidence.[51] As Creps points out, "the persuasive force of the conspiracy case is produced not by a single portion of testimony, but by the simultaneous consideration of hundreds of pieces of evidence...."[52]

The article in the *Nation* contains a great deal of evidence that is only tangentially related to the points at issue: Did the RC-135 rendezvous with Flight 007? Did US radar pick up the errant jetliner? Was the airliner on a spy mission for the US? A clear example of the effect this tactic can have on narrative structure is found in the following passage:

> [I]n 1960 ... a U.S. RB-47 reconnaissance aircraft packed with long-range cameras, mapping camera and electronic equipment for checking sites and frequencies of aircraft detection systems was attacked by two Soviet MiG-17 fighters over the Barents Sea ... (p. 106).

The wealth of trivial detail in the participial construction **packed ... systems** serves no true informational function—after all, what other kind of equipment would one expect to be carried by a reconnaissance plane? But the writer, by providing this detailed description and using the verb **packed** (rather than **equipped** or **carrying**) gives the reader the subconscious impression that this RB-47 was somehow different, "extraordinary," rather than a routine, scheduled flight over international waters. The detail assumes the burden of demonstrating the author's point. In this way, the onus on the Soviets for shooting down the plane is somewhat lessened.[53]

249

In the next section, entitled "The Role of the RC-135," Pearson asks what might explain the proximity of the reconnaissance plane to KAL 007 prior to the airliner's intrusion over Kamchatka. This segment contains the notion of US monitoring of a Soviet missile test (a function explicitly allowed by the SALT agreements), as well as a more sinister possibility—that the RC-135 was watching as Soviet radar reacted to KAL, an intelligence opportunity the author terms "extraordinary" and a "bonanza." The passage is dominated by a wealth of faulty technical detail and logistical information, running to about 1100 words, but the question posed at the outset ("What was a reconnaissance aircraft doing in such close proximity to an intruder in Soviet airspace?") is never actually answered. Rather, the author concludes that, regardless of the reason for the presence of the RC-135, it "must have observed the Korean airliner and had ample time to correct its course, but it did not do so" (p. 115). The unanswered question which initiated this segment of the article has been obscured by a proliferation of tangential facts.

EMOTIVE LANGUAGE USE

As communication scholars know well, emotional responses to persuasive language are not accidental; they stem from the underlying semantics of the words themselves. Indeed, it has been argued that such responses are unavoidable:

> The inherent character of language makes it impossible to use "pure" reason in any human context. Since all words may possess "emotive" as well as "descriptive" significance, even the most logical argument may be expected to contain a modicum of emotional appeal.[54]

Accordingly, responses can be manipulated by a rhetor and controlled, at least to some extent. As Ogden and Richards have commented, "Words are so powerful ... that by the excitement which they provoke through the emotive force, discussion is for the most part rendered sterile."[55]

Linguistically marked lexical choices, such as the use of **packed** noted above, recur often within this text. Another instance of such manipulation is found in the statement, "Although the airliner's instruments should have conclusively indicated the deviation, the pilot of KAL 007 falsely reported to air traffic control that his airliner had passed Bethel [Alaska] on course" (p. 107). Elimination of the adverbs

conclusively and **falsely** results in no loss of information; thus, their inclusion may be regarded as gratuitous. A neutral emotional reading can be obtained simply by deleting both words.[56] But the use of **falsely** is much more invidious than might be apparent initially, because, in a linguistic sense, the word entails the presumption of willfulness on the part of the KAL pilot, a willfulness which is essential to the conspiratist scenario. In other words, by labeling the position reports **false**, Pearson, in effect, accuses the pilot of consciously lying. Another rhetor might have chosen an adverb that would have been equally biased, but in the direction of inadvertence, such as **mistakenly**. As it is, the burden of proof for the conspiracy allegation is borne, in large part, by the language used to describe an otherwise innocuous occurrence.

Particularly for qualitative adjectives and adverbs, one can establish degrees of neutrality or bias and compare words of similar meaning on that basis alone:[57]

falsely	HIGHLY BIASED: conspiracy, premeditation
erroneously	MILDLY BIASED: conspiracy, premeditation
—no adverb—	—NEUTRAL—
incorrectly	MILDLY BIASED: accident, inadvertence
mistakenly	HIGHLY BIASED: accident, inadvertence

Just two pages later, while attempting to demonstrate that another Korean Air Lines jet, Flight 015, "could have been playing a supporting role in the events that were to follow," Pearson states that 015 was flying "about six to eight minutes behind the location it falsely reported for Flight 007" (p. 109). Again, the lexical choice prejudges the situation and has the effect of imputing collusion, hence conspiracy, to the activities of both airplane crews.

DISCUSSION

In the shocked aftermath of the tragedy, the public psyche demanded an explanation. How could a modern airliner with sophisticated guidance mechanisms and numerous fail-safe systems have gone so badly off-course over proscribed territory? Obviously, a rhetorical situation had been created which required an adequate response. However, a majority of Americans felt that the US government was withholding important information about the crisis, and, further, that the US should wait for a full explanation from the Soviets before taking retaliatory action.[58] Complicating this episode were the questions that can never be answered. The flight recorder was never found, the Soviets have never provided any hard data, and the US and Japanese governments are apparently withholding transcripts of Soviet ground personnel, as well as analyses of Soviet radar data.

In such a vacuum, any forceful statement that is at least possibly true gains credibility. And, in an age of skepticism nourished by Watergate and the Iran-Contra scandal, government complicity does not seem unreasonable. Indeed, conspiracy theories are almost never completely unreasonable; they are merely too monistic.

In most instances of the genre, much of the credibility of the conspiratist's rhetoric relies on the promise of "inside information" or data to which the ordinary citizen cannot have access; thus the reliance on defectors, secret memoranda, or unanswerable questions for proof that the claimed conspiracy exists. Similarly, one reason Pearson's article succeeds is the author's reliance on the technical ignorance of his audience. Fisher tells us that the role of experts in public moral argument should be to act as counselors, lest they prematurely stifle public debate.[59] "Only experts can argue with experts, and their arguments ... cannot be rationally questioned by nonexperts." Yet Fisher sheds no light on what one should do with a case such as the present one. Pearson is not an "expert" in the sense that Hans Bethe and Edward Teller are experts on nuclear weapons. Nevertheless, as noted, Pearson provides an overwhelming amount of technical detail (which helps in the development of the rhetorical world view he is creating); the reader, however, is in no position to judge the accuracy, the significance, or the relevance of this information.

For example, Pearson claims that KAL's pilot took on 9800 pounds of additional fuel prior to leaving Anchorage, fuel that was "neither needed for his scheduled flight nor accounted for in his subsequent position reports to air traffic controllers" (p. 107).[60] Such details are crucial to the narrative probability and narrative fidelity of Pearson's account, yet their accuracy can be tested only if experts argue in the mode excluded by Fisher's paradigm. The effect of accumulating such detail is to enhance the believability of Pearson's story.

The spy-plane scenario developed in this article is further aided by the love-hate relationship Americans have with sophisticated machinery. While individually many of us have had mixed experiences with technology, in the aggregate Americans seem to believe in the infallibility of "high-tech" devices. Until recently, the average person certainly had no knowledge of the frequency with which commercial airplanes fly off-course.[61] Analogizing to everyday experience with automobiles, most of us assume that planes stay on course—or know if they deviate. Certainly, we like to believe in the reliability of the expensive, complex defense tracking systems the US has in the Pacific. The average person would have difficulty believing that, with all of the technology and surveillance apparatus the US has installed there, neither the US military nor its intelligence services had the Boeing 747 on radar or were in a position to warn it. The idea that two sets of equipment—the aircraft's trebly redundant internal guidance and US military tracking systems—might not perform to assumed standards strains credulity. Likewise, most people do not realize that on the long commercial routes across the Pacific there are extended periods of time when aircraft are not on anyone's radar—at least, not on any friendly civilian radar.

Such a confluence of ignorance and belief provided fertile ground for those who argued that the US must have been controlling the airplane for espionage purposes. Therefore, at one level, to paraphrase Fisher, the Pearson article is persuasive simply because it tells a more coherent 'story.' Pearson is able to exploit a convergence of public knowledge [about past espionage activities, traditional American distrust of government, a concomitant faith in technology, and the administration's unwillingness to reveal sources and methods of intelligence]. His task is made easier by the romantic nature and intrigue of the spy story in Western culture,[62] a genre, like that of the detective novel, in which no event is random or without meaning.

Consequently, we have suggested that it is fruitful to view conspiratist rhetoric from the standpoint of persuasion *versus* coercion, of rhetorical behavior intended to expand possibilities for meaningful dialog and compromise *versus* strategies which limit real communication. Like propaganda, conspiratist rhetoric attempts to vitiate competing sources of knowledge; the difference is that conspiratist argument absorbs the competing data, turning that information to its own purposes. For example, one major aspect of much conspiratist rhetoric which has not been discussed by previous authors is the overweening use of the false dilemma as a rhetorical strategy. In our opinion, the use of logical fallacy—particularly the false dilemma—exemplifies coercive, rather than persuasive, communication, since its goal is to polarize, reducing the alternatives available to the audience. Indeed, "The conspiracy argument functions to *create* fundamental differences...."

> by suggesting that the apparent similarity in views is only the tip of the iceberg. The legitimacy of the conspiracy claim may stem partly from the "useful" work done by the argument in forcing a wedge between apparently similar positions and thereby requiring of the people a real choice.[63]

Forcing audiences into a simple binary choice between alleged "good" and alleged "evil" is a standard ploy which has ancient roots: "HE WHO IS NOT WITH US IS AGAINST US." One can also pose an issue in such a manner that the audience is offered a choice between willful evil and inadvertent evil—but evil nonetheless. Thus, Robert Welch, founder of the John Birch Society, characterized President Eisenhower as either a conscious Soviet agent or an unwitting dupe of the communist conspiracy. Similarly, David Pearson argues that US claims of failure to monitor KAL 007 indicate a concerted attempt to cover up either a failed intelligence operation or, at the very least, a major US intelligence breakdown. After setting up this dichotomy, Pearson then argues for his perception of a malevolent reality, with inadvertent evil reserved as the only refuge for non-believers.

The appeal of the conspiratist's story is its self-sealing nature: it provides a world view which is complete, capable of answering—by subsuming—all uncomfortable questions. Its internal cohesiveness provides the narrative fidelity and probability that makes it persuasive. The mass of irrelevant data adduced gives the appearance of evidence but, in reality, merely serves as camouflage for inference; and the use of inference in place of more traditional supporting material allows the audience to participate in the authorizing process. Thus, conspiratist argument proves Fisher's narrative theory correct: auditors test a story by their own lights. Yet, because the narrative paradigm is not normative, analysis of conspiratist argument also provides the rationale for resisting the seduction of Fisher's position, a position which explains the believability (credibility) but not the facticity of the conspiratist argument.[64] For as long as credibility is an audience-centered rather than a message-centered concept, critics of rhetoric need an external standard to assess the content of the conspiratist argument.

254

Approaching the conspiratist argument from this vantage point, one arrives at a symbiosis of poetics and argumentation: various logical fallacies are utilized as artistic devices in the structure of a conspiratist tract *qua* rhetorical text, while consciously crafted language carries the intellectual burden of argument farther by use of emotion than the rhetor could otherwise achieve through induction. In this way, Pearson (and perhaps other conspiratists) can be seen to utilize structural devices to create the anomalies which are then explained by claims of conspiracy. In so doing, he transforms the rhetorical act, distorting its communicative nature from persuasion to coercion.

Ironically, perhaps, those same factors conspire to deny the author conclusive proof for his theories. Nevertheless, Pearson effectively associates his hypothetical premises and conclusions with what is known about the incident. Association/dissociation is probably the most powerful instrument of rationality and the most basic human thought process. It is the means by which we classify experience. As a rhetorical tool it is not only the standard by which stories are judged; it is the very substance of the narrative act. Thus, the lack of definitive evidence allows association to prevail; and the associative power of the narrative mode allows circular reasoning to succeed. Hypothetical premises, as well as the conclusions drawn from them, take on the status of proven fact and can be repeated as such in subsequent arguments. Each argument becomes an artistic element in the narrative development, and traditional rhetorical fallacies are utilized as artistic devices. Thus, it is to the traditionalist approach that we must turn in order to assess the conspiratist rhetor: the premises assumed, the structuring of arguments, the use of language, and the types of evidence brought to bear.

Of course, this is the view of argument which Fisher and others tell us is inadequate as a means of explaining public discourse.[65] Certainly, it is incomplete as a means of explaining how argument comes to be accepted by the public. Nevertheless, we would argue that it is the best, perhaps the only, means of coming to grips with conspiratist argumentation—argumentation which relies on the trappings of reasoned discourse while consciously violating the standards of rational argument.

CHAPTER NINE

NOTES

[1]R. W. Johnson, "007: License to Kill?"; Anonymous (P.Q. Mann), "Reassessing the Sakhalin Incident"; Sampson & Bittorf, "'Sinken auf eins-null-tausend." Similar articles also appeared in *L.A. Weekly, Seattle Weekly,* and *People's World* .

[2]*The Nation,* August 18-25, 1984, pp. 104-24. Page references to this article are inserted into the text.

[3]See, for instance, the ad in *The New York Times,* October 25, 1984.

[4]*The New York Times,* September 7, 1984 and October 21, 1984. See also: Wicker's columns of September 3 and 6, 1985 and September 21, 1986.

[5] *COMPILATION,* p. 1.

[6] Sayle, "A Conspiracy of Coincidence," p. 49. Pearson's position is underscored by the title of his recent book: *KAL 007: Cover-up (Why the True Story Has Never Been Told).*

[7] See: Cutler; and Michael Parenti, *Inventing Reality. The Politics of the Mass Media* (New York: St. Martin's Press, 1986), especially pp. 156-60.

[8]While the information is anecdotal, a perusal of comments elicited by two call-in talk shows indicates this is the case: *Larry King Live,* CNN, telecast September 2, 1986 (guests included John Keppel and Nicola Truppin, the daughter of two KAL 007 victims); *Donohue,* nationally syndicated telecast, September 16, 1986 (guests included Truppin, two other family members of victims, and Seymour Hersh).

[9]A stratified random sample of 1500 Americans was polled June 7-11, 1986, by the G. Lawrence Company of Santa Ana, California, for the National Strategy Information Center. One question asked during the survey was:

Three years ago this coming fall, the Soviet Union shot down a Korean Air Lines passenger jumbo jet. From everything you've heard and read since then, which comes closest to your own opinion?

The airliner accidentally strayed off course	1	(72%)
The airliner was equipped with devices for spying and intentionally went off course to spy	2	(25%)
No Opinion	3	(4%)

We are grateful to Ronald H. Hinckley, formerly a Senior Fellow at NSIC, for providing this information.

[10]To commemorate the second anniversary of the tragedy *The Nation* published "Journey Into Doubt: New Pieces in the Puzzle of Flight 007," by David Pearson and John Keppel. Both Pearson and Keppel are Contributing Editors of *The KAL 007 Information Bulletin & Newsletter*, an irregular periodical published in Washington by The Fund for Constitutional Government.

[11]Fisher, "Public Moral Argument," p. 12. Fisher cites Thomas B. Farrell and G. Thomas Goodnight, "Accidental Rhetoric: The Root Metaphor of Three Mile Island," *Communication Monographs*, 48:4 (December 1981), 271-300.

[12]Goodnight and Poulakos (p. 301). According to a poll taken three weeks after the event, three-fifths of the American public believed the United States government was not telling everything "important" to judging the truth of the incident. See *ABC News/Washington Post Poll, Survey # 0084*. See also note 9, above.

[13]Indeed, were it not true that an atmosphere existed in which the espionage theory was credible, it is unlikely that this article would have been published in *The Nation*. According to Victor Navasky, the magazine's editor, Pearson's major professor at Yale, Charles Perrow, asked for Navasky's help in placing the manuscript. Because of the sensational nature of Pearson's allegations and the existing public doubt, Navasky offered exposure in *The Nation*, despite the fact that the article was far longer than any the magazine had ever published. Navasky provided this information during a January, 1986 interview in New York.

[14]As Goodnight and Poulakos remarked in their discussion of Watergate, "in conspiracy rhetoric a struggle emerges where both sides compete for the public's belief" (p. 306). Further, "the President assumed that he himself was the highest source of the definition of reality . . . " (p. 316). Earlier (Chapter Two) we observed that in his analysis of presidential rhetoric concerning KAL, Donald Smith stated, "The President is, for all intents and purposes, The Source of information on 007." Such an assumption is implicitly challenged by all claims of official conspiracy: indeed, it is this presumption that conspiratists must overcome in order to emerge victorious.

[15]Kneupper, p. 184.

[16]Although often broadcasting the 'American line,' it is the express function of VOA and RFE/RL (along with other transnational stations such as the BBC) to attempt to provide an alternate voice challenging the official Soviet 'Party line.'

[17]Lt. Col. Iu. Borin, "Zametaiut sledy" ["Covering its Tracks"], *Krasnaia zvezda*, September 21, 1986, p. 3. See Chapter Seven. Obviously, the Soviet Union is not alone in doing this: Larry Speakes admits in his memoirs that on at least two occasions, the KAL controversy being one, he made up quotes and distributed them to reporters as the words of Ronald Reagan. See: Speakes, *Speaking Out*, p. 121; "Officials blast Speakes over fake Reagan quotes," *Tallahassee Democrat*, April 13, 1988, p. 9A; and "Reagan didn't know about fake quotes," *Tallahassee Democrat*, April 14, 1988, p. 3A.

[18]See: Robert Jervis, "Hypotheses on Misperception," in Robert J. Art and Robert Jervis, eds., *International Politics. Anarchy, Force, Political Economy and Decision Making* (Boston: Little, Brown, 1985), 2nd ed., 510-26, pp. 513-14. [originally published in *World Politics,* 20:3 (April 1968), 454-79.]

[19]It would appear that the idea of "sensitive moments"—the coincidence of suspicious overflights to ongoing or upcoming international negotiations—was first broached by a September 7, 1983 Soviet television commentary that was subsequently translated and published in *Moscow News* . "Even the time seems to have been specially chosen: it happened . . . not long before the meeting . . . in Madrid, not long before the resumption of the Geneva talks on nuclear arms in Europe. . . ." (See: *MN,* September 18-24, 1983, p. 3).

[20]Jervis, *Perception and Misperception,* p. 321.

[21]Pearson relies, it would seem, on the reader being aware of the long-standing collaboration between the CIA and its Korean counterpart. In his book, Pearson devotes much of Chapters Five and Six to making the CIA/KCIA connection explicit.

[22]He also suggests that evasive action taken by military aircraft is evidence of ulterior motives rather than the desire to avoid a forced landing, whatever the reason for the intrusion. Yet, we have been told that crews of aircraft carrying sophisticated electronic equipment have standing orders prohibiting capture.

[23]Edward Stankiewicz, "Poetic and non-poetic language in their interrelation," *Poetics* (Warszawa: Panstwowe wydawnictwo naukowe, 1961), p. 20. Lubomir Dolezel and Karel Hausenblas created the term "linguistic stylistics" to describe the study of "not only the style of belles lettres, but equally, all areas and means of utilizing language, especially literary language." The poetic resources of a language "do not form a special [linguistic] system"; rather, artistic style "depends on other styles of language." See: "O sootnoshenii poètiki i stilistiki" ["On the Interrelation of Poetics and Stylistics"], *Poetics,* pp. 39, 43; Paul Garvin, trans. and ed., *A Prague School Reader on Esthetics, Literary Structure and Style* (Washington: Georgetown University Press, 1964); and Frank R. Silbajoris, ed., *The Architecture of Reading. Essays on Russian Literary Theory and Practice,* OSU Slavic Papers No. 3 (Columbus: Ohio State University), 21-34. For a rhetorical perspective, see also: Richard Weaver, "Some Rhetorical Aspects of Grammatical Categories," Chapter Five in *The Ethics of Rhetoric* (Chicago: Henry Regnery Co, 1953), pp. 115-42. The interested reader might also consult I. A. Richards, *The Philosophy of Rhetoric* (New York: Oxford University Press, 1965).

[24]For a diametrically opposed view, see Oberg, *Uncovering Soviet Disasters,* pp. 32-49, *et passim.*

[25]However, the ICAO reached a different conclusion: "There was no evidence that complete visual identification procedures were employed. Such visual identification should have resulted in a recognition of the type of aircraft involved as well as the civilian airline markings" (*ICAO REPORT,* p. 43). Further: "The USSR authorities

assumed that KE007 was an intelligence aircraft and, therefore, did not make exhaustive efforts to identify the aircraft through in-flight visual observations" (p. 56).

[26]Soviet propagandists noted the irony of the airliner's flight number, mentioning it as an aside in one of their news releases.

[27]Fisher, "Public Moral Argument," p. 8; Fisher, "Elaboration," p. 364.

[28]The typical "mission orbit" of an RC-135 is a figure eight paralleling the coastline of the USSR. The Soviet government contends that as the RC-135 was returning to its base in the Aleutians, it made an unexpected turn to the southeast in order to position itself near the flight-path of KAL 007 and effect a rendezvous; in a diagram presented by Ogarkov at his September 9, 1983 press conference, this alleged "second loop" enabled the RC-135 to fly parallel to the route of KAL 007 (See: FBIS, "KAL Incident," *Daily Report. Soviet Union*, September 12, 1983, pp. DD 1-43.). The US government, of course, denies the existence of this anomaly in the route of the RC-135.

[29]This was the allegation that served as the centerpiece of the P. Q. Mann article, for which Korean Airlines received an out-of-court settlement from *Defence Attaché* [See: *The New York Times*, November 20, 1984].

[30]Michael Dobbs, *Washington Post*, September 20, 1983, p. A 11.

[31]Perelman and Olbrechts-Tyteca, pp. 193-94.

[32]This line of reasoning was observed in Soviet argumentation, as well, when it was claimed that sophisticated navigational systems never malfunction. See Chapter Six.

[33]Hersh has confirmed what many suspected all along: that the tragedy was indeed monitored in real time, but the radar operators did not realize the significance of their intercepts (p. 64). However, certain knowledge of this information was not available in 1984.

[34]As we have indicated, there exist two independent facts which argue that Ogarkov's map is a fabrication: (a) the passenger plane is depicted as having turned to a course heading of 300° over Sakhalin, which is contradicted by the air-to-ground tapes, Soviet interviews with the interceptor pilots, and other Soviet maps; (b) on Ogarkov's map the time of the shooting was placed at 1824 GMT, two minutes earlier than that indicated in all US and Japanese materials, including the voice activated tape of Soviet fighter pilots. No one else has ever challenged the authenticity of 1826 GMT as the time at which the airplane was destroyed or that it was still in Soviet airspace when fired upon.

[35]In fact, the Soviets never presented evidence to support any of their allegations. Dallin has pointed out that "the Soviet authorities failed to provide [the ICAO with] copies or transcripts of taped communications and records of radar tracking, falling back on legal arguments that under the Chicago Convention they were not obliged to do so" [*Black Box*, p. 91]. One may infer from the facts in this and the preceding note that the

Soviets did not record their own radar, hence could not know for certain where KAL 007 was at the moment it was hit and did not know what US intelligence might be able to prove. For a different interpretation, see: Pearson, *KAL 007: The Cover-Up*, p. 321.

[36]See: Jervis, *Perception and Misperception*, p. 321.

[37]*ICAO REPORT*, p. 40. To date, neither the USSR nor the United States has released the radar traces which would resolve this question.

[38]Informed sources indicate that Cobra Dane's circuitry blocks signals from low-flying, relatively slow-moving vehicles (*i.e.*, aircraft) so that they cannot interfere with the reception of high-altitude telemetry information from Soviet missiles. This point is confirmed by Frederic Golden, who derided the use of "flat-earth physics" ("Seeing a Conspiracy in the Sky," *Discover*, December 1984, p. 8). Accordingly, it is virtually certain that Cobra Dane would <u>not</u> have tracked KAL 007, even if the airliner were within range. The efficacy of this rhetorical strategy, however, was borne out in a conversation we had with a prominent magazine editor in January, 1986. The editor asked why we did not believe, based on the evidence Pearson presented, that Cobra Dane could 'see' over the horizon. His position was that if Cobra Dane could 'see' 2,000 miles into space, there was no telling what else it could do.

[39]As demonstrated in Chapter Four, the linguistic evidence provided by the Russian transcript indisputably contradicts Pearson's allegations. In a December, 1984 telephone interview Pearson acknowledged that he knew no Russian and had not consulted anyone who did. The fact that analysis of the pilot transcript remains essentially unchanged in Pearson's 1987 book—despite his having had access to contrary evidence—is further testimony, in our opinion, to his conspiratorial *Weltanschauung*.

[40]The *ICAO REPORT* supports our interpretation. "The information contained in the USSR preliminary report states that the aircraft lights were 'off.' This contradicted the monitored air-to-ground communications" (p. 43).

[41]Pearson does not retreat from these assertions in his book (p. 73, *et passim*); rather, he augments them with charges that KAL 007 made several abrupt changes in altitude. In order to reach this conclusion he must dismiss as biased the statements of Japanese Defense Agency officials and ignore the well-attested inaccuracy of ground-based height-seeking radar, even though he quotes published data showing that such radar is accurate only to within +/- 3,000 feet at the range from which the data were collected (pp. 320-25). [While KAL 007 was being trailed by the SU-15, and shortly before it was struck by the missiles, the crew received permission to increase altitude from 32,000 feet to 35,000 feet.]

[42]*ANC REPORT*, p. 8.

[43]It should be noted that even if the Soviet pilot had made a call to KAL 007 on the International Hailing Frequency (121.5 MHz), such a voice call would not appear on the transcripts because the frequency is different from that being monitored. Likewise, these transcripts would not contain any response made by KAL 007. US representatives,

particularly Ambassadors Kirkpatrick and Lichenstein, failed to point this out in their presentations at the United Nations. Pearson ignores this fact as well. Presumably, however, references to such a call would appear. In any event, the emergency frequencies are constantly monitored by satellites and ground installations scattered throughout the world.

[44]See Perelman and Olbrechts-Tyteca: "Qualification, insertion into a class, may be expressed by use of a coordinating conjunction, such as 'and,' 'or,' or 'nor,' instead of by use of a notion already developed" (p. 128).

[45]Jervis, *Perception and Misperception*, p. 321.

[46]Creps, pp. 96, 100.

[47]Some commentators assume an opposite view of this point. For example, in "Conspiracy of Coincidence," Sayle took the position that a voice call on 121.5 MHz probably was made. In a 1985 letter to us, Sayle explained why he adopted this stance: "I think you are probably right and it was [IFF], but the Soviet statement to ICAO says that they called on the guard frequency and I can't show that they did not." At the time, Sayle was unaware of statements by Duane Freer of the ICAO, cited in Chapter Four, that directly refute the Soviet claim. He has subsequently stated his complete acceptance of our position on this matter (telephone conversation, November 1987).

[48]Stephen E. Toulmin, *The Uses of Argument* (Cambridge: Cambridge University Press, 1958).

[49]Contrary to Pearson's claim, the *ICAO REPORT* also concluded there was no evidence of the interceptor pilot having made any significant effort to follow international procedures for intercepting aircraft (p. 43).

[50]In this regard, the *ICAO REPORT* states that the "monitored communications . . . did not specifically refer to the use of the emergency channel (121.5 MHz) in calls directed to the intercepted aircraft . . . " (p. 43). Furthermore, the Air Navigation Commission concluded:

> There is no record or other information of any calls on 121.5 MHz having been heard by any civil or military ground unit or by other aircraft within VHF range of the intercepting aircraft, or any record of such transmissions having been received via the search and rescue satellite (SARSAT) system (p. 9).

Pearson continued to overlook these refutations in his book.

[51]For an early discussion of this phenomenon, see: Baskerville.

[52]Creps, p. 45; see, also: Hofstadter, pp. 36-37.

[53]See: Perelman and Olbrechts-Tyteca, p. 150-51: "In order to discern the argumentative use to which a term is being put, it is important to know the words or expressions the speaker might have used and to which he preferred the word he selected. . . . The

terms comprising a [word-] family form an aggregate by relation to which any given term is specifically determined: they are . . . the background against which the selected term stands out." One of Perelman's primary interests is determination of the "relation between art and argumentation" (p. 153).

[54]Murty, p. 29. In this context Murty cites Charles L. Stevenson, *Ethics and Language* (New Haven: Yale University Press), pp. 59-62, 141-42.

[55]Quoted in Andrews, p. 12.

[56]Perelman and Olbrechts-Tyteca argue that epithets are used "without justification" when they are "supposed to set forth unquestionable facts" (p. 126). Adverbs are particularly well-suited to this purpose (p. 163). Further: "Analysis of the argumentative role of certain variations in expression can be carried out only in terms of divergence from the expression that goes unnoticed" (pp. 151-52).

[57]Weaver singles out the adverb as "peculiarly a word of judgment" because it is "used frequently to express an attitude which is the speaker's projection of himself" (p. 133). In modern linguistics this phenomenon is called "deixis". It is specifically the sum of linguistic resources available to express the speaker's point of view and assessment of truth value. Recent rhetorical theory seems to have bypassed such language studies.

[58]*ABC News/Washington Post Poll, Survey # 0084* .

[59]Fisher, *Human Communication as Narration*, p. 72. It is not clear what should be the role or the subject of the "counsel" Fisher espouses. If experts refute technical error, they are engaging in the discourse-stifling practices that Fisher condemns. On the other hand, failure to provide refutation leaves the public as ignorant and error-prone as before. See: Rowland, pp. 271-73.

[60]Harold Ewing has demonstrated that this allegation is false (telephone conversation, September 30, 1986). However, even if the pilot had taken on extra fuel, no sinister intent need be read into such an act. Adding fuel before a long trip is not unusual—indeed, it is often done. The quantity does sound impressive, though, and it is easy to imagine that an uninformed reader would impute nefarious intent to the pilot's alleged action. But in fact 9,800 pounds of fuel would have amounted to only 3.8% of the minimum required for the flight and would have constituted, in the view of many experienced pilots, a prudent reserve referred to as "grandmother fuel" [See: Maertens, p. 29]. One should not minimize the rhetorical effect of citing such figures, however. As Perelman and Olbrechts-Tyteca observe, "Generally speaking, absolute figures have a greater impact on the imagination [than relative figures] . . . " (p. 148).

[61]According to testimony before the House Committee on Science and Technology, this happens fairly often (See: U. S. House of Representatives, *Aircraft Navigation Technology and Errors*). State Department sources indicate that in the year immediately following the KAL tragedy, there were 55 such instances over the North Atlantic

alone. These events were not common knowledge in 1984, and Pearson's article might have been received somewhat differently had it been published in 1988.

[62]Compare Pearson's account of the flight of the Korean airliner with the theories about the final flight of Amelia Earhart. The proof that Earhart flew over the Marshall Islands in order to spy on the Japanese is no more definitive, yet a determined minority believe that to be the cause of her disappearance. Of course, the KAL mystery is enhanced by the serendipitous similarity of the aircraft's flight number with the code name for James Bond.

[63]Zarefsky, "Conspiracy Argument," p. 73.

[64]Fisher, *Human Communication as Narration*, p. 66.

[65]Fisher, "Public Moral Argument," p. 12; See also: Charles Arthur Willard, *Argumentation and the Social Grounds of Knowledge* (University: University of Alabama Press, 1983); idem., "Argument Fields," in J. Robert Cox and Charles Arthur Willard, eds., *Advances in Argumentation Theory and Research*, 24-77; idem., "Argument Fields, Sociologies of Knowledge and Critical Epistemologies," presented at the annual conference of the Speech Communication Association, 1982.

CONCLUSION

PROPAGANDA, CONSPIRACY, AND COMMUNICATION

PROPAGANDA, CONSPIRACY, AND COMMUNICATION

In the preceding chapters we have examined various aspects of the rhetorical aftermath of the Korean Air Lines tragedy. We discussed the nature of the foreign policy decision-making process in the Reagan Administration at the time of the shootdown; the nature of public information in the Soviet Union; and the concepts of propaganda and conspiracy theory. We also posited some theoretical notions relating to these ideas. In this final chapter, we will attempt to develop our positions more fully and offer some generalizations about conspiracy theories, propaganda, and Soviet rhetoric.

The political aftermath of the destruction of Korean Airlines flight 007 was an exercise in the "creation of truth." The governments of both the United States and the USSR were less than forthright, subordinating accuracy to the ends of foreign and domestic policy and allowing ideology to cloud judgment. (On the whole, the US was guilty of sins of omission, the Soviets—sins of commission.) Leaders in both countries, in turn, faced a rhetorical situation that required a "fitting response." In the United States, the requirement is imposed upon the government by its "instant accountability to the American Press."[1] As for the Soviet Union, the impetus came from without, but its exigency was no less real.

The rhetorical matrix in any situation consists of a reflexive interaction among the contextual situation, the rhetor, the audience, and the text. But the kinds of response that might meet this requirement will be different for various matrices, including dissimilar societies. Intrinsic to this relationship is Bitzer's notion of public knowledge, which serves as the warranting process for public discourse. Bitzer, we believe, would accept wholeheartedly Huntington and Dominguez's concept of the 'political culture' of any society, defined as consisting of "the empirical beliefs about expressive political symbols and values and other orientations of members of the society toward political objects."[2] Brown proposed that this concept be understood as "the subjective perception of history and politics, the fundamental beliefs and values, the foci of identification and loyalty, and the political knowledge and expectations which are the product of the specific historical experience of nations and groups."[3] Remington characterizes

267

"patterns of perceptions" as "the basis for the unity of a cultural community."[4]

Most societies probably have both an official and an unofficial public knowledge. Official public knowledge—what Brown calls 'official political culture'[5]—consists of the ideals and values to which all members of a society pay lip-service, the information and policies promulgated by the government, the laws and public practices of the society. Unofficial public knowledge is more diverse, culturally-based, and historically situated. In the open societies, unofficial public knowledge may, over time, become part of the official public knowledge; more importantly, since the two varieties are never far removed from one another, both must be taken into account by rhetors who would be persuasive. The differences between the two forms of public knowledge are more distinct in the USSR. There, unofficial public knowledge is seldom acknowledged in public discourse, and it is rare that such perceptions ever become part of the recognized official political culture.

Because of the greater flexibility of public knowledge in the West, information must go through several developmental stages before becoming part of that corpus. For our purposes, the most salient aspect of that process is the reciprocal, reflexive relationship among the components: text, context, the rhetor, and the auditor. One can point to the steady re-evaluation of the AIDS threat as an example of this process. AIDS was initially perceived to be a disease affecting only a minority class. More became known about the disease and those it affects, however, and the context for discourse about the virus changed. As the threat spread, the focus changed from cure to prevention, and a campaign was undertaken to provide information to those at risk.

Obviously, the media play a decisive role in the rhetorical process, for they are the primary purveyors of information to society at large. Consequently, the media also exist as part of the reflexive relationship, part of the perceptual matrix. Media reports about any event are instrumental in determining the context in which that event is viewed; frequently they are responsible for alterations in perceptions. The Vietnam War, Watergate, and the recent Iran-Contra affair are examples of this phenomenon.

In an atmosphere of crisis, the primary demand is for information, which heightens the reflexivity of the elements of discourse. Public discourse, official and unofficial, both responds to and reshapes the context. In the case of the destruction of Korean Air Lines Flight 007, a dramatic event received considerable coverage in the media; but information was held primarily in the hands of the government, and the crisis context of the tragedy was determined by the Reagan Administration's decision to treat the shootdown as a part of the struggle between The Forces of Good and Evil.[6]

Jervis's analysis of premature cognitive closure presents a persuasive framework for understanding the process of decision-making on the night of August 31/September 1. The danger of preconceptions does not lie in the preconceptions themselves; on the contrary, they can be quite useful in managing information and in reacting quickly to crises. The problem arises when decision makers fail to realize that they are working from a preconceived perceptual framework:

> Not being aware of the inevitable influence of beliefs upon perceptions often has unfortunate consequences. If a decision-maker thinks that an event yields self-evident and unambiguous inferences when in fact these inferences are drawn because of his pre-existing views, he will grow too confident of his views and will prematurely exclude alternatives because he will conclude that the event provides independent support for his beliefs.[7]

It is fairly obvious that this is exactly what occurred in the case of the Korean airliner incident. Presented with a heinous act, and given the Administration's preconceptions about the barbaric nature of the Soviet Union, decision makers drew from the event reinforcement and confirmation of previous belief. Invoking the rational actor model of Soviet behavior,[8] American decision makers concluded almost immediately that the shootdown was a deliberate act, and no amount of discrepant information was going to dislodge that conclusion. The evidence—i.e., the various audio tapes and, presumably, intercepted radar tracks—was perused for data that would support those conclusions. Jervis postulates a close relationship between "being too closed to discrepant information and forming one's hypothesis too soon, before sufficient evidence is available."[9] Thus, the Administration forced the early release of the air-to-ground transcripts, to 'strike while the iron was hot,' because it was convinced that there could be no disconfirm-ing information in the unintelligible portions of the intercepted conversation between the Soviet pilot and his ground control.

Once the hypothesis of deliberateness was formed, it was virtually impossible, given the decision-making atmosphere and the mind-set of the Reagan advisers, to amend that hypothesis, a condition which Jervis has described: "[I]nitial incorrect hypotheses will not be quickly altered in light of later evidence but will delay accurate perception for a long time."[10] In the prevailing atmosphere, the play of events was virtually inevitable, because the tendency to form early images is

> greater the more ambiguous the information, the more confident the actor is of the validity of his image, and the greater his commitment to the established view.... Commitment here means not only the degree to which the person's power and prestige are involved but also—and more importantly—the degree to which this way of seeing the world has proved satisfactory and has become internalized."[11]

Certainly, Reagan had made a considerable investment in his 'get tough' attitude towards the Soviet Union—the evoked set shared by him and his closest advisors. This perceptual framework guaranteed that the United States would take full advantage of every opportunity to manifest that philosophy.[12]

Because the US government couldn't control the information flow, however, subsequent events presented a rhetorical situation in which multiple rhetors continuously redefined the context in which the shootdown was interpreted. As new information came to light, both from official sources and through the investigative efforts of the media, public preknowledge evolved. As we have shown, official American rhetorical efforts failed to take this evolution into account.

The situation in the Soviet Union was somewhat different. Part of the official public knowledge in that country is the realization that no event is critical enough to warrant public disclosure without first having been situated within the matrix of communist ideology. Thus, the demands for information are different, and both text and context are determined by the state. The general lack of competing information sources enables the government to control not only the rhetorical situation, but the specifics of public discourse, as well. Indeed, had it not been for the public clamor in the West, the Soviet people might never have learned of the shootdown at all.

The most challenging part of this study has been the application of principles of rhetorical theory and criticism to the Russian language material. Rhetorical theory, from classical times to the present, has been based on the Western democratic model, and thus presumes open competition in the marketplace of ideas. However, despite frequent discussion of the role of ideology in rhetorical studies, no systematic attempt has been made to develop a comparable theory for authoritarian societies such as the USSR. The assumption seems to have been that theories obtaining in the so-called 'open societies' will prevail in the information-restricted cultures as well. However, this notion has not been tested, as neither rhetorical theory nor principles of rhetorical criticism have been systematically applied to Soviet discourse. And logic dictates that it may well not hold true; if words and symbols can have different meanings in different cultures, why not forms of communication?[13] Perhaps the barrier to such theory construction is linguistic: few present-day 'closed societies' are English-speaking; and such studies of communication as exist in these milieus have not been shared with the West (in contrast to theoretical advances developed, say, in Belgium and Germany).[14]

It is our hope that this study will lay a foundation on which a theory of communication for closed societies might be developed. Our assumption is, to borrow an architectural phrase, that form follows function: when a government views the primary role of public communication as indoctrination/education, forms of communication will differ materially to accord with that function. Concurrently, we anticipate that effect will flow from form. That is, the effect of a discourse is dependent upon its relationship to its auditors, its creators, and the rhetorical situation. Thus, one assumes, there will exist theoretical differences between rhetoric in a pluralistic setting and rhetoric in a monistic setting.[15]

Most closed societies hold the belief that the truth is known only to a few and the general citizenry cannot be trusted to discern it for themselves if presented with a morass of conflicting information. As a result, argumentation takes a different form in the Soviet Union, because it serves a very different function. The proffering of claims backed by evidence is a rhetorical structure intrinsic to the operation of Western democracies. In the Soviet Union there has existed no tradition of public argumentation as we know it, except, perhaps, within the highest circles of the party and the government. One of the fundamental characteristics of argumentation is risk-taking: those who argue risk not only losing the argument but becoming convinced of the truth of other side.[16] In a monistic system, such public risk-taking is impossible.[17]

Likewise, evidence—at least as it is characterized in the argumentatively based institutions of the West—is also a casualty of the authoritarian system, a notion amply illustrated by similar regimes of the past, such as Germany under Hitler. The pluralistic concept of the need for an informed citizenry underlies the fundamental differences apparent in the nature and use of evidence within open and closed systems. Since authoritarian governments do not recognize the validity of political pluralism, they do not face the requirement of providing their citizens the information necessary to make political choices; the need, rather, is for the populace to be provided the true interpretation of events. The function of both the news media and the educational establishment is to inform the populace of that truth.[18]

Accordingly, rhetoric in the Soviet Union is viewed as an instrument for propagating the state approved ideology. Hence, it functions as an instrument for social control and, to that extent, is coercive by its very nature: Soviet society provides no approved outlets for alternate information and no opportunity to openly apply rational processes to opinion formation.[19] This is not to suggest that competing information does not exist in the Soviet Union, nor that opinions contrary to state-approved doctrine are not formed, simply that there are no institutionalized mechanisms for implementing these cherished Western values. Thus, all public communication is of a piece—the print media, television, the classroom, the local agitprop meeting, or the discussion group: public communication is designed to reinforce the society's official political culture, to create and maintain national unity.[20] Western distinctions, fuzzy as they may be, among persuasion, argumentation, propaganda, indoctrination, and education are irrelevant.

The primary rhetorical feature of the aftermath of the destruction of KAL 007 was a propaganda war between the United States and the USSR. In the Introduction, we defined propaganda as discourse which attempts to conceal evidence and subvert rational processes. Certainly that was the case with the rhetoric which flowed between the two superpowers in the Fall of 1983. Both sides exhibited what Jervis has called "the tendency of [political] actors to believe that the hostile behavior of others is to be explained by the other side's motives and not by its reaction to the first side."[21] In so doing, each opponent created a closed loop of mutually reinforcing rhetorical behaviors.

The United States, for its part, hinted at extensive evidence, but released only the pilot tape. The remainder of the American campaign consisted primarily of exhortation designed to isolate the Soviet Union from the community of civilized nations. The USSR, on the other hand, released little evidence of any sort (other than a television interview with the pilot of the SU-15), but relied almost entirely on revelations from the West and the standard topoi of Soviet rhetoric vis-a-vis the United States. In that sense, the Soviets, too, engaged in exhortation. Neither government presented the type of arguments which would allow an individual to reach a rational determination of sociopolitical reality. Moran would call this pseudocommunication:

> The Stated and Observed Purposes tend toward being different in that the stated purposes are unclear, hidden, or contradictory to the observed purposes, or in that the stated purposes are not verifiable by empirical observation, or in that the methods of analysis are determined by the sender only.[22]

We commented in Chapter Five that the Soviet system is essentially deductive in nature, with all arguments stemming from the axioms—the universal truths—of Marxist-Leninist doctrine. That has not changed. Nevertheless, the Soviet propaganda campaign over KAL 007 represented a concerted attempt to win the assent of the population through the use of argument and reason giving. Surprisingly, in this controversy the logical structure of the arguments that were advanced was inductive rather than deductive. Soviet propagandists relied on inference from past example, using the technological capabilities of the United States as a bridge. In contrast to the American side, Soviet propagandists had a clearer picture of the goals they hoped to achieve with their rhetorical campaign. Taken in its entirety, it was more realistic, better coordinated—despite obvious inconsistencies and mistakes—and appeared more likely to achieve its purpose than was the vacillating American performance.

The Soviet Union, of course, based most of its domestic campaign on the allegation that the overflight was deliberate—an espionage mission under the sponsorship of the United States. As always, the goal was to preserve the insularity of the Soviet people: since truth is known, there is no need for competing sources of knowledge. What outside news did get through was absorbed into the propaganda effort and became part of the proof for the government position, creating a self-sealing quality similar to that identified for conspiratist argument.

Indeed, Western conspiratists made similar claims, chaining a series of inferences based on the presumed technological capabilities of the US defense establishment and its known penchant for spying. In the course of this analysis, we have commented on the striking similarities between propaganda and conspiratist rhetoric. In fact, if Soviet propaganda rhetoric has a Western counterpart in substance and in methodology, that counterpart is the conspiratist model of argument. While these are not consubstantial phenomena, both are essentially pseudo-communication processes and, thus, they overlap in method: both seek to conceal evidence and both attempt to subvert rational processes, by adopting the garb of evidence and the appearance of logic. Accordingly, when discussing KAL, Soviet propagandists clothed their rhetoric in the trappings of argumentation: They made extensive use of 'evidence' and 'reason-giving', endeavoring to foster the impression of logical processes. Nevertheless, this was done mostly napokaz, 'for show.' Like propaganda, conspiracy rhetoric attempts to subsume discrepant information; the difference is that conspiracy argument absorbs the competing data, turning that information to its own purposes. By relying on rhetorical devices to achieve the appearance of rationality, both propaganda and conspiracy argument approach the coercion end of the persuasion-coercion axis.

It is in this mutual reliance on coercion that we discern the effective point of congruence between propaganda and conspiracy argument. Burgess characterizes a coercive situation as one in which "negative cues conspire to achieve pinpoint clarity of desired response by inhibiting all responses except the one invited." "The key tactic," Burgess argues, "is to preclude verbal and nonverbal alternatives to the demanded act."[23] Andrews, it will be recalled, claimed rhetoric that was non-rational or that limited the options of auditors "becomes less persuasive and more coercive."[24] Certainly, any rhetorical system which restricts evidence and subverts rational processes conforms to the notion of coercion, for one of the most effective means of limiting choice is limiting information.[25] The auditor is left with two alternatives: adhering to the tightly constructed world of the rhetor, with its promise of unrevealed knowledge, or rejecting it in favor of the unknown. This simple, binary choice provides an effective means of polarization and is consistently reflected in the rhetorical strategies adopted by conspiratists and propagandists of all persuasions.

The practical difficulty encountered by the critic (and the target) of conspiracy argument, as we pointed out in Chapter Eight, is that the argument is self-sealing. All attempts at refutation are simply absorbed as proof that the conspiracy still exists, rendering the argument virtually impossible to disprove. As Moran points out, "[T]he pseudocommunicator is always endeavoring to have us accept a simplified view of life. In pseudocommunication, a ready answer is always available and provides the receiver with a ready defense against conflicting evidence."[26] This is one of the ways of distinguishing conspiratist rhetoric as a genre of discourse (*i.e.*, a way of viewing the world) amidst the broader category of all rhetoric which alleges a conspiracy.

To that end, we have proposed three standards for evaluating conspiracy argument which might apply equally well to propaganda analysis:

1. A determination of factual accuracy;

2. An examination of logical structure;

3. An exposition of artistic choices.

In applying these criteria to one example of Western conspiracy argument, the David Pearson article in *The Nation*, we found that the author made numerous factual errors, utilized the appearance of careful reasoning as a rhetorical tactic, and relied on artistic devices such as juxtaposition, repetition, and emotive language choices to carry the weight of his argument. This construction becomes coercive in part because it presents a dichotomous view of the world, and in part because, while claiming to assemble proofs, it substitutes for evidence verbal artistry and the discursive structure of narrative. Moreover, it illustrates one of the basic factors that makes conspiratist rhetoric effective: the facility with which narrative structure employs parataxis (associative thinking) to subsume anomalous—even contradictory—details within its explanatory apparatus. It is this characteristic of conspiratist argumentation that renders the genre problematical as an instrument of epistemology. With respect to logical processes, rhetorical fallacies such as the false dilemma abound in conspiratist rhetoric. Neither the Pearson article nor the Soviet defense of its action against the airliner is an exception to this characterization.

It proved appropriate, therefore, to apply to the Soviet campaign the same three categories advanced for the evaluation of conspiracy argument: factual accuracy, rhetorical structure, and artistic choices. We have noted throughout this book the extent to which Soviet commentators distorted—or simply fabricated—factual material, a task made easier by the complex technical nature of the information surrounding the destruction of the Korean jetliner. The propagandists traded on the ignorance of their audience, and depended upon the lack of alternate sources of information—a tactic used to advantage by their Western counterparts, as well. Indeed, one could posit the similarity of effect on public discourse attributable to highly technical subject matter, on the one hand, and to the tactic of suppressing or overlooking alternate sources of information. Both rely on the inability of the audience to arrive at a reasoned judgment regarding the evidentiary value of the arguments being presented. Compounding the auditor's difficulty was the fact that the USSR produced no evidence of its own, relying instead, as did Pearson, on logical structure and artistic choices to carry the burden of proof.

The USSR advanced three claims: the airliner could not have strayed accidentally; it could have been warned by the US; and, therefore, it was a spy plane and the USSR was justified in shooting it down. While each of these is treated as a separate argument, the validity of the third is dependent on the first two. Thus, taken together, they form a chain of inference leading to the conclusion, a tactic reminiscent of the McCarthy era and, more recently, of the John Birch Society. Yet each component is dependent on rhetorical fallacies which reduce the alternatives to a false dilemma, a tactic we have identified as coercive. When logical or rhetorical fallacy is so consistently employed as a means of proof, it becomes an artistic device, a stylistic choice designed to conceal, yet giving the appearance of careful reasoning.

It is in the category of artistic devices that the similarities between Soviet rhetoric and conspiracy rhetoric are most obvious. The same devices—juxtaposition, repetition, emotive language, and the appearance of careful reasoning—can be found in both. Soviet propagandists juxtaposed the KAL incident with previous known incidents, such as the U-2 overflights, the KAL 902 intrusion in 1978,[27] and images of World War II to demonstrate a continuing phenomenon of invasion.[28] Assertions about KAL 007 appearing in one medium are repeated, often as proof of additional claims, both in that medium and in others. Finally, Soviet allegations that the airliner could not have strayed by accident and that it could have been warned, although unproven except by continued assertion and repetition, function as proof for argument three, that KAL 007 was engaged in an espionage mission.

Language choices are always indicative of the ideological orientation of a rhetor.[29] For example, while US spokesmen were referring to an **"unarmed, civilian airliner"** and an **"act of wanton murder,"** Soviet rhetors labelled KAL 007 as an **"intruder,"** **"intruder aircraft,"** or **"spy plane,"** choices which not only depersonalize the incident but also give it ominous overtones. Other Soviet appellations included "this aircraft" (or "plane"),[30] "the South Korean aircraft", or "the Boeing 747," none of which indicate KAL's civilian status. The destruction was referred to as the **"incident"**, as in "the incident involving the South Korean aircraft," thus minimizing its tragic nature. In this same vein, the Soviet interceptor pilot **"struggled"** to alert the airliner under conditions of **"great risk,"** while the Americans **"relentlessly** tracked the movements of the intruder by satellite." This latter passage underscores the Soviet claim that the US willingly and knowingly sacrificed the 269 persons on board the Korean jetliner, despite the best efforts of the Soviet pilot to avoid a fatal confrontation. It also reinforces the impression that US technological capability ruled out an accidental overflight. Claiming that the US frequently used foreign passenger aircraft to **"cover"** for reconnaissance flights, a Soviet commentator remarked, "spyplanes **loaded** with electronic equipment literally **poise** themselves above passenger liners," language which is reminiscent of that used by Pearson.

One of the most commonly used devices of conspiratists is the citation of 'evidence' from 'the other side'. Several commentators, including Hofstadter, have remarked on the frequency of the 'convert' as a source of proof for the conspiracy argument.[31] In a variation of this technique, Soviet rhetors use material from Western sources to condemn the United States with its own words. Such evidence justifying the Soviet argument must necessarily carry greater credibility, particularly since the first information Soviet citizens received about the shootdown came from Western transnational broadcasting.

While citing one another's articles and commentaries is not a new practice for Soviet rhetors, quoting Western sources is a relatively recent development and is representative of the anomalies in the Soviet response to the Korean airliner tragedy. Most of these anomalies, however, function as a means of maintaining control over the information flow within the Soviet Union.

In dealing with the Korean airliner incident, the Politburo was faced with an unusual situation: the information that had been disseminated during the first six days following the inception of this crisis came from the West, either through travellers returning home or in the form of broadcasts by VOA, Radio Liberty, BBC, Deutsche Welle, or one of the other foreign stations received on short-wave radio. As we pointed out earlier, initially the issue was factual, not interpretive: either the PVO had shot down a passenger aircraft or they had not; the six-day silence by the Soviet government lent credibility to Western accounts. Thus, the situation was particularly serious, from the point of view of the state: unless the government provided a context within which to view the shootdown, the response of most individuals would be shock and disapproval. The infallibility of the state was threatened along with its ability to control information. No doubt tradition played a role in this as well: to the extent that audience expectations serve as a limitation on rhetoric, the state could not simply admit culpability and apologize for making a mistake, even if US rhetoric had left them that option.

One goal of the Soviet propaganda campaign had to be to blunt the effectiveness of alternate information sources. The primary tactic in this campaign seems to have been the appearance of openness and forthrightness on the part of the Soviet government. Thus, in addition to admitting that the PVO did, indeed, "terminate" the flight of the "intruder," the government held a press conference where a top military official answered questions from the domestic and foreign press; part of the press conference was televised domestically (on tape delay) and the authorities allowed a live feed to Western television; the press conference was re-broadcast by Soviet radio; and *Pravda* and *Izvestiia* each reported the event. The very uniqueness of this press conference and the coverage it received bolstered the credibility of the Soviet story domestically. Likewise, the interview with the pilot who shot down KAL 007, featured on *Vremia* the evening after the press conference, was an unusual event which gave the impression that the government had nothing to hide. Indeed, the uniqueness of the methods employed—including the techniques of quoting the Western media, and, later, reporting the conspiracy theories that developed in the West— served to enhance the believability of the Soviet government campaign.

Examination of the content of this propaganda campaign (using the three criteria we stipulated) reveals, however, that its purpose was to enable the state to regain control of public knowledge by vitiating the impact of information disseminated from outside sources. The aim was to create a context, a rhetorical situation, in which the destruction of the airliner could be interpreted in light of communist doctrine, the action justified, and blame for the tragedy shifted to the United States.

In this one sense, there occurred a real change in the approach of the Soviet government: providing reasons for the actions of its armed forces. One can only assume that the uniqueness of the situation, coupled with the intensity of the outcry worldwide, had forced the Soviets to re-evaluate their propaganda tactics. Reason-giving is a reflection of the Western concept of a social contract between citizen and state, a relationship which rests on the assumptions that the state will not act capriciously and that the citizen is entitled to know the rationale behind state actions. The very fact of the Ogarkov press conference, combined with the specific denial that the destruction of the Korean airliner had occurred by accident, appeared to signal Soviet acceptance of these parameters.[32]

However, what has gone unnoticed throughout the many discussions of this incident is the fundamental inconsistency of the Soviet position. On the one hand, Soviet citizens were asked to accept that the interceptor pilot could not possibly have known the aircraft was a civilian passenger plane; on the other, destroying the aircraft was not a mistake, and the Soviet government was prepared if necessary to defend its borders in the same manner in the future. The second argument can stand alone within Soviet political culture, so there was no necessity for making the first. But in making the first argument, Soviet propagandists should have completely undercut the validity of the second. Why, then, did they go to such extremes in the fabrication of evidence to demonstrate the first assertion? The answer, we believe, lies in the clash with information that was reaching inside the State borders via transnational broadcasting. By proclaiming the brutality of the Soviet state, Western radio challenged the fundamental legitimacy of the government—that is to say, of the Party. By appealing in the shrillest manner possible to the unofficial public knowledge, consistently ignored by the state throughout the Soviet era, Western radio forced the official public knowledge to take cognizance of that shadow political culture, a culture that knew full well exactly how brutal the Soviet state could be. The Soviet government might not be able to insulate its state borders from intrusion over the airwaves; but it certainly could repulse intrusions by foreign aircraft.

"The Voices" emphasized the premeditated attack on innocent civilians. By concentrating on emotional aspects, however, and neglecting to respond to the specific counter-charges lodged by the Soviet government, Western radio failed to exhibit the fundamental inconsistency of the American position, which becomes clear if one examines official American statements closely and compares them with the only tangible evidence that was released to the public—the air-to-ground transcript—evidence which undercuts the American rhetorical position.

The irreducible minimum charge emanating from the West was that the Soviet PVO had followed KAL 007 on radar for over two hours and absolutely knew that the aircraft was civilian prior to destroying it. However, when the Soviet side, in order to deflect this charge, maintained that the crew of the airliner ignored a number of attempts to draw attention to its situation, the US rushed in to fill the evidence void with its tape. And, indeed, the Russian language transcript proves beyond any reasonable doubt that these Soviet claims were almost completely fabricated. The victory, however, is best described as Pyrrhic. For in accomplishing this, the US also proved the falsity of its own claim. If the Soviet pilot made an IFF inquiry minutes prior to shooting down the aircraft, then it must not be true that military officials knew all along what sort of aircraft they were dealing with. As we stated in Chapter Four, all the IFF interrogation proved was that KAL 007 was not a Soviet military aircraft. Had that been clear for over two hours, there would have been no necessity to complete such an electronic inquiry so late in the interception sequence.[33]

Of course, as we have demonstrated, the Reagan Administration manifested little interest in establishing the truth for public consumption.[34] Rather, it engaged in many of the same tactics in its propaganda war against the Soviet Union as the Soviets themselves had employed. The American government controlled the flow of technical data: Except for the Japanese, who followed the US lead, no one else had any real information. Initially, the Americans released only that which seemed to support their position, asking the world to accept their interpretation uncritically. Thus, in effect, there were no competing sources of information. From the beginning of this controversy up through the present, the US government has controlled the relevant data; it has chosen to release some, but much remains secret. We have seen the extent to which this decision blunted much of the rhetorical effort made by the Reagan Administration, how much it contributed to reinforcing the expectancy of disbelief among Americans that is the *sine qua non* for any plausible conspiracy theory.

By comparison, how successful was the Soviet propaganda campaign? This is a difficult question to answer. However, some insight can be gained from the results of audience research conducted by RFE/RL. Soviet Area Audience and Opinion Research interviewed 274 Soviet citizens travelling in Europe between early September and mid-November 1983. Forty-five per cent of the respondents cited Western radio as one source of information on the KAL incident (many respondents named several sources). RFE/RL found a strong correlation between the respondents' source of information and their attitude toward the incident. Approximately 50% of the Western radio listeners "accepted the Western version of events and expressed disapproval of the Soviet action." Of the non-listeners in the sample 79% found the Soviet version most credible; seventy per cent supported the decision to 'terminate' the flight. SAAOR points out that the value of this study lies in these correlations between attitude and information source. Another interesting finding was that 26% of the Western radio listeners cited word-of-mouth as a source of information. According to the SAAOR report, this conforms to earlier findings showing that "Western radio listeners rely more on word of mouth sources for international news than do non-listeners," indicating a greater proclivity toward unofficial sources; it also indicates that "the information obtained from the outside world by Western radio is undergoing continued discussion and dissemination."[35] Certainly, one could argue that the Reagan Administration's rhetoric about KAL 007 was effective on large numbers of the Soviet citizens who heard it. Evidently, the Soviet government's concern about the impact of Western transnational broadcasting was not misplaced.

In Chapter Seven we elaborated the role played by Voice of America and Radio Liberty in the continuing US campaign to present its version of the Korean airliner tragedy. Significant numbers of the Soviet citizens listened, primarily to Voice of America;[36] and the Soviet government felt compelled to react. By presenting discrepant factual information and an interpretation of events not authorized by the Soviet state, Western transnational broadcasting alters the rhetorical process of this closed society. In particular it stimulates the growth of an unofficial public knowledge—truly, a counterculture of 'blackmarket information'—that competes and conflicts with the authorized version. In affect, it creates a situation in which the Soviet government must pay heed to a warranting process that previously could be ignored, a warranting process which in the past had been nonexistent, or at least not meaningful, in Soviet society.

It would not be an exaggeration, we believe, to claim that Western transnational broadcasting fulfills a role in certain segments of Soviet society not unlike the role played by an established free press in the West. By challenging the unlimited control over dissemination of information within society, each organ forces power centers to explain and justify their policies and actions. Although the effects of this influence within the Soviet Union do not extend to all, or even most, avenues of state control, Western radio had forced modifications in the verbal behavior of the state.

More than any other medium, the counter-programming of Western radio has the potential to challenge Soviet hegemony over its domestic public communication. While no Soviet government has ever succeeded in totally controlling the flow of information, it is equally true that the challenge from external sources has never been greater. Recognizing this fact, Soviet policy planners have gradually introduced changes into their communication industry. One of the most surprising findings of RFE/RL listener polling is the decreased influence of the Soviet "prestige press"—*Pravda* and *Izvestiia*.[37] Television has assumed greater importance, paralleling Western experience, a trend which can only increase over time. TV is becoming such a factor that even Western radio has felt its effect: According to Sherwood Demitz, VOA's Soviet audience decreases at 9:00 p.m. local time, when the TV news program *Vremia* goes on the air, and increases immediately after *Vremia* is over.[38]

As we have documented throughout this study, the Soviet government has taken cognizance of Western radio. The USSR has modified its propaganda in order to counter specific information and arguments entering the public realm from outside the country—turning that information back against its promulgators and, like conspiratists in the West, incorporating it into the Soviet scenario. In addition, Soviet domestic propagandists have changed the manner in which their message is presented: citations of Western sources[39] and the use of TASS wire service reports from foreign cities have become the predominant tactics of newspaper propaganda. The Ogarkov press conference and the *Vremia* interview with the pilot of the SU-15 indicate that Party officials are making more sophisticated use of television.[40]

If it is true that rhetorical conventions place limitations on future discourse, the Korean Airline disaster may have affected the course of Soviet rhetoric, at least in times of crisis. According to Black, such expectations exist not only in the auditor but in the rhetor as well, making a reversal of style difficult. In this context, the 1986 nuclear power disaster at Chernobyl provides a striking example of Soviet communication in a state of flux. A detailed analysis of the Chernobyl rhetoric is hardly appropriate here, but some observations are certainly in order.

Elements of traditional rhetorical conventions were evident in the delayed public recognition of any problem at the Chernobyl plant, charges that reactionary forces in the West (particularly the US) were slandering the Soviet state, the curious use of "you-too-ism" (If the West has problems with nuclear power—submarines, underground tests, the Hanford nuclear reactor—why be surprised if we do, too? This is an effective use of the enthymeme, involving the audience in the inferential process).[41]

Some of the elements seen first in the KAL controversy reappeared in the Soviet discourse about the reactor accident, including different treatment of domestic and foreign audiences, citation of Western non-communist sources, and reaction to VOA & RL (once again, the first news that Soviet citizens received of the disaster was from Western transnational broadcasts).

However, there were some totally new elements as well, including actual news reports about the accident and positive public treatment of foreign experts such as bone marrow specialist Dr. Robert Gale of the United States and Hans Blix of the International Atomic Energy Agency (a UN agency). General Secretary Gorbachev addressed the nation on television (albeit, over two weeks later) and was pictured in newspapers shaking hands with Dr. Gale—certainly unusual occurrences in the USSR.[42]

Most startling, however, was the admission of a major Soviet problem—implying for what might be the first time that the Soviet system is not infallible. Many Western observers are encouraged by what appears to be a new openness in the Soviet Union—Gorbachev's policy of glasnost' . What remains to be seen is whether this policy represents actual change or is simply an alternate form of coercion, a way to regain control of the dissemination of information by creating the impression that the government has nothing to hide. Nevertheless, it is clear that the difficulties encountered by the Soviet government in selling their case at home and abroad during the KAL crisis are, in large measure, responsible for whatever reassessment of rhetorical methods has taken place. KAL—Chernobyl—glasnost' . Whatever the relationship among these phenomena, it will be difficult for the Soviet Union to return to its old ways, at least in terms of its relationship with the outside world.[43] Wilensky has noted the tendency of leaders to become captives of their own rhetoric, of the media image which they present to the world; evidence suggests that Soviet leaders are no exception. While Wilensky's observation carried a slightly pejorative tone, in this instance, the effect may prove salutary.

Thus, in the end, the ultimate irony of the destruction of Korean Air Lines flight 007 may be this: the more the two superpowers strove to control the flow of information, the more each lost control of the situation. As a result, neither government succeeded in retaining the unquestioning assent of the publics most critical to its immediate interests.

NOTES

[1] Hugo, p. 48. Recall that news reports had already begun streaming in from Japan and Korea by the time Secretary Shultz began his press conference September 1, 1983.

[2] Samuel P. Huntington and Jorge I. Dominguez, "Political Development," in Fred I. Greenstein and Nelson W. Polsby, eds., *Handbook of Political Science, vol. III: Macropolitical Theory* (Reading, MA, 1975), p. 15. [Quoted by Brown in his introduction to *Political Culture and Communist Studies*, p. 2.]

[3] Archie Brown and Jack Gray, eds., *Political Culture and Political Change in Communist States* (New York: Holmes and Meier, 1977), p. 1. [Quoted by Brown in his introduction to *Political Culture and Communist Studies*, p. 2.]

[4] Remington, *The Origin of Ideology*, p. 12. Obviously, Remington sees a relationship between culturally based perceptual patterns and ideology; an interesting question to pursue is whether or not there can exist both official and unofficial ideologies.

[5] Brown, "Soviet Political Culture through Soviet Eyes," p. 103.

[6] For a discussion of Reagan's perception of the Cold War as Good versus Evil, see Erickson.

[7] Jervis, *Perception and Misperception*, p. 181.

[8] Jervis believes that political actors evaluate information "in light of the small part of [their] memory that is presently active—the 'evoked set '." In addition, they "tend to see the behavior of others as more centralized, disciplined, and coordinated than it is.... Further, actors see others as more internally united than they in fact are and generally overestimate the degree to which others are following a coherent policy." See: "Hypotheses on Misperception," pp. 519, 521.

[9] Jervis, *Perception and Misperception*, p. 188. This notion is borne out by the information released by Congressman Hamilton in January 1988: that the US was aware soon after the tragedy that the Soviets did not realize the airliner was a civilian craft when they shot it down. Nevertheless, Reagan's advisers went forward with the charge that the Soviets deliberately destroyed an unarmed airliner. See: Chapter One, note 60; also, Chapter Two.

[10] Jervis, *Perception and Misperception*, p. 188.

[11] Jervis, *Perception and Misperception*, pp. 195-96.

[12]The strength of the "evoked set" is described in a chilling anecdote that has particular relevance to the story of KAL 007. Jervis points out that "people perceive incoming information in terms of the problems they are dealing with and what is on their minds when the information is received." Re-orienting one's attention in an atmosphere of crisis can be nearly impossible. Jervis's example is the cockpit conversation on board the Libyan airliner shot down over Israel in 1973. As Jervis describes the scene, "the crew was so immersed in their task of finding the Cairo airport that they paid little attention to the fighters that suddenly appeared. Even the firing of warning shots could not jog their minds into realizing that they were facing a very different problem." The transcript of those conversations reveals the tenacity with which one's mind can focus on an absorbing problem:

Captain:	Now is that Lima Uniform [code for Cairo airport] on your right?
Captain:	Did you have the ILS? [instrument landing system]
Captain:	What's that you have there?
Co-pilot:	Ah, we have rockets.
Captain:	Eh?
Co-pilot:	I have seen some rockets here.
Captain:	Oh, eh?

(A 15 second beep was heard, signaling that the undercarriage was being lowered as if for landing. Noise of aircraft passing the airliner.)

Engineer:	You have the ILS. Is it descending?
Captain:	No
Captain:	Check the ILS on yours.
Co-pilot:	What?
Captain:	The ILS of Cairo.

Evoked sets can be so dominant that actors often assume their perceptions are shared by those with whom they are interacting. Accordingly, Jervis contends, the Israeli interceptor pilots took for granted that the Libyan crew saw them, understood the situation, and chose to attempt an escape. It never occurred to the Israelis that the Libyans were so engrossed in their own task they failed to comprehend that they were being intercepted; had anyone suggested this to the fighter pilots, they would have rejected the notion as incredible. "Actors thus overestimate the degree to which each understands what the other is trying to say" (pp. 214-15). Perhaps that is why the US failed to perceive the admission of culpability which the Soviets claimed was contained in the initial September 2 announcement about the attempted interception of KAL 007.

[13] In their discussion of speech communication in East Germany, McGuire and Berger observe that "ideological commitment to Marxism precedes and shapes the teaching of communication and does not result incidentally from it." See: Michael McGuire and

Lothar Berger, "Speech in the Marxist State," *Communication Education*, **28**:3 (July 1979), 169-78, p. 174.

[14] McGuire and Berger take note of the existence of rhetorical studies in West Germany. They cite two references: Frederick Trautmann, "Rhetoric Far and Near: Lessons for Americans, from German Books," *Quarterly Journal of Speech*, **61**:3 (October 1975) 328-36; and, Joachim Dyck, "Rhetorical Studies in West Germany, 1974-1976: A Bibliography," *The Rhetoric Society Quarterly*, 7 (Winter 1977), 1-18, with "Addenda" by Peter Jehn, 18-19.

[15] McGuire and Berger discuss the relationship between ideology and communicative behavior, arguing that "despite carefully reasoned and Whorfian explanations that our communicative behavior (certainly use of a language counts as such) makes our ideology, the fact of the matter is that our ideology determines our very definitions of competent communication, whether we as speech scholars acknowledge or obscure that fact" (p. 178). Certainly when one considers communication as epistemic, as a way of knowing, one must recognize the importance of ideology to the form of communication, especially an ideology such as Marxism-Leninism, which depends on first principles. Unfortunately, a discussion of the relationship between ideology and communication theory is beyond the scope of the present volume.

[16] See Henry W. Johnstone, Jr., "Some Reflections on Argumentation," in Maurice Natanson and Henry W. Johnstone, Jr., *Philosophy, Rhetoric, and Argumentation* (University Park: Pennsylvania State University Press, 1965), 1-9; and Douglas Ehninger, "Argument as Method: Its Nature, Its Limitations and Its Uses," *Speech Monographs*, 37:2 (June 1970), 101-110, especially, pp. 103, 104.

[17] Conditions are changing somewhat within the Soviet Union—witness the recent public controversy over Boris Yeltsin's role within the current Soviet leadership; also the current debate over the pace of reform and the extent to which correction should be made in public understanding of the history of the Stalinist era. Both of these controversies have been publicized in the Soviet press.

[18] Perhaps there is some gentle irony in the names of the two major daily Soviet newspapers: *Pravda* (Truth) and *Izvestiia* (News). A common Soviet aphorism may be apt: "There is no news in *Pravda* and no truth in *Izvestiia*," Gospozha Ul'ianova raised no fools.

[19] In his 1964 explication of *The Art of Oratory*, Butler (p. 239) notes:

And if a Soviet student desires to analyze and define, for instance, the word '"logic,"'he will find an entire page in the *Great Soviet Encyclopedia* devoted to it, but defined in strict terms of dialectical materialism. The translation of *Oratory* reveals that there is no great omission or concealment of the liberal principles of classical rhetoric in Soviet speech-craft; however, there are official interpretations of those principles based on their unique application to Communism.

[20]"Regardless of type, therefore, Soviet speech has a primary or secondary objective of propagating the state-approved ideology. To ensure uniformity and coordination of speech and source material, the ideology is kept current by official interpretation, and controlled throughout the established speech apparatus. This is why Communist doctrine and dogma is found not only in Soviet political forums, but in academic halls, factories, public auditoriums, theatres, and even courtrooms." See: Butler, p. 238.

[21]Jervis, "Hypotheses on Misperception," p. 522.

[22]Moran, p. 186.

[23]Parke G. Burgess, p. 67. Burgess's constructions entail a threat, or at least an implied threat, of violence. He argues that the nature of the threat is rhetorical. We argue that the constructions apply as well to intellectual coercion, since the goal of both forms is the elimination of alternative courses of action or belief.

[24]Andrews, p. 10. Most rhetoricians view coercion as involving physical violence, or, at least, the threat of violence; Burgess includes Andrews in this category. Nevertheless, the point Andrews makes applies equally to a form of intellectual coercion exemplified by the elimination of alternatives, since that is the goal of "coercive persuasion." See: Burgess, p. 71. For other discussions of the persuasion-coercion phenomenon, see: Herbert W. Simons, "Persuasion in Social Conflicts: A Critique of Prevailing Conceptions and a Framework for Future Research," *Speech Monographs*, 39:4 (November 1972), 227-47; and Douglas H. Parker, "Rhetoric, Ethics, and Manipulation," *Philosophy and Rhetoric*, 5:2 (1972), 69-87.

[25]In political systems, this tactic is the root of coercive—*i.e.,* authoritarian—governments.

[26]Moran, p. 192. In his review of Jerry F. Hough, *The Struggle for the Third World: Soviet Debates and American Options* (Washington, DC: Brookings, 1986), Peter Shearman notes Hough's argument that "the Reagan administration has tended to view the world in simplistic bipolar terms, almost resembling Stalin's two-camp thesis. He suggests that those who claim that Soviet ideology is 'monolithic and unaffected by events . . . are being far more ideological than their Soviet counterparts' (p. 262). See: *International Affairs*, 62:3 (Summer 1986), 542.

[27]This brings to mind Pearson's "sensitive moments."

[28]It should be noted that World War II and the incredibly heavy toll in human life and suffering endured by the USSR serves as a rhetorical icon in the Soviet Union.

[29]Hugo decried this fact as "an odium inescapable by the humblest writer on political technique. Strive as he will for objectivity and neutrality, he can not avoid the commitments and the overtones of the words he uses" (p. 189).

[30](ètot) samolet.

[31]Hofstadter observes that the mind-set which allows a person to belong to an extremist group of one persuasion also predisposes that same person to "convert" to a mirror-image group of the opposite persuasion. Thus, we have the phenomenon of "Jews for Christ" and former Communist Party members who have joined the John Birch Society. Hofstadter also notes that these converts become a prime source of testimony, their credibility established by their previous affiliation.

[32]Although Western experts now believe that the shootdown was not the result of a coherent policy decision, at the time these factors reinforced the West's misconception that the Soviet government had acted rationally—that is, deliberately.

[33]To our knowledge, the first individual to assemble these facts correctly was Professor Sugwon Kang. Faced with our linguistic evidence, Kang was compelled to repudiate the assertions he had made based on incorrect information obtained from David Pearson's article in *The Nation*, but he nonetheless refused (justifiably, it turns out) to accept the American government's position uncritically. See: Launer, Young, and Kang, p. 70.

[34]Hersh's assertion that NSA linguists continued to revise the Russian language transcripts of their audio tapes until at least 1985 demonstrates the lengths that US intelligence agencies must go to establish as reliably as possible the true sequence of events and the actual state of knowledge at every point in the Soviet military chain of command. But those data will be sealed from public scrutiny for several decades at least.

[35]Mihalisko and Parta. None of those interviewed was emigrating from the USSR. These figures represent unweighted frequency counts. SAAOR cautions that the sample for this study is skewed in favor of urban educated males of Russian nationality who are members of the Communist Party. Consequently, the results of the study cannot be projected to the Soviet population as a whole—hence, the stress on the relationship between source of information and attitude toward the shootdown. One interesting result of the survey is the 30% of listeners (to Western radio) and the 16% of non-listeners who expressed no opinion about the two versions of the event; with regard to attitude toward the downing of the aircraft, 31% of listeners and 20% of non-listeners expressed no opinion. One should keep in mind, however, that those with the proclivity to defy the government and the Party by listening to Western radio in the first place, might have a proclivity to reject the official Soviet version and disapprove of the action.

[36]Mihalisko and Parta.

[37]Mihalisko and Parta. Only 19% of respondents cited the Soviet press as a source of information on the KAL 007 tragedy.

[38]Demitz is Chief of Media Research in the USIA Office of Research. He was interviewed in Washington, DC during January, 1987. *Vremia* is broadcast from 9:00 - 9:30 p.m. in every Soviet time zone.

[39]L. Jameson, p. 23.

[40]As an indication of television's growing impact, in the SAAOR survey cited above (see footnote 31), 35% of the listeners and 53% of the non-listeners cited television as a source of information. Based on the correlation of attitudes toward the shootdown with sources of information, SAAOR concludes that "Soviet television was the most effective means of persuading the public of the government's position." By contrast, agitprop occupied in third place and print media—sixth. We attribute the dominance of Soviet television to the Ogarkov press conference and the pilot interview. Nevertheless, long-range political propaganda will probably remain the province of the print medium, which is better suited to the task. It will be interesting to follow the impact of television on the ideological mission of Soviet journalism.

[41]This technique recalls the *Jeune Afrique* articles on the 1973 Israeli destruction of a Libyan passenger plane and the rhetorical device of asking what the US would have done if a Soviet plane had flown over Los Alamos and ignored all signals to land. Clearly, the intent was to mitigate Soviet responsibility for destroying KAL. The technique was that much more potent for allowing the audience to reach the obvious conclusion. See Chapter Seven.

[42]At the time, few Western observers credited Gorbachev with the political astuteness and courage manifested by his televised address to the nation. Rather, he was criticized for providing little of the information Westerners would have expected from a leader at home. But it should be remembered that the Soviet people simply had no precedent for such a statement by any Soviet leader. In 1983 no public statement about the Korean airliner was attributed to Andropov until four weeks had passed; in 1986, the political leadership did not distance itself from the tragic events at Chernobyl.

[43]Testimony to actual changes within Soviet society may be provided by recent Associated Press wire stories. In a well publicized Russian article, venerable Soviet historian Dmitri Likhachev urged that officials at the Academy of Sciences library in Leningrad be fired for lying about the extent of damage inflicted by a fire that destroyed more than 400,000 books and periodicals. Over three million other priceless books and documents suffered severe water damage. Likhachev charged that library administrators reacted "according to the 'model' programmed by the mistakes of the Chernobyl catastrophe—they tried to [minimize] the cultural loss in the grossest manner." The day after the fire broke out TASS reported that the most valuable collections and bequests had been spared, with total damage amounting to about $4,800. See: "Soviet academic says library fire is a 'cultural Chernobyl'" (AP S9398, 27 March 1988); and "Soviet scholar calls library fire 'a national disaster'" (AP S55695, 1 April 1988). We are grateful to Robert Broedel of Florida State University for providing these references.

APPENDIX

This appendix contains synopses of the contents and arguments provided in many of the English language books that have been published about the Korean airliner. These are separated into two groups: a large collection of works that, while spanning the political spectrum from left to right, may properly be described as 'mainstream'; plus a smaller group of extremist views. In both groups, the books are listed in the chronological order of their publication.

MAINSTREAM STUDIES

Massacre 747
Major-General Richard Rohmer
Markham, Ontario: PaperJacks, Ltd., 1984, 213 pages

Rohmer, who holds the Distinguished Flying Cross, is a former WWII fighter pilot and squadron commander who brings his expertise to bear on the events surrounding the loss of Korean Air Lines Flight 007. **Massacre 747** was one of two early books to provide a serious and relatively complete discussion of the facts. Rohmer has little sympathy for American political posturing or bungling, but absolutely none for Soviet rationalizations of its actions: "the shooting down of a civilian airliner has no justification in human, moral or civilized terms" (p. 213). The book contains considerable information regarding Korean Air Lines, and it provided the earliest significant analysis of the United Nations debate. Rohmer's basic contention is that the captain of KAL 007 deliberately flew over Soviet territory to reduce flying time and save fuel.

> The causal links between Flight 007's presence over Soviet territory, the investigation and the grounding of [10 senior KAL] pilots are direct and impossible to ignore. There may be some other explanation as to why Captain Chun and his crew flew into Soviet airspace en route direct to Seoul. However, in the permanent absence of the black boxes,... all the evidence points to an attempt to "cut the corner" (pp. 212-13).

Rohmer calls for greater international cooperation to completely eliminate any possibility that such incidents might recur.

Black Box. KAL 007 and the Superpowers
Alexander Dallin
Berkeley: University of California Press, 1985, 130 pages

Of all the books on this topic, **Black Box** has received the most consistently favorable reviews, due in large part to the author's eminence as a historian. Dallin examines potential reasons for KAL's route over the Soviet Union and describes the political process that ensued. Published after Rohmer's book and the Pearson article, **Black Box** accepts

> three possible explanations: (1) a calculated attempt by the crew to save fuel—the least plausible and the least likely of these alternatives; (2) innocent error, of which at least two variants provide technically possible though humanly rather unrealistic explanations for what took place; and (3) an intelligence assignment, perhaps to trigger a higher stage of Soviet air-defense alert for U.S. equipment to record, or perhaps with a different objective (p. 56).

Regarding a possible intelligence mission, Dallin concludes:

> [T]he logic of that argument is strong, but that is a far cry from suggesting ... that this is indeed what must have taken place, especially since a plausible motive or mission remains to be supplied. By the same token, this possibility must not be ruled out simply because of the political embarrassment which its validation would occasion. In fact, it must be acknowledged that with the passage of time this argument, unlike all others, looms stronger than before (p. 57).

Dallin's discussion of the political ramifications relies on experience gained from a long and distinguished career. He correctly decries the reliance of leaders in both countries on a rational-actor model for explaining the actions of the adversary, and claims—as we would agree—that preconceptions in both capitals played an inordinately great role in determining the political aftermath. But Dallin believes that both governments were more successful in convincing their domestic audiences of the rectitude of their respective actions and positions than do we. In addition, while recognizing that Moscow "surely has been capable of brazenly insisting on would-be facts which are demonstrably not so" (p. 96), he accepts at face value many such Soviet assertions regarding the interception and destruction of the airplane. Moreover, one sometimes gets the impression that he has bent over backwards in his attempt to rationalize the Soviet rhetorical effort.

KAL Flight 007: The Hidden Story
Oliver Clubb
Sag Harbor, NY: Permanent Press, 1985, 174 pages

Oliver Clubb, a political science professor, is the son of O. Edmund Clubb, a former US diplomat whose career was destroyed by the Joseph McCarthy purges. This book offers virtually no indication of any particular competence that the author brought to his task, nor of any research undertaken.

Clubb alleges that KAL 007 was engaged in an intelligence mission; he also alleges that the 1978 flight of KAL 902 was similarly engaged. The exposition rests almost exclusively on ideas and assertions promulgated by the Soviet Union or by Pearson in *The Nation*, with particular emphasis on the notion that the primary purpose to be achieved by KAL 007 was to ensure the deployment of Pershing II and cruise missiles in Western Europe and to derail the disarmament process.

The KAL 007 Massacre
Franz A. Kadell
Alexandria, VA: The Western Goals Foundation, 1985, 341 pages.

The Western Goals Foundation, an arch-conservative organization, was established in 1979 by Larry McDonald, a passenger on the Korean airliner. In the words of Foundation Director Linda Guell, this book recounts a "story of unbelievable terror: a cruel, overt act designed to intimidate, horrify and mesmerize every American" (p. i).

Considering the bias of the organization that commissioned this work, Franz Kadell has written a remarkably objective and balanced treatment. Kadell, a political reporter from West Germany, produced a well researched story of the flight and a detailed reiteration of the political controversy through September 16, 1983. He specifically denigrates Jeffrey St. John's assertions (in *Day of the Cobra*, a book that focuses on Rep. McDonald's anti-Soviet views) that the Soviet government used secret electronic equipment to redirect the plane's flight path in order to murder the Congressman:

> [N]othing has come to light to support the theory that the KAL 902 in 1978 or KAL 007 in 1983 were lured into Soviet airspace by an electronic device. There is also no evidence to support the assumption that the Soviets shot down KAL 007 because Larry McDonald was aboard the plane, or that they confused KAL 007 and KAL 015 in an attempt to kill other members of Congress (p. 82).

A rumor current among the anti-conspiratists in late 1985 alleged that leaders of Western Goals were highly displeased with this conclusion.

Much of Kadell's book traces the political aftermath of KAL 007. Many statements by American and Soviet officials are reprinted verbatim, although the text suffers in spots from dubious translations. Kadell was particularly interested in Jeane Kirkpatrick's presentation of the air-to-ground recording at the United Nations; considerable attention is devoted to Charles Wick, USIA Director and a close friend of Ronald Reagan, and to the intensive efforts by USIA staff to prepare and stage the UN show. Kadell's description accords well with information we received from Sherwood Demitz at USIA.

The ultimate purpose of the book is well disguised until the concluding pages, where it becomes clear that the political aftermath received such attention in order to demonstrate the manner in which the liberal press in the United States wrote apologia for the Soviet Union. Without naming either the writer or title, Kadell describes the contents of David Shribman's October 6, 1983 *New York Times* article ("U.S. Experts Say Soviet Didn't See Jet Was Civilian," pp. A 1, A 10), stating that the newspaper "took the lead in distorting the story about KAL 007" (p. 337). He continues:

> There are strong indications which give good reason to assume that *The New York Times* story was deliberately shoved onto the front page to influence public opinion in order to go easy on the Soviets (p. 338).

Kadell claimed that there was "more and more ground for the assumption" that articles like Shribman's "were only part of a campaign to hammer a factually inaccurate and garbled version of the airline massacre into public opinion" (p. 339). He closes his book by quoting a statement attributed to General George Keegan, former chief of Air Force intelligence, that "a conscious, political decision [had been] made somewhere to tone down the rhetoric to free the Soviet leaders from responsibility" (p. 341).

Shootdown: Flight 007 and the American Connection
R. W. Johnson
New York: Viking, 1986, 335 pages.
First published in London: Chatto & Windus, 1986 as
    Shootdown: The Verdict on KAL 007

R. W. Johnson is a Fellow in Politics at Oxford. He has published extensively, with much of his previous work emphasizing Africa. In December, 1983, he published an article in *The Guardian* that posited US culpability in the fate of KAL 007. **Shootdown** is Johnson's effort to substantiate that view.

Johnson saw as the impetus behind an American spy mission the fact that Soviet authorities had begun building an extensive radar installation at Abalakovo near Krasnoyarsk in central Siberia. According to Johnson, intelligence officials needed to ascertain whether or not a 'hole' existed in the Soviet anti-ballistic missile radar defense system that the Abalakovo installation might fill: if capable of being used in such a manner, the radar site would violate the ABM Treaty. Although Johnson has amassed an impressive collection of press treatments of the tragedy, his book contains virtually no new evidence. Moreover, in asserting the alleged motivation for the overflight, Johnson ignored information that had been published in *Aviation Week & Space Technology*, an authoritative publication, stating that CIA experts were not worried about such a possibility. [There is no question that Johnson was aware of this information, because he had corresponded for over a year with Philip Klass of the *AW&ST* staff.]

In 1987, in a startling development attributed to glasnost' and the spirit of cooperation engendered between General Secretary Gorbachev and President Reagan, a delegation of American Congressmen and aides specializing in military affairs visited the Abalakovo installation, which was still under construction. See: Michael R. Gordon, "U.S. Presses Plans to Upgrade Radar Despite Concerns," *The New York Times*, December 28, 1986, pp. A 1, A 6; Philip J. Klass, "U. S. Scrutinizing New Soviet Radar," *Aviation Week & Space Technology*, August 22, 1983, pp. 19-20; William J. Broad, "Inside a Key Russian Radar Site: Tour Raises Questions on Treaty," *The New York Times*, September 7, 1987, pp. A 1, A 8; idem., "Soviet Radar on Display," *The New York Times*, September 9, 1987, pp. A 1, A 6; and an editorial, "Breaching the Wall at Krasnoyarsk," *The New York Times*, September 10, 1987, p. A 24.

We have already published a decidedly negative review of **Shootdown**. That opinion has not changed. Johnson, even more than Pearson, demonstrates a facility for distorting information, for ignoring a large body of fact that conflicts with his interpretation, and for treating his opponents with disdain. With specific reference to the Russian language materials, we can assert unequivocally that nearly every statement made by Johnson is incorrect in fact or interpretation. His book exemplifies Jervis's classic description of the extent to which the interpretation of political events can be directed to promoting a preconceived viewpoint. In addition, it provides glaring proof of what might happen if Fisher's strictures against expert participation in policy debate were implemented completely, leaving the discussion to others less well versed in the technical issues that impinge on nearly every contemporary public argument.

"The Target Is Destroyed"
Seymour M. Hersh
New York: Random House, 1986, 282 pages.

Seymour Hersh is the most celebrated of all the authors who have chosen to write about the Korean airliner. Formerly a reporter for *The New York Times*, Hersh has won a Pulitzer Prize (for uncovering the My Lai massacre and the subsequent cover-up by Army investigators) and a National Book Critics Circle Award (for his study of Henry Kissinger). He is justly considered one of the best—if not the best—investigative reporter in America. Hersh concluded that there was no spy mission but that the airliner crew and the Soviet Air Defense Forces demonstrated incredible incompetence, all of which resulted in the deaths of 269 people.

In our review of Hersh's latest book we disagreed with those reviewers who described it as his best work ever (for instance, Thomas Powers, writing in the *New York Times Book Review*, September 21, 1986, p. 3); but this study is challenged only by Alexander Dallin's *Black*

Box for its authenticity and authoritative research. In particular, we do not accept Hersh's position regarding the non-existence of the ground-to-air recordings.

The strength of Hersh's book is the inside look at how intelligence officers reach their conclusions and what happens to those assessments once they are turned over to policy makers. Having detailed the unique position occupied by William Casey in his dual roles as trusted advisor to the president and as the director of Central Intelligence—and the pernicious effect this situation had upon the political process—Hersh would no doubt agree with the assessments of Allen Dulles and General "Bull" Donovan that were cited in Chapter One.

As we have noted elsewhere, Hersh enjoys incomparable respect among mid- and upper level military and intelligence personnel for his honesty and deeply held belief in the difficult work they do. But high-ranking officials less interested in operations than policy formation probably would prefer to see him jailed. Hersh also has an uncanny ability to get people to talk. Both traits continue to have repercussions within the American intelligence establishment: not only have operational changes been instituted as a result of his revelations, but former intelligence specialists indicate that the personnel changes which followed in the wake of his book rippled throughout the system, as personnel from Misawa and Wakkanai were shuffled to other installations world-wide in an effort to break up the teams that talked. NSA officials were fuming.

Hersh's book also contains Hal Ewing's now famous reconstruction of what may have happened to get KAL Flight 007 so far off course. Ewing demonstrated that it <u>was</u> possible to construct an accidental scenario that would contradict no known facts, yet take the aircraft to a position of mortal danger over Sakhalin Island in Soviet airspace. As far as we have been able to determine, the scenario appears in the book primarily as the result of a marketing decision by Hersh's editor, who feared that the lack of a "sexy" conclusion—Hersh candidly admits that he expected to find evidence of American complicity, but uncovered none—left Random House with a manuscript that might not recoup the hefty advance Hersh's reputation had warranted.

KAL 007: The Cover-Up
David E. Pearson
New York: Summit, 1987, 462 pages

When Pearson wrote his article in *The Nation*, he was a doctoral student in Sociology at Yale University. He subsequently took time off from his graduate studies to devote his efforts to writing this book.

The Cover-Up contains the most detailed discussion of all facets of the Korean airliner tragedy. Personnel at *The Nation* arranged for the services of a Japanese translator, allowing Pearson to provide the most complete account of relevant events and publications in Japan. With financial support provided by The Nation Institute and The Fund for Constitutional Government, he was able to travel to Anchorage to interview traffic control personnel, to contract for two different acoustic studies of ATC tapes obtained in Alaska, and to arrange for a comprehensive search of all published materials. As a result, the book provides the most complete bibliography published on this topic.

Pearson continues to insist that the Korean airliner was engaged in a spying mission for American intelligence. As a result, he charges that the US government has engaged in a systematic cover-up in order to escape censure for its actions. In all candor, it must be admitted that no reasonable justification can be found for US Air Force personnel destroying radar tapes that might have shed light on KAL 007's precise location and heading as it left Alaska in a west-south-westerly direction toward the Soviet Far East. Further, as Dallin wrote in **Black Box**, it was Pearson who first detailed in public the extent of the American surveillance network in that part of the world, rendering it quite difficult for anyone to believe that even at 3:00 a.m. no one knew where KAL 007 was or what it was doing.

Nonetheless, despite all of this time, money, and effort, Pearson continues to rely on doubtful information, leading him to incorrect conclusions. For instance, his discussion of the contents of the Russian air-to-ground recordings remains essentially unchanged from 1984— Pearson simply ignored the contrary information available in the public domain. To increase the acceptability of his tape interpretation, however, Pearson cites Sugwon Kang's article as his source, conveniently ignoring the fact that Kang had cited Pearson's original article in *The Nation* as <u>his</u> source.

The one piece of potentially important new information that Pearson brings to bear on the case is the acoustic reconstruction of a tape recording made in Anchorage ATC; this recording purportedly contains an inadvertent comment to the effect that someone should warn the Korean airliner it was nearing Soviet airspace. There are two reasons for considering this evidence suspect: one is the fact that Pearson had access to a sworn affidavit by the FBI's leading acoustic expert; that affidavit, filed in Federal District Court in Washington, D.C., states that there are no intelligible words contained on the tape segment in question.

In addition, in Chapter 22 of his book, Pearson details the two investigations of this tape that he commissioned. The first, performed by Dr. Malcolm Brenner, resulted in a conclusion equivalent to that in the sworn affidavit—there were no incriminating statements anywhere on the tape. Pearson then gave the tape to another expert, Lawrence L. Porter, who found evidence to support Pearson's claim that Anchorage ATC was aware of KAL 007's position.

Our conclusion remains that Pearson has provided no credible evidence substantiating any US involvement in planning or executing an intelligence mission involving Korean Airlines Flight 007. Nevertheless it is undoubtedly true that the US government failed to make a full public accounting of the information in its possession regarding the event.

EXTREMIST STUDIES

Flight 007
M. Kalyanasundaram, M.P.
Delhi: New Literature, 1983, 80 pages

One of the earliest books out on the topic, **Flight 007** contributed nothing of substance. The essential point is that the Central Intelligence Agency is infamous for its espionage activities, and the Korean airliner is but the latest such event.

President's Crime: Who ordered the espionage flight of KAL 007?
Akio Takahasi
Japanese version—Tokyo: Ningensha, 1984
Russian and English versions—Novosti Press Agency, 1985
Also published in New Delhi as
Truth Behind KAL FLIGHT 007

Takahasi's book—127 pages long in Russian, only 80 pages long in English—amounts to no more and no less than a compilation of Soviet assertions and allegations. As we have indicated, Murray Sayle believes that the project is a simple piece of <u>dezinformatsiia</u>, the primary function of which was to present as foreign commentary the legal justification for actions taken by Soviet PVO forces.

Explo 007: Evidence of Conspiracy
R. B. Cutler
Beverly Farms, MA: R. B. Cutler, 183 pages

This handsomely crafted volume, produced by a talented callig-raphist, is by far the most interesting of the so-called 'crackpot' books on the Korean airliner. Cutler, who identifies himself as an "assassin-ologist," has devoted the last two decades to studying political assas-sinations in America, beginning with the deaths of JFK, Martin Luther King, Jr., and RFK. Cutler includes in his recapitulation the murder of Mary Jo Kopechne and the multiple murder of 269 innocent people aboard Korean Airlines Flight 007. All of these crimes have been com-mitted, he is convinced, by the Professional War Machine, Cutler's version of the military-industrial complex.

The simplicity of Cutler's conspiracy scenario is exquisite: an American RC-135 penetrates Soviet airspace, allowing itself to be tracked by radar until it draws fire from Soviet defense forces, then instantaneously deploys a super-secret shield (à la the Starship Enter-prise?) to deflect the air-to-air missiles fired at it by a Soviet fighter pi-lot. Simultaneously, a message is flashed to an attacker flying near a South Korean passenger airliner that is innocently and totally without suspicion of danger flying over the Pacific Ocean along NOPAC Route Romeo-20. The attacker destroys KAL 007, which had just radioed to Air Traffic Control at Narita Airport, Tokyo, to announce reaching NOKKA, an over-ocean waypoint along R-20.

All this was motivated, Cutler contends, because America was losing its sense of the Soviet Union as the enemy, and needed to be reminded of that fact in an unambiguous manner.

Except for the fact that only two seconds separated the firing of missiles by the SU-15 from their impact into KAL 007's rear-mounted engines—which seems hardly enough time to sense the attack and deploy the 'stealth technology' defense system—Cutler's scenario conforms perfectly to all known facts and even explains many of the 'anomalies' attendant to the flight of KAL 007, particularly the lack of correspondence between the routine position and status reports emanating from the airliner with the various in-flight maneuvers claimed by Soviet spokespersons (now seen to have been a true reflection of the activities designed to draw fire from Soviet defense forces, which correctly identified the intruder as a US reconnaissance aircraft). Nice.

REFERENCES

Due to the subject of our research, many citations in this book refer to radio, television, and newspaper accounts of the KAL tragedy and its political aftermath. Listing all of these accounts is not only impractical, it would contribute little to the purpose of verifying or replicating our work beyond what is achieved by citations contained within the body of the text. Accordingly, we have not included in this bibliography the following sources:

(1) articles published in the *Los Angeles Times, The New York Times,* and *Washington Post,* for the period September 1—October 31, 1983;

(2) transcripts of news specials and regularly scheduled news programs on the ABC, CBS, and NBC television networks during September, 1983;

(3) coverage in the newsmagazines *Newsweek, Time,* and *U.S. News & World Report* during September, 1983;

(4) English language transcripts of correspondent reports and regularly scheduled news programs broadcast by Voice of America for the period September 1, 1983—April 1988 [we did not have the opportunity to travel to Munich, where Radio Liberty's Russian language transcripts are preserved; VOA's Russian transcripts are not archived];

(5) Federal Broadcast Information Service translations of Russian, Japanese, and Korean media reports;

(6) transcripts of Soviet radio and television news programs for the period September 1, 1983—April 1988;

(7) articles published in Soviet national daily newspapers for the period September 1, 1983—April 1988.

ABC NEWS/WASHINGTON POST POLL, Survey #0084, September 22-26, 1983 [Peter Begans, analyst, and Karen Ivy Wright, compiler].

Jan S. Adams, "Critical Letters to the Soviet Press: An Increasingly Important Public Forum," in Donald E. Schulz and Jan S. Adams, eds., *Political Participation in Communist Systems,* Pergamon Policy Studies on International Politics (New York: Pergamon, 1981), 108-37.

Hannes Adomeit, "Ideology in the Soviet View of International Affairs," in Christoph Bertram, ed., *The Prospects of Soviet Power in the 1980s* (Hamden, CT: Archon Books, 1980), 103-10.

"Aeroflot's Intelligence Activities," *armed forces JOURNAL international,* May 1981, pp. 55-7.

Airplane Missing Near Sakhalin May Be a Soviet Airliner," *Tallahassee Democrat,* May 17, 1985, p. 6A.

James R. Andrews, "Confrontation at Columbia: A Case Study in Coercive Rhetoric," *Quarterly Journal of Speech*, 55:1 (February 1969), 9-16.

Anonymous (P.Q. Mann), "Reassessing the Sakhalin Incident," *Defence Attache*, June 1984, 41-56. [Russian translation: P. K. Mann, "Pereotsenka sakhalinskogo intsidenta," *Za rubezhom*, June 29—July 5, 1984, pp. 10-11.]

G. Arbatov, "O Sovetsko-amerikanskikh otnosheniiakh" ["On Soviet-American Relations"], "Kommunist" [*Communist*], #3 (February 1973), p. 101-113.

Georgi Arbatov, *The War of Ideas in Contemporary International Relations*, David Skvirsky, trans. (Moscow: Progress Publishers, 1973) [original title: "Ideologicheskaia bor'ba v sovremennykh mezhdunarodnykh otnosheniiakh"].

Georgi Arbatov, *Soviet-American Relations: Progress and Problems* (Moscow: Novosti Press Agency, 1976).

Georgi A. Arbatov and Willem Oltmans, *The Soviet Viewpoint* (New York: Dodd, Mead, 1983).

"The Arms Race in Space," *SIPRI Yearbook, 1978. World Disarmament and Armaments*, (New York: Crane, Russell, 1978), 114-24.

Robert Arnold and Peter Fedynsky, "KAL 007 Disinformation Exposed," American Viewpoints #85-17, Voice of America, April 29, 1985.

Robert J. Art and Robert Jervis, eds., *International Politics. Anarchy, Force, Political Economy and Decision Making* (Boston: Little, Brown, 1985), 2nd ed.

J. Jeffery Auer, ed., *The Rhetoric of Our Times* (New York: Appleton-Century-Crofts, 1969).

V. G. Baikova, "Ideologicheskaia rabota KPSS v usloviiakh razvitogo sotsializma" [CPSU Ideological Work under Developed Socialism] (Moscow: Mysl', 1977).

Desmond Ball, *A Suitable Piece of Real Estate: American Installations in Australia* (Sydney: Hale & Iremonger, 1980).

V. William Balthrop, "Argumentation and the Critical Stance: A Methodological Approach," in Cox and Willard, eds., 238-58.

V. William Balthrop, "Culture, Myth, and Ideology as Public Argument: An Interpretation of the Ascent and Demise of 'Southern Culture,'" *Communication Monographs*, 51:4 (December 1984), 339-52.

James Bamford, *The Puzzle Palace* (Boston: Houghton Mifflin, 1982).

James Bamford, "The Last Flight of KAL 007," *Washington Post Magazine*, January 8, 1984, 4-8.

Frederick C. Barghoorn, *Politics in the USSR*, 2nd ed., The Little, Brown Series in Comparative Politics (Boston: Little, Brown, 1972).

Felicity Barringer, "Changing Times Turn Tables On a 'Saint' of the Stalin Era," *The New York Times*, March 21, 1988, pp. 1, 8.

John Barron, *The KGB Today: The Hidden Hand* (New York: Reader's Digest Books, 1983).

F. C. Bartlett, "The Aims of Political Propaganda," in F. C. Bartlett, *Political Propaganda* (London: Cambridge University Press, 1940), 1-22. [Reprinted in: D. Katz, et al., eds., *Opinion and Propaganda* (New York: Holt, 1954), 463-70.]

Barnet Baskerville, "The Illusion of Proof," *Western Speech*, 25:4 (Fall 1961), 236-42.

Richard Bayley, "Soviet Journalism and the Assimilation of Science," *Journalism Quarterly*, 43:4 (Winter 1966), 733-38.

Viktor Belenko, "What Really Happened to KAL Flight 007," *Reader's Digest*, January 1984, 72-78.

George Belknap and Angus Campbell, "Political Party Identification and Attitudes Toward Foreign Policy," *Public Opinion Quarterly*, 55 (Winter 1951-1952), 601-23.

Coral Bell, "Decision-Makers and Crises," *International Journal*, 39:2 (Spring 1984), 324-36.

W. Lance Bennett, Lynne A. Gressett, and William Haltom, "Repairing the News: A Case Study of the News Paradigm," *Journal of Communication*, 35:2 (Spring 1985), 50-68.

G. Bensi, L. Roitman, and L. Predtechevskiy, *Sachalin—befehl zum Mord. Der erste vollstandige Hintergrundbericht* (Munchen: L. Roitman Verlag, 1983).

Morton Berkowitz, P. G. Bock, and Vincent J. Fuccillo, *The Politics of American Foreign Policy: The Social Context of Decisions* (Englewood Cliffs, NJ: Prentice-Hall, 1977).

Tom Bernard and T. Edward Eskelson, "U.S. Spy Plane Capable of Interceding in Attack on Korean Jet," *Denver Post*, September 13, 1983, p. 3B.

L. B. Berzin and Yu. P. Davydov, "Propaganda na sluzhbe vneshnei politiki" ["Mass Media and Foreign Policy"] in G. A. Trofimenko, ed., "Sovremennaia vneshniaia politika SShA" [*Current U.S. Foreign Policy*] (Moscow: Nauka, 1984), vol. 2, 91-112.

Seweryn Bialer, "The International and Internal Contexts of the 26th Party Congress," in Bialer and Gustafson, eds., 7-38.

Seweryn Bialer and Joan Afferica, "Reagan and Russia," *Foreign Affairs*, 61:2 (Winter 1982/83), 249-71.

Seweryn Bialer and Thane Gustafson, eds., *Russia at the Crossroads: The 26th Congress of the CPSU* (London: George Allen & Unwin, 1982).

Lloyd F. Bitzer, "The Rhetorical Situation," in Walter R. Fisher, ed., *Rhetoric: A Tradition in Transition* (East Lansing: Michigan State University Press, 1974), 247-60.

Lloyd F. Bitzer, "Rhetoric and Public Knowledge," in Don M. Burks, ed., *Rhetoric, Philosophy, and Literature: An Exploration* (West Lafayette: Purdue University Press, 1978), 67-94.

Edwin Black, "The Second Persona," *Quarterly Journal of Speech*, 56:2 (April 1970), 109-119.

305

Edwin Black, *Rhetorical Criticism: A Study in Method*, 2nd ed. (Madison: University of Wisconsin Press, 1978).

Edwin Black, "A Note on Theory and Practice in Rhetorical Criticism," *Western Journal of Speech Communication*, 44:4 (Fall 1980), 331-36.

Ernest G. Bormann, "Fantasy and Rhetorical Vision: The Rhetorical Criticism of Social Reality," *Quarterly Journal of Speech*, 58:4 (December 1972), 396-407.

Kenneth Boulding, "National Images and International Systems," *Journal of Conflict Resolution*, 3 (1959), 120-31.

Robert J. Branham and W. Barnett Pearce, "Between Text and Context: Toward a Rhetoric of Contextual Reconstruction," *Quarterly Journal of Speech*, 71:1 (February 1985), 19-36.

Alex Braun, "Has 007's 'Black Box' Been Found?", *Microwave Systems News*, 13:11 (November 1983), p. 48.

Michael Brecher, "'Vertical' Case Studies: A Summary of Findings," in Michael Brecher, ed., *Studies in Crisis Behavior* (New Brunswick, NJ: Transaction Books, 1978), 264-76.

Archie Brown, "Soviet Political Culture through Soviet Eyes," in Brown, ed., 100-114.

Archie Brown, ed., *Political Culture and Communist Studies* (London: Macmillan, 1984).

Archie Brown and Jack Gray, eds., *Political Culture and Political Change in Communist States* (New York: Holmes and Meier, 1977).

William R. Brown, "Television and the Democratic National Convention of 1968," *Quarterly Journal of Speech*, 55:3 (October 1969), 237-46.

John Bunzel, *Anti-Politics in America* (New York: Knopf, 1967).

John Burgess, "KAL Punishment Policy Cited In 007 Disaster," *The Guardian*, January 11, 1987, p. 17.

Parke G. Burgess, "Crisis Rhetoric: Coercion vs. Force," *Quarterly Journal of Speech*, 59:1 (February 1973), 62-73.

Tom Burgess, "Book says Walker action encouraged KAL shooting," *San Diego Union*, October 24, 1987, p. A-2.

Fëdor Burlatskii, "Kakoi sotsialism nuzhen narodu" ["What Kind of Socialism Do the People Need?"], *Literaturnaiia gazeta*, 20 April 1988, p. 2.

Don M. Burks, ed., *Rhetoric, Philosophy and Literature: An Exploration* (West Lafayette: Purdue University Press, 1978).

John F. Burns, "Soviet Seems to Fault Pilot Who Downed Jet," *The New York Times*, January 8, 1984, pp. 1, 6.

Jack H. Butler, "Russian Rhetoric: A Discipline Manipulated by Communism," *Quarterly Journal of Speech*, 50:3 (October 1964), 229-39.

Robert F. Byrnes, ed., *After Brezhnev: Sources of Soviet Conduct in the 1980s* (Bloomington: Indiana University Press, 1983).

Randall L. Bytwerk and Stuart J. Bullion, "In Others' Words: Foreign News Media Citations in Neues Deutschland," paper presented to the 1985 annual convention of the Association for Education in Journalism and Mass Communication, Memphis TN (August 1985).

L. T. Caldwell and Robert Legvold, "Reagan Through Soviet Eyes," *Foreign Policy*, 52 (Fall 1983), 3-21.

Peter Calvocoressi, "How Russia hit an 'own goal,'" *Sunday Times*, September 11, 1983, p. 16.

Karlyn Kohrs Campbell and Kathleen Hall Jamieson, "Form and Genre in Rhetorical Criticism: An Introduction," in Campbell and Jamieson, eds., *Form and Genre: Shaping Rhetorical Action* (Falls Church, VA: Speech Communication Association, 1976), 9-32.

James Canan, *War In Space* (New York: Harper & Row, 1982).

Cho Kap Che, "KAL007: Choihu eui Mokkyukja" ["The Last Witness"], *Chosun Review* [Seoul, South Korea], December 1986.

James W. Chesebro and Caroline D. Hamsher, "Contemporary Rhetorical Theory and Criticism: Dimensions of the New Rhetoric," *Speech Monographs*, 42:4 (November 1975), 311-34.

Marianna Tax Choldin, *A Fence Around the Empire: The Censorship of Foreign Books in Nineteenth-Century Russia*, Diss. University of Chicago, 1979 (Ann Arbor, MI: UMI, 1980).

Marianna Tax Choldin, *A Fence around the Empire. Russian Censorship of Western Ideas under the Tsars*, Duke Press Policy Studies (Durham: Duke University Press, 1985).

Oliver Clubb, *KAL Flight 007, The Hidden Story* (Sag Harbor, NY: Permanent Press, 1985).

Andrew Cockburn, *The Threat: Inside the Soviet Military Machine* (New York: Random House, 1983).

Bernard Cohen, "The Relationship Between Public Opinion and Foreign Policy Maker," in Melvin Small, ed., *Public Opinion and Historians: Interdisciplinary Perspectives* (Detroit: Wayne State University Press, 1970), 65-80.

Bernard C. Cohen, *The Public's Impact on Foreign Policy* (Boston: Little, Brown, 1973).

Stephen F. Cohen, *Sovieticus: American Perceptions and Soviet Realities* (New York: W. W. Norton, 1986).

Farrel Corcoran, "The Bear in the Back Yard: Myth, Ideology, and Victimage Ritual in Soviet Funerals," *Communication Monographs*, 50:4 (December 1983), 305-20.

Farrel Corcoran, "KAL 007 and the Evil Empire: Mediated Disaster and Forms of Rationalization," *Critical Studies in Mass Communication*, 3:3 (September 1986), 297-316.

Frank Cormier, James Deakin, and Helen Thomas, *The White House Press on the Presidency. News Management and Co-option*, Kenneth W. Thompson, ed. (Lanham, MD: University Press of America, 1983).

J. Robert Cox and Charles Arthur Willard, eds., *Advances in Argumentation Theory and Research* (Carbondale: Southern Illinois University Press, 1982).

Edward Crankshaw, "Case History of an Unfree Press," *New York Times Magazine*, December 2, 1962, pp. 35, 131, 135.

Earl G. Creps III, *The Conspiracy Argument as Rhetorical Genre*, Diss. Northwestern University, 1980 (Ann Arbor: UMI, 1981).

Hugh M. Culbertson, "Leaks--A Dilemma for Editors as Well as Officials, *Journalism Quarterly*, **57**:3 (Autumn 1980), 402-408.

R. B. Cutler, *Explo 007: Evidence of Conspiracy* (Beverly Farms, MA: R. B. Cutler, 1986).

Alexander Dallin, "The United States in the Soviet Perspective," in Christoph Bertram, ed., *The Prospects of Soviet Power in the 1980s* (Hamden, CT: Archon Books, 1980), 31-39.

Alexander Dallin, *Black Box: KAL 007 and the Superpowers* (Berkeley: University of California Press, 1985).

Alexander Dallin and Gail W. Lapidus, "Reagan and the Russians: United States Policy Toward the Soviet Union and Eastern Europe," in Kenneth A. Oye, Robert J. Lieber, and Donald Rothchild, eds., *Eagle Defiant. United States Foreign Policy in the 1980s* (Boston: Little, Brown, 1983), 191-236.

David Brion Davis, ed., *The Fear of Conspiracy* (Ithaca: Cornell University Press, 1971).

W. Phillips Davison, "The Role of Research in Political Warfare," *Journalism Quarterly*, **29**:1 (Winter 1952), 18-30.

E. Michael DelPapa, *Meeting the Challenge: ESD and the COBRA DANE Construction Effort on Shemya Island* (Bedford, MA: Electronic Systems Division, 1979).

Martin Dewhirst and Robert Farrell, *The Soviet Censorship* (Metuchen, NJ: Scarecrow Press, 1973).

Lubomir Dolezel and Karel Hausenblas, "O sootnoshenii poètiki i stilistiki" ["On the Interrelation of Poetics and Stylistics"], *Poetics* (Warszawa: Panstwowe wydawnictwo naukowe, 1961).

John C. Donovan, *The Cold Warriors: A Policy-Making Elite* (Lexington, MA: D.C. Heath, 1974).

Alan Dowty, "United States Decision-Making in Middle East Crises: 1958, 1970, 1973," *Jerusalem Journal of International Relations*, **7**:1-2 (1984), 92-106.

Theodore Draper, "Reagan's Junta," *New York Review of Books*, January 29, 1987, 5-14.

P. Albert Duhamel, "The Function of Rhetoric as Effective Expression," *Journal of the History of Ideas*, **10** (June 1949).

John L. Dunning, "The Kennedy Assassination as Viewed by Communist Media," *Journalism Quarterly*, 41:2 (Spring 1964), 163-9.

Joachim Dyck, "Rhetorical Studies in West Germany, 1974-1976: A Bibliography," *The Rhetoric Society Quarterly*, 7 (Winter 1977), 1-18, with "Addenda" by Peter Jehn, 18-19.

Martin Ebon, *The Soviet Propaganda Machine* (New York: McGraw-Hill, 1987).

Roland Eggleston, "A Year Since the Destruction of the Korean Airliner," Radio Liberty Research, RL 326/84, August 28, 1984.

Douglas Ehninger, "Argument as Method: Its Nature, Its Limitations and Its Uses," *Speech Monographs*, 37:2 (June 1970), 101-110.

Jacques Ellul, "An Aspect of the Role of Persuasion in a Technical Society," *et cetera*, 36:2 (Summer 1979), 147-51.

A. Ralph Epperson, *The Unseen Hand: An Introduction to the Conspiratorial View of History*, (Tucson: Publius Press, 1985).

Paul D. Erickson, *Reagan Speaks. The Making of an American Myth* (New York: New York University Press, 1985).

T. Edward Eskelson and Tom Bernard, "A Personal View: Former RC-135 Crewmen Question U.S. Version of Jet Liner Incident," *Baltimore News American*, September 15, 1983, p. 8.

V. S. Evseev, "Partiinoe vozdeistvie pressy" [*The Influence of the Press in Support of the Party*] (Moscow: Izdatel'stvo politicheskoi literatury, 1980).

Thomas B. Farrell, "Critical Models in the Analysis of Discourse," *Western Journal of Speech Communication*, 44:4 (Fall 1980), 300-14.

Thomas B. Farrell and G. Thomas Goodnight, "Accidental Rhetoric: The Root Metaphors of Three Mile Island," *Communication Monographs*, 48:4 (December 1981), 271-300.

Dante B. Fascell, ed., *International News. Freedom Under Attack* (Beverly Hills: Sage Publications, 1979).

Erwin W. Fellows, "Propaganda and Communication: A Study in Definitions," *Journalism Quarterly*, 34:4 (Fall 1957), 431-42.

Walter R. Fisher, "A Motive View of Communication," *Quarterly Journal of Speech*, 56:2 (April 1970), 131-39.

Walter R. Fisher, *Rhetoric: A Tradition in Transition* (East Lansing: Michigan State University, 1974).

Walter R. Fisher, "Genre: Concepts and Applications in Rhetorical Criticism," *Western Journal of Speech Communication*, 44:4 (Fall 1980), 288-99.

Walter R. Fisher, "Narration as a Human Communication Paradigm: The Case of Public Moral Argument," *Communication Monographs*, 51:1 (March 1984), 1-22.

Walter R. Fisher, "The Narrative Paradigm: An Elaboration," *Communication Monographs*, 52:4 (December 1985), 347-67.

Walter R. Fisher, "Assessing Narrative Fidelity: The Logic of Good Reasons," Chapter Five in Walter R. Fisher, *Human Communication as Narration: Toward a Philosophy of Reason, Value, and Action* (Columbia: University of South Carolina Press, 1987), 105-123.

Walter R. Fisher, *Human Communication as Narration: Toward a Philosophy of Reason, Value, and Action* (Columbia: University of South Carolina Press, 1987).

Dick Fitzpatrick, "America's Campaign of Truth Throughout the World," *Journalism Quarterly*, 28:1 (Winter 1951), 3-14.

Foreign Broadcast Information Service, *The Public Soviet Response to the KAL Incident*, FBIS Analysis Report FB 83-10041, September 21, 1983.

Daniel Frei, ed., *Managing International Crises* (Beverly Hills: Sage Publications, 1982).

Maurice Friedberg, "Cultural and Intellectual Life," in Robert F. Byrnes, ed., *After Brezhnev: Sources of Soviet Conduct in the 1980's* (Bloomington: Indiana University Press, 1983), 250-89.

Theodore H. Friedgut, *Political Participation in the USSR* (Princeton: Princeton University Press, 1979).

John Lewis Gaddis, *The United States and the Origin of the Cold War, 1941-1947* (New York: Columbia University Press, 1972).

John Lewis Gaddis, *Strategies of Containment: A Critical Appraisal of Postwar National Security Policy* (New York: Oxford University Press, 1982).

John Lewis Gaddis, "The Rise, Fall and Future of Detente," *Foreign Affairs*, 62:2 (Winter 1983/84), 354-77.

Richard A. Garver, "Polite Propaganda: 'USSR' and 'America Illustrated'," *Journalism Quarterly*, 38:4 (Autumn 1961), 480-484.

Paul Garvin, trans. and ed., *A Prague School Reader on Esthetics, Literary Structure and Style* (Washington: Georgetown University Press, 1964).

Frederic Golden, "Seeing a Conspiracy in the Sky," *Discover*, December 1984, p. 8.

General-polkovnik aviatsii S. Golubev, "Zadacha gosudarstvennoi vazhnosti" ["A Problem of Great Importance to the State"], *Aviatsiia i kosmonavtika*, January 1984, 1-3.

G. Thomas Goodnight, "Ronald Reagan's Re-formulation of the Rhetoric of War: Analysis of the 'Zero Option,' 'Evil Empire,' and 'Star Wars' Addresses," *Quarterly Journal of Speech*, 72:2 (November 1986), 390-414.

G. Thomas Goodnight and John Poulakos, "Conspiracy Rhetoric: From Pragmatism to Fantasy in Public Discourse," *Western Journal of Speech Communication*, 45:4 (Fall 1981), 299-316.

Colin S. Gray and Rebecca Strode, "The Imperial Dimension of Soviet Military Power," *Problems of Communism*, November-December 1981, 1-15.

A. V. Grebnev, "Gazeta, organizatsiia raboty redaktsii" [*The Newspaper: The Organization of Editorial Operations*], (Moscow, 1974).

Felix Greene, *A Curtain of Ignorance* (Garden City, NY: Doubleday, 1964).

Leland M. Griffin, "The Rhetorical Structure of the 'New Left' Movement: Part I," *Quarterly Journal of Speech,* 50:2 (April 1964), 113-35. [Reprinted in J. Jeffery Auer, ed., *The Rhetoric of Our Times* (New York: Appleton-Century-Crofts, 1969), 15-44.]

Kazimierz Grzybowski, "Propaganda and the Soviet Concept of World Public Order," in Clark C. Havighurst, ed. *International Control of Propaganda* (Dobbs Ferry, NY: Oceana, 1967), 41-67.

Michael Haas, *International Conflict* (Indianapolis: Bobbs-Merrill, 1978).

Michael Haas, "Research on International Crisis: Obsolescence of an Approach," *International Interactions,* 13:1 (1986), 23-58.

Alexander M. Haig, jr, *Caveat: Realism, Reagan, and Foreign Policy* (New York: Macmillan, 1984).

Julian Hale, *Radio Power.Propaganda and International Broadcasting* (Philadelphia: Temple University Press, 1975).

Louis J. Halle, *The Cold War As History* (New York: Harper & Row, 1967).

Louis J. Halle, *The Ideological Imagination* (Chicago: Quadrangle Books, 1972).

Conn Hallinan, *The Curious Flight of KAL 007* (New York: U. S. Peace Council, 1984).

Roger Hamburg, "Political and Strategic in Soviet Relations with the West: Soviet Perceptions," in Kanet, ed., 197-230.

Peter L. Haratonik, "INFORMATION/PROPAGANDA: Analects from a Technological Society," *et cetera,* 36:2 (Summer 1979), 153-56.

Farooq Hassan, "A Legal Analysis of the Shooting of Korean Airlines Flight 007 by the Soviet Union," *Journal of Air Law and Commerce,* 49:3 (1984), 555-88.

Clark C. Havighurst, ed. *International Control of Propaganda* (Dobbs Ferry, NY: Oceana, 1967).

Baruch A. Hazan, *Soviet Propaganda. A Case Study of the Middle East Conflict* (New Brunswick, NJ: Transaction Books, 1976).

Robert L. Heilbroner, *The Worldly Philosophers* (New York: Simon & Schuster, 1962), 2nd ed.

Alfred O. Hero, *Americans in World Affairs* (Boston: World Peace Foundation, 1959).

Alfred O. Hero, jr, "Non-profit Organizations, Public Opinion, and United States Foreign Policy," *International Journal,* 33:1 (Winter 1977-78), 150-76.

Seymour M. Hersh, "(But Don't Tell Anyone I Told You)", *New Republic,* December 9, 1967, pp. 13-4.

Seymour M. Hersh, *"The Target Is Destroyed"* (New York: Random House, 1986).

311

Seymour M. Hersh, "The Target Is Destroyed," *Atlantic Monthly,* September 1986, 47-69.

Roger Hilsman, Jr., *Strategic Intelligence and National Decisions* (Glencoe, IL: Free Press, 1956).

Roger Hilsman, Jr., "Intelligence and Policy-Making in Foreign Affairs," in James N. Rosenau, *International Politics and Foreign Policy* (Glencoe, IL: Free Press, 1961), 209-19.

Gayle Durham Hollander, *Soviet Political Indoctrination. Developments in Mass Media and Propaganda Since Stalin* (New York: Praeger, 1972).

David Holloway, "Military Power and Political Purpose in Soviet Policy," *Daedalus,* 109:4 (Fall 1980), 13-30.

Ole R. Holsti, "Cognitive Dynamics and Images of the Enemy," in John C. Farrell and Asa P. Smith, eds., *Image and Reality in World Politics* (New York: Columbia University Press, 1967), 16-39.

Mark Hopkins, *Russia's Underground Press* (New York: Praeger, 1983).

Richard Hofstadter, "The Paranoid Style in American Politics," in *The Paranoid Style in American Politics and Other Essays* (New York: Knopf, 1965), 3-40.

Jerry F. Hough, "The World As Viewed from Moscow," *International Journal,* 37:1 (Winter 1981/82), 183-97.

Jerry F. Hough, *The Struggle for the Third World: Soviet Debates and American Options* (Washington: Brookings, 1986).

Neal D. Houghton, "The Cuban Invasion of 1961 and the U.S. Press, in Retrospect," *Journalism Quarterly,* 42:3 (Summer 1965), 422-32.

"How Hard To Say Sorry," *The Economist,* September 10, 1983, p. 13-4.

Russell Warren Howe, "What Happened to Flight 007?", *The Washingtonian,* November 1985, 147-60.

Barry B. Hughes, *The Domestic Context of American Foreign Policy* (San Francisco: W. H. Freeman, 1978).

Grant Hugo, *Appearance and Reality in International Relations* (London: Chatto and Windus, 1970).

Samuel P. Huntington, "Social and Institutional Dynamics of One-Party Systems," in Samuel P. Huntington and Clement H. Moore, eds., *Authoritarian Politics in Modern Society* (New York: Basic Books, 1970), 3-47.

Samuel P. Huntington and Jorge I. Dominguez, "Political Development," in Fred I. Greenstein and Nelson W. Polsby, eds., *Handbook of Political Science, vol. III: Macropolitical Theory* (Reading, MA: Addison-Wesley, 1975), Addison-Wesley Series in Political Science.

Bruce Hurwitz, "Threat Perception, Linkage Politics and Decision Making: The October 1973 Worldwide Alert of US Military Forces," *Jerusalem Journal of International Relations,* 7:3 (1985), 135-45.

Alex Inkeles, *Public Opinion in Soviet Russia* (Cambridge: Harvard University Press, 1950).

Alex Inkeles, ed., *Social Change in Soviet Russia* (Cambridge: Harvard University Press, 1968).

Alex Inkeles and Raymond Bauer, *The Soviet Citizen* (New York: Atheneum, 1968).

Alex Inkeles and H. Kent Geiger, "Critical Letters to the Soviet Press," in Alex Inkeles, ed., 291-324.

Iurii Ivashchenko, "Shchit otechestva," *Nedelia*, April 7-13, 1986, p. 6. [Translated as "The Fatherland's Shield," *Soviet Press Selected Translations*. Current News Special Edition, No. 1528, December 30, 1986, 181-86].

Alain Jacob, "Circonstances atténuantes?", *Le Monde*, September 10, 1983.

Kathleen Jamieson, "The Rhetorical Manifestations of *Weltanschauung*," *Central States Speech Journal*, **27**:1 (Spring 1976), 4-14.

Lisa Jameson, "Soviet Propaganda: On the Offensive in the 1980's," in Richard F. Staar, ed., *Public Diplomacy: USA Versus USSR* (Stanford: Stanford University Press, 1986), 18-45.

"Jamming the Free Radio Stations," *The Conflict of INFORMATION--'Detente,' Freedom and Constraint*, Conflict Studies, No. 56 (April 1975), 21-3.

Irving L. Janis, *Groupthink*, 2nd ed. (Boston: Houghton Mifflin, 1982).

"Japan: KAL Pilot Gave Incorrect Altitude," *Tallahassee Democrat*, May 17, 1985, p. 6A.

Robert Jervis, "Hypotheses on Misperception," in Art and Jervis, eds., 510-26. [originally published in *World Politics*, **20**:3 (April 1968), 454-79.]

Robert Jervis, *Perception and Misperception in International Politics* (Princeton: Princeton University Press, 1976).

David M. Johnson, *Korean Airlines Incident: U.S. Intelligence Disclosures* (Cambridge: Harvard University, Center for Information Policy Research, 1984), Program on Information Resources Policy. Incidental Paper [I-84-2].

R. W. Johnson, "007: Licence to Kill?", *The Guardian*, December 17, 1983, p. 15. [Russian translation: R. V. Dzhonson, "Velikii obman" ("The Big Lie"), *Literaturnaia gazeta*, January 18, 1984, p. 14.]

R. W. Johnson, *Shootdown: Flight 007 and the American Connection* (New York: Viking, 1986).

Henry W. Johnstone, jr, "Some Reflections on Argumentation," in Maurice Natanson and Henry W. Johnstone, jr, *Philosophy, Rhetoric, and Argumentation* (University Park: Pennsylvania State University Press, 1965), 1-9.

Nancy C. Jones, "U. S. News in the Soviet Press," *Journalism Quarterly*, **43**:4 (Winter 1966), 687-96.

R. Jones, *Self-Fulfilling Prophesies: Social, Psychological, and Physiological Effects of Expectancies* (Hillsdale, NJ: Lawrence Erlbaum, 1977).

Carey B. Joynt and Percy E. Corbett, "Rival Explanations in International Relations," Chapter nine in *Theory and Reality in World Politics* (Pittsburgh: University of Pittsburgh Press, 1978).

John M. Joyce, "The Old Russian Legacy," *Foreign Policy*, 55 (Summer 1984), 132-53.

Franz A. Kadell, *The KAL 007 Massacre* (Alexandria, VA: Western Goals Foundation, 1985).

Robert G. Kaiser, *Russia: The People and The Power* (New York: Atheneum, 1976).

The KAL Information Bulletin and Newsletter (Washington: The Fund for Constitutional Government) [irregular periodical—5 issues to date].

M. Kalyanasundaram, M.P., *Flight 007* (Delhi: New Literature, 1983).

Roger E. Kanet, ed., *Soviet Foreign Policy in the 1980s* (New York: Praeger, 1982).

Sugwon Kang, "Flight 007: Was There Foul Play?", *Bulletin of Concerned Asian Scholars*, 17:2 (April—June 1985), 30-48.

Charles W. Kegley, jr and Eugene R. Wittkopf, "Beyond Consensus: The Domestic Context of American Foreign Policy," *International Journal*, 38:1 (Winter 1982-83), 77-106.

Paul Kelly, "NSA, The Biggest Secret Spy Network in Australia," *National Times*, May 23-28, 1977.

Peter Kenez, *The Birth of the Propaganda State: Soviet Methods of Mass Mobilization, 1917-1929* (New York: Cambridge University Press, 1985).

George F. Kennan (as 'X'), "The Sources of Soviet Conduct," *Foreign Affairs*, 25 (July 1947), 566-82.

George F. Kennan, *Memoirs: 1925-1950* (Boston: Little, Brown, 1967).

John Keppel, "Was KAL Incident Really an Accident?", *USA Today*, August 31, 1984, p. 10A.

Marshal aviatsii P. Kirsanov, "Fakty izoblichaiut Vashington" ["The Facts Expose Washington"], *Pravda*, September 20, 1983, p. 4.

Henry A. Kissinger, *The Necessity of Choice* (Garden City, NY: Doubleday, 1982).

Henry A. Kissinger, *Years of Upheaval* (London: George Weidenfield and Nicolson, 1982).

Philip J. Klass, *Secret Sentries In Space* (New York: Random House, 1971).

Philip J. Klass, "USAF Tracking Radar," *Aviation Week & Space Technology*, October 25, 1976, pp. 41ff.

Philip J. Klass, "U. S. Scrutinizing New Soviet Radar," *Aviation Week & Space Technology*, August 22, 1983, pp. 19-20.

Charles W. Kneupper, "Rhetoric, Public Knowledge and Ideological Argumentation," *Journal of the American Forensic Association*, 21:4 (Spring 1985), 183-95.

Gabriel Kolko, *The Politics of War* (New York: Random House, 1968).

Elie D. Krakowski, "The Korean Air Line Massacre: The Broader Context," unpublished analyst's report, U. S. Department of Defense, no date.

Leopold Labedz, "Ideology and Soviet Foreign Policy," in Christoph Bertram, ed., *The Prospects of Soviet Power in the 1980s* (Hamden, CT: Archon Books, 1980), 22-30.

Walter Lafebre, *America, Russia and the Cold War 1945-1980* (New York: Wiley, 1980).

Harold D. Lasswell, *Propaganda Technique in World War I* (Cambridge: M.I.T. Press, 1971).

Michael K. Launer, "Yolki-palki!--Fiddlesticks or Fir Trees," *No Uncertain Terms*, 2:2 (Summer 1987), 4-6.

Michael K. Launer, Marilyn J. Young, and Sugwon Kang, "Correspondence," *Bulletin of Concerned Asian Scholars*, 18:3 (July--September 1986), 67-71.

"The Law on the USSR State Border,"*The Current Digest of the Soviet Press*, 34:51 (January 19, 1983), 15-20. ["Zakon o gosudarstvennoi granitse SSSR," *Pravda* and *Izvestiia*, November 26, 1982, pp. 1-3.]

Alfred McClung Lee and Elizabeth Briant Lee, *The Fine Art of Propaganda* (New York: Harcourt, Brace, 1939).

Gary Lee, "Donohue's Russian Revelations," *Washington Post*, February 7, 1987, p. C11.

Michael Leff, "Textual Criticism: The Legacy of G. P. Mohrmann," *Quarterly Journal of Speech*, 72:4 (November 1986), 377-89.

Robert Legvold, "The Nature of Soviet Power," *Foreign Affairs*, 57:1 (Fall 1977), 49-71.

Robert Legvold, "The Concept of Power and Security in Soviet History," in Christoph Bertram, ed., *The Prospects of Soviet Power in the 1980s* (Hamden, CT: Archon Books, 1980), 5-12.

Robert Legvold, "The 26th Party Congress and Soviet Foreign Policy," in Bialer and Gustafson, eds., 156-77.

V. I. Lenin, *What Is To Be Done?* (New York: International Publishers, 1969).

Howard H. Lentner, "The Concept of Crisis as Viewed by the United States Department of State," Chapter Six in Charles F. Herman, ed., *International Crises* (New York: Free Press, 1972).

"The Lessons Learned," *Newsweek*, November 12, 1962, pp. 21-9.

Todd Leventhal, "FOCUS: The Korean Airliner Shootdown: One Year Later," Voice of America Special Report #4-0877, August 30, 1984.

Todd Leventhal, "FOCUS: The Korean Airliner Shootdown Revisited," Voice of America Special Report #4-1948, September 17, 1986.

Anthony Mark Lewis, "The Blind Spot of U.S. Foreign Intelligence," *Journal of Communication*, 26:1 (Winter 1976), 44-55.

Dave Lindorff, "Why Meese Spoke," *The Nation*, March 21, 1987, p. 349.

Walter Lippman, *The Public Philosophy* (Boston: Little, Brown, 1955).

D. Richard Little, "Bureaucracy and Participation in the Soviet Union," in Schulz and Adams, eds., 79-107.

Jonathan Samuel Lockwood, *The Soviet View of U.S. Strategic Doctrine* (New Brunswick, NJ: Transaction Books, 1983).

Thomas Maertens, "Tragedy of Errors," *Foreign Service Journal*, 62:8 (September 1985), 24-31.

Robert A. Manning, "A Chase for the Elusive KAL Story," *U.S. News & World Report*, September 1, 1986, p. 69.

Paul Marantz, "Changing Soviet Conceptions of East-West Relations," *International Journal*, 37:2 (Spring 1982), 220-40.

James W. Markham, *Voices of the Red Giants* (Ames: The Iowa State University Press, 1967).

David Marks, "Broadcasting Across the Wall: The Free Flow of Information Between East and West Germany," *Journal of Communication*, 33:1 (Winter 1983), 46-55.

Ronald J. Matlon, comp., *Index to Journals in Communication Studies Through 1979* (Annandale, VA: Speech Communication Association, 1980).

Rose Matuz, "TV News in the Framework of Television Political Programmes," *Radio and Television*, 2(1963), 3-6.

Charles A. McClelland, "Access to Berlin: The Quantity and Variety of Events, 1948-63," in J. David Singer, ed., *Quantitative International Politics* (New York: Free Press, 1968), 159-86.

Herbert McClosky and John E. Turner, *The Soviet Dictatorship*, McGraw-Hill Series in Political Science (New York: McGraw-Hill, 1960).

Patrick McGarvey, *The CIA: The Myth and the Madness* (Baltimore: Penguin, 1972).

Michael Calvin McGee and Martha Anne Martin, "Public Knowledge and Ideological Argumentation," *Communication Monographs*, 50:1 (March 1983), 47-65.

Ralph McGehee, *Deadly Deceits: My Twenty-Five Years in the CIA* (New York: Sheridan Square Publications, 1983).

Michael McGuire and Lothar Berger, "Speech in the Marxist State," *Communication Education*, 28:3 (July 1979), 169-78.

John W. Meaney, "Propaganda as Psychical Coercion," *Review of Politics*, 13 (January 1951), 64-87.

John Meisel, "Communications and Crisis: A Preliminary Mapping," in Frei, ed., 61-75.

Richard L. Merritt, "Improbable Events and Expectable Behavior," in Frei, ed., 77-86.

Sig Mickelson, *America's Other Voice. The Story of Radio Free Europe and Radio Liberty* (New York: Praeger, 1983).

Ellen Propper Mickiewicz, *Media and the Russian Public*, Praeger Special Studies (New York: Praeger, 1981).

K. Mihalisko and R. Parta, "The Korean Airline Incident: Western Radio and Soviet Perceptions," RFE-RL Soviet Area Audience and Opinion Research, AR 4-84, April 1984.

David W. Miller, "007's Analysis of KAL's Flight 007," *The International Journal of Intelligence and Counterintelligence,* 1:1 (Spring 1986), 109-119.

C. Wright Mills, *The Power Elite* (New York: Oxford University Press, 1956).

Terence P. Moran, "Propaganda as Pseudocommunication," *et cetera,* 36:2 (Summer 1979), 181-97.

Walter S. Mossberg, "Soviet Military, Civilian Leaders Clash Over Downed KAL Plane, U.S. Contends," *Wall Street Journal,* September 27, 1983, p. 38.

"Murder First, Lies Later," *Economist,* September 10, 1983, 33-37.

Geoffrey Murray, "Under Soviet Eyes, U.S. and Japan Hold Sea Exercises," *Christian Science Monitor,* September 22, 1983, p. 6.

B. S. Murty, *Propaganda and World Public Order. The Legal Regulation of the Ideological Instrument of Coercion* (New Haven: Yale University Press, 1968).

Joel O. Naidus, "Spy Gear on Flight 007? Baloney!", *Microwave Systems News,* 13:10 (October 1983), p. 48.

National Strategy Information Center, *National Survey 6320,* June 7-11, 1986 (Washington: NSIC).

Franz Neuman, *The Democrat and the Authoritarian State* (Glencoe, IL: Free Press, 1957).

Richard E. Neustadt, *Presidential Power: The Politics of Leadership* (New York: John Wiley & Sons, 1960).

Robert P. Newman, "Under the Veneer: Nixon's Vietnam Speech of November 3, 1969," *Quarterly Journal of Speech,* 56:2 (April 1970). [Reprinted in Windt with Ingold, 204-23.]

Robert P. Newman, "Foreign Policy: Decision and Argument," in Cox and Willard, eds., 318-42.

Robert P. Newman and Dale R. Newman, *Evidence* (Boston: Houghton Mifflin, 1969).

THE NEW YORK TIMES/CBS NEWS POLL, September 14, 1983. [Reported by Adam Clymer, "Nation Is Confused About Jet Downing, Latest Poll Suggests," *The New York Times,* September 16, 1983, pp. A1, A8.]

D. Nikolaev, "Informatsiia v sisteme mezhdunarodnykh otnoshenii. Organizatsiia i funktsionirovanie informatsionnykh organov vneshnepoliticheskogo mekhanizma SShA" [*Information in International Relations. The Organization and Operations of Information Agencies within the US Foreign Policy Establishment*] (Moscow: Mezhdunarodnye otnosheniia, 1978).

North Atlantic Treaty Organization. Advisory Group for Aerospace Research and Development (AGARD/NATO), *First Supplement to AGARD Aeronautical Multilingual Dictionary. Premier supplement a AGARD Dictionnaire aeronautique multilingue,* A. H. Holloway, ed. (Oxford: Pergamon, 1963).

North Atlantic Treaty Organization. Advisory Group for Aerospace Research and Development (AGARD/NATO), *Multilingual Aeronautical Dictionary. Dictionnaire aeronautique multilingue* (London: Pergamon, 1980).

James E. Oberg, "Sakhalin: Sense and Nonsense," *Defence Attaché,* January/February 1985, 37-47.

James E. Oberg, "Sense and Nonsense: A Reader's Guide to the KE007 Massacre," *American Spectator,* October 1985, 36-39.

James E. Oberg, "The Sky's No Limit to Disinformation," *Air Force Magazine,* March 1986, 52-56.

James E. Oberg, *Uncovering Soviet Disasters. Exploring the Limits of Glasnost* (New York: Random House, 1988).

William E. Odom, "Who Controls Whom in Moscow," *Foreign Policy,* **14** (Summer 1975), 109-22.

"Officials blast Speakes over fake Reagan quotes,"*Tallahassee Democrat,* April 13, 1988, p. 9A.

Paul O'Higgins, *Censorship in Britain* (London: Nelson, 1972).

James H. Oliver, "A Comparison of Four Western Russian-Language Broadcasters," *Journalism Quarterly,* **54**:1 (Spring 1977), 126-34.

Organization of the Joint Chiefs of Staff. Special Operations Division, *"KRASNAIA ZVEZDA. Soviet News and Propaganda Analysis,* 3:9 (September 1983); 3:10 (October 1983).

Jack E. Orwant, "Effects of Derogatory Attacks in Soviet Arms Control Propaganda," *Journalism Quarterly,* **49**:1 (Spring 1972), 107-15.

Douglas H. Parker, "Rhetoric, Ethics, and Manipulation," *Philosophy and Rhetoric,* 5:2 (Spring 1972), 69-87.

R. E. Parta and M. S. Rhodes, "Information Sources and the Soviet Citizen. Domestic Media and Western Radio," RFE-RL Soviet Area Audience and Opinion Research, AR 5-81, June 1981.

Anthony Paul, "Shot Down Over Russia! The Mysterious Saga of Flight 902," *Reader's Digest,* November 1978, 139-44.

David Pearson, "K.A.L. 007: What the U.S. Knew and When We Knew It," *The Nation,* August 18-25, 1984, 104-24. [Russian translation: Dèvid Pirson, "Iuzhnokoreiskii samolet v raiony sovetskoi oborony napravilo TsRU" ("It Was The CIA That Sent The South Korean Airplane Into Soviet Defense Areas"), *Za rubezhom,* August 24-30, 1984, pp. 17-19.]

David E. Pearson, *KAL 007: The Cover-Up (Why the True Story Has Never Been Told)* (New York: Summit, 1987).

David Pearson and John Keppel, "Journey Into Doubt: New Pieces in the Puzzle of Flight 007," *The Nation*, August 17-24, 1985, 104-10.

Winslow Peck, "U.S. Electronic Espionage: A Memoir," *Ramparts*, August 1972, 36-50.

Chaim Perelman and L. Olbrechts-Tyteca, *The New Rhetoric: A Treatise on Argumentation*, John Wilkinson and Purcell Weaver, trans. (Notre Dame: University of Notre Dame Press, 1969).

V. F. Petrovskii, *Amerikanskaia vneshne-politicheskaia mysl'* [*American Foreign Policy Thought*] (Moscow: Mezhdunarodnaia otnosheniia, 1976).

Richard Pipes, "Militarism and the Soviet State," *Daedalus*, 109:4 (Fall 1980), 1-12.

"Plane Triggers Soviet Scramble," *Denver Post*, November 7, 1985, p. 23A.

Karl Popper, "Prediction and Prophecy in the Social Sciences," in Patrick Gardiner, ed., *Theories of History* (New York: Free Press, 1959).

Neil Postman, "Propaganda," *et cetera*, 36:2 (Summer 1979), 128-33.

James W. Pratt, "An Analysis of Three Crisis Speeches," *Western Speech*, 34:3 (Summer 1970), 194-202.

"Preserving the past confronts today's Soviets," *Tallahassee Democrat*, April 17, 1988, pp. 1B, 7B.

Presidential Study Commission on International Broadcasting,*The Right to Know* (Washington: U. S. Government Printing Office, 1973).

The Press in Authoritarian Countries (Zurich: International Press Institute, 1959), Survey No. 5.

Terence H. Qualter, *Propaganda and Psychological Warfare*, Series in Political Science (New York: Random House, 1962).

Terence E. Qualter, *Opinion Control in the Democracies* (London: Macmillan, 1985).

Eleanor Randolph, "Casey Warns Writers, Publishers About Putting Secrets in Books," *Washington Post*, June 26, 1986, p. A11.

Richard D. Raum and James S. Measell, "Wallace and His Ways: A Study of the Rhetorical Genre of Polarization," *Central States Speech Journal*, 25:1 (Spring 1974), 28-35.

"Reagan didn't know about fake quotes," *Tallahassee Democrat*, April 14, 1988, p. 3A.

Rodger Allen Remington, *The Function of the "Conspiracy Theory" in American Intellectual History*, Diss. St. Louis University, 1965 (Ann Arbor: UMI, 1966).

Thomas Remington, *The Origin of Ideology* (Pittsburgh: University of Pittsburgh, University Center for International Studies, 1974).

Thomas Remington, *Soviet Public Opinion and the Effectiveness of Party Ideological Work* (Pittsburgh: University of Pittsburgh, Russian and East European Studies Program, 1983), The Carl Beck Papers in Russian and East European Studies, No. 204.

James Reston, *The Artillery of the Press: Its Influence on American Foreign Policy* (New York: Harper & Row, 1967).

RFE-RL, *Information Sources and the Soviet Citizen: Domestic Media and Western Radio*, Soviet Area Audience and Opinion Research, AR 5-81, June 1981.

RFE-RL, *The Korean Airline Incident: Western Radio and Soviet Perceptions*, Soviet Area Audience and Opinion Research, AR 4-84, April 1984.

I. A. Richards, *The Philosophy of Rhetoric* (New York: Oxford University Press, 1965).

Jeffrey Richelson, *The United States Intelligence Community* (Cambridge: Ballinger, 1985).

Jeffrey Richelson, *Sword and Shield. The Soviet Intelligence and Security Apparatus* (Cambridge: Ballinger, 1986).

Jeffrey Richelson, *American Espionage and the Soviet Target* (New York: William Morrow, 1987).

Jeffrey Richelson and Desmond Ball, *The Ties That Bind--The UK-USA Intelligence Network* (London: Allen & Unwin, 1985).

Major-General Richard Rohmer, *Massacre 747* (Markham, Ontario, Canada: PaperJacks Ltd., 1984).

Robert C. Rowland, "Narrative: Mode of Discourse or Paradigm?" *Communication Monographs*, 54:3 (September 1987), 264-75.

Anthony Sampson, "What Happened to Flight 007?", *Parade Magazine*, April 22, 1984, pp. 12-3.

Anthony Sampson and Wilhelm Bittorf, "'Sinken auf eins-null-tausend...' Der Todesflug des Korea-Jumbo" ["'Dropping to One-Zero-Thousand...' The Death Flight of the Korean Jumbo Jet"], *Der Spiegel*, September 24 and October 1, 8, and 15, 1984 (four parts).

Murray Sayle, "KE007: A Conspiracy of Coincidence," *New York Review of Books*, April 25, 1985, 44-54.

Murray Sayle, "Bad Year in the Air," *Quarterly Review*, Winter 1986, 21-25.

Murray Sayle, "Shooting on suspicion: The final secrets of KE007," unpublished manuscript, 1987.

Leonard Schapiro, "The International Department of the CPSU: Key to Soviet Policy," *International Journal*, 32:1 (1976-77), 41-55.

Robert Scheer, *With Enough Shovels* (New York: Random House, 1982).

Charles P. Schliecher, *International Behavior: Analysis and Operations* (Columbus: Charles E. Merrill, 1973).

Wilbur Schramm, ed., *One Day in the World's Press* (Stanford: Stanford University Press, 1959).

Donald E. Schulz and Jan S. Adams, eds., *Political Participation in Communist Systems*, Pergamon Policy Studies on International Politics (New York: Pergamon, 1981).

Morton Schwartz, *Soviet Perceptions of the United States* (Berkeley: University of California Press, 1978).

Dietrich G. Schwarzkopf, "Responsibility of National States for Hostile Propaganda Campaigns," *Journalism Quarterly*, 29:2 (Spring 1952), 194-206.

Peter Shearman, review of Hough, *The Struggle for the Third World: Soviet Debates and American Options*, in *International Affairs*, 62:3 (Summer 1986), 542.

Lawrence Sherwin, "The KAL Incident: Analysis of a Soviet Propaganda Campaign," Radio Liberty Research, RL 371/83, October 4, 1983.

Milton Shieh, "Red China Patterns Controls of Press on Russian Model," *Journalism Quarterly*, 28:1 (Winter 1951), 74-80.

Vladimir Shlapentokh, *Soviet Public Opinion and Ideology. Mythology and Pragmatism in Interaction* (New York: Praeger, 1986).

Marshall Shulman, *Stalin's Foreign Policy Revisited* (Cambridge: Harvard University Press, 1963).

Marshall Shulman, *Beyond the Cold War* (New Haven: Yale University Press, 1966).

Richard H. Shultz and Roy Godson, *Dezinformatsia. Active Measures in Soviet Strategy* (McLean, VA: Pergamon-Brassey's, 1984).

Lee Sigelman and Carol K. Sigelman, "Presidential Leadership of Public Opinion: From 'Benevolent Leader' to 'Kiss of Death'?", *Experimental Study of Politics*, 7:3 (1981), 1-22.

Frank R. Silbajoris, ed., *The Architecture of Reading. Essays on Russian Literary Theory and Practice*, OSU Slavic Papers No. 3 (Columbus: Ohio State University, Department of Slavic Languages and Literatures).

Dimitri K. Simes, "The New Soviet Challenge, " *Foreign Policy*, 55 (Summer 1984), 113-31.

Dimitri K. Simes, "America's New Edge," *Foreign Policy*, 56 (Fall 1984), 24-43.

Herbert W. Simons, "Persuasion in Social Conflicts: A Critique of Prevailing Conceptions and a Framework for Future Research," *Speech Monographs*, 39:4 (November 1972), 227-47.

Solomon Simonson, "Report of the Committee on Propaganda," *Journal of Communication*, 1:2 (November 1951), 73-74.

Donald C. Smith, "KAL 007: Making Sense of the Senseless," unpublished paper presented to the 1985 annual convention of the Speech Communication Association, Denver, CO (November 1985).

"Soviet academic says library fire is a 'cultural Chernobyl'" (Associated Press, 27 March 1988) [S9398].

"Soviet scholar calls library fire 'a national disaster'" (Associated Press, 1 April 1988) [S55695].

"Soviet Union Discontinues Jamming of BBC Broadcasts," *Tallahassee Democrat*, January 23, 1987, 5A.

321

"The Soviet's Lie About Censorship," *U. S. News & World Report*, January 13, 1956, 68-76.

Larry Speakes with Robert Pack, *Speaking Out. The Reagan Presidency from Inside the White House* (New York: Charles Scribner's Sons, 1988).

Polkovnik G. Spiridonov, "Trassery b'iut po tseli" ["Tracers Hit the Target"], *Aviatsiia i kosmonavtika*, September 1984, pp. 42-43.

J. Michael Sproule, "The Institute for Propaganda Analysis: Public Education in Argumentation, 1937-1942," in Zarefsky, Sillars, and Rhodes, eds., 486-99.

J. Michael Sproule, "Propaganda Studies in American Social Science: The Rise and Fall of the Critical Paradigm," *Quarterly Journal of Speech*, 73:1 (February 1987), 60-78.

J. Michael Sproule, "What Ever Happened to Propaganda? Attitudes Toward Mass Persuasion in Twentieth Century America," presented at the 1987 Biennial Convention of The World Communication Association, Norwich, England, August 1987.

Harold and Margaret Sprout, "Environmental Factors in the Study of International Politics," *Journal of Conflict Resolution*, 1 (December 1957), 327-28.

Edward Stankiewicz, "Poetic and non-poetic language in their interrelation," *Poetics* (Warszawa: Panstwowe wydawnictwo naukowe, 1961).

"Statement of William D. Reynard, Manager, Aviation Safety Reporting System, [NASA]" in United States House of Representatives, "Aircraft Navigation Technology and Errors," Hearings before the Subcommittee on Transportation, Aviation, and Materials of the Committee on Science and Technology, 19 September 1983 (pp. 3-19).

Kenneth J. Stein, "Cobra Judy Phased Array Radar Tested," *Aviation Week & Space Technology*, August 10, 1981, pp. 70-3.

Thomas M. Steinfatt, "Evaluating Approaches to Propaganda Analysis," *et cetera*, 36:2 (Summer 1979), 157-80.

Charles L. Stevenson, *Ethics and Language* (New Haven: Yale University Press, 1944).

Jeffrey St. John, *Day of the Cobra* (Nashville: Thomas Nelson Publishers, 1984).

Akio Takahasi, *President's Crime: Who ordered the espionage flight of KAL007?* (Tokyo: Ningensha, 1985). Russian translation: "Prestuplenie prezidenta. Provokatsiia s iuzhnokoreiskim samoletom sovershena po prikazu Reigana" [*The President's Crime: The South Korean Airliner Provocation Was Carried Out On Reagan's Orders*] (Moscow: Izdatel'stvo Agentstva pechati Novosti, 1984).

Strobe Talbott, *The Russians and Reagan* (New York: Vintage Books, 1984).

Elizabeth Teague, "The Foreign Departments of the Central Committee of the CPSU," *Radio Liberty Research Bulletin*, October 27, 1980.

Stephen E. Toulmin, *The Uses of Argument* (Cambridge: Cambridge University Press, 1958).

Frederick Trautmann, "Rhetoric Far and Near: Lessons for Americans from German Books," *Quarterly Journal of Speech*, 61:3 (October 1975), 328-36.

G. A. Trofimenko, ed., "Sovremennaia vneshniaia politika SShA" [*Current US Foreign Policy*] (Moscow: Nauka, 1984), 2 vols.

Robert W. Tucker, "The Role of Defense in the Foreign Policy of the Reagan Administration," *Jerusalem Journal of International Relations*, 7:1-2 (1984), 47-56.

United Nations Organization. International Civil Aviation Organization, *Destruction of Korean Air Lines Boeing 747 Over Sea of Japan, 31 August 1983, Report of the ICAO Fact-Finding Investigation*, December 30, 1983.

United Nations Organization. International Civil Aviation Organization. Air Navigation Commission, *1818th Report to Council by the President of the Air Navigation Commission*, Document C-WP/7809, February 16, 1984.

United States Congress, House Committee on Foreign Affairs, Subcommittee on Europe and the Middle East, *Developments in Europe, September 1983* (Washington: U. S. Government Printing Office, 1984).

United States Congress. House Permanent Select Committee on Intelligence, *Soviet Active Measures* (Washington: U. S. Government Printing Office, 1982).

United States Congress. House Permanent Select Committee on Intelligence, *Declassified Intelligence Assessments of 1983 KAL Shootdown at Variance With Prevailing Administration Statements* (Washington: U.S. House of Representatives, Committee on Foreign Affairs, January 12, 1988).

United States Department of State. Bureau of Public Affairs, *KAL Flight #007: Compilation of Statements and Documents. September 1-16, 1983*, Washington, DC.

United States House of Representatives, *Aircraft Navigation Technology and Errors*. Hearings before the Subcommittee on Transportation, Aviation and Materials of the Committee on Science and Technology, September 19, 1983 (Washington, DC: U. S. Government Printing Office, 1983).

United States Information Agency, *The Shootdown of KAL 007: Moscow's Charges--and the Record* (Washington, 1983).

United States Information Agency, "The Death of KAL 007: 'This appalling and Wanton Misdeed' (Chronology: Soviet shootdown and world reaction)", POL405, August 16, 1984.

United States Information Agency. Office of Research, *Soviet Propaganda Alert*, No. 16 (October 7, 1983); No. 17 (December 6, 1983); No. 18 (January 31, 1984).

The University of Miami. Advanced International Studies Institute, "Moscow's Reactions to Prior Downings of Civilian Aircraft Reveal Blatant Double Standards," *Press Reports on Soviet Affairs*, September 22, 1983, Washington, DC.

Joan Barth Urban, "The West European Communist Challenge to Soviet Foreign Policy," in Kanet, ed., 171-93.

323

U. S. News & World Report, "The Soviet's Lie About Censorship," January 13, 1956, pp. 68-76.

Gerard de Villiers, *Le vol 007 ne repond plus* (Paris: Librairie Plon, 1984).

Leonid Vladimirov, "Problems of the Soviet Journalist," in *The Conflict of INFORMA-TION--'Detente,' Freedom and Constraint,* Conflict Studies, No. 56 (April 1975), 3-10.

Voice of America, "Murkier Still," Editorial 0-0715, September 22, 1983.

Voice of America, "An Impartial Report," Editorial 0-0800, Dec. 18, 1983.

Voice of America, "Memory and Resolve," Editorial 0-1057, Sept. 1, 1984.

Voice of America, "Unfriendly Skies," Editorial 0-1287, April 19, 1985.

Voice of America, "KAL 007: Three Years Later," Editorial 0-2069, August 31, 1986.

Vladimir Voinovich, "Yolki-palki" *Novoe russkoe slovo,* October 28, 1983, p. 3.

Philip Wander, "The Rhetoric of American Foreign Policy," *Quarterly Journal of Speech,* 70:4 (November 1984), 339-61.

Barbara Warnick, "The Narrative Paradigm: Another Story," *Quarterly Journal of Speech,* 73:2 (May 1987), 172-82.

Granville Watts, "Year After KAL Disaster Mystery Remains on Why Plane Strayed," Reuter, Seoul, South Korea, August 29, 1984.

William Watts and Lloyd Free, eds., *State of the Nation* (New York: Universe Books, 1973).

Michael Weatherly, "Propaganda and the Rhetoric of the American Revolution," *Southern Speech Journal,* 36:4 (Summer 1971), 352-63.

Richard Weaver, "Some Rhetorical Aspects of Grammatical Categories," Chapter Five in *The Ethics of Rhetoric* (Chicago: Henry Regnery Co., 1953), 115-42.

Michael Westlake, "On Course for Disaster," *Far Eastern Economic Review,* October 13, 1983, p. 32.

Ralph K. White, *Fearful Warriors* (New York: Free Press, 1984).

Stephen White, *Political Culture and Soviet Politics* (London: Macmillan, 1979).

Stephen White, "Soviet Political Culture Reassessed," in Brown, ed., 62-99.

The White House. Office of the Press Secretary, "Press Briefing by Larry Speakes," September 4, 1983.

Harold L. Wilensky, *Organizational Intelligence* (New York: Basic Books, 1967).

Charles Arthur Willard, "Argument Fields," in Cox and Willard, eds., 24-77.

Charles Arthur Willard, "Argument Fields, Sociologies of Knowledge and Critical Epistemologies," unpublished paper presented to the annual convention of the Speech Communication Association, 1982.

Charles Arthur Willard, *Argumentation and the Social Grounds of Knowledge* (University, AL: University of Alabama Press, 1983).

Theodore Otto Windt, jr, "Administrative Rhetoric: An Undemocratic Response to Protest," *Communication Quarterly*, 30:3 (Summer 1982), 245-50.

Theodore Windt with Kathleen Farrell, "Presidential Rhetoric and Presidential Power: The Reagan Initiatives," in Windt with Ingold, 310-22.

Theodore Windt with Beth Ingold, *Essays in Presidential Rhetoric* (Dubuque, IA: Kendall/Hunt, 1983).

Paula Wolfson and De Smith, "FOCUS: The Fate of Flight Seven," Voice of America Special Report #4-0389, September 6, 1983.

Roy V. Wood, James J. Bradac, Sara A. Barnhart, and Edward Kraft, "The Effect of Learning About Techniques of Propaganda on Subsequent Reaction to Propagandistic Communications," *Speech Teacher*, 19:1 (January 1970), 49-53.

Bob Woodward, "Casey Revived Demoralized CIA," *Washington Post*, February 3, 1987, pp. A1, A9.

Kunio Yanagida, "Shooting Down the KAL Spy Plane Theory," *Japan Echo*, Spring 1985, 74-80.

Marilyn J. Young, *The Conspiracy Theory of History as Radical Argument: The John Birch Society and Students for a Democratic Society*, Diss. University of Pittsburgh, 1974 (Ann Arbor: UMI, 1975).

Marilyn J. Young and Michael K. Launer, "007--Conspiracy or Accident?", *Commonweal*, September 12, 1986, 472-73 [review article: R. W. Johnson, *Shootdown: Flight 007 and the American Connection*].

Marilyn J. Young and Michael K. Launer, "Flight 007," *Washington Book Review*, 2:1 (January 1987), 9-11. [review article: Seymour M. Hersh, "The Target Is Destroyed"].

"Zaiavlenie general'nogo sekretaria TsK KPSS, predsedatelia Presidiuma Verkhovnogo soveta SSSR Iu. V. Andropova," *Pravda*, September 29, 1983, p. l.

David Zarefsky, "Conspiracy Argument in the Lincoln-Douglas Debates," *Journal of the American Forensics Association*, 21:2 (Fall 1984), 63-75.

David Zarefsky, "The Lincoln-Douglas Debates Revisited: The Evolution of Public Argument," *Quarterly Journal of Speech*, 72:2 (May 1986), 162-84.

David Zarefsky, Malcolm O. Sillars, and Jack Rhodes, eds., *Argument in Transition: Proceedings of the Third Summer Conference on Argumentation*, (Annandale, VA: Speech Communication Association, 1983).

G. T. Zhuravlev, "Sotsiologicheskie issledovaniia èffektivnosti ideologicheskoi raboty" [*Sociological Investigations into the Effectiveness of Ideological Work*] (Moscow: Mysl', 1980).

V. V. Zhurkin and V. A. Kremeniuk, "Podkhod SShA k mezhdunarodnym krizisnym situatsiiam" ["The US Approach to International Crisis Situations"], in G. A. Trofimenko, ed., "Sovremennaia vneshniaia politika SShA" [*Current US Foreign Policy*] (Moscow: Nauka, 1984), vol. 1, 370-92.

Nikolai Zhusenin, "Beriia," *Nedelia*, 12-18 February 1988, pp. 11-12.

William Zimmerman, "Rethinking Soviet Foreign Policy: Changing American Perspectives," *International Journal*, 35:3 (Summer 1980), 548-62.

William Zimmerman, "What Do Scholars Know About Soviet Foreign Policy?", *International Journal*, 37:2 (Spring 1982), 198-219.

Harold Zyskind, "A Rhetorical Analysis of the Gettysburg Address," *Journal of General Education*, 4 (April 1950), 202-12.

INDEX